From Writer to Reader

From Writer to Reader

STUDIES IN EDITORIAL METHOD

───

PHILIP GASKELL

OXFORD

AT THE CLARENDON PRESS

1978

Oxford University Press, Walton Street, Oxford OX2 6DP

OXFORD LONDON GLASGOW
NEW YORK TORONTO MELBOURNE WELLINGTON
KUALA LUMPUR SINGAPORE JAKARTA HONG KONG TOKYO
DELHI BOMBAY CALCUTTA MADRAS KARACHI
IBADAN NAIROBI DAR ES SALAAM CAPE TOWN

British Library Cataloguing in Publication Data
Gaskell, Philip
    From writer to reader.
    1. Editing—Case studies
    I. Title
    820'.9   PN162   77-30111
    ISBN 0-19-818171-X

*Printed in Great Britain
at the University Press, Oxford
by Vivian Ridler
Printer to the University*

FOR DADIE

PREFACE

THE brief section on the theory and practice of textual bibliography in my *New introduction to bibliography*[1] offered conclusions which now seem to have been too positive and clear-cut. I have tried to do better here by presenting extracts from the early texts of twelve works of literature, and seeing how the evidence might be used in the production of editions for various classes of readers.

The method of following an extract from a text through its surviving stages from writer to reader, while it cannot illustrate all the problems that an editor of that text would meet, has enabled me to cover a lot of ground in a book of moderate length, and to encompass a variety both of subject and of treatment. The examples were therefore chosen not only because they are important as works of art but also on account of the quantity and variety of the surviving textual evidence.[2]

The examples were not chosen because they proved a theory or supported a preconception. As it turned out, the possible solutions to which the evidence led me were in almost every case surprising, and if this book has a message it is that the editor should not base his work on *any* predetermined rule or theory. In general he will try to produce an edited text that is free from accidental error and from unauthorized alteration, and is presented in a way that is convenient for its intended readers. Beyond this every case is unique and must be approached with an open mind.

Although the extracts are short they are meant to be typical of the works from which they are taken. Facsimiles of the originals are in most cases fitted together to make the extracts continuous (which also saves space). Reproductions of extracts from manuscripts are transcribed in type-facsimile.[3]

In writing this book I have been most generously helped by friends and colleagues and by specialists in the subjects of my examples. The whole book has benefited enormously by discussions with Marie Axton, Carl and Helen Baron, Peter Blayney, Tom Davis, and Edgar Harden. Invaluable criticism of the individual sections was given by Glenn Black (Harington);

[1] Gaskell, P., *A new introduction to bibliography*, Oxford 1972 (repr. with corrections 1974), pp. 336–60. On the terminology of textual bibliography see p. 2 and n. 3 below.

[2] One of the reasons for choosing these particular examples was that we have authors' manuscripts for all but one of them (the exception is Example 3). Many nineteenth- and twentieth-century authors' manuscripts have survived, but relatively few from earlier periods.

[3] I have done my best to transcribe accurately, but there are sure to be mistakes; I should be grateful to be told of them.

Mary Ann Radzinowicz (Milton); Duncan Eaves and Peter Sabor (Richardson); David Woolley (Swift); Brian Jenkins (Scott); Christopher Ricks and Susan Shatto (Tennyson); Nina Burgis (Dickens); Edgar Harden (Thackeray); Tom Davis (Hawthorne); Simon Gatrell, Dale Kramer, and Alan Manford (Hardy); Hans Walter Gabler and Michael Groden (Joyce); Peter Blayney, Peter Holland, and Tom Stoppard (Stoppard). I am also very grateful for advice on individual points given me by Alan Bell, Peter Croft, and John Yearwood.

PHILIP GASKELL

Trinity College
Cambridge
1975-6

ACKNOWLEDGEMENTS

The author and publisher gratefully acknowledge permission to publish copyright material as follows:

Basil Blackwell & Mott Ltd. (pp. 98-9)
The Bodleian Library, Oxford (p. 16)
The Bodley Head (pp. 225, 234)
The British Library Board (pp. 18, 24, 186)
J. M. Dent & Sons Ltd. (p. 79)
Dorset County Museum and the Thomas Hardy Memorial Collection Trustees (pp. 200, 207)
Doubleday & Co. Inc. (pp. 56, 59, 61)
E. P. Dutton & Co. Inc. (p. 79)
Faber & Faber Ltd. (pp. 226, 240, 248, 251, 253, 255, 257, 259)
The Fitzwilliam Museum, Cambridge (p. 125)
Grove Press Inc. (pp. 248, 251, 253, 255, 257, 259)
The Houghton Library, Harvard University (pp. 229-30, 241)
The Trustees of the James Joyce Estate and the Society of Authors (pp. 224-34, 236-7, 240-3)
Longman Group Ltd. (pp. 59, 140)
Macmillan & Co. (p. 206)
The Trustees of the National Library of Scotland (p. 108)
State University of New York at Buffalo (Lockwood Poetry Collection) (pp. 228, 231-2, 240, 242)
Ohio University Press (p. 193)
Oxford University Press (pp. 26-7)
Random House Inc. (pp. 225, 234)
The Philip H. and A. S. W. Rosenbach Foundation (pp. 226, 240)
Tom Stoppard (pp. 248, 250-9, 260)
The Duke of Sutherland (pp. 34-5, 45)
Lord Tennyson, and the Tennyson Trustees (pp. 120, 122, 125, 126, 128, 130, 132)
University of Texas at Austin (Humanities Research Center) (pp. 233, 243)
The Master and Fellows of Trinity College, Cambridge (pp. 33, 44, 86, 120, 122, 126, 128, 130, 132, 160, 162, 164, 169-70, 174)
The Victoria and Albert Museum (pp. 88, 148, 150)

CONTENTS

ABBREVIATIONS

THE following abbreviations are used:

DNB   *The dictionary of national biography* (2nd edn., 1908–12)

NIB   Gaskell, P., *A new introduction to bibliography*, Oxford 1972 (repr. with corrections 1974)

OED   *The Oxford English dictionary*

PBSA   *Papers of the Bibliographical Society of America*

PMLA   *Publications of the Modern Language Association of America*

STC   Pollard, A. W., and Redgrave, G. R., *A short-title catalogue of books printed in England* [etc.] *1475–1640*, London 1926 (2nd edn. in progress)

Wing   Wing, D. G., *Short-title catalogue of books printed in England* [etc.] *1641–1700*, 3 vols., New York 1945 (2nd edn. in progress)

Explanations of the abbreviations used for particular manuscripts and editions are given in each example.

INTRODUCTION

EDITING WORKS OF LITERATURE

MOST of the major works of English literature are readily available today only in versions that are sadly inadequate. There are few reliable specialist editions; much worse, the majority of the paperback texts of English and American authors that are sold in their millions to students and general readers are corrupt and misleading.[1] This is as unnecessary as it is undesirable. By combining critical judgement with an understanding of textual bibliography an editor can establish a 'critical text' that is as authoritative as the evidence allows, and can present it in the form best suited to his intended audience. The examples given in this book are intended to show how this may be done.

The author of a work of literature that is to be published as a printed book commonly alters the text by correcting and revising his working manuscript as he goes along, by writing out new drafts, and by making corrections and revisions[2] in the printed proof; and he may return to the work after publication to make further alterations for subsequent editions. This is the *variation of composition*, and it is a normal part of the process of creative writing. The variant readings which are superseded do not become part of the completed work of art, but they may be worth recording for the light they throw on its development and on the author's mind and art.

The text of the work will also be affected by the *variation of transmission* which results from the processes and controls of copying, editing, printing, and publication, and which is part accidental, part deliberate. There are nearly always copying errors and similar accidental mistakes made by the author himself, by copyists, and by compositors; and there is usually deliberate interference with the text, mostly by printers and publishers, for the sake of regularity or conformity. Apart from the printer's normalization of the details of the text, which may be unobjectionable when it was approved or at least accepted by the author, most transmission variants are detrimental to the work, and are seldom worth recording for their own sake.

---

[1] This is especially true of prose fiction, though every literary genre is plagued by bad editing. For a recent survey see Tanselle, G. T., 'Problems and accomplishments in the editing of the novel', *Studies in the novel*, vii, 1975, pp. 323–60, and the references given therein.

[2] In this book the term 'correction' is used for an alteration intended to put right an error (usually of transcription), while 'revision' is used for one intended to improve what is already correctly transcribed. Corrections are commonly made by printers as well as by authors; revision is usually, but not invariably, authorial.

(It is of course often difficult to know whether variation resulting from the alteration of a document which is now missing was authorized or not.)

The editor of a work of literature investigates the circumstances of its composition and transmission, the probable intentions of its author, and the forms in which it reached its original audiences. In the light of what he discovers, and of the needs of his own intended audience, he presents a text purged as far as possible of accidental errors and of deliberate but un-authorized alterations; he equips it with a record of those surviving variants of composition which he thinks readers of the edition will find useful, and supports it with an apparatus of textual notes and of the more important variants of transmission which explains and justifies his version.

Ordinarily the words of the early versions of a text are found to be more authoritative than its spelling, punctuation, etc., and the editor's first priority must always be to get the words of the text right. He will of course endeavour to get the details right as well, but this is generally less important (although he is likely to find it disproportionately difficult).

It is not only works of literature that are written, printed, and published in these ways and to which such editorial procedures can be applied. But although any work that is worth editing at all ought to be produced in an accurate and authoritative version, few non-literary works are of such textual interest that they need an apparatus of notes and variants.

The editor—or, to call him by another name, the textual critic[3]—acts both as *textual bibliographer*, one who establishes texts and readings by finding out how and with what intentions they were written and reproduced, and as *literary critic*, one who judges texts and readings as works of art and says which of them he prefers. As critic, too, he may expound the meaning and quality of the work. This is not to suggest that, in editing, bibliography is the servant of criticism or vice versa, for they are essentially interdependent activities. The relationship of the surviving texts of a work, and the nature of the variants, are established bibliographically; texts are chosen and variants are evaluated critically; and there can be no critical text unless the editor performs both functions.[4]

[3] Formerly the term 'textual criticism' referred primarily to the establishment of early texts from manuscript sources, but nowadays it is also applied to editorial work in a more general sense (as in James Thorpe's *Principles of textual criticism*, 1972).

[4] For a conspectus of the theoretical background to mid twentieth-century editing see the following extracts:

Reynolds, L. D., and Wilson, N. G., *Scribes and scholars*, 2nd edn., Oxford 1974, pp. 186–213.

McKerrow, R. B., *Prolegomena for the Oxford Shakespeare*, Oxford 1939 (repr. 1969), pp. 1–18.

Greg, W. W., 'The rationale of copy-text', *Studies in bibliography*, iii, 1950-1, pp. 19–36; repr. in *Collected papers*, Oxford 1966, pp. 374–91.

Bowers, F. T., 'Practical texts and definitive editions', in Hinman, C., and Bowers, F. T., *Two lectures on editing*, Columbus 1969, pp. 21–70.

The examples which are presented here investigate particular editorial problems and offer possible solutions. But first we should consider a few general questions.

AUTHORS' INTENTIONS[5]

It is desirable that a reproduction of a work of literature should as far as possible conform to its author's intentions. As far as the larger features of a work of literature are concerned, the author is likely to have worked through the various stages of its composition towards an end that he purposed and foresaw, although he may not have formulated these intentions precisely, even to himself, and although he may have changed his mind about what he wanted to do either during or after composition. In general, too, we can usually see what he intended. The last, largely rewritten, version of *Pamela* (Example 3) certainly represents Richardson's final intentions for the book, whether or not we happen to like it better than the first version. Similarly Hardy's progressive, detailed revision of *The woodlanders* (Example 10) resulted in a final text that he preferred to the first published version of twenty-five years earlier. It is not possible in either case to conflate the different versions into one, so the editor has to decide which version he is going to edit; and, although he may know for instance that the last version of *Pamela* represented Richardson's final intentions for the novel, he may nevertheless decide on critical grounds to edit the first version—which of course did at one time represent Richardson's intentions.

In matters of textual detail and typographical presentation an author may not have had intentions for his work so much as expectations. The printers and publishers of works of literature have always acknowledged a duty to set the words of their copy in type as exactly as possible, without change, omission, or addition;[6] but at the same time they have considered it equally their duty to ensure that the spelling, capitalization, italicization, and contraction of the printed transcript should accord with the standards and conventions of their own time.

Thorpe, J., *Principles of textual criticism*, San Marino 1972, pp. 3–49.

Tanselle, G. T., 'Problems and accomplishments in the editing of the novel'; and Freehafer, J., 'Greg's theory of copy-text and the textual criticism in the CEAA editions', *Studies in the novel*, vii, 1975, pp. 323–60, 375–88.

Davis, T., 'The CEAA and modern textual editing', *The Library*, xxxii, 1977, pp. 61–74.

[5] The subject is full of philosophical traps; but see Peckham, M., 'Reflections on the foundations of modern textual editing', *Proof*, i, 1971, pp. 122–55; and Tanselle, G. T., 'The editorial problem of final authorial intention', *Studies in bibliography*, xxix, 1976, pp. 167–211.

[6] Provided that there was not some obvious error (such as a word omitted, or impossible grammar). The printers and publishers of non-literary works have always been liable to go further than this, and even today may try to improve the text by amending the words; see Butcher, J., *Copy-editing*, Cambridge 1975, pp. 18–20.

Punctuation differs from the largely formal details of spelling, etc., because much of it has a grammatical function and affects the meaning of the words; and printers and publishers have tended not to alter authors' punctuation of verse since the earlier eighteenth century (though sometimes supplying punctuation where there was none) or authors' punctuation of prose fiction since the later nineteenth century. A few authors—Tennyson, Hardy, and Joyce are examples—wanted to control the way that their texts were punctuated in print. Others, contrariwise, actually asked the printer or publisher to supply the punctuation (Scott and Charlotte Brontë did this, and so more surprisingly did Gray, Byron, and Yeats);[7] or, like Thackeray, they simply omitted punctuation from the manuscript and left the printer to make it good. But most authors—including amongst our subjects Harington and Hawthorne and perhaps several others—took the normalization of their texts so much for granted that it may not have occurred to them that their books could appear in any other way.

When an author merely acquiesced in the normalization of his text he may have expected it, and he may not have objected to it, but he did not necessarily intend it. Even when an author actively accepted the printer's normalized details by revising them and then passing them in proof (as Dickens did, Example 7), it may be supposed that he would have revised and passed in proof his own original system of punctuation if the printer had followed it. Whether such an author's intentions are better represented by the normalized punctuation which he revised and accepted, or by some version of his manuscript punctuation (which he would presumably have revised if it had been presented to him in proof), is something of a puzzle.

COPY-TEXT

A critical edition of a work of literature must be based on some previous version or versions of the text. Usually one particular version will appear to offer a better basis for the edited text than any other, and it is therefore chosen as 'copy-text' for the critical edition. No one previous text, however, will be so flawless that it cannot be improved. Each of the surviving pre-publication documents is likely to have been superseded in some of its readings by later authoritative revision, while the published texts—and probably some of the pre-publication documents as well—are almost certain to have been affected by unauthorized changes, both deliberate and inadvertent.

The copy-text is therefore converted into a critical text by means of a technique of controlled eclecticism whereby the editor, in the light of all the evidence, emends the copy-text by substituting readings from another text

---

[7] For instances see *NIB*, p. 339; Thorpe, J., *Principles of textual criticism*, San Marino 1972, pp. 141-51.

or by supplying new ones himself; he does this where he believes that the alterations represent the author's intended text more closely than the copy-text readings, because they correct errors, omissions, or unauthorized alterations. The resulting critical text, whether it be reset or reproduced photographically from an emended copy of an existing version, usually resembles one or more of the previous versions of the work very closely, but is not precisely the same as any one of them. If it has been skilfully edited it will be an improvement on all previous texts in accuracy, completeness, authority, and authenticity.

A theory of copy-text, intended to indicate which of the early versions of a work should be chosen as copy-text for an edition and how far it should be followed, was formulated by Sir Walter Greg and published in 1950 as 'The rationale of copy-text'.[8] This influential paper offered sound advice to the editors of Renaissance texts. It argued essentially that the earliest in an ancestral series of printed editions[9] should be chosen as copy-text, and should be followed both in words (which Greg called 'substantives') and in non-verbal details (the punctuation, spelling, capitalization, italicization, and contraction, which were liable to normalization by the printer and which Greg called 'accidentals'), unless the editor believed that verbal variants from another source had greater authority. The copy-text would then be amended in accordance with the editor's critical judgement.

Greg was concerned solely with the problems of editing Renaissance texts, and his theory is an inadequate guide to editors of nineteenth- and twentieth-century works of which (as is commonly the case) the author's manuscript has survived, and in the printing and reprinting of which the author had taken an active interest. Priority alone does not make the manuscript the best copy-text; while the distinction between substantives and accidentals is likely to be less important in such cases than the distinction between those elements of the text which affect its meaning and those which do not.[10] There are six important nineteenth- and twentieth-century novels amongst our examples; we have the authors' manuscripts of all of them, but in only one case (Example 9) is it clear that the manuscript should be used as copy-text.

It is usually convenient to use as copy-text the version with the best details, for the editor will in any case adopt what he considers to be the most authoritative words, and these should be the same whichever copy-text is chosen. What a potential copy-text offers is a system of punctuation,

[8] *Studies in bibliography*, iii, 1950-1, pp. 19-36; reprinted in Greg, W. W., *Collected papers*, Oxford 1966, pp. 374-91.
[9] That is, a series in which each new edition is set from the last.
[10] Here I shall say 'words', 'punctuation', 'spelling', etc., rather than 'substantives' and 'accidentals'.

spelling, etc., which may give a particular tone to the text as a whole, depending on whether it derives from the author's manuscript, from an early printed edition, or from the editor's revision of an early text.

Every textual situation is unique, and the editor must base his procedures on his own critical judgement as much as on general principles. But in deciding which copy-text to use he may consider whether the choice of a particular version will result in a system of punctuation, spelling, etc., in the edited text which is more likely than another to represent the author's own intentions for the form of the work; whether the resulting system is better critically than one that would result from a different choice; and whether it is the system most likely to be acceptable to readers of the edition. There may also be the question of whether a potential copy-text contains the whole work or only part of it.

These considerations may conflict. Where the editor believes that he can make a good guess at the author's intentions for the form of the work, he will probably try to follow them even if (for example) this means rejecting a coherent printed text and repointing a defective manuscript himself. But more often the evidence for the author's intentions for the form of the work will be inadequate, and the editor might decide for instance to follow the version that is best on critical grounds; or to follow the author's manuscript, whatever its merits, because it is what the author himself first wrote; or to follow the first printed edition, whatever its merits, because the author passed it in proof and it is what the original audience read. But, whatever he does, the editor should base his decisions, not on rules, but on his bibliographical and critical judgement of the circumstances of each case.

PRESENTATION AND ANNOTATION

It may be tempting for an editor to suppose that he should present all the evidence concerning every version of his text, and should annotate practically every word of it; tempting because the inclusion of everything would relieve him of the difficulty of deciding what to omit, and would also guard him against possible criticism for having omitted what he should have included. But of course any hope of producing an all-inclusive edition would be vain and delusive: it is impossible to present and annotate *everything*; and if it were possible no one would want to read the result.

In presenting and annotating his text, the editor must record at least his verbal emendations of the copy-text; then he should use his critical judgement to select those items of information which his readers are likely to need, and to omit everything else. He may well find it easier to choose and emend a copy-text than to decide how far he should go in annotating it, and he will often want to record his hard-won expertise even when it does not directly illuminate the text. But his job is to convey the author's work to his readers, not to show off his own scholarship; and the readers are interested not in the editor but in the edition.

Every case, again, is unique, and the evidence must be presented in the way that is best for the particular edition: sometimes footnotes are better than appendices, sometimes it is the other way round; a type of list which is convenient in one case may be less so in another; and so on. Neither can there be any rules governing the extent to which textual annotation should be carried. Important variants, no doubt, should be annotated, but only the editor can decide which of the variants are important. The proper nature and extent of critical and explanatory annotation, finally, is even harder to judge: linguistic usage and local reference which will be plain to a reader of a particular nationality, age, education, and social class will be obscure to one of a different background; and it is obviously impossible to give an explanation sufficient for one that is not too much or too little for the other.

A reset critical text will of course require extreme care in proof-reading if serious new errors of transmission are to be avoided, and it is inevitable that *any* reset text—which is after all a new edition of the work—will introduce at least minor errors.[11] The only way of avoiding new transmission errors is to reproduce a good early version of the text photolithographically with the editor's emendations incorporated in it, a method which also has the advantage of being very much cheaper than setting and correcting a new edition (see Example 10). However, photolithographic reprinting for a critical text is practicable only where few editorial emendations are necessary; if there has to be much emendation resetting is unavoidable.

REGULARIZATION AND MODERNIZATION

In the course of emending the copy-text the editor may come across a good deal of minor inconsistency which is either directly attributable to the author, or has been accepted by him. In his manuscripts Dickens was inconsistent in his use of spelling, hyphenation, and the conventions of punctuation; and similar inconsistencies are found in his printed texts, some of them copied from manuscript, some of them introduced by the compositors. Editors—who are tidy-minded by profession—are prone to think that such inconsistency must be wrong, and to eliminate it without question. Nevertheless it is often clear (as in Dickens's texts) that such irregularity was a normal feature of the author's or printer's style, and that no one was much upset by it at the time. Where this was so it can hardly be classed as an error; and the only reason for eliminating it is to satisfy the

[11] See the 'Addendum' to Fredson Bowers's 'Scholarship and editing', *PBSA*, lxx, 1976, pp. 185–8.

expectations of modern readers. It is arguable that to 'correct' inconsistencies where they are characteristic of the copy-text and where they do not affect its meaning is to act unhistorically; and that by imposing our modern fondness for consistency upon the author's or printer's indifference to it, we are unconsciously modernizing the text.

The deliberate modernization of the spelling, punctuation, etc. of an early text is undesirable because it suggests that the modern meaning of the words of the text is what the author meant by them; because it conceals puns and rhymes; because it causes the editor to choose where the author was ambiguous; and because it deprives the work of the quality of belonging to its own period.

Nevertheless there are texts which even the most scrupulous editor may be obliged to modernize. Not Middle English texts, of course, where modernization of the spelling will conceal rather than reveal the meanings of the words; or texts from the eighteenth century onwards, where the original details do not hinder anyone's comprehension; but texts of the sixteenth and seventeenth centuries edited for the use of students and general readers. It is not that the objections to modernization outlined here are not applicable in this period—indeed they apply with particular force to the modernization of sixteenth- and seventeenth-century texts—but that the relatively difficult old spelling, etc., is liable to put off non-specialist readers to the extent that they simply will not read in old spelling texts which they would be prepared to try in modernized versions. Where this is so the editor must be prepared to modernize, however much he dislikes it. By way of consolation it may be said, first, that the modernization for students even of seventeenth-century texts is not inevitable, as our Milton example shows; and secondly that we have all read Shakespeare and the 1611 Bible in modernized texts without coming to much harm.

The modernization of later texts should be sedulously avoided. Anyone who can read an early eighteenth-century (or later) author will have no real difficulty with the original spelling and punctuation, quickly becoming accustomed to the styles of capitalization and italicization that were characteristic of the period. There is no need, incidentally, for an editor to reproduce the early printer's long ſ (which some readers find tiresome), for the distinction between ſ and s was a typographical convention that was connected with the positions of the letters in the words, and was of no textual significance. Similar considerations apply to the alternative forms of *i* and *j*, *u* and *v* found in sixteenth- and early seventeenth-century printing.

WORKS NOT INTENDED FOR PUBLICATION AS PRINTED BOOKS

These are chiefly (1) stage plays; (2) works circulated in manuscript copies; and (3) private papers not written for publication.

(1) Plays are different from the works of literature that we have been considering so far because they are completed and primarily communicated not as books to be read but as performances in the theatre, in which the playwright's chief collaborators—the director and the actors—contribute essentially to the realization of the play as a work of art. Indeed, plays are so different from books that they might well be classed as belonging to another art form altogether; but we consider them to be part of literature because they can be communicated in a secondary way as written texts, and because such reading texts and the performances we derive from them are all that remain to us of the plays of the past. (Some plays, of course, are written for the study, not for the theatre, but they can be treated as books. Milton's *Maske*, though it was written for amateur performance, never belonged to the professional stage, and it remained essentially a dramatic poem.)

Editing a play text is in many ways similar to editing a poem or a novel, but it may include elements deriving from theatrical performance as well as from the author's script. To show how the reading text of a play may be developed by production and performance, we have the example of a recent work by Tom Stoppard, in which we are able to consider not only the published text, but also the texts of actual performances, and to have the author's own account of his procedures and intentions.

(2) Publication in manuscript was resorted to either for the purpose of restricting circulation to a coterie (as with Shakespeare's 'sugred Sonnets among his private friends'), or because publication in the ordinary way would have got those concerned into trouble with the authorities. In both cases publication was by means of the private circulation between individuals of transcripts of the author's manuscript. Most of such transcription was done by amateur copyists, and it commonly resulted in marked textual deterioration.

We do not know much about the mechanics of manuscript publication in the sixteenth and early seventeenth centuries, the period when it was commonest in England. A good deal of coterie verse was circulated in this way, but the lines of textual descent were complicated and too few early copies have survived to enable us to follow their textual history in detail. The evidence for clandestine publication in England (which belongs to the same period) is even less complete, though there is a parallel, if a rather distant one, in the *samizdat* (self-published) literature of modern Russia.[12]

(3) Although they were not written for publication, the literary quality of diaries, collections of letters, etc., may be great, and they may be edited for publication. Here it is the original document itself that is the finished product, and there is every reason to take the manuscript as copy-text and to reproduce it without normalization. The only difficulty is likely to be that of representing the author's manuscript conventions readably and economically by means of typographical symbols.[13]

CONCLUSION

Finally it should be stressed yet again not only that every textual situation is unique and should be approached without editorial preconceptions, but also that there is seldom only one right way of editing a work of literature. The needs of the various classes of readers differ and, apart from this, there is generally more than one useful way of approaching a work editorially even for the same readers. The fact that important works of literature are found in editions which differ from each other but which are intended for essentially the same audience should not surprise or distress us. Shakespeare is an obvious example; but it is implicit in all the examples given in this book—and explicit in many of them—that the suggested editorial procedures are not necessarily the only possible or satisfactory ones. Each editor, in short, should use his knowledge, skill, and judgement to make his contribution to the better understanding of his subject in his own way.

[12] See *The Soviet censorship*, ed. Dewhirst, M., and Farrell, R., Metuchen, N.J. 1973, pp. iv–vi; *Solzhenitsyn, a documentary record*, ed. Labedz, L., London 1970, pp. 121, 122; Mood, C., *Solzhenitsyn*, Edinburgh 1973, pp. 15–16.

[13] See Halsband, R., 'Editing the letters of letter-writers', *Studies in bibliography*, xi, 1958, pp. 25–37; and Bowers, F. T., 'Transcription of manuscripts: the record of variants', *Studies in bibliography*, xxix, 1976, pp. 212–64.

EXAMPLE 1

Harington, Ariosto's *Orlando furioso*, 1591

HARINGTON'S translation of *Orlando furioso*—the first and still the best rendering into English of Ariosto's huge poem—is an unusually well-documented example of the progress from writer to reader of a work of literature in the late Elizabethan period.[1] We have two manuscripts, one of them written out for the most part by Harington himself and then used as printer's copy for the first edition; three early printed editions, two of them probably emended by Harington; and a recent critical edition. Taken together these documents show how an author and his printer actually dealt with a literary text at the end of the sixteenth century, and how it has come down to us.

Orlando furioso is an immensely long poem—this English version runs to close on 33,000 lines of verse, longer than ten average plays of the period, with much prose in addition—which Harington translated when he was about thirty years old, during a period of banishment from Court. No draft or working manuscript has survived, but there are two early transcripts, the first (called here MSa) made by a scribe, and the second (MSb) copied out for the most part by Harington himself, both of which appear to derive from a single lost draft.[2]

---

[1] For Harington's background, and for that of the *Orlando*, see the Introduction to McNulty's great edition: Ariosto, L., *Orlando furioso, translated into English heroical verse by Sir John Harington*, ed. McNulty, R., Oxford 1972; and the references given therein.

[2] MSa: Bodleian MS. Rawl. Poet. 125. This manuscript has hitherto been believed to be in Harington's autograph, but in fact Harington wrote out only the first stanza on fo. 1, presumably as a model, and then handed over to the scribe; he later added the few shoulder notes in italic, and made a few emendations to the text. (See Lea, K. M., 'Harington's Folly', *Elizabethan and Jacobean studies presented to Frank Percy Wilson*, Oxford 1959, pp. 42–58.)

MSb: British Library MS. Add. 18920. This manuscript has hitherto been thought to be wholly in Harington's autograph, and indeed most of it is; but a scribe's hand appears on fos. 134ᵃ–136ᵇ, and shares fo. 137ᵃ with Harington (Book 28); the scribe then copies fos. 171ᵇ–177ᵃ (Book 32), and much of the verse—but not the prose—from fo. 280 to the end (Book 43). (See Greg, W. W., 'An Elizabethan printer and his copy', *The Library*, iv, 1923, pp. 102–18; Simpson, P., *Proof-reading*, Oxford 1935 (repr. 1970), pp. 71–5.)

The two hands (see p. 16 and p. 18), which derive from the same model, formed most of the individual letters in similar ways; though it will be seen, for instance, that the scribe of MSa usually formed 'e' by means of a continuous loop whereas Harington in MSb commonly made 'e' with two strokes. But the essential difference between the two hands lies in their general character, that of the scribe being rounder and more sprawling than Harington's. (I am most grateful to Peter Croft and Helen Baron for help in investigating these manuscripts.)

The earlier, scribal manuscript (MSa) is a copy of the first twenty-four of the forty-six Books of the poem on paper, now bound as a small quarto volume. Apart from the first stanza and a few notes which were entered by Harington, the whole manuscript is written in an unidentified but elegant 'secretary' hand; it lacks most of the marginal notes and all of the prose Arguments and Annotations. Three plates and a number of smaller cuts have been pasted in. As to its text, MSa must have been copied directly or indirectly from the lost working manuscript, but it does not show Harington's own characteristic spellings, and it is scarcely punctuated at all. If the spelling of the lost manuscript is fairly represented by Harington's own fair copy, then the scribe of MSa altered the spelling of every third or fourth word.

The other manuscript (MSb, also a small-quarto paper book) is a fair copy of three-quarters of the poem, from Book 14 to the end. It is mostly in Harington's own hand, but there are several substantial passages totalling about a seventh of the whole in someone else's hand, probably that of the scribe of MSa. It represents a later stage of the text than MSa, and where the two overlap in Books 14 to 24 MSb shows a number of verbal changes, some of which were written into MSa as corrections by the scribe and by Harington himself. MSb was at first lightly punctuated, but somebody (probably Harington) went over it after it was copied out and added a much heavier punctuation.[3] MSb, together with a manuscript now lost of the first thirteen Books and of most of the prose, was used by the printer Richard Field as copy for setting the first edition of 1591.

This first printed edition of 1591,[4] which was a small folio set in double columns and well printed for its period, generally followed the words of MSb; the few changes were probably made by Harington in proof. The heavy additional punctuation of the manuscript was refined, and the spelling, capitalization, italicization, and contraction were normalized. Harington himself was concerned with the production of this edition; indeed he may have backed it financially, for no publisher is named in the colophon, and there are notes in the manuscript which give Field detailed typographical instructions. The book has an engraved title-page and forty-six other plates, all made according to Harington's directions.

Field also printed the second edition of the poem in 1607,[5] this time probably as an ordinary commercial venture, 'for John Norton and Simon Waterson'. It was set from a copy of *1591*, which it followed in words except

---

[3] Deduced from the evidence of passages later corrected by paste-on slips (e.g. on fos. 188[b] and 278[a]). Something similar seems to have happened to the punctuation of some manuscript verses which Harington wrote out in 1600 on the endpapers of a presentation copy of the 1591 edition of his *Orlando furioso* (Univ. Lib. Cam. Adv.b.8.1).

[4] STC 746, hereafter *1591*.   [5] STC 747, hereafter *1607*.

for a number of emendations which were probably made by Harington himself, and also generally in punctuation and spelling, etc. The third edition, again an ordinary commercial one, was printed after Harington's death by George Miller in 1634.[6] It was set from *1607*, the words of which it followed apart from transcription errors and from some apparently unauthorized alterations; the punctuation and spelling, etc., were modernized. Both *1607* and *1634* had illustrations printed from the original set of plates which had been made for *1591*, and which were touched up and re-hatched as they became worn.

There was no further edition of Harington's Ariosto until modern times. A fourth edition was set somewhat inaccurately from *1634* and published in 1962 without either Harington's apparatus or the illustrations.[7] Finally a critical text edited by Robert McNulty appeared in 1972, which presented Harington's text, apparatus, and illustrations with a critical and explanatory introduction, together with a register of the substantial textual variation between the two manuscripts and the three early editions of the poem.[8]

The relationship between the early versions of the work appears to have been as follows:

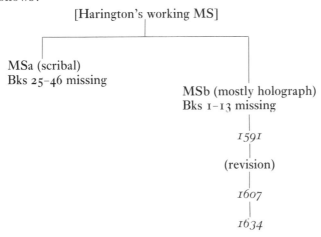

[Haringxon's working MS]

MSa (scribal)
Bks 25–46 missing

MSb (mostly holograph)
Bks 1–13 missing

1591

(revision)

1607

1634

There are still some gaps in the evidence—the working manuscript, the missing parts of MSa and MSb, and the proofs—but there is much more of it than the editor of a sixteenth-century work usually has when he considers the choice and emendation of a copy-text.

McNulty prepared his critical edition of Harington's Ariosto in the belief that both MSa and MSb were copied out by Harington himself. Since it

---

[6] STC 748, hereafter *1634*.   [7] Ed. Hough, G. G., London 1962.
[8] Ariosto, L., *Orlando furioso, translated into English heroical verse by Sir John Harington*, ed. McNulty, R., Oxford 1972.

appears that virtually the whole of MSa and a substantial fraction of MSb were scribal copies, it is worth reconsidering the basic editorial questions, and doing so in the light of the early versions of an extract from the text. The passage chosen is stanzas 28–33 of Book 16, a part of the poem that is represented in both the surviving manuscripts. We begin with MSa, the scribal copy (see pp. 16–17).

This is a handsome manuscript written in a fast, rounded secretary hand, probably by a professional scribe; it includes elsewhere a few entries made by Harington (notably the first stanza, copied out by Harington as a model, and some shoulder notes added at the beginning in italic). The spelling of MSa, which appears to be mostly the scribe's personal orthography, differs considerably from that of Harington's own transcript, the scribe spelling 'you', 'if', etc., where Harington prefers 'yow' and 'yf'; but the occasional use in MSa of 'yow', etc. (as here at 28.7) suggests that it may have been copied from a holograph draft.

There are also verbal variants between this copy of the extract and Harington's own transcript, MSb, which we consider next (see pp. 18–19).

This is another well-executed manuscript—evidently Harington, although a statist, did not hold it a baseness to write fair—with the main text in a neat, spiky, secretary hand and the shoulder notes in italic (Harington wrote both styles with facility). This was the copy used by the printer of *1591*, who made marks in the manuscript to show where the new sheets began in the printed version.[9] Harington's spelling ('yow', 'yf', etc.) was old-fashioned by the printing-house standards of the 1590s, and it was not wholly self-consistent (compare the rhyme-words in stanzas 29, 30, 32, and 33); but it was by no means as eccentric as manuscript spelling of the period could be. The added punctuation, which was probably Harington's, was somewhat ponderous but again was better than that of most manuscripts of the period.

These are the verbal variants between the two manuscripts:

stanza line	MSa (*scribal transcript*)	MSb (*holograph transcript*)
28.2	to	into
28.7	faythe	fame
29.2	offered	offerd[10]
30.5	now	,
31.5	their	thease
32.5	thowsand	townsman
32.8	shall	shold [overwritten]
33.2	overcome	over ronne

[9] Examples of the printer's annotations are reproduced by Greg and by Simpson (see p. 11 n. 2 for references).

[10] This may be no more than a spelling variant, but it is included because it could indicate a different pronunciation.

If both MSa and MSb were copied from the same working manuscript, it would appear that several of the MSa readings in this list were copying errors: certainly 'thowsand' and 'overcome', and perhaps others as well, although it is possible that Harington revised the working manuscript after MSa had been transcribed and also that he revised while he was actually transcribing MSb.

We can now compare MSb with the first edition text, *1591* (see p. 20). The first edition was set from MSb, the words of which it followed with very little change. In this extract there is only one verbal alteration, 'The' for 'then' (33.4), where neither reading is obviously superior to the other, and where the change could just as well have been made by the printer as by Harington.

There was rather greater change to the punctuation, but even so the final punctuation of MSb was refined rather than replaced. In the extract there were 11 changes of punctuation at line endings; 7 internal commas were deleted, and 2 internal commas and 1 parenthesis were added.

Changes to the spelling were another matter, for here Field's compositors normalized vigorously. There are 390 words in the extract, and the printers altered the spelling of 149 (38 per cent) of them. Most of these changes were from an old-fashioned form used by Harington to one that is still in use (76 per cent of the changes), but there were also changes from a form which has survived to one which has not (14 per cent) and from one non-current form to another (10 per cent); the compositor also shared 15 spellings with MSb which have not survived. In all 143 (37 per cent) of the MSb spellings are no longer in use, compared with only 44 (11 per cent) of the *1591* spellings.

In addition to all this there were a number of relatively minor graphical changes: the outsetting of the first line of each stanza; and capitals placed at the beginning of each line, not just at the beginning of sentences.

The next edition, *1607*, was set from *1591*, and at the same printing house (see p. 21). It followed the first closely in layout and typographical style. There were a few further changes of spelling, the number of non-current forms, forty-seven here, being slightly higher than in *1591*; they presumably represent the preferences of the *1607* compositor. More important were a number of verbal changes made throughout the poem. In the extract the verbal changes were:

	1591	*1607*
28.3	Onely I	I onely
28.6	Giuing but	But giuing
28.8	haue	all
31.4	Out of	From out

(*continued on p.* 22)

[16]

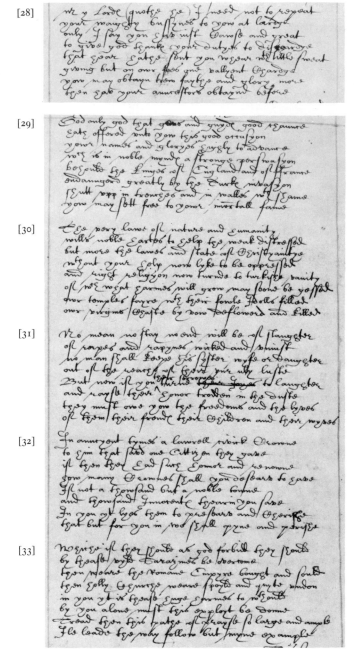

MSa (scribal) of Harington's *Orlando furioso* xvi. 28–33 (Bodleian MS. Rawl. Poet. 125, pp. 256–7; × 0·73). For a note on the handwriting see p. 11 n.

[28]   My Lords (quothe he) I need not to repeat
your waighty bussynes to yow at lardge
only I say you hav just Cawse and great
to give god thanks your dutyes to dischardge
that hear hathe sent you whear wth little sweat
giving but on owr foes one vallyent Chardge
yow may obtayn trew faythe and glory more
then hav your auncestors obtaynd before

[29]   God only god that gevs and guyds good chaunce
hath offered vnto yow this good occasyon
yowr names and gloryes highly to advance
wch is in noble mynds a stronge perswasyon
behould the Kinges of England and of France
endaungerd greatly by the Turks invasyon
shutt vpp in trenches and in walles wth shame
yow may sett free to yowr imortall fame

[30]   The very lawe of nature and humanity
wills noble hartes to help the weak distressed
but more the lawes and state of Christyanitye
wthout your help now lyke to be oppressed
and right religyon now turnde to turkishe vanity
of wch what harmes will grow may soone be gessed
owr temples fayre wth their fowle Idolls filled
owr virgins Chaste by vow deflowerd and killed

[31]   No mean no stay no end will be of slaughter
of rapes and rapynes wicked and vniust
no man shall keepe his syster wyfe or Daughter
out of the reache of their vnruly luste
              their sorrowes
But now if you ʌ turne ~~their Ioyes~~ to laughter
and rayse their honor trodden in the duste
they must owe yow the freedoms and the lyves
of them their frends their Children and their wyves

[32]   In auncyent tymes a lawrell civick Crowne
to him that savd one Cittizen they gave
if then they had such honnor and renowne
how many Crownes shall you desearv to have
If not a thowsand but a noble towne
and thowsand Innocents thearin you save
In you yt lyes them to presearv and Cherishe
that but for you in wo shall pyne and perishe

[33]   Whiche if they should as god forbidd they should
by thease vyld Sarazines be overcome
then weare the Romane Empyre bought and sould
then holly Churche weare spoyld and quyte vndon
in you yt is thease huge harmes to wthould
by you alone must this exployt be donne
Tread then this pathe of prayse so large and ample
Ile leade the way follow but myne example

My Lord (quoth he) I need not to repeat

Renaldos oration. from 28 to the 34.

28

29

30

31

Civica corona

32

33

MSb (autograph) of Harington's *Orlando furioso* xvi. 28–33 (British Library MS. Add. 18920, fos. 23ᵃ–23ᵇ; ×0·74). For a note on the handwriting see p. 11 n.

28

My Lords (quoth he) I need not to repeat,
yowr wayghty busynes vnto yow at large,
Only I say yow have iust cawse and great,
to geve god thanks, yowr dewtyes to dyscharge,
that heer hath sent yow, whear with lytle sweat,
geving but on owr foes on valyent charge,
yow may obtayn true fame and glory more
then have yowr awncestors obtaynd before.

*Renaldos
oration.
from 28 st.
to the 34.*

29

God, only god that gyvs and guyds good chawnce,
hath offerd vnto yow this good occasyon,
yowr nams and gloryes hyghly to advawnce,
which ys in noble mynds a strong perswasion,
Behold the kings of England and of Frawnce,
endawngerd greatly by the Turks invasion,
shut vp in trenches, and in walls with shame,
yow may set free to yowr immortall fame. /

30

The very law of Nature and humanytie,
wills noble harts, to help the weake dystressed,
but more the laws, and state of Chrystianitye,
withowt yowr help now lyke to be oppressed,
and ryght rellygion, turnd to turkysh vanytie,
of which what harms will grow may soon be gessed,
Owr temples fayr with theyr fowle Idolls filled,
owr vyrgins (chast by vow) deflowrd and killed

31

No mean no stay, no end will be of slawghter,
of Rapes, and rapins wycked and vniust,
no man shall keep his syster, wyfe, or dawghter,
owt of the reache of theyr vnruly lust.
But now yf yow thease sorrows turn to lawghter,
and rayse theyr honor troden in the dust,
they must ow yow the freedoms and ye lyves,
of them theyr frends, theyr children and theyr wyves.

32

Civica corona

In awncyent tymes a lawrell cyvicke crown,
to him that savd on cytisen they gave,
yf then they had soch honor and renown,
how many crowns shall yow desarve to have,
yf (not a townsman/ but) a noble town,
and thowsand innocents thearin yow save.
In yow yt lyes them to preserv and cherysh,
that but for yow in woe shold pyne and peryshe.

33

which yf they showld (as god forbyd they shold)
by thease vyle saracyns, be over ronne:
then wear the Roman Empyre bowght and solde,
then holly Church wear spoyld, and quyte vndonne.
In yow yt ys thease huge harms to withold,
by yow alone must this exployt be donne,
tred then this path of prayse so large & ample,
Ile lead the way, follow but myne exaumple. /

Transcript of p. 18

28

Rinaldos oratiõ
Tom 28. ft. 10
at 34.

My Lords (quoth he) I need not to repeat,
    Your weightie bufnesse vnto you at large,
    Onely I fay you haue iuft caufe and great,
    To giue God thankes,your dueties to difcharge,
    That here hath fent you,where with little fweat,
    Giuing but on our foes one valiant charge,
    You may obtaine true fame and glorie more,
    Then h aue your auncefters obtaind before.

29

God, onely God that giues and guyds good chance,
    Hath offerd vnto you this good occafion,
    Your names and glories highly to aduance,
    Which is in noble minds a ftrong perfwafion:
    Behold the kings of England and of France,
    Endaungerd greatly by the Turkes inuafion,
    Shut vp in trenches and in walls with fhame,
    You may fet free to your immortall fame.

30

The verie law of nature and humanitie,
    Wills noble hearts to helpe the weake diftreffed;
    But more the lawes and ftate of Chriftianitie;
    Without your helpe now like to be oppreffed,
    And right religion turnd to Turkifh vanitie, (fed,
    Of which what harms will grow may foon be guef-
    Our Temples faire with their foule idols filled,
    Our virgins (chaft by vow) deflourd and killed.

31

No meane, no ftay, no end will be of flaughter,
    Of rapes and rapines wicked and vniuft;
    No man fhall keepe his fifter,wife,or daughter,
    Out of the reach of their vnruly luft:
    But now if you thefe forrowes turne to laughter,
    And raife their honour troden in the duft,
    They muft ow you the freedomes and the liues,
    Of them, their friends, their children and their
                                              (wiues.

32

In auncient times a laurell cyuicke crowne,   Ciuica corona.
    To him that fau'd one citizen they gaue,
    If then they had fuch honour and renowne:
    How many crownes fhall you deferue to haue,
    If (not a townfman but) a noble towne,
    And thoufand innocents therein you faue?
    In you it lies them to preferue and cherifh,
    That (but for you) in woe fhould pine and perifh.

33

Which if they fhould (as God forbid they fhould)
    By thefe vile Sarazens be ouer runne:
    Then were the Romaine Empire bought & fold,
    The holy church were fpoild and quite vndone,
    In you it is thefe huge harmes to withhold,
    By you alone muft this exploit be done:
    Tread then this path of praife fo large and ample,
    Ile lead the way, follow but mine example.

1591, xvi. 28-33 (Harington, Sir J., *Orlando furioso*, London 1591, p. 123; Trin. Coll. Cam. Capell I.1;
× 0·91)

28

illustration
&c. to the My Lords (quoth he) I need not to repeate
Your weightie bisnesse vnto you at large,
I onely say, you haue iust cause and great,
To giue God thankes, your duties to discharge,
That here hath sent you, where with little sweat,
But giuing on our foes one valiant charge,
You may obtaine true fame and glorie more,
Then all your aunceftors obtaind before.

29

God, onely God that giues and guides good chance,
Hath offerd vnto you this good occasion,
Your names and glories highly to aduance,
Which is in noble minds a strong perswasion:
Behold the Kings of England and of France,
Endangerd greatly by the Turks inuasion,
Shut vp in trenches and in wals with shame,
You may set free to your immortall fame.

30

The very law of nature and humanitie,
Wils noble hearts to helpe the weake distressed,
But more the lawes and state of Christianitie,
Without your helpe now like to be oppressed,
And right Religion turnd to Turkish vanitie,
Of which what harms wil grow, may soon be guessed
Our temples faire with their foule idols filled,
Our virgins (chast by vow) deflourd and killed.

31

No meane, no stay, no end will be of slaughter,
Of rapes and rapines wicked and vniust;
No man shall keepe his sister, wife or daughter,
From out the reach of their vnruly lust:
But now if you these sorrowes turne to laughter,
And raise their honor troden in the dust,
They must ow you the freedomes and the liues,
Of them, their friends, their children and their wiues.

32

In auncient times a laurell Ciuick crowne   *Ciuica corona.*
To him that sau'd one citizen they gaue,
If then they had such honor and renowne,
How many crownes shall you deserue to haue,
If (not a townsman, but) a noble towne,
And thousand innocents therein you saue?
In you it lies them to preserue and cherish,
That (but for you) in wo should pine and perish.

33

Which if they should (as God forbid they should)
By these vile Saracens be ouerrunne,
Then were the Romaine Empire bought and sold,
The holy Church were spoyld and quite vndone:
In you it is these huge harmes to withhold,
By you alone must this exploit be done,
Tread then this path of praise so large and ample,
Ile leade the way, follow but mine example.

1607, xvi. 28–33 (Harington, Sir J., *Orlando furioso*, London 1607, p. 123; Trin. Coll. Cam. Capell G.3²; ×0·91)

The general tendency of the verbal alterations found in *1607* was to improve the text, and it seems most likely that they were Harington's own revisions.

The only other early edition is *1634*:

28

aldo's My Lords(quoth he) I need not to repeat
oa from   Your weighty businesse unto you at large,
ft after the I onely say,you have just cause and great,
   To give God thanks your duties to discharge,
That here hath sent you,where with little sweat,
   But giving on your foes one valiant charge,
You may obtaine true fame and glory more,
   Than all your ancestors obtain'd before,

29

God,onely God that gives and guides good chance,
   Hath offer'd unto you this good occasion,
Your names and glories highly to advance,
   Which is in noble minds a strong perswasion :
Behold the kings of *England* and of *France*,
   Endanger'd greatly by the *Turks* invasion,
Shut up in trenches and in wals with shame,
   You may set free to your immortall fame.

30

The very law of nature and humanity
   Wils noble hearts to help the weak distres'd,
But more the lawes of state and Christianity,
   Without your help now like to be oppres'd,
And right Religion turn'd to Turkish vanity,
   Of which what harms will grow, may soon be guest,
Our temples faire with their foule idols fil'd,
   Our virgins (chast by vow) deflour'd and kil'd.

31

No mean,no stay,no end will be of slaughter,
   Of rapes and rapines wicked and unjust,
No man shall keep his sister,wife,or daughter,
   From out the reach of their unruly lust :
But now if you these sorrowes turn to laughter,
   And raise your honour troden in the dust,
They must owe you the freedomes and the lives
   Of them,their friends,their children, and their wives.

32

In ancient times a lawrell Civick crown   *Civica corona*
   To him that sav'd one citizen they gave,
If then they had such honour and renown,
   How many crownes shall you deserve to have,
If (not a townsman,but) a noble town,
   And thousand innocents therein you save ?
In you it lies them to preserve and cherish,
   That (but for you) in wo should pine and perish.

33

Which if they should (as God forbid they should)
   By these vile *Saracens* be over-run,
Then were the *Romane* Empire bought and sold,
   The holy Church were spoil'd and quite undone :
In you it is these huge harms to with-hold,
   By you alone must this exploit be done,
Tread then this path of praise so large and ample,
   Ile lead the way,follow but mine example.

1634, xvi. 28-33 (Harington, Sir J., *Orlando furioso*, London 1634, p. 123; Trin. Coll. Cam. VI. 12.27;
× 0·89)

The third edition was a line-for-line reprint of *1607*, but with the spelling modernized (there are only twenty-three non-current forms in the extract, half as many as before). There were also a few verbal changes, those in the extract being:

	1607	*1634*
28.6	our	your
30.3	and . . . of	of . . . and
31.6	their	your

The general tendency of the verbal alterations in *1634* (unlike those in *1607*) was to degrade the text, and these three look like copying errors. It is unlikely that any of them derived from an authoritative source such as a copy of *1607* marked up by Harington.

We can now go on to consider how and for whom Harington's Ariosto might most usefully be edited, and to see how McNulty's recent edition meets the requirements. It is important to establish at the outset the quality of the work that is to be edited. Harington was not a major creative writer, and his translation of Ariosto's epic is not a central work of English literature. It must also be reckoned a very long poem, even for an epic. Now a sixteenth-century poem 33,000 lines long of moderate literary quality is not going to appeal to the general reader however it is edited, and there is no point in trying to produce an edition for non-specialists who dislike old spelling and footnotes. Nevertheless Harington's Ariosto was a considerable achievement, and still interests specialists as a contribution to the booming literary culture of the 1590s; so that there is a place for a scholarly edition— or at least for a good reproduction—of the text.

In choosing the copy-text for such an edition of Harington's Ariosto we can eliminate three of the five early versions without much difficulty. The scribal MSa of Books 1–24 is unauthoritative in its spelling and other details, and although it contains some interesting verbal variants it will not do as copy-text. The third printed edition, *1634*, can also be eliminated straight away: produced after Harington's death, its verbal variants appear to have been unauthorized, and its details were modernized. The second edition, *1607*, is more promising, and indeed a cautious editor of fifty years ago would probably have chosen it as copy-text; arguing that, since it was the last edition produced in the author's lifetime and was revised by him, it represents his final intentions in detail as well as in general. Nowadays, however, an editor would probably believe that, if Harington ever proof-read the details of the text with care, he did so for the first edition, not for the second; and that alterations of detail introduced in the second edition are unlikely to have caught his attention. If this is so, *1591* is preferable to

1607, and the choice is either to take the first edition as copy-text for the whole work, or to take it for Books 1–13 only, using MSb for Books 14–46.

MSb, the largely autograph manuscript of two-thirds of the poem, gives us Harington's own spelling and probably his punctuation; and its details, although differing from the conventions of printed texts of the period, are not so eccentric as to give a specialist any real difficulty. If our chief concern were with Harington as an author, we might well decide to take MSb as copy-text for Books 14–46 in order to present the text with Harington's own details, even though we should have to use *1591* as copy-text for Books 1–13. There would be inconsistency of detail between the two parts, but not such as to cause the reader inconvenience.

It does seem likely, however, that most potential readers of an edition of Harington's Ariosto are going to be concerned with it primarily as a feature of the literary landscape of the 1590s, not on account of its poetic quality; and that they will want to be presented with the text that its original audience read. In this case the copy-text for a reset version would be the first edition, *1591*, which has the additional advantages of being complete (including the whole text, the prose commentaries, and the plates), and of being presented in a spelling more modern than that of Harington's manuscript. It is moreover the finished product towards which Harington was consciously working, for he took a great and explicit interest in the details of its production, even to the extent of specifying the fount of type in which parts of it were to be set.[11] He undoubtedly foresaw his book in its printed form, he was in a position to control its details, and it is a reasonable inference that he approved of the result.

---

[11] Harington wrote the following note to his printer at the end of the last book of the poem (MSb, fo. 336ª; ×0·69):

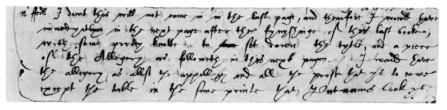

Mr Feeld I dowt this will not come in in the last page, and thearfore I wowld have immedyatly in the next page after the fynyshinge of this last booke, with some prety knotte: to ⟨ ⟩ set down the tytle, and a peece of the Allegory as followeth in this next page. / I would have the allegory (as allso the appollygy and all the prose that ys to come except the table [)] in the same printe that Putnams book ys./

The 'prety knotte' used by Field on p. 405 of *1591* was a rectangular woodcut used as a headpiece to the 'Allegorie'. 'Putnams book' was presumably George Puttenham's *Arte of English poesie*, printed by Field in 1589 (STC 20519); the 'Apologie' of Harington's book (which comes at the beginning but was printed last), the 'Allegorie', and the other prose at the end were in fact all set in the fount of pica roman that had been used for the text of Puttenham's book.

A photographic facsimile of *1591* itself would meet most scholarly needs, but it is also worth considering the criteria for a reset version based on *1591*. Such an edition for the specialist—or at least for the enthusiast—would be unmodernized, for its readers would not be repelled by the spellings of *1591*, some ninety per cent of which are still current. There is however much to be said for getting rid of long ſ and for modernizing the positional use of *i* and *j*, *u* and *v*.

The editor would therefore follow the details of *1591*, emending only undoubted errors. Similarly he would follow its words, except that he would probably incorporate the revisions made apparently by Harington to the text of *1607*. Just possibly he would decide not to incorporate these revisions on the ground that the first edition text is more interesting than the second because it is the one read by Harington's original audience in the 1590s; but *1607* appeared at what was also an interesting time, and there would seem to be good critical grounds for allowing Harington his verbal revisions.

This leaves the question of how the editor should present the evidence on which his text is based. The textual variation between the early versions of the poem, though of some technical interest, is of little historical or literary importance; but the editor is likely to feel that he should at least record the verbal variants in all the texts up to *1607*, and note departures from the details of the copy-text. Whether he should record the multitudinous variation of detail between the early texts, and the apparently unauthorized verbal variants of *1634*, is doubtful. An immensely detailed apparatus is an unreadable one. Those who want to study the punctuation, spelling, etc., of the manuscripts or of *1607* can do so in microform; and for the sake of the majority who do not, it is better to omit all but essential verbal variants from the critical edition.

Appendices of variants are unattractive and, since there is no case here for anything so elaborate and costly as parallel texts, the variants that are recorded may be given as footnotes to the poem, where they can easily be used, and do not seriously detract from the impact of the work (as may happen if a novel is presented with textual footnotes).

Robert McNulty's great critical text of Harington's Ariosto appeared in 1972. It was in fact the fifth printed edition of the work, and there is unlikely to be a sixth on anything like the same scale in the foreseeable future. McNulty reached several of the editorial decisions that have been proposed here, but not always by the same routes. Believing that both MSa and the whole of MSb had been copied out by Harington, he concluded that 'Harington seems to have cared almost nothing about spelling or punctuation'.[12] He therefore took *1591* as copy-text, following it in spelling, capitalization,

---

[12] McNulty's edition of Harington's Ariosto (see p. 13 n.), p. liii.

22

Nor doth the cruell rage and furie cease
With seing of so many people slaine,
But rather still it growes and doth encrease
Against those other that alive remaine,
Nor graunts he to the Churches any peace,
But ev'n as though the walls could suffer paine
He maketh furious warres against the walls
And flings against them store of firie balls.

23

Their houses all were built in Paris then
Of timber (and I judge this present houre
Of bricke and stone there are not sixe of ten)
Which made the Pagan then to bend his powre
To burne the houses, having killd the men,
And though that fire do of it selfe devour,
Yet he doth helpe the fire and overthrew them,
And those that lurkt within, he spoyld and slew
    them.

24

Had *Agramant* had like successe without
As had within this wicked *Rodomount*,
The walls of Paris had not kept him out
On which so oft he did assay to mount;
But now this while the Angel brought about
Renaldo *Renaldo* stout, the floure of Clarimount,
Both with the English and the Scots supplies
As secretly as Silence could devise,

25

And that they might them more unwares assaile
They cast a bridge a league above the towne
And passe the river to their best availe
And so in battle order comming downe
Not doubting, if their footing do not faile,
To get that day great glorie and renowne;
And still among the rankes *Renaldo* rides
And for things needfull evermore provides.

26

Two thousand horse in good Duke *Edmonds* guid
And thrise two thousand archers he doth send
To get to Paris on the tother side
To helpe within the cittie to defend.
(The cariages and other lets beside
To leave behind a while he doth entend.)
These succours greatly helpe the towne within,
And at Saint *Dennis* gate they let them in.

27

Renaldo takes the conduct of the rest,
Appointing each his office and his place
As in his skill and judgement seemeth best,
Sev'ring each band from other with a space
And seeing ev'rie one was prone and prest
As was to be required in such case.
He calleth all the Lords and Leaders chiefe,
And usd to them this pithy speech and breefe:

28

My Lords (quoth he) I need not to repeat   Renaldos
Your weightie busnesse unto you at large;   oration from
I onely say you have just cause and great   28 st. to the
                                                  34
To give God thankes, your dueties to discharge,
That here hath sent you, where with little sweat,
But giving on our foes one valiant charge,
You may obtaine true fame and glorie more
Then all your auncestors obtaind before.

29

God, onely God, that gives and guyds good
    chance,
Hath offerd unto you this good occasion
Your names and glories highly to advance,
Which is in noble minds a strong perswasion.
Behold the Kings of England and of France
Endangered greatly by the Turkes invasion,
Shut up in trenches and in walls with shame,
You may set free to your immortall fame.

22. *1. the ABC. his ab.   4. Against those other BC. towards the others a. Towards those
other bA. [b: as a; 'the' overwritten to 'those'; 's' of 'others' crossed out.]   5. Churches
aBC. churches bA.   6. ev'n bABC. even a.   8. And flings BC. Flinging abA.   firie AB. fyery a. fyry
b. fiery C.   23. 2. (and bABC. ᴀand a.   howre bABC. hower a.   *3. are not sixe of ten) ABC. is
one of tenneᴀ a. ys not six of ten ᴀ b. [b: 'ys not one of ten'; 'one' lined out; 'six' interlined.] [AR: 26. 7–8: 'E
ben creder si può, che in Parigi ora / De le diece le sei son così ancora.'] [NOTE: H. between a and b
has consulted AR.]   **4. powre abAB. power C.   6. fire bABC. fyer a.   devour bABC. devower a.
7. fire bABC. fyer a.   24. 1. Had bABC. And a.   3. him abABC. [a: 'them'; 't' struck out;
'e' overwritten to 'i'.]   **6. flowre bAB. flower aC.   25. 3. And passe BC. Passing abA.
6. great glorie and BC. glorie and great abA.   26. 1. in good Duke BC. under duke abA.   *Edmonds*
bABC. Edmond a.   5. (The bABC. ᴀ the a.   6. entend) bABC. intend ᴀ a.   *7. helpe ABC.
holp ab.   27. 3. As abABC. [a: 'and' overwritten to 'as'.]   **4. Sev'ring bABC. severing a.   other
abAB. others C.   7. Leaders BC. leaders abA.   8. And usd BC. Using abA.   28. 2. busnesse
unto A. bussynes to a. busynes unto b. bisnesse unto B. business unto C.   3. I onely BC. Onely I abA.
**6. But giving BC. Giving but abA.   our abAB. your C.   7. fame bABC. faythe a. [AR: 32. 8: 'Sopra
ogni nation vi doni onore.']   8. all BC. have abA   29. 2. offerd bABC. offered a   *5. Kings
aB. kings bAC.

Harington, Sir J., *Orlando furioso*, ed. McNulty, R., Oxford 1972, p. 178; ×0·77

30

The verie law of nature and humanitie
Wills noble hearts to helpe the weake dis-
tressed,
But more the lawes and state of Christianitie,
Without your helpe now like to be oppressed,
And right Religion turnd to Turkish vanitie,
Of which what harms will grow may soon be
guessed:
Our temples faire with their foule idols filled,
Our virgins (chast by vow) deflourd and killed.

31

No meane, no stay, no end will be of slaughter,
Of rapes and rapines wicked and unjust;
No man shall keepe his sister, wife, or daughter
From out the reach of their unruly lust;
But now if you these sorrowes turne to laughter
And raise their honour troden in the dust,
They must ow you the freedomes and the lives
Of them, their friends, their children and their
wives.

32

Civica corona In auncient times a laurell Civick crowne
To him that sav'd one citizen they gave.
If then they had such honour and renowne,
How many crownes shall you deserve to have
If (not a townsman but) a noble towne
And thousand innocents therein you save?
In you it lies them to preserve and cherish
That (but for you) in woe should pine and perish.

33

Which if they should (as God forbid they should)
By these vile Sarazens be over runne,
Then were the Romaine Empire bought and sold,
The holy Church were spoild and quite undone.
In you it is these huge harmes to withhold,
By you alone must this exploit be done.
Tread then this path of praise so large and
ample;
Ile lead the way, follow but mine example.

34

This speech by him pronounc'd with so good
spright,
With voice so audible, with comly grace,
Incensed them with such desire to fight
That tedious seem'd to them each little space,
And as we see in riding, men delight   Simile
To spurre a horse although he runne apace,
So stird *Renaldo* with this exhortation
Those of the English and the Scottish nation,

35

And having thus confirmd their forward hearts
And promis'd largely in his masters name
Great recompence to ev'rie mans desearts,
Unto the river walls he closely came.
His armie he devides in sundrie parts
Least breach of order bring them out of frame,
And with the Irish band he first indents
To spoile their lodgings and to rob their tents.

36

The rest he thus in prudent sort devides:
The vaward *Zerbin* hath in goverment;
The Duke of Lancaster the battell guides;
The Duke of Clarence with the rereward went.
Renaldo with some chosen men besides
Gives first the charge by generall consent;
Then on a sodaine they do raise a shout,
And fild our side with courage, theirs with doubt.

37

Renaldo riding out afore the rest
(With mind to do as much as he had said)
Puts spurs to horse and sets his speare in rest.
His onely sight the Pagans greatly fraid.
With fainting hearts, pale lookes, and panting
brest
They shew most certaine signes of minds dis-
maid;
Yet stout king *Puliano* shewes no token
Of heart astonished or courage broken,

---

30. 5. Religion ˄ turned BC. religyon now turnde a. religion ˄ turnd bA.   *7. temples abBC.
Temples A.   8. (chast by vow) bABC. ˄chaste by vow˄ a.   deflourd bABC. deflowerd a.
31. 4. From out BC. Out of abA.   5. these sorrowes bABC. their sorrowes a. [a: 'if you turne their
Joyes to laughter'; 'their Joyes' lined out; 'their sorrowes' interlined after 'you'. b: 'theyr' overwritten to
'thease'.]   **6. their abAB. your C.   32. 1. Civick BC. cyvicke abA.   4. deserve ABC.
desearv a. desarve b.   5. (not a townsman but) bABC. ˄not a thousand but˄ a.   *8. (but for you) ABC.
˄but for you˄ ab.   should bABC. shall a. [b: 'shall' overwritten to 'shold'.]   33. 1. (as . . . should)
bABC. ˄as . . . should˄ a.   *2. vile bABC. vyld a.   Sarazens A. Sarazines a. saracyns b. Saracens BC.
over runne bABC. overcome a.   *4. The ABC. then ab.   Church abBC. church A.   34. 1. pronounc'd BC. utterd abA.   2. audible, with bABC. audible and wth a.   3. desire bABC. desyer a.
35. **3. desearts A. desarts abB. deserts C.   36. Duke aBC. duke bA.   4. Duke aBC. duke bA.
Clarence BC. Clarens abA.   6. first the BC. the first abA.   7. a sodaine BC. the sodaine abA.
8. And fild BC. Filling abA.   37. 2. (with mind . . . said) BC. ˄meaning . . . sayd˄ a. (Meaning . . . said)
bA.   *3. Puts BC. setts a. Set b. Put A.   5. pale aBC. pall bA.   6. certaine aABC. carten b.
7. yet stout BC. Onely abA.

Harington, Sir J., *Orlando furioso*, ed. McNulty, R., Oxford 1972, p. 179; ×0·77

and italicization, and also in words except for the revisions of *1607*. His main
alteration of the copy-text was to replace its punctuation with a new punctuation of his own. He gave a full record in footnotes of the variants in all the
early texts up to *1634*, including details of capitalization but not of punctuation or of spelling (see pp. 26–7).

This is a massive work of scholarship, achieved with estimable accuracy.
There are a few mistakes in the text—in the extract McNulty misread a
broken 'ſi' ligature in 'buſineſſe' in *1591*, 28.2, as plain 'ſ'; and he missed
the variant word order in *1634*, 30.3—but they are certainly not many in
a task of such size and complexity.

McNulty chose the right copy-text, but his misunderstanding of the
nature and relationship of the manuscripts helped him to make the unfortunate decision to modernize the punctuation of *1591*, which he found
'confusing', and which he was willing to alter because he thought that
Harington cared almost nothing about spelling or punctuation. In fact it
looks as if Harington carefully amended the punctuation of MSb; and the
further refinement of the MSb punctuation in *1591* resulted in a system
which is seldom really confusing, and which is apparently authoritative.
It should have been kept.

McNulty's footnote apparatus, which would of course be substantial even
if it recorded no more than the verbal variants up to *1607*, is longer than it
needs to be because of the inclusion of the unauthoritative variants from
1634—for which no reason is given, for McNulty does not argue that they
are Harington's—and of such minutiae as variants of capitalization (see the
footnotes to 29.5, 30.7, 32.1, and 33.4 of McNulty's edition of the extract).
It is particularly pointless to record such detailed variants when no indication is given of the much more important emendation of the punctuation.

All the original illustrations are reproduced; and the editor has provided
a critical and historical introduction that is a model of its kind.

EXAMPLE 2

Milton, *A maske (Comus)*, 1634

MILTON wrote the dramatic entertainment which we know as *Comus* but
which he called simply *A maske* to honour and entertain the Earl of Bridgewater and his family and friends on the day Bridgewater became Lord
President of Wales.[1] The invitation to write it was extended to Milton,
perhaps at the instance of the court musician Henry Lawes, when the poet
was twenty-four or twenty-five years old and had published nothing but the
epitaph on Shakespeare which had appeared in the Second Folio of 1632.
This masque was composed, with music by Lawes, for a particular performance at Ludlow Castle, the official residence of the Lord President, on
Michaelmas day 1634.

The court masque, a well-established but not rigidly fixed form of entertainment, was characteristically a spectacular dramatization of morality,
compliment, and dance, performed by professional actors, singers, and
dancers, and by noble masquers who joined in a ceremonial measure at the
end.[2] The form of Milton's masque was necessarily different, for it had to
do without elaborate spectacle and (apart from Lawes himself) without
trained performers; and it was required moreover that three of the principal
parts should be played by children of the Earl, a girl of fifteen and two of
her brothers aged eleven and nine. Consequently there was more emphasis
than was usual in a masque on theme and on poetry, while the children's
parts had to be kept within their capacity to memorize and to speak. Nevertheless it was explicitly *A maske*, not a play or a poem, even though it had
in it notable elements of drama, and especially of poetry.

It is hard to divine Milton's original attitude to the work. He certainly
wrote it for the single performance in 1634, but after that he seems to have
been in no hurry to publish it; perhaps he was inhibited by his father's
disapproval of theatrical shows; perhaps he was thinking of keeping it for

[1] For the background, see W. R. Parker's great biography, *Milton*, 2 vols., Oxford 1968. The number
of books and papers about *A maske* is enormous, but there is a convenient summary in Hughes, M. Y.,
Woodhouse, A. S. P., and Bush, D., *A variorum commentary on the poems of John Milton*, ii. 3, London
1972, pp. 735–990. For references to the major studies of the text, see p. 30 n. 8 below.

Milton's masque was called *Comus* at least as early as 1698, and *Comus* has been its common name
since the early eighteenth century; but there is a modern tendency to revert to calling it *A maske*.

[2] *A variorum commentary*, ii. 3, pp. 740–55.

a substantial volume of poems such as the one he eventually published in 1645. Then in 1637 Henry Lawes, wearied he said with copying out Milton's masque by hand for his friends, published the first edition of *A maske presented at Ludlow Castle, 1634*, without giving Milton's name but with a note saying 'Although not openly acknowledg'd by the Author, yet it is a legitimate off-spring';[3] and it is certain that Milton had in fact prepared a revised text of the work for this first printing. The same revised text, with a few further amendments, was included in the acknowledged *Poems* of 1645, and it was reprinted with little further change in 1673.

Five early versions of *A maske* survive, two manuscript and three printed. The first is a manuscript in Milton's own hand (the Trinity manuscript, here called TMS),[4] which is the earliest version of the text that we have, but which also contains later revision. Next is a scribal copy (the Bridgewater manuscript, here BMS),[5] which postdates TMS and has some rearrangement of the text. (There is also an early manuscript of the words and music of the five songs written by Lawes; its verbal variants, not found elsewhere, appear to be unauthorized, and it will not concern us further.)[6] Finally there are the three editions printed in Milton's lifetime, and called here *1637*, *1645*, and *1673*;[7] the text which they reproduce is later and longer than that of TMS or BMS.

The precise textual status of TMS (a foolscap folio notebook of 24 leaves) has not been certainly established. We can be pretty sure that the holograph text of *A maske* in this notebook is a working copy which Milton made for private reference, but just how and when he wrote out the main text and revised it is still a matter for debate.[8] The most likely course of events is that Milton copied out the main text up to the end of the first version of the epilogue from rough drafts, and also made some of the alterations before

---

[3] STC 17937, A2ᵃ.

[4] Trinity College, Cambridge, MS. R.3.4; for facsimiles see p. 54 n. 21.

[5] Now in the library of the Duke of Sutherland, Mertoun, Roxburghshire.

[6] British Library MS. Add. 53723.

[7] STC 17937; Wing M2160; Wing M2161.

[8] See Diekhoff, J. S., 'The text of *Comus*, 1634 to 1645', *PMLA*, lii, 1937, pp. 705-27; Shawcross, J. T., 'Certain relationships of the manuscripts of *Comus*', *PBSA*, liv, 1960, pp. 38-56, 293-4. S. E. Sprott has since surveyed all the evidence in an impressive monograph (Milton, J., *A maske, the earlier versions*, Toronto and Buffalo 1973), which includes parallel transcripts of TMS, BMS, and *1637*, and transcripts of the British Library manuscripts of the songs. While these authorities all agree about the essential relationships of the early texts, Sprott is unconvinced by Diekhoff's hypothesis that the whole of the TMS text was a transcript from an earlier draft, though allowing that Milton may have drafted passages on rough sheets as he went along; and Sprott does not accept Shawcross's argument from the evidence of Milton's handwriting that not only the later corrections and additions but also the main text of TMS (and therefore also that of BMS) was written in 1637, rather than in 1634. Although Sprott's analysis of the alterations in TMS and of the hypothetical transcript made from it seems to me over-complicated, I accept his case in the main and have based my own account on it. But even if Sprott is wrong, and Diekhoff and Shawcross are right, our view of the genealogical relationship between TMS, BMS, and the printed texts is not affected.

the performance of the masque in 1634; but that most of the other alterations and the second version of the epilogue were added by Milton in 1637, in the course of preparing a revised text for Lawes's edition.

BMS is a scribal transcript of the masque, made perhaps for presentation to the Earl of Bridgewater or to Lord Brackley at about the time of the original performance. Its text is related to the earlier (1634) stage of the TMS text, after some but not all of Milton's alterations had been made, but it was not copied directly from TMS; there was an intermediate transcript, probably made by Milton, and perhaps an actors' version or set of parts. BMS also incorporates a number of rearrangements and cuts which appear to represent adaptations made for the performance of the masque.[9]

The first printed edition, *1637*, was also set from a transcript of TMS, probably the one which had been used by the scribe of BMS, but updated in 1637 by the incorporation of the later TMS alterations and by the addition of thirty-seven extra lines and a number of other alterations which did not appear in TMS. This revised and expanded text was essentially the final version of *A maske*. The authorized second edition, *1645*, which was set from the first, and the third edition, *1673*, which was set from the second, each incorporated only a handful of relatively minor changes.

It is suggested, then, that Milton wrote out the first full copy of his masque from rough work-sheets as a working manuscript in a private note-book, TMS. This was in 1634, but Milton was to keep the notebook by him for many years and to use it for noting down later alterations to the text. After revising the TMS text, he made a fair copy (now lost) from which the performance text of 1634 was derived, as was a scribal copy (BMS, also 1634), and probably the copies Lawes made for his friends. Three years later, in 1637, Milton further revised the text for publication, making drafts for some of the new readings in TMS, and transferring them together with further alterations to the fair copy. The fair copy, thus revised and expanded, was used by the compositor of *1637*; from which derived successively, and with only minor change, *1645* and *1673* (see p. 32).

Having considered the probable relationship between the early texts of Milton's masque, we can try to choose the copy-text for an edition and to decide how it might be perfected and presented. We will begin by comparing extracts from the early texts. Two passages are illustrated, first by means of

---

[9] The main adaptations in BMS, which do not appear in any other surviving text, were (1) the transfer of part of the first epilogue to the beginning, to make a prologue; (2) the distribution of some of the Demon's lines to the two Brothers; and (3) the omission of two substantial and four short passages. Some of the changes may have been made by Lawes, others by Milton himself; see S. E. Sprott's Milton, J., *A maske* . . ., pp. 19–23.

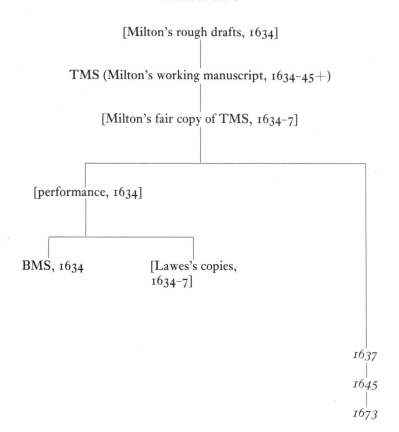

[Milton's rough drafts, 1634]

TMS (Milton's working manuscript, 1634-45+)

[Milton's fair copy of TMS, 1634-7]

[performance, 1634]

BMS, 1634   [Lawes's copies, 1634-7]

1637

1645

1673

facsimiles of their appearance in TMS, BMS, *1637*, and *1645*; and then by means of parallel transcripts[10] of the TMS, BMS, and *1637* versions.

The first passage is from the opening of the masque: the first 34 lines of TMS (a1-a34), the first 38 lines of BMS (b1-b38), and the first 18 lines of *1637* and *1645* (c1-c18, d1-d18) (see pp. 33-41).

Besides differing in detail from each other and from the printed texts, the two manuscript versions of the opening of the masque have major differences that are peculiar to them. The holograph TMS, first, has a passage of 15 lines (a5-a19, a6 being crossed out and repeated as a8) which Milton composed—this looks like a first draft—revised, and finally deleted, so that it does not appear in any of the other texts; and he also deleted line a23. It seems that all the changes made to this passage in TMS were early ones,

(*continued on p.* 42)

[10] The transcripts are based on those in S. E. Sprott's Milton, J., *A maske . . .*, Toronto and Buffalo 1973.

A maske   1634.
                    the first scene discovers a wilde wood.

A Guardian spirit, or Dæmon

Before the starrie threshold of Joves court
my mansion is, where those immortall shapes
of bright aëreall spirits live insphear'd
in regions mild of calme & serene aire
amidst the gardens hesperian gardens, on whose bankes

bedew'd with nectar & celestiall songs
æternall roses yeild & hyacinth
& fruits of golden rind, on whose faire tree
the scalie harnest wachfull dragon keeps
his unenchanted eye & round the verge
& sacred limits of this happie Isle blissfull
the jealous ocean that old river winds
his farr-extended armes till with steepe fall
halfe his waste flood ye wide Atlantique fills
& halfe the slow unfadom'd poole of Stygian poole   (wonder
but to those I was not sent to court yor
                                              strange removed clim
yet thence I come and oft fro thence behold

above the smoke & stirre of this dim spot
with men call earth, & with low-thoughted care
strive to keepe up a fraile & feaverish beeing
beyond the written date of mortall change
confind & pesterd in this pinfold heere
unmindfull of the crowne that Vertue gives
after this mortall change to her true servants
amoungst the enthron'd gods on sainted seats
yet some there be that by due steps aspire
to lay thire just hands on that golden key
that opens the palace of æternitie   ope?
to such my errand is, & but for such
I would not soyle these pure ambrosiall weeds
with the rank vapours of this sin-worne mould
but to my now Neptune whose sway besids the sway

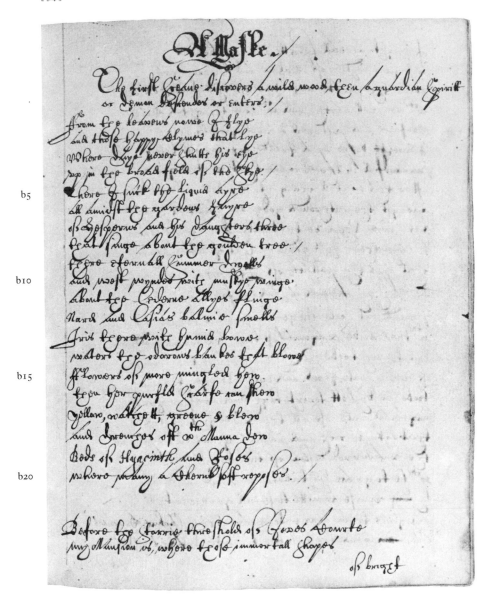

BMS (The Bridgewater MS. of *A maske*, fo. 2ᵃ; ×0·80)

of bright aereall spirits live insphear'd
in regions mylde of Calme and serene ayre
b25 above the smoake and stirre of this dim spott
wch men call earth, and wth low-thoughted care
confind and pester'd in this pinfold heere
strive to keepe up a fraile & feavourish beeinge
unmindfull of the crowne that vertue gives
b30 after this mortall chaunge to her true servants
amongst the enthron'd gods, on sainted seats
yet some there be that by due stepps aspire
to lay theyr just hands on that golden key
that opes the pallace of eternitie:
b35 to such my errand is, and but for such
I would not soile these pure ambrosiall weeds
wth the ranke vapours of this sin-worne mould
but to my taske; Neptune besides the swaye

BMS (The Bridgewater MS of *A maske*, fo. 2^{b}; ×0·80)

(1)

A MASKE

PERFORMED BEFORE

the Præfident of WALES

at *Ludlow*, 1 6 3 4.

The firſt Scene diſcovers a wild
wood.

The attendant Spirit deſcends or enters,

Before the ſtarrie threſhold of *Ioves* Court
My manſion is, where thoſe immortall ſhapes
Of bright aëreall Spirits live inſphear'd
In Regions mild of calme and ſerene aire,
c5　Above the ſmoake and ſtirre of this dim ſpot
Which men call Earth, and with low-thoughted care
Confin'd, and peſter'd in this pin-fold here,
Strive to keepe up a fraile, and feaveriſh being
Vnmindfull of the crowne that Vertue gives
c10　After this mortall change to her true Servants
Amongſt the enthron'd gods on Sainted ſeats.
Yet ſome there be that by due ſteps aſpire

B　　　　　　　　　To

(2)

To lay their juſt hands on that golden key
That ope's the palace of Æternity:
c15　To ſuch my errand is, and but for ſuch
I would not ſoile theſe pure ambroſial weeds
With the ranck vapours of this Sin-worne mould.
But to my task. *Neptune* beſides the ſway

1637 ([Milton, J.], *A maske presented at Ludlow Castle*, *1634*, London 1637, pp. 1-2; Trin. Coll. Cam.
Capell Q.14.3; ×0·83)

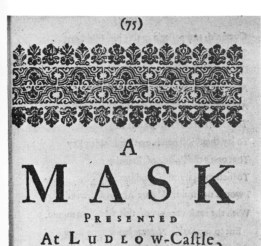

(75)

A MASK

PRESENTED
At LUDLOW-Castle,
1634. &c.

The first Scene discovers a wilde Wood.

The attendant Spirit descends or enters.

Efore the starry threshold of *Joves* Court
My mansion is, where those immortal shapes
Of bright aëreal Spirits live insphear'd
In Regions milde of calm and serene Ayr,
Above the smoak and stirr of this dim spot,
Which men call Earth, and with low-thoughted care
Confin'd,

1645 (Milton, J., *Poems*, London 1645, pp. 75-6; Trin. Coll. Cam. C.11.151; ×0·84)

(76)

Confin'd, and pester'd in this pin-fold here,
Strive to keep up a frail, and Feaverish being
Unmindfull of the crown that Vertue gives
d10 After this mortal change, to her true Servants
Amongst the enthron'd gods on Sainted seats.
Yet som there be that by due steps aspire
To lay their just hands on that Golden Key
That ope's the Palace of Eternity :
d15 To such my errand is, and but for such,
I would not soil these pure Ambrosial weeds,
With the rank vapours of this Sin-worn mould,
But to my task. *Neptune* besides the sway

A maske   1634.   13

the first scene discovers a wild wood

A Guardian spirit, or Dæmon

Before the starrie threshold of Ioves court

my mansion is, where those imortall shapes

of bright aereall spirits live insphear'd

in regions mild of calme & serene aire ~~where the banks~~

A Maske./

A MASKE

PERFORMED BEFORE

the Præsident of WALES

at *Ludlow*, 1634.

The first sceane discovers a wild wood, then a guardian spiritt
or demon descendes or enters. /

The first Scene discovers a wild

wood.

The attendant Spirit descends or enters.

   From the heavens nowe I flye

and those happy Clymes that lye

Where daye never shutts his eye

up in the broad field of the skye. /

b5   There I suck the liquid ayre

all amidst the gardens fayre

of Hesperus and his daughters three

that singe about the goulden tree. /

there eternall summer dwells

b10   and west wyndes with muskye winge

about the Cederne allyes flinge

Nard and Casias balmie smells

Iris there with humid bowe

waters the odorous bankes that blowe

b15   Flowers of more mingled hew

then her purfld scarfe can shew

yellow, watchett, greene & blew

and drenches oft wth Manna dew

Beds of *Hyacinth* and Roses

b20   where many a Cherub soft reposes. /

Before the starrie threshold of Ioves Courte

my Mansion is, where those immortall shapes

of bright aereall spiritts live inspheard

in regions mylde of Calme and Cerene ayre

B Efore the starrie threshold of *Ioves* Court

My mansion is, where those immortall shapes

Of bright aëreall Spirits live insphear'd

In Regions mild of calme and serene aire,

Transcript of *A maske* lines 1–18 in TMS, BMS, and *1637*

a5   amidst the ~~gardens~~ Hespian gardens, ~~on , whose bancks~~

2

~~æternall roses grow & hyacinth~~

bedew'd wth nectar & celestiall songs

               *yeeld   *   *

                                                blow grow ~~blosme~~

aeternall roses ~~grow~~, & hyacinth

& fruits of golden rind, on whose faire tree

                      ever

a10   the scalie-harnest ~~watchfull~~ dragons ∧ keeps

         uninchanted

his ~~never charmed~~ eye, & round the verge

& sacred limits of this *happie Isle ~~blissfull~~ *blisfull

the jealous ocean that old river winds

his farre-extended armes till wth steepe fall

a15   halfe his wast flood ye wide Atlantique fills

                                       (wonder

& halfe the slow unfadom'd ~~poole of styx~~ [|] stygian poole

~~I doubt me gentle mortalls these may seeme~~ but soft I was not sent to court yor

~~strange distances to heare & unknowne climes~~ wth distant worlds, & strange removed clim[e]

yet thence I come and oft frō thence behold

             a

a20 above the smoke & stirre of this dim,~~[narrow]~~ spot

wch men call earth, & wth low-thoughted care

  2 strive to keepe up a fraile & feavourish beeing

   ~~beyond the written date of mortall change~~

  1 confin'd & pester'd in this pinfold heere

a25   unmindfull of the crowne that vertue gives

after this mortall change to her true servants

amoungst the enthron'd gods on sainted seates

yet some there be that by due steps aspire

to lay thire just hands on that golden key

a30   that *shews the palace of æternity   *

                                     ope's

to such my errand is, & but for such

I would not soyle these pure ambrosiall weeds

wth the ranck vapours of this sin-worne mould

      taske

but to my ∧ ~~buisnesse now.~~ Neptune ~~whose sway~~ besids the sway b25 above the smoake and stirr of this dim spott

wᶜʰ men call earth, and wᶜʰ low-thoughted Care

Confinde and pestered in this pinfold heere

strive to keepe vp a fraile & fevourish beeinge

vnmindfull of the Crowne that vertue gives

b30 after this mortall change to her true servants

amongst the enthroned gods, on sainted seats

yet some there be that with due stepps aspire

to laye their lust hands on that goulden keye

that opes the pallace of *Æternitie:*

b35 To such my errand is, and but for such

I would not soile theese pure ambrosiall weedes

wᵗʰ the ranke vapours of this sin-worne moulde

but to my taske; *Neptune* besides the swaye

c5 Above the smoake and stirre of this dim spot

Which men call Earth, and with low-thoughted care

Confin'd, and pester'd in this pin-fold here,

Strive to keepe up a fraile, and feaverish being

Vnmindfull of the crowne that Vertue gives

c10 After this mortall change to her true Servants

Amongst the enthron'd gods on Sainted seats.

Yet some there be that by due steps aspire

To lay their just hands on that golden key

That ope's the palace of Æternity:

c15 To such my errand is, and but for such

I would not soile these pure ambrosial weeds

With the ranck vapours of this Sin-worne mould.

But to my task. *Neptune* besides the sway

Transcript of *A maske* lines 1–18 in TMS, BMS, and *1637* (continued)

dating from 1634 rather than 1637: the deleted lines, the reversal of the order of lines a22 and a24, and the verbal alterations in lines a20, a30, and a34, appear in their corrected form in BMS as well as in the printed texts. The changing form of the stage direction at the beginning seems to run successively from TMS through BMS to *1637*.

BMS too has a passage which is peculiar to it, but one of a different sort: here the masque opens with 20 lines, b1–b20, which have been transferred with one necessary verbal alteration from the cancelled version of the epilogue at the end of the TMS text.[11] This change was presumably made (perhaps by Lawes) to provide an opening song for the performance in 1634.

The remaining lines of TMS (a1–a4, a20–a22, a24–a34, with a22 and a24 reversed) and of BMS (b21–b38) parallel the first 18 lines of the printed texts (c1–c18, d1–d18), and these passages in the manuscripts may now be compared in detail with each other and with the equivalent passages in the printed versions.

Two words are changed in BMS: 'wth' in TMS a21 is 'w^{ch}' in BMS b26; and 'by' in a28 is 'with' in b32: both the BMS readings appear to be copying errors. There are no differences of words between TMS and the printed versions.[12]

The spelling which varies most from TMS is that of BMS, which was written by a scribe whose spelling habits were both personal and old-fashioned. Occasionally (though not in this particular passage) he reproduces an obviously Miltonic spelling, but for the most part he goes his own way, deviating from his copy (presumably Milton's transcript) in ways which do not seem to have any significance; here there are 27 differences of spelling, but they are not worth listing. More interesting is the relative lack of spelling variation between TMS and *1637*, only 10 of the 142 TMS spellings being altered (Harington's compositor altered more than one word in three): heere/here (a24/c7), feavourish beeing/feaverish being (a22/c8), amoungst, seates/Amongst, seats (a27/c11), thire/their (a29/c13), soyle, ambrosiall/soile, ambrosial (a32/c16), taske, besids/task, besides (a34/c18). This lack of spelling difference between TMS and *1637* suggests that the

---

[11] TMS p. [28], where the first line of the cancelled epilogue reads 'To the Ocean now I fly'; this line is altered in the BMS prologue to 'From the heavens nowe I flye'.

[12] For the purpose of comparing the texts of *A maske* the differences between their various elements are defined as follows:

Differences of *words* are words changed in the lines of verse, and do not include altered stage directions or speech headings.

Differences of *spelling* are alterations of letters, and do not include changes of capitalization, italicization, hyphenation, and word division, or the use of internal apostrophes where no letters are altered, or the expansion of contractions, or the equivalent use of i/j f/s u/v.

Differences of *punctuation* are additions or deletions of punctuation marks, and do not include the substitution of one mark for another.

intermediate transcript of TMS used by the printer had been made by Milton himself. The compositor of *1645*, setting from a copy of *1637*, followed 9 of the 10 non-TMS spellings from *1637* (the tenth, 'soil' in d16, is a new variant), but he introduced a further 16 spelling changes of his own: starrie/starry (a1/d1), immortall/immortal (a2/d2), aereall/aëreal (a3/d3), mild, calme, aire/milde, calm, Ayr (a4/d4), smoake, stirre/smoak, stirr (a20/d5), keepe, fraile/keep, frail (a22/d8), crowne/crown (a25/d9), mortall/mortal (a26/d10), some/som (a28/d12), æternity/Eternity (a30/d14), ranck, worne/rank, worn (a33/d17); 'snch' in d15 is a misprint.

The punctuation of TMS is light and rhetorical. In the 18 lines of this passage which are paralleled by the printed versions, TMS has only 4 punctuation marks: the internal commas in lines a2, a21, and a31, and the full stop at the end of the sentence in a34: a hint (all Milton needed, no doubt) at how the lines were to be spoken. The punctuation of BMS, unlike its spelling, generally follows that of TMS; here there is no more than an extra comma in b31. The punctuation of *1637*, however, adds a number of grammatical stops, especially at the ends of lines which Milton did not normally punctuate: all the TMS stops are reproduced, together with 2 more internal commas (c7, c8) and 5 stops at the ends of lines c4, c7, c11, c14, and c17. The punctuation of *1645* is heavier still, Milton's punctuation and the additional stops of *1637* all being retained, and 4 more being added (an internal comma in d10 and stops at the ends of d5, d15, and d16).[13]

Thus comparison of the texts of this first passage from *A maske* suggests that the spelling and punctuation of *1637* is closer to Milton's own manuscript practice than *1645*; and this is confirmed by further investigation. Here is a second passage for comparison, from the dialogue of the two Brothers, about a third of the way through the masque (see pp. 44–51).

In this second extract the major revisions are late, not early ones. The TMS text was written out in 1634 with 36 lines (e1–e29, e46–e52), which were followed in BMS (f1–f36). Then in 1637 10 lines (e20–e29) were reworked: 3 of them (e27–e29) were cancelled and replaced by 9 new lines, and the revised passage of 16 lines was copied out on a slip of paper which was attached to margin of p. 19 of TMS, with a direction to it written opposite lines e20–e22 on the facing p. [18] (it probably said 'read the paper over against'). During the nineteenth century this slip was broken off and was then negligently lost by a Librarian of Trinity, leaving only the left-hand margin which shows the first letter or two of ten of the added lines;

(*continued on p. 52*)

---

[13] Milton may well have read proof for *1637* and *1645*, but there is no particular reason to suppose that he altered or controlled the punctuation, spelling, or capitalization of these editions.

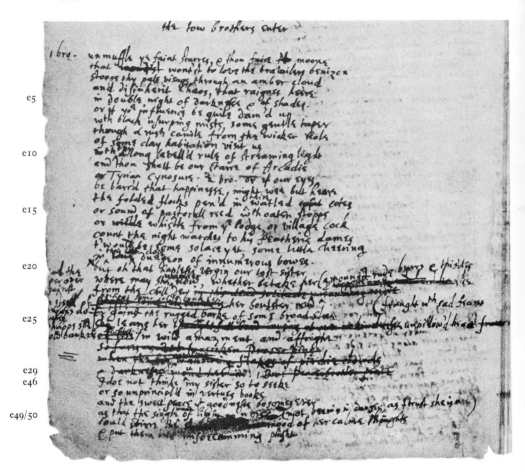

TMS (Trin. Coll. Cam. MS. R.3.4, p. 18; ×0·66)

The two brothers.

Unmuffle yee faint starrs, and thou fair moone
that woust to love the travailors benizon
Stoope thy pale visadge through an amber clonde
and disinherit Chaos, that raignes heere
in double night of, darknes, and of, shades
or if yo'ur influence be quite dam'd up
w'th black usurpinge mists, some gentle taper
though a rushe candle, from the wicker hole
of, some clay habitacon visit us
w'th thy long levell'd rule of streaming light
and thou shalt be o'r starr of, Arcady
or Tirian Cynosure. 2 bro: or if our eyes
be barrd that happines might wee but heare
the folded flocks pend in their wattled cotes
or sound of, pastorall reede w'th sweet stopps
or whistle from the lodge, or village cock
count the night watches to his feathery dames
t'would be some solace yet, some little cheering
in this lone dungeon of, innumerous boows,
but O that hapless virgin o lost sister
where may she wander now, wher'er shee be
from the chill dewe, amongst rude burrs & thisthes
p'haps some cold bank is her bolster now
or against the ruggod barke of, some broade Elme
leanes her unpillow'd head fraught w'th sad feares
or els in wilde amazement and affright,
                                        &c.

for theres no div. fantahon Proserpine
when the bigg rowlinge flakes of, pitchey clonds
and darknes wound her in: El. bro: peace brother peace
I doe not thinke my sister soe to seeke
or soe unprincipled in vertues booke,
and the sweete peace that goodnes bosoms ever
as that the single want of, light and noise
(not beinge in danger, as I hope shee is not)
could stirr the constant moode of, her calme thoughts
and put them into misbecominge plight

BMS (The Bridgewater MS. of *A maske*, fos. 7^b–8^a; ×0·72)

The two Brothers.

Eld.bro. Vnmuffle yee faint ſtars,and thou fair moon
That wontſt to loue the travailers benizon
Stoope thy pale viſage through an amber cloud
And diſinherit *Chaos*, that raigns here
In double night of darkneſſe, and of ſhades ;
Or if your influence be quite damm'd up
With black uſurping miſts, ſome gentle taper,
Though a ruſh candle from the wicker hole
Of ſome clay habitation viſit us
With thy long levell'd rule of ſtreaming light,
And thou ſhalt be our ſtarre of *Arcadie*
Or *Tyrian* Cynoſure.   *2 Bro.* Or if our eyes
Be barr'd that happineſſe, might we but heare
The folded flocks pen'd in their watled cotes,
Or ſound of paſtoral reed with oaten ſtops,
Or whiſtle from the Lodge, or village cock

Count

(13)

Count the night watches to his featherie Dames,
T'would be ſome ſolace yet, ſome little chearing.
In this cloſe dungeon of innumerous bowes.
But ô that hapleſſe virgin our loſt ſiſter
Where may ſhe wander now, whether betake her
From the chill dew, amongſt rude burs and thiſtles ?
Perhaps ſome cold banke is her boulſter now
Or 'gainſt the rugged barke of ſome broad Elme
Leans her unpillow'd head fraught with ſad fears.
What if in wild amazement, and affright.
Or while we ſpeake within the direfull graſpe
Of Savage hunger, or of Savage heat ?
Eld: bro. Peace brother, be not over exquiſite
To caſt the faſhion of uncertaine evils ;
For grant they be ſo, while they reſt unknowne
What need a man foreſtall his date of griefe
And run to meet what he would moſt avoid ?
Or if they be but falſe alarms of Feare.
How bitter is ſuch ſelfe-deluſion ?
I doe not thinke my ſiſter ſo to ſeeke
Or ſo unprincipl'd in vertues book
And the ſweet peace that goodneſſe boſoms ever
As that the ſingle want of light, and noiſe
(Not being in danger, as I truſt ſhe is not)
Could ſtir the conſtant mood of her calme thoughts
And put them into miſbecomming plight.

g5
g10
g15
g20
g25
g30
g35
g40

1637 ([Milton, J.], *A maske presented at Ludlow Castle, 1634,* London 1637, pp. 12-13; Trin. Coll. Cam. Capell Q.14.3; ×0·77)

(90)

The two Brothers.

Eld. Bro. Unmuffle ye faint ſtars, and thou fair Moon
That wontſt to love the travailers benizon,
Stoop thy pale viſage through an amber cloud,
And diſinherit *Chaos*, that raigns here
h5   In double night of darknes, and of ſhades ;
Or if your influence be quite damm'd up
With black uſurping miſts, ſom gentle taper
Though a ruſh Candle from the wicker hole
Of ſom clay habitation viſit us
h10 With thy long levell'd rule of ſtreaming light,
And thou ſhalt be our ſtar of *Arcady*,
Or *Tyrian* Cynoſure *2 Bro.* Or if our eyes
Be barr'd that happines, might we but hear
The folded flocks pen'd in their watled cotes,
h15 Or ſound of paſtoral reed with oaten ſtops,
Or whiſtle from the Lodge, or village cock
Count the night watches to his feathery Dames,
T'would be ſom ſolace yet, ſom little chearing
In this cloſe dungeon of innumerous bowes.
h20 But O that haples virgin our loſt ſiſter
Where may ſhe wander now, whether betake her
From the chill dew, amongſt rude burrs and thiſtles ?
                                    Perhaps

1645 (Milton, J., *Poems*, London 1645, pp. 90–1 ; Trin. Coll. Cam. C.11.151 ; ×0·75)

(91)

Perhaps ſom cold bank is her boulſter now
Or 'gainſt the rugged bark of ſom broad Elm
h25 Leans her unpillow'd head fraught with ſad fears.
What if in wild amazement, and affright,
Or while we ſpeak within the direfull graſp
Of Savage hunger, or of Savage heat ?
   Eld. Bro. Peace brother, be not over-exquiſite
h30 To caſt the faſhion of uncertain evils;
For grant they be ſo, while they reſt unknown,
What need a man foreſtall his date of grief,
And run to meet what he would moſt avoid ?
Or if they be but falſe alarms of Fear,
h35 How bitter is ſuch ſelf-deluſion ?
I do not think my ſiſter ſo to ſeek,
Or ſo unprincipl'd in vertues book,
And the ſweet peace that goodnes booſoms ever,
As that the ſingle want of light and noiſe
h40 (Not being in danger, as I truſt ſhe is not)
Could ſtir the conſtant mood of her calm thoughts,
And put them into miſ-becoming plight.

the tow brothers enter

1 bro. unmuffle ye faint starres, & thou faire ~~N~~ moone

that ~~wont'st~~ wont'st to love the travailers benizon

stoope thy pale visage through an amber cloud

and disinherit Chaos, that raignes heere

e5 in double night of darknesse & of shades.

or if yor influence be quite dam'd up

wth black usurping mists, some gentle taper

though a rush candle from the wicker hole

of some clay habitation visit us

          thy
e10 wth ∧ ~~a~~ long levell'd rule of streaming light

and thou shalt be our starre of Arcadie

or Tyrian Cynosure. 2 bro. or if our eyes

be barr'd that happinesse, might wee but heare

          thire
the folded flocks pen'd in ∧ watled e[~~osat~~] cotes

e15 or sound of pastorall reed wth oaten stopps

or ~~wistle~~ whistle from ye lodge, or village cock

count the night watches to his featherie dames

t'would be some solace yet, some little cheering

          this ~~sad~~ close
in ∧ ~~lone~~ ∧ dungeon of innumerous bowes.

              ×
e20 ead the   but oh that haplesse vergin our lost sister

              wander   (amoungst rude burrs & thistles
per over __   where may she ∧ now, whether betake her ~~phapps some cold hard banke~~

gainst /   from the chill dew ~~in this dead solitude surrounding wilde,~~

        /   perhaps some cold bank is   ∧ ∧
[n]ste[a]d of ~~phapps some cold banck[e] is~~ her boulster now   (fraught wth sad feares

[/]s do-   or 'gainst the rugged barke of some broad elme

  wne /   *
e25 happs sōe   she leans her ~~thoughtfull head musing at our unkindne~~sse unpillow'd head ~~frau~~

              what if
old banke is ~~or else~~ in wild amazment, and affright

──────   ~~so fares as did forsaken Proserpine~~

                  ~~rowling~~
──────   ~~when the big ∧ wallowing flakes of pitchie clowds~~

                              u
──────   ~~& darkness wond her in~~. 1 Bro[.] ~~Peace brother peace~~

                      ∧

1637

The two brothers

El: bro Vnmuffle yee fainte starrs, and thou faier moone
  that wonst to love the travailers benizon
  stoope thy pale visadge through an amber cloude
  and disinherit Chaos, that raignes heere
f5 in double night of darkness, and of shades
  or if yor influence be quite damm'd vp
  wth black vsurpinge mists, some gentle taper
  though a rushe candle, from the wicker hole
  of some claye habitacō visite vs
f10 wth thy long levell'd rule of streaming light
  and thou shalt be o^r starr of Arcady
  of Tirian Cynosure: *2 bro:* or if o^r eyes
  be barr'd that happines might wee but heare
  the folded flocks pen'd in their watled cotes
f15 or sound of pastorall reede with oaten stopps
  or whistle from the lodge, or village Cock
  count the night watches to his featherie dames
  t'would be some solace yet, some little cheeringe
  in this lone dungeon of inumerous bows,
f20 but O that haples virgin o^r lost sister
  where may she wander nowe? whether betake her
  from the chill dewe, amongst rude burrs & thistles
  phaps some could banke is her boulster nowe,
  or gainst the rugged barke of some broade Elme
f25 leanes her vnpillow'd head fraught wth sad feares
  or els in wild amazement and affright,
  soe fares as did forsaken *Proserpine*
  when the bigg rowling flakes of pitchie clouds
  and darkness wound her in: *El bro:* peace brother peace

The two Brothers.

Eld. bro. Vnmuffle yee faint stars, and thou fair moon
  That wontst to love the travailers benizon
  Stoope thy pale visage through an amber cloud
  And disinherit *Chaos*, that raigns here
g5 In double night of darknesse, and of shades;
  Or if your influence be quite damm'd up
  With black usurping mists, some gentle taper
  Though a rush candle from the wicker hole
  Of some clay habitation visit us
g10 With thy long levell'd rule of streaming light
  And thou shalt be our starre of *Arcadie*
  Or *Tyrian* Cynosure. *2 Bro.* Or if our eyes
  Be barr'd that happinesse, might we but heare
  The folded flocks pen'd in their watled cotes,
g15 Or sound of pastoral reed with oaten stops,
  Or whistle from the Lodge, or village cock
  Count the night watches to his featherie Dames,
  T'would be some solace yet, some little chearing
  In this close dungeon of innumerous bowes.

Transcript of *A maske* lines 331–72 in TMS, BMS, and *1637*

[ ] ⟨Reconstructed '[pa]per over [a]gainst'⟩

e30 bu[t O that haplesse virgin our lost sister]

wh[ere may she wander now, whether betake her]

fr[om the chill dew amoungst rude burrs & thistles]

[phapps some cold banke is her boulster now]

o[r gainst the rugged barke of some broad elme]

e35 l[eans her unpillow'd head fraught wᵗʰ sad feares]

w[hat if in wild amazment, & affright]

or [while we speake wᵗʰin the direfull graspe]

o[f salvage hunger or of salvage heate]

1 [bro. peace brother be not over exquisit]

e40 t[o cast the fashion of uncertaine evills]

[wᶜʰ grant they be so while they rest unknowne]

his
[what need a man forestall ~~the~~ date of greife]

[and run to meet what he would most avoid]

[or if they be but false alarms of feare]

such
e45 [how bitter is ~~this~~ selfe delusion]

I doe not thinke my sister so to seeke

or so unprincipl'd in vertues booke

and the sweet peace yᵗ goodnesse bosomes ever

want
e49/50 as that the single ˄ of light & noise (not beeing in danger, as I trust she is not)

could stirre the ~~s[tabl]e~~ [co]nstant mood of her calme thoughts

& put them into misbecomming plight

g20 But ô that haplesse virgin our lost sister

Where may she wander now, whether betake her

From the chill dew, amongst rude burs and thistles?

Perhaps some cold banke is her boulster now

Or 'gainst the rugged barke of some broad Elme

g25 Leans her unpillow'd head fraught with sad fears.

What if in wild amazement, and affright

Or while we speake within the direfull graspe

Of Savage hunger, or of Savage heat?

    Eld: bro. Peace brother, be no over exquisite

g30 To cast the fashion of uncertaine evils,

For grant they be so, while they rest unknowne

What need a man forestall his date of griefe

And run to meet what he would most avoid?

Or if they be but false alarms of Feare

g35 How bitter is such selfe-delusion?

f30 I doe not thinke my sister soe to seeke	I doe not thinke my sister so to seeke
or soe vnprincipl'd in vertues booke,	Or so unprincipl'd in vertues book
and the sweete peace that goodness bosoms ever	And the sweet peace that goodnesse bosoms ever
as that the single want of light and noise	As that the single want of light, and noise
(not beinge in danger, as I hope she is not)	g40 (Not being in danger, as I trust she is not)
f35 could stirr the constant mood of her calme thoughts	Could stir the constant mood of her calme thoughts
and put them into misbecominge plight	And put them into mis-becomming plight.

Transcript of *A maske* lines 331–72 in TMS, BMS, and *1637* (continued)

but it was transcribed before it disappeared, and lines e30–e45 of the transcript given here are a reconstruction of its contents made by S. E. Sprott.[14]

There remain 26 comparable lines (201 words): e1–e19, e46–e52; f1–f19, f30–f36; and g1–g19, g36–g42. It appears that their differences in words, spelling, and punctuation broadly parallel those of the first extract. Between TMS and BMS there are 2 differences of words (e19/f19, where BMS uses a cancelled reading, and e50/f34), 30 differences of spelling, and 5 of punctuation.[15] There are no verbal differences between TMS and the printed versions, but between TMS and *1637* there are 14 differences of spelling and 6 of punctuation, while between TMS and *1645* there are 32 differences of spelling and 13 of punctuation.

To put the differences for both extracts in another way: 17 per cent of the spellings in BMS differ from those in TMS; 7 per cent of those in *1637*; and 17 per cent of those in *1645*. As to punctuation, there is 1 difference from TMS in 7·3 lines of BMS; 1 in 3·4 lines of *1637*; and 1 in 1·8 lines of *1645*.

In order to discover whether the differences found in the total of 44 lines, 343 words, of the extracts are typical of these texts as a whole, a random sample of 100 lines, 720 words, was checked.[16] In the sample lines, 16 per cent of the spellings in BMS differ from those in TMS (compared with 17 per cent in the extracts); 6 per cent of those in *1637* (7 per cent); and 15 per cent of those in *1645* (17 per cent). This is a very close correspondence; but there are more differences of punctuation in the sample than in the extracts: there is 1 difference from TMS in 2·1 lines of the BMS sample (compared with 1 in 7·3 lines of the extracts); 1 in 1·7 lines of *1637* (1 in 3·4); and 1 in 1·3 lines of *1645* (1 in 1·8). The actual number of differences of punctuation in the sample was again least in BMS and most in *1645*.

As to words, the sample showed 9 differences in the 90 lines of BMS, which all appeared to be copying errors; and 6 differences each in the 100 lines of *1637* and *1645*, which were probably intentional alterations.

To sum up: it seems that BMS was transcribed from Milton's fair copy without much regard for copy spelling but with only moderate alteration of the punctuation, and that the scribe made a good many copying errors. The compositor of *1637*, however, seems to have followed the spelling of

---

[14] See the *Variorum commentary*, ii. 3, pp. 904–5, and S. E. Sprott's Milton, J., *A maske . . .*, pp. 11, 94. The slip had disappeared by the time Aldis Wright became Librarian in 1863.

[15] See p. 42 n. 12.

[16] A consecutive series of three-digit numbers of the lines to be sampled were taken from a table of random numbers, passing over duplicated numbers. All the lines sampled were comparable between TMS and the printed texts; but 10 of the sample lines came in passages which had been cut in BMS, so the BMS sample totalled only 90 lines, 645 words.

the presumed copy quite closely, and he was verbally accurate; we cannot know whether his additions to the punctuation were his own or whether they had been added to the copy. The compositor of *1645*, finally, who was setting from a copy of *1637*, continued the process of normalizing the spelling and of adding to the punctuation; he too got the words right.[17]

As to the nature and purpose of the differences of spelling and punctuation between TMS and the printed texts, the spelling changes seem indeed to have been no more than printers' normalizations of Milton's personal spellings. Although Milton's orthography was identifiably his own, and therefore subject to the compositor's urge to regularize, it was not in itself either consistent or indicative of pronunciation. J. T. Shawcross concluded: 'We see that Milton cared less about spelling than has previously been thought. He did not write certain words or groups of words in any rigid way, and even those which seem to be consistent do not give evidence of a grand scheme of improved spelling. Rather, such distinctive spellings as are seen represent practice, not philosophical ideas. No spelling system appears. The evolution of certain forms simply lies in the direction of simplicity, suggestion of pronunciation, or clarity.'[18] If this is so, it is not surprising that Milton did not prevent the partial normalization of his spellings in *1637*, or the more comprehensive normalization that took place in the authorized edition of *1645*. Perhaps he did not much care about it one way or the other.

The changes in the punctuation of the printed versions of *A maske*, on the other hand, were not so much the printers' ordinary normalization as the addition of a new system of pointing. As we have seen, Milton's punctuation in TMS had been rhetorical, not grammatical, and it was moreover no more than a sketchy indication of how the lines might be spoken, not a complete or finished punctuation even of its own sort.[19] In the printed versions most of Milton's rhetorical stops were retained, but they were supplemented (more heavily in *1645* than in *1637*) by a grammatical punctuation which marked

---

[17] The fact that *1637* is much closer to TMS in spelling and punctuation than *1645* has not always been apparent to editors of *A maske*. In her edition of Milton's *Poetical works*, Helen Darbishire wrote surprisingly (ii, Oxford 1955, p. xi): 'A glance at the first printed texts of *A mask (Comus)*, 1637, and *Lycidas*, (1638), will be enough to convince a critical reader that in all the minutiae of spelling and punctuation they represent Milton himself very imperfectly: the printer has done pretty much as he liked, according to the current conventions of the printing-house. A close scrutiny of the volume of 1645 reveals a careful printer who followed Milton's copy with what he would have thought reasonable faithfulness, but took his own line freely in what were to him accepted conventions or variations.' As far as *A maske* is concerned this suggests the reverse of the actual situation.

[18] Shawcross, J. T., 'What we can learn from Milton's spelling', *Huntington Library quarterly*, xxvi, 1962-3, p. 361. Shawcross took essentially the same position in his later 'Orthography and the text of *Paradise Lost*', in Emma, R. D., and Shawcross, J. T., *Language and style in Milton*, New York 1967, ch. 5. See also in the same collection Dobson, E. J., 'Milton's pronunciation', loc. cit., ch. 6.

[19] See Treip, M., *Milton's punctuation*, London 1970, especially pp. 10-13.

off clauses and ended sentences. Again we have no evidence of Milton's own reaction to the change except that he did not prevent it; but it is quite possible that he wrote out the transcript from which *1637* appears to have been set with a heavier, more grammatical, punctuation than he had used in TMS, his private notebook.[20]

We can now return to the problems of editing Milton's masque. It is a work that has been much edited before, and several specialist editions are available, besides facsimiles of all the early texts.[21] But, while there would seem to be little need at the moment for another full-dress edition for specialists, none of the editions available to students and general readers today, good as they are in many ways, offers a wholly satisfactory text of *A maske*. We will therefore look at the problems of editing the work with the need for a reliable students' edition in mind; and first at the question of choosing the best copy-text.

There are five early versions to be considered: the two manuscripts TMS and BMS, and the first three printed editions *1637*, *1645*, and *1673*. Since we are dealing with a major work by one of the greatest of poets the holograph TMS immediately suggests itself as being the version closest to Milton, and the only certain authority for his own spelling and punctuation. Yet in other ways TMS would make an unsatisfactory copy-text. This rough working draft of the masque in a private notebook was not the version which Milton expected or wanted people to read; he thoroughly revised the words of the text for publication, and perhaps the details as well. It is moreover an incomplete as well as an unrevised version of the work, thirty-seven lines shorter than the final text. Although Milton's revised manuscript might have done as copy-text, TMS will not.

BMS is worse still. This scribal transcript also represents an intermediate, incomplete version of the masque, lacking not only the material added in 1637 but also a number of original passages which were cut for performance; and it was inaccurately copied, with unauthorized spelling and punctuation. Of course we can learn a great deal about Milton and his masque by studying the manuscripts, but this can easily be done with the aid of the published

---

[20] Milton added to the punctuation of Sonnet 13 when he copied it out (both his rough draft and his fair copy are on p. 43 of TMS), though in this case he did not change his essentially rhythmical pointing to a more grammatical form.

[21] Major specialist editions: the Columbia *Works* of Milton, ed. F. A. Patterson, New York 1931- , with *A maske* in vol. i, pts. 1 and 2; Milton's *Poetical works*, ed. Helen Darbishire, Oxford 1952–5, with *A maske* in vol. ii; and Milton's *A maske, the earlier versions*, ed. S. E. Sprott, Toronto and Buffalo 1973. Facsimiles and transcripts: TMS: ed. W. Aldis Wright, Cambridge 1899; Scolar Press, with Wright's transcript (Menston 1970, 1972). BMS: Milton's *Complete poetical works in facsimile*, ed. H. F. Fletcher, Urbana, Ill., 1943–8, with *A maske* in vol. i, *1637*: facsimile in Fletcher's edition, transcript in Sprott's edition. *1645*: facsimile in Fletcher's edition; also Scolar Press, Menston 1970. *1673*: facsimile in Fletcher's edition.

facsimiles and transcripts (or of excerpts from them in a students' edition), and it is as unnecessary as it is undesirable to use either of them as copy-text for an edition.

This leaves the three printed editions, *1637*, *1645*, and *1673*; and it may surprise those who have followed this example so far to learn that, while a number of recent editors of *A maske* have chosen *1673* as copy-text, and a rather smaller number have chosen *1645*, none has yet chosen *1637*.[22] Certainly Milton took pains with the arrangement and editing of the poems in *1645*, and made some further corrections in *1673*; yet it is clear from our examination of the early texts that it is the *1637* version of *A maske*, not the versions in *1645* or *1673*, which contains the minimum of apparently un-authorized alteration of detail. There are of course authorized alterations in the second and third editions, but we should not suppose that, because Milton made some corrections in these later texts, he also normalized the spelling and added to the punctuation; or even, if these detailed changes were made by someone other than Milton, that he consciously approved of them. All we know is that he did not prevent these changes of spelling and punctuation from taking place; all we may suppose is that he accepted them. The copy-text for our edition, therefore, will be *1637*, emended by the usual editorial procedures, including the incorporation of those alterations in *1645* and *1673* which appear to have been made by Milton.

Next there is the question of how to present the spelling and punctuation of the copy-text in the edited version, and especially whether there should be any modernization of either. Mid-seventeenth-century orthography comes just on that borderline between old and new spelling where the few remaining archaic forms do not really interfere with a modern reader's comprehension of the text, but where their antique appearance may be enough to put him off; and one would rather that Milton were read in modern spelling than not at all. Nevertheless actual modernized texts of *A maske* (such as the Longman annotated text edited by John Carey, which

[22] The many editions of *A maske* based on *1673* include the Columbia Milton's *Works* edited by F. A. Patterson, 1931– , and the semi-modernized texts in B. A. Wright's new Everyman *Poems*, 1956, and John Carey's Longman *Complete shorter poems*, 1968. The reason for choosing *1673* appears in most cases to have been the editorial principle (widely accepted before the 1940s, and still not quite without influence) that the copy-text should be the last edition with which the author himself could have been concerned.

The editions of *A maske* based on *1645* include those of Helen Darbishire in Milton's *Poetical works*, 1952–5, and J. T. Shawcross in *Complete poetry*, revised edn., 1971. Those who have chosen *1645* as copy-text may have been influenced by the fact that this first edition of the *Poems*, with which Milton himself took a lot of trouble, is undoubtedly the right copy-text to choose for most of its contents, while failing to see that the text of *A maske* is not in the same category as the poems published in *1645* for the first time (cf. p. 53 n. 17).

The modernized texts of M. Y. Hughes in Milton's *Complete poems and major prose*, 1957, and of Douglas Bush in *Poetical works*, 1966, follow *1645* in substantive variants.

we shall be looking at in a moment) suggest that more is likely to be lost by modernization than to be gained by it; while John Shawcross's unmodernized student text (also to be looked at shortly) has in fact gained wide acceptance.

So an old-spelling text is proposed. It would even be possible to go further, and to replace those spellings of *1637* which appear to have been normalized with the forms originally used by Milton in TMS. But, since this would affect only about one word in two lines of *1637* and since we do not know for certain that Milton did not alter these spellings himself when he transcribed TMS, it is probably best to leave the spelling of the copy-text as it is.

As to punctuating the edited version, there is every reason to follow the punctuation of *1637*. Although it includes a few mistakes—which, like other mistakes, can be emended—it provides a light but perfectly adequate framework for the masque, and one which seems more likely to be Milton's work than the heavy-handed grammatical punctuation of *1645* and *1673*.

To illustrate these points, transcripts of four of the early texts (TMS, *1637*, *1645*, and *1673*) of the first nineteen lines of my second extract are set out here for comparison with the same passage in two students' texts which are in widespread use today: Milton's *Complete poetry* edited by John T. Shawcross, New York, Doubleday, 1963, revised 1971; and Milton's *Complete shorter poems* edited by John Carey, London, Longman, 1968 (see pp. 58-9).

Shawcross summarizes his editorial principles as follows:

A text given in this edition follows the copy available which seems to have been closest to Milton; alterations are made when authority is found in another text, when (as with punctuation) they are necessary for easy understanding of a line, when an error seems certain, and when meter dictates. In addition a few spellings are changed to more standard (and Milton's later) forms: these include the dropping of most redundant final "e's." The result of these principles is, unfortunately, inconsistency; but it represents the kind of text offered the seventeenth-century reader without being an uncritical duplication of an original printing.[23]

Shawcross chooses *1645* as copy-text (perhaps because it was the first acknowledged text, for it was not otherwise closest to Milton),[24] and follows it with fair consistency. In this extract he emends the spellings 'here' to 'heer' (h4/j4), 'their' to 'thir' (h14/j14), and 'bowes' to 'bows' (h19/j19). Milton's spellings in TMS were 'heere', 'thire', and 'bowes' (e4, e14, and e19), and the forms used by Shawcross (derived presumably from his principle of dropping final 'e's) are not found in any of the early texts. But the spelling of Shawcross's edition, although it is further from Milton's own practice than if he had followed *1637*, is mostly of the period.

[23] Shawcross's Milton, 1971, p. 621.   [24] But see p. 55 n. 22.

The adoption of the *1645* punctuation, on the other hand, is inhibiting. For instance the pointing of the Elder Brother's speech in *1637* (g1–g12), which follows TMS pretty closely, is light yet perfectly adequate; but the extra commas taken from *1645* at the ends of lines j2, j3, j10, and j11 retard the movement of the verse, and only one of them (at j10) helps to make the passage more comprehensible. Shawcross adds stops from *1645* at the ends of 14 of the 60 lines of my extracts, most of which are redundant.

But on the whole, while it may be argued that Shawcross would have done better to take *1637* as his copy-text, this respectful but critical treatment of the version of *1645* has resulted in a useful old-spelling text for students. Carey, on the other hand, takes a more radical line with the text with less satisfactory results.

Carey does not consider the possibility of using *1637* as copy-text, believing (mistakenly) that *1637* was 'based on the Trinity MS at an early stage of correction';[25] and he argues that, since it seems that some of the corrections in *1673* were made in accordance with Milton's wishes, Milton 'was too closely connected with the production of *1673* for any editor to jettison the *1673* variants'.[26] As he puts it: 'If some of *1673*'s divergences from *1645* are evidently Milton's, it would appear unsafe to assume, without evidence to the contrary, that all are not.'[27] (I would put it the other way round: although some of *1673*'s divergences from *1645*—and of *1645*'s divergences from *1637*—are evidently Milton's, it would be unsafe to assume that all are.) Carey therefore chooses *1673* as copy-text.

Carey then argues that the spelling and the punctuation of the copy-text should each be treated differently in the edited version: that the spelling should be modernized because orthography indicates only vocabulary, not grammar; but that the punctuation should be retained because it has a grammatical function like word order and inflection. Carey is surely right not to change the punctuation, although it is a pity that he is committed to the pointing of *1673*, which is worse even than that of *1645*. For instance *1673*, followed by Carey, omits the internal comma in line i18/k18; Milton in TMS included it, as did the compositors of *1637* and *1645*; the line is difficult to read without it. Again, the punctuation of *1673* is generally heavier than that of *1645*, and Carey prints stops at the ends of fifteen lines of the two extracts which were not in *1637*.

Carey's argument for modernizing the spelling of *1673* is only superficially attractive, and in practice his modernization detracts from the

[25] Carey's Milton, p. 168. Here Carey is repeating C. S. Lewis; on the same page he mentions Shawcross's argument that *1637* was set from a revised intermediate copy of TMS.

[26] Carey's Milton, p. 4.

[27] Carey's Milton, p. 3.

TMS

1 bro. unmuffle ye faint starres, & thou faire ~~N~~ moone
　　　that ~~wont'st~~ wont'st to love the travailers benizon
　　　stoope thy pale visage through an amber cloud
　　　and disinherit Chaos, that raignes heere
e5　　in double night of darknesse & of shades.
　　　or if yor influence be quite dam'd up
　　　wth black usurping mists, some gentle taper
　　　though a rush candle from the wicker hole
　　　of some clay habitation visit us
e10　　wth ^{thy} ~~a~~ long levell'd rule of streaming light
　　　and thou shalt be our starre of Arcadie
　　　or Tyrian Cynosure. 2 bro. or if our eyes
　　　be barr'd that happinesse, might wee but heare
　　　　　　　　　　　　thire
　　　the folded flocks pen'd in ∧ watled ~~e[osat]~~ cotes
e15　　or sound of pastorall reed wth oaten stopps
　　　or ~~wistle~~ whistle from ye lodge, or village cock
　　　count the night watches to his featherie dames
　　　t'would be some solace yet, some little cheering
　　　　　　this　~~sad~~ close
　　　in ∧ ~~lone~~ ∧ dungeon of innumerous bowes.

1637
　　　Eld. bro.　Vnmuffle yee faint stars, and thou fair moon
　　　That wontst to love the travailers benizon
　　　Stoope thy pale visage through an amber cloud
　　　And disinherit *Chaos,* that raigns here
g5　　In double night of darknesse, and of shades;
　　　Or if your influence be quite damm'd up
　　　With black usurping mists, some gentle taper
　　　Though a rush candle from the wicker hole
　　　Of some clay habitation visit us
g10　　With thy long levell'd rule of streaming light
　　　And thou shalt be our starre of *Arcadie*
　　　Or *Tyrian* Cynosure. *2 Bro.*　Or if our eyes
　　　Be barr'd that happinesse, might we but heare
　　　The folded flocks pen'd in their watled cotes,
g15　　Or sound of pastoral reed with oaten stops,
　　　Or whistle from the Lodge, or village cock
　　　Count the night watches to his featherie Dames,
　　　T'would be some solace yet, some little chearing
　　　In this close dungeon of innumerous bowes.

1645
　　　Eld. Bro. Unmuffle ye faintstars, and thou fair Moon
　　　That wontst to love the travailers benizon,
　　　Stoop thy pale visage through an amber cloud,
　　　And disinherit *Chaos,* that raigns here
h5　　In double night of darkñes, and of shades;
　　　Or if your influence be quite damm'd up
　　　With black usurping mists, som gentle taper
　　　Though a rush Candle from the wicker hole
　　　Of som clay habitation visit us
h10　　With thy long levell'd rule of streaming light,
　　　And thou shalt be our star of *Arcady*,
　　　Or *Tyrian* Cynosure 2 Bro. Or if our eyes
　　　Be barr'd that happines, might we but hear
　　　The folded flocks pen'd in their watled cotes,
h15　　Or sound of pastoral reed with oaten stops,
　　　Or whistle from the Lodge, or village cock
　　　Count the night watches to his feathery Dames,
　　　T'would be som solace yet, som little chearing
　　　In this close dungeon of innumerous bowes.

   Eld. Bro. Unmuffle ye faint Stars, and thou fair Moon
That wontst to love the travellers benizon,
Stoop thy pale visage through an amber cloud,
And disinherit *Chaos*, that raigns here
i5 In double night of darkness, and of shades;
Or if your influence be quite damm'd up
With black usurping mists, som gentle taper
Though a rush Candle from the wicker hole
Of som clay habitation visit us
i10 With thy long levell'd rule of streaming light,
And thou shalt be our star of *Arcady*,
Or *Tyrian* Cynosure. 2. *Bro.* Or if our eyes
Be barr'd that happines, might we but hear
The folded flocks pen'd in their watled cotes;
i15 Or sound of pastoral reed with oaten stops,
Or whistle from the Lodge, or Village Cock
Count the night watches to his feathery Dames,
'Twould be som solace yet som little chearing
In this close dungeon of innumerous bowes.

Shawcross
   Elder Brother. Unmuffle ye faint stars, and thou fair moon
That wontst to love the travailers benizon,
Stoop thy pale visage through an amber cloud,
And disinherit *Chaos*, that raigns heer
j5 In double night of darknes, and of shades;
Or if your influence be quite damm'd up
With black usurping mists, som gentle taper
Though a rush candle from the wicker hole
Of som clay habitation visit us
j10 With thy long levell'd rule of streaming light,
And thou shalt be our star of *Arcady*,
Or *Tyrian* Cynosure.
    2 Brother.   Or if our eyes
Be barr'd that happines, might we but hear
The folded flocks pen'd in thir watled cotes,
j15 Or sound of pastoral reed with oaten stops,
Or whistle from the lodge, or village cock
Count the night watches to his feathery Dames,
'Twould be som solace yet, som little chearing
In this close dungeon of innumerous bows.

Carey
Eld. Bro. Unmuffle ye faint stars, and thou fair moon
That wont'st to love the traveller's benison,
Stoop thy pale visage through an amber cloud,
And disinherit Chaos, that reigns here
k5 In double night of darkness, and of shades;
Or if your influence be quite dammed up
With black usurping mists, some gentle taper
Though a rush-candle from the wicker hole
Of some clay habitation visit us
k10 With thy long levelled rule of streaming light,
And thou shalt be our star of Arcady,
Or Tyrian Cynosure.
Sec. Bro.   Or if our eyes
Be barred that happiness, might we but hear
The folded flocks penned in their wattled cotes,
k15 Or sound of pastoral reed with oaten stops,
Or whistle from the lodge, or village cock
Count the night-watches to his feathery dames,
'Twould be some solace yet some little cheering
In this close dungeon of innumerous boughs.

meaning of the text as well as depriving it of the quality of belonging to the seventeenth century. His spelling 'traveller's' (k2) is a case in point. TMS, *1637*, and *1645* all spell this word 'travailers', which refers, perhaps intentionally, to 'travail' as well as to 'travel'—either spelling could then be used for either word—and which gives no indication of whether the word refers to one person or to more than one. While it is possible, though improbable, that the blind Milton altered the 'travailers' of *1645* to the 'travellers' of *1673*, the *1673* text still did not say whether there was one or more of them. Carey's 'traveller's' both suppresses the original reference to travail and puts the word unambiguously in the singular; which is at least as bad as altering the punctuation.[28]

Altogether Carey's students' text is an unhappy compromise: he chooses as copy-text the early version that is furthest from Milton's manuscript, he rejects its contemporary spelling, and he accepts its frequently defective punctuation.

There is finally the question of how best to present the textual apparatus in a non-specialist text. Here it will be necessary at least to give a summary of the relationship between the five early texts, to say why one of them has been chosen as copy-text, and to indicate how it has been followed, both by giving a general account and by recording the major variants in the other texts. There should be no difficulty in providing a brief textual introduction; the problem here will be how to present the evidence of the other texts, and especially how to record the large number of variants (including cancelled words and passages) in TMS. Because there are so many variants, the usual method of gathering them into footnotes or a textual appendix will result in records that are unreadably dense, and therefore of little use in this sort of edition. Here is an extract from the textual appendix in Shawcross's edition (where the amount of information given is minimal, not for instance including the cancelled readings in TMS) (see facing page).

Students and general readers are not really going to make much of this. Textual footnotes may be better, but they can be confusing if they have to be fitted in with critical and explanatory notes. The best answer may be to record the isolated TMS variants and the variants in the other printed texts in footnotes—they do not add up to very many altogether—but to give transcripts in an appendix of those passages in TMS where the variation is great.

---

[28] Later on in the same passage (at e21 of TMS, g21 of *1637*, etc.) TMS and the early printed editions (including *1673*) all agree in reading 'whether betake her', but Carey emends this to 'whither betake her'. 'Whether' and 'whither' are another pair of words of which each could be spelt in either way in the seventeenth century; so that modernization again suppresses possible ambiguity.

632   THE COMPLETE POETRY OF JOHN MILTON

(214) flittering *TM* / hovering *1645, 1673, TM in scribe's hand.* (223) sable / sables *1637.* (226) hallow / hollowe *BM.* (229) off. / hence *TM, BM.* (231) cell *TM* / shell *1637, 1645, 1673, BM.* (241) *of* / to *BM.* (243) *And give resounding grace* / And hould a Counterpoint *BM.* (dir., 243–44) Comus looks in and speaks *TM, BM.* (252) she *TM* / it *1645, 1673.* (270) prosperous / prosperinge *BM.* (291) Two such / Such tow *TM.* (294) 'em *TM* / them *1637, 1645, 1673.* (300) colours / cooleness *BM.* (304) To / *omitted, but given as catchword BM.* (312) wide *TM* / wilde *1645, 1673,* wild *TM in scribe's hand, 1637.* (317) roosted / rooster *BM.* (dir., 330–31) the tow brothers enter *TM.* (349) this close / lone *BM.* (356) What if / or els *BM.* (357–65) *missing* TM, BM; *three other lines are found:* so fares as did forsaken Proserpine | when the big rowling flakes of pitchie clowds | & darknesse wound her in. 1 bro. Peace, brother peace |. (370) trust / hope *BM.* (384) walks in black vapours, though the noone tyde brand *BM.* (385) blaze in the summer solstice *BM.* (390) a / an *1637, BM.* (399) treasure / treasures *BM.* (401) on / at *BM.* (402) let / she *BM.* (403) wild / wide *TM, BM.* (409) controversie: / question, no *TM, BM.* (409 ff.) *TM, BM give five additional undeleted lines:* I could be willing though now i'th darke to trie | a tough encounter wth the shaggiest ruffian | that lurks by hedge or lane of this dead circuit | to have her by my side, though I were sure | she might be free from perill were she is |. (410) Yet / but *TM, BM.* (413) banish gladly *TM* / gladly banish *1637, 1645, 1673, BM.* (415) imagine, / imagine brother *TM, BM.* (417) if you mean / if meane *1637.* (428) there, / even *TM, BM.* (432) Som say / naye more *BM.* (433) moorie *TM* / moorish *1637, 1645, 1673, BM.* (437) Has *TM* / Hath *1645, 1673.* (438) ye / you *BM.* (443) she / we *1637.* (444) naught *TM* / nought *1637, 1645, 1673, BM.* (448) That / the *BM.* (460) Begin / begins *BM.* (465) But / and *TM, BM;* lewd and lavish / lewde lascivious *BM.* (472) Hovering, *TM* / Lingering, *1645, 1673.* (474) sensualty / sensuality *1637, 1673, BM.* (481) off / of *1673, BM;* hallow / hollowe *BM.* (dir., 488–89) he hallows the guardian Dæmon hallows agen & enters in the habit of shepheard *TM,* he hallowes and is answered, the guardian dæmon comes in habited like a shepheard. *BM.* (493) fathers *TM* / father *1637, 1645, 1673.* (497) thou / *omitted BM;* Swain? / shepheard, *TM, BM.* (498) his *TM* / the *1637, 1645, 1673, BM.* (513) you. *TM* / ye, *1645, 1673.* (520) *not indented* TM. (547) mediate / mediate upon *1673.* (553) frighted / flighted *TM.* (555) soft / sweete, *BM.* (556) a / the softe *BM;* steam / stream *1673;* rich / *omitted BM.* (563) did / might *TM, BM.* (572) knew) / knowe) *BM.* (581) ye / yon *BM.* (605) buggs *TM* / forms *1645, 1673.* (608) and cleave his scalp *TM* / to a foul death, *1645, 1673.* (609) Down to the hipps. *TM* / Curs'd as his life. *1645, 1673.* (610) Thy / The *BM.* (616) thy self / *omitted BM.* (626) ope / open *BM.* (632–37) *missing* BM. (637) Which *TM* / That *1637, 1645, 1673, BM.* (657) Ile / I *TM, BM.* (dir., 657–58) *State 1 of l. 1 found in British Museum copy (C.34.d.46) of 1637; soft Musick,* / *missing* TM, BM; *appears* / is discover'd *TM; to whom . . . rise.* / she offers to rise *TM.* (678A) poore ladie thou hast neede of some refreshinge *BM.* (679–87) *missing* BM. (688) have / hast *BM.* (689) have / hast *BM;* but / heere *BM.* (697–700) *missing* BM. (698) forgeries *TM* / forgery *1637, 1645, 1673.* (709) sallow / shallow *BM.* (731) multitude / inultitude *1637.*[29]

[29] Shawcross's Milton, 1971, p. 632.

EXAMPLE 3

Richardson, *Pamela*, 1741

SAMUEL RICHARDSON was a fat, successful master printer of London, who at the age of fifty was inspired to write a first novel about a resourceful servant-girl that was an artistic and technical prodigy. Completed in only two months, *Pamela* was a huge success, yet the book had the crudity as well as the vigour of new-found inspiration, and Richardson—who was of course his own printer—tinkered with the text each time it was reset for a new edition, polishing and refining the work in detail. But in the end detailed revision alone did not satisfy him and, towards the end of his life (when he had written another two novels with more deliberation and care than before), he set about revising the whole text of *Pamela* in a more general way, deleting, adding, and recasting major sections of the novel, and leaving scarcely a sentence unchanged. Richardson himself did not print this last version of *Pamela*, but it was preserved by his family and finally published in 1801, forty years after his death.[1]

Thus there were three main versions of *Pamela*: the first-edition text, Pamela's lively entry into the world; the refined version of this text that resulted from Richardson's detailed revision of the early editions; and the fully revised—almost rewritten—version published posthumously. Of the three, the intermediate, refined version is perhaps the least important, although it is the one which is most easily available and therefore most commonly read.

The original two-volume *Pamela* was printed in duodecimo at Richardson's own shop, and was published in November 1740 (though it was dated 1741). Richardson printed four more duodecimo editions in 1741, each one being set from an amended copy of its predecessor; of these, the second

---

[1] The best general study of Richardson and his work is Eaves, T. C. D., and Kimpel, B. D., *Samuel Richardson, a biography*, Oxford 1971; but there is a fuller account of his printing in two important books by W. M. Sale: *Samuel Richardson, a bibliographical record of his literary career with historical notes*, New Haven 1936, and *Samuel Richardson, master printer*, Ithaca, N.Y. 1950.

The text of *Pamela* is studied in Eaves and Kimpel's excellent 'Richardson's revisions of *Pamela*', *Studies in bibliography*, xx, 1967, pp. 61–88.

See also van Marter, S., 'Richardson's revisions of *Clarissa* in the second edition', *Studies in bibliography*, xxvi, 1973, pp. 107–32; ibid., 'Richardson's revisions of *Clarissa* in the third and fourth editions', *Studies in bibliography*, xxviii, 1975, pp. 119–52; and Pierson, R. C., 'The revisions of Richardson's *Sir Charles Grandison*', *Studies in Bibliography*, xxi, 1968, pp. 163–89.

incorporated a considerable amount of detailed revision (841 'substantive changes');[2] the third and fourth were only slightly revised (59 and 48 substantive changes respectively); and the fifth was again much revised (950 substantive changes). During the same year, 1741, *Pamela* was pirated, parodied, adapted, praised, attacked, and even continued, by others. In fact three unauthorized continuations of the story appeared, which provoked Richardson into producing his own continuation: volumes 3 and 4 of *Pamela*, published first in December 1741, and thereafter as part of each new edition of the book; but, as so often happens, the sequel did not live up to the promise of the original.

The next edition, the sixth, interrupted the series of small duodecimos: this was an octavo with illustrations published in four larger volumes in May 1742, which again incorporated a considerable amount of revision (633 substantive changes in the first two volumes), and which Richardson was later to take as the basis for his final, major revision of the novel. But, although Richardson seems to have thought that the octavo was the best of the early texts of *Pamela*, he put out three more duodecimo editions with some further revision, but not incorporating the larger number of changes he had made for the octavo. These were the 'sixth' edition of 1746 (26 substantive changes from the fifth edition in the first two volumes); the 'seventh' edition of 1754 (35 more changes in the first two volumes); and the 'eighth' edition dated 1762 (but actually published in October 1761, just after Richardson's death), which incorporated a further 251 substantive changes in the first two volumes.

The early editions of Pamela *vols. 1 and 2*

Edition number	Format	Date	Number of changes from preceding edition
[1st]	12°	1741 [6 Nov. 1740]	—
2nd	12°	1741 [12 Feb.]	841
3rd	12°	1741 [12 Mar.]	59
4th	12°	1741 [5 May]	48
5th	12°	1741 [22 Sept.]	950
6th	8°	1742 [8 May]	633
'6th'	12°	1746 [18 Oct.]	26 (from 5th)
'7th'	12°	1754	35
'8th'	12°	1762 [28 Oct. 1761]	251

[2] These figures for textual changes in *Pamela*, vols. 1 and 2, are taken from Eaves and Kimpel's 'Richardson's revisions of *Pamela*' (see p. 63 n. 1). They counted as substantive all changes of words, including the order of words, but did not count changes of punctuation, spelling, capitalization, italicization, etc.; but since, as they say (p. 62), 'either an added paragraph or a "was" altered to "were" counts as one change, the numbers are of course only roughly indicative'. They are at least indications both of the order of magnitude of the number of alterations, and of their relative frequency in the various editions.

Richardson's chief aim in making these detailed changes to the early editions of *Pamela* was to elevate and dignify the tone of the novel. Thus the changes in the second edition served mainly to refine Pamela's language; at first her words were apt to be plebeian, and Richardson sought to make her speak more like a lady. Linguistic refinement was again the point of the second main group of changes, in the fifth edition, but these tended to affect whole phrases rather than individual words. The third and fourth main groups of changes, in the sixth and 'eighth' editions, were more miscellaneous, but always tending towards greater elegance, better form, in the narration.

These many individual alterations—2,531 in the first two volumes up to the sixth octavo edition, and a further 312 in the last three duodecimos—made a real difference to the manner of *Pamela*, but they left its essential character unchanged. Richardson's final revision, however, published long after his death in 1801, was another matter. This time Richardson virtually rewrote the book in his artistic maturity, producing a version of *Pamela* with the skill and assurance of *Clarissa* and *Grandison*. The changes he made, probably in an interleaved copy of the 1742 octavo, were so great, involving the addition, deletion, and recasting of whole pages and groups of pages, that it is pointless to try to compare them numerically with the relatively minor substantive changes of the earlier revisions.[4] Scarcely a sentence of the original text remained unaltered, and this time Richardson not only continued to refine the tone of his novel but also and more fundamentally he attempted to shift its whole moral balance.

To see how all this was done, let us look at three passages from the first two volumes of *Pamela* in the first edition, 1741; in the sixth octavo edition, 1742; and in the posthumously published revision, 1801.

---

[4] Eaves and Kimpel do attempt the comparison. Their figure for the number of alterations in the first two volumes of the 1801 edition is 'over 8400', although they do say later that some of the changes are 'so great as to make comparison impossible' (*Studies in bibliography*, xx, 1967, pp. 78, 79).

· Well, said he, I will set this down by itself, as the
first Time that ever what I advis'd had any Weight
with you. And I hope, said I, as the first Advice
you have given me of late, that was fit to be follow'd!
a5 —I wish, said he, (I'm almost asham'd to write it,
impudent Gentleman as he is! I wish) I had thee as
quick another Way, as thou art in thy Repartees —
And he laugh'd, and I tripp'd away as fast as I could.

Ah! thinks I, marry'd! I'm sure 'tis time you was
a10 marry'd, or at this Rate no honest Maiden will live
with you.

Why, dear Father and Mother, to be sure he
grows quite a Rake! Well, you see, how easy it is
to go from bad to worse, when once People give
a15 way to Vice!

How would my poor Lady, had she liv'd, have
griev'd to see it! But may-be he would have been better then!—Tho', it seems, he told Mrs. *Jervis*, he had
an Eye upon me in his Mother's Life-time; and he
a20 intended to let me know as much by the Bye, he told
her! Here's Shamelessness for you! — Sure the ·
World must be near an End! for all the Gentlemen
about are as bad as he almost, as far as I can hear!—
And see the Fruits of such bad Examples: There is
a25 'Squire *Martin* in the Grove, has had three Lyings-
in, it seems, in his House, in three Months past, one
by himself; and one by his Coachman; and one by
his Woodman; and yet he has turn'd none of them
away. Indeed, how can he, when they but follow
a30 his own vile Example. There is he, and two or three
more such as he, within ten Miles of us; who keep
Company and hunt with our fine Master, truly; and
I suppose he's never the better for their Examples.
But, God bless me, say I, and send me out of this
a35 wicked House!

Pamela, first extract:
  a1–a55: 1st edn., 1741 (Trin. Coll. Cam., Rothschild 1745, i, pp. 84–6; ×1·0)
  b1–b64: 6th edn., 1742 (Brit. Lib., 1457.e.14, i, pp. 107–9; ×0·67)
  c1–c55: 1801 edn. (Univ. Lib. Cam., Syn.7.80.75, [i], pp. 82–3; ×0·74)

WELL, reply'd he, I will set this down by itself, as the first Time that ever what I advis'd had any Weight with you. And I will add, said I, as the first Advice you have given me of late, that was fit to be follow'd!——I wish, said he, (I'm almost asham'd to write it, impudent Gentleman as he is! I wish) I had thee as *quick another way*, as thou art in thy Repartees! ——And he laugh'd, and I snatch'd my Hand from him, and tripp'd away as fast as I could. Ah! thought I, marry'd! I'm sure 'tis time you were marry'd, or at this Rate no honest Maiden ought to live with you!

WHY, dear Father and Mother, to be sure he grows quite a Rake! How easy it is to go from bad to worse, when once People give way to Vice!

HOW would my poor Lady, had she liv'd, have griev'd to see it! But may-be he would have been better *then*!—— Tho', it seems, he told Mrs. *Jervis*, he had an Eye upon me in his Mother's Life-time; and he intended to let me know as much by-the-bye, he told her! Here's Shamelessness for you! Sure the World must be near at an End! for all the Gentlemen about are as bad as he almost, as far as I can hear!——And see the Fruits of such bad Examples! There is 'Squire *Martin* in the Grove has had three Lyings-in, it seems, in his House, in three Months past; one by himself, and one by his Coachman, and one by his Woodman; and yet he has turn'd none of them away. Indeed, how can he, when they but follow his own vile Example! There is he, and two or three more such as he, within ten Miles of us; who keep Company, and hunt with our fine Master, truly; and I suppose, he's never the better for their Examples. But, Heaven bless me, say I, and send me out of this wicked House!

I will set this down by itself, replied he, as the first time that ever what I advised had any weight with you.—And I will add, returned I, as the first advice you have given me of late, that was fit to be followed!

He laugh'd, and I snatch'd my hand from him, and hurried away as fast as I could. Ah! thought I, marry'd! I'm sure 'tis time you were marry'd, or at this rate no honest maiden ought to live with you.

How easy is it to go from bad to worse, when once people give way to vice!—But do you think, my dear father, that my master shew'd any great matter of wit in this conversation with his poor servant? But I am now convinc'd that *wickedness* is *folly* with a witness. Since, if I may presume to judge, I think he has shewn a great deal of foolishness, as well in his sentiments and speeches, as in his actions to me; and yet passes not for a silly man, on other occasions, but the very contrary. Perhaps, however, he despises me too much to behave otherwise than he does to such a poor girl.

How would my poor lady, had she liv'd, have griev'd to see him sunk so low!—But perhaps, in that case, he would have been better. Tho' he told Mrs. Jervis he had an eye upon me, in his mother's life-time; and that he intended to let me know as much by-the-bye! Here's shamelessness! Sure the world must be near at an end; for all the gentlemen about are almost as bad as he!—And see the fruits of such examples! There is 'Squire Martin in the Grove has had three lyings-in in his house, in three months past; one by himself, and one by his coachman, and one by his woodman; and yet he has turn'd neither of them away. Indeed, how can he, when they but follow his own vile example?

But, dear Father and Mother, what Sort of Creatures muſt the Womenkind be, do you think, to give way to ſuch Wickedneſs? Why, this it is that makes every one be thought of alike: And, alack-a-day! what a World we live in! for it is grown more a Wonder that the Men are reſiſted, than that the Women comply. This, I ſuppoſe, makes me ſuch a Sawce-box, and Boldface, and a Creature; and all becauſe I won't be a Sawce-box and Boldface indeed.

But I am ſorry for theſe Things; one don't know what Arts and Stratagems theſe Men may deviſe to gain their vile Ends; and ſo I will think as well as I can of theſe poor Creatures, and pity them. For you ſee by my ſad Story, and narrow Eſcapes, what Hardſhips poor Maidens go thro', whoſe Lot is to go out to Service; eſpecially to Houſes where there is not the Fear of God, and good Rule kept by the Heads of the Family.

You ſee I am quite grown grave and ſerious; ſo it becomes

Your dutiful Daughter.

Pamela, first extract (continued)

This gave me a Doubt, whether ſhe knew of my Maſter's Intimation of that ſort formerly; and I asked her, if ſhe had Reaſon to ſurmize, that that was in View? No, ſhe ſaid; it was only her own Thought; but it was very likely that my Maſter had either that in View, or ſomething better for me. But, if I approv'd of it, ſhe would propoſe ſuch a thing to her Maſter directly; and gave a deteſtable Hint, that I might take Reſolutions upon it, of

bringing ſuch an Affair to Effect. I told her, I abhorr'd her Inſinuation; and as to Mr. *Williams*, I thought him a civil good ſort of Man; but as on one ſide, he was above me; ſo on the other, of all Things, I did not love a Parſon. So finding ſhe could make nothing of me, ſhe quitted the Subject.

Pamela, second extract:
d1–d16: 1st edn., 1741 (Trin. Coll. Cam., Rothschild 1745, i, pp. 186–7; ×1·0)
e1–e17: 6th edn., 1742 (Brit. Lib., 1457.e.14, i, p. 235; ×0·63)
f1–f31: 1801 edn. (Univ. Lib. Cam., Syn.7.80.75, [i], pp. 188–9; ×0·75)

BUT, dear Father and Mother, what Sort of Creatures must the Women-kind be, do you think, to give way to such Wickedness? Why, this it is that makes every one be thought of alike: And, Alack-a-day! what a World we live in! for it is grown more a Wonder, that the Men are *resisted*, than that the Women *comply*. This, I suppose, makes me such a a Sauce-box, and Bold-face, and a Creature; and all because I won't be a Sauce box and Bold-face indeed.

BUT I am sorry for these Things; one don't know what Arts and Stratagems Men may devise to gain their vile Ends; and so I will think as well as I can of these poor undone Creatures, and pity them. For you see by my sad Story, and narrow Escapes, what Hardships poor Maidens go thro', whose Lot it is to go out to Service; especially to Houses where there is not the Fear of God, and good Rule kept by the Heads of the Family.

YOU see I am quite grown grave and serious: Indeed it becomes the present Condition of

Your dutiful Daughter.

But what sort of creatures must the women be, do you think, to give way to such wickedness? This it is that makes every one be thought of alike. What a world do we live in! for it is grown more a wonder, that the men are *resisted*, than that the women *comply*. This, I suppose, makes me such a sauce-box, and bold-face, and a creature; and all because I won't be indeed what he calls me.

But I pity these poor creatures: one knows not what arts and stratagems men may devise to gain their vile ends. For do I not see, by my narrow escapes, what hardships poor maidens go thro', whose lot it is to go out to service; especially to houses where there is not the fear of God, and good rule kept by the heads of the family.

But it is time to put an end to this letter, which I do, by subscribing myself, what I shall ever be,

Your dutiful Daughter.

THIS gave me a Doubt, whether she knew of my Master's Intimation of that sort formerly; I asked her, If she had Reason to surmise, that *that* was in View? No, she said; it was only her own Thought; but it was very likely, that my Master had either that in View, or something better for me. But, if I approv'd of it, she would propose such a Thing to her Master directly; and gave a detestable Hint, that I might take Resolutions upon it, of bringing such an Affair to Effect. I told her, I abhorr'd her vile Insinuation; and as to Mr. *Williams*, I thought him a good civil sort of Man; but as on one side, he was above me; so on the other, I said, of all Things, I did not love a Parson. So, finding she could make nothing of me, she quitted the Subject.

This gave me a doubt, whether she knew of my master's intimation of that sort formerly: I asked her, if she had reason to surmise, that *that* was in view?—No, she said; it was only her own thought; but it was very likely, that my master had either that in view, or something better for me. But, if I approv'd of it, she would propose such a thing to our master directly.

She then gave a detestable hint, that I might take resolutions upon it, of bringing such an affair to effect. I abhorr'd her vile insinuation; and as to Mr. Williams, I thought him a good civil sort of man; but as, on one side, he was above me; so on the other, I said, of all professions, I should not like a clergyman for my husband. She wonder'd at that, she said, as I had such a religious turn.—Why, Mrs. Jewkes, said I, my dislike of a clergyman proceeds not from disrespect to the function. Far otherwise.—Why, indeed, as you say, answered she [I did *not* say so] there are a great many fooleries among lovers, that would not so well become a starched band and cassock. E'fackins, thou hast well considered of the matter. And then she *neighed*, as I may say, if neighing be the laugh of a horse. I think I do hate her. Must not, my dear mother, this woman be a bad woman to the very core? She turns every thing into wickedness. She saw I was very angry, by my colouring at her, I suppose; but I said nothing; and finding she could make nothing of me, she changed the discourse.

He was going to speak; but I said, to drive him from thinking of any more; And I muſt beg you, Sir, to read the Matter favourably, if I have exceeded in any Liberties of my Pen.

g5   I think, said he, half-ſmiling, you may wonder at my Patience, that I can be ſo eaſy to read myſelf abus'd as I am by ſuch a ſaucy Slut.—Sir, said I, I have wonder'd you ſhould be ſo deſirous to ſee my bold Stuff; and for that very Reaſon, I have thought it
g10 a very *good* or a very bad *Sign*. What, said he, is your *good* Sign?—That it may not have an unkind Effect upon your Temper, at laſt, in my Favour, when you ſee me ſo ſincere. Your *bad* Sign? Why, that if you can read my Reflections and Ob-
g15 ſervations upon your Treatment of me, with Tranquillity, and not be mov'd, it is a Sign of a very cruel and determin'd Heart. Now, pray Sir, don't be angry at my Boldneſs, in telling you ſo freely my Thoughts. You may, perhaps, said he, be leaſt
g20 miſtaken when you think of your bad Sign: God forbid! said I.

   So I took out my Papers; and said, Here, Sir, they are. But, if you pleaſe to return them, without breaking the Seal, it will be very generous: And
g25 I will take it for a great Favour, and a good Omen.

Pamela, third extract:
   g1-g59: 1st edn., 1741 (Trin. Coll. Cam., Rothschild 1745, ii, pp. 27-8; ×1·0)
   h1-h64: 6th edn., 1742 (Brit. Lib., 1457.e.14, i, pp. 399-401; ×0·66)
   i1-i37: 1801 edn. (Univ. Lib. Cam., Syn.7.80.75, [i], pp. 318-19; ×0·75)

HE was going to fpeak; but I faid, to drive him from thinking of any more, And I muft beg you, Sir, to read the Matter favourably, if I have exceeded in any Liberties of my Pen.

I THINK, faid he, half-fmiling, you may wonder at my Patience, that I can be fo eafy to read myfelf abus'd as I am by fuch a faucy Slut.——Sir, faid I, I have wonder'd you fhould be fo defirous to fee my bold Stuff; and for that very Reafon, I have thought it a very *good*, or a very *bad* Sign. What, faid he, is your *good* Sign?——That it may have an Effect upon your Temper, at laft, in my Favour, when you fee me fo fincere, Your *bad* Sign? Why, that, if you can read my Reflections and Obfervations upon your Treatment of me, with Tranquillity, and not be mov'd, it is a Sign of a very cruel and determin'd Heart. Now, pray, Sir, don't be angry at my Boldnefs, in telling you fo freely my Thoughts. You may, perhaps, faid he, be leaft miftaken, when you think of your bad Sign: God forbid! faid I.

So I took out my Papers; and faid, Here, Sir, they are. But if you pleafe to return them, without breaking the Seal, it will be very generous: And I will take it for a great Favour, and a good Omen.

He was going to fpeak; but I faid, to drive him from thinking of any more, than that parcel—And I muft beg of you, fir, to read them with favour, in fuch places as I may have treated you with freedom; and allow for the occafions: but if you will be pleafed to return them, without breaking the feal, it will be very generous: and I will take it for a great favour, and a good omen.

He broke the Seal inftantly, and open'd them. So
much for your Omen, faid he. I am forry for it,
faid I; and was walking away. Whither now, faid
g30 he? Sir, I was going in, that you might have Time
to read them, if you thought fit. He put them into
his Pocket, and faid, You have more than thefe. Yes,
Sir; but all that they contain you know, as well as
I. — But I don't know, faid he, the Light you put
g35 Things in; and fo give them me, if you have not a
Mind to be fearch'd.

Sir, faid I, I can't ftay, if you won't forbear that
ugly Word. — Give me then no Reafon for it. Where
are the other Papers? Why then, unkind Sir, if it
g40 muft be fo, here they are. And fo I gave him out of
my Pocket the fecond Parcel, feal'd up, as the former, with this Superfcription; *From the naughty
Articles, down, thro' fad Attempts, to* Thurfday *the
42d Day of my Imprifonment.* This is laft *Thurfday,*
g45 is it? — Yes, Sir; but now you *will* fee what I
write, I will find fome other way to employ my
Time: For I can neither write fo free, nor with
any Face, what muft be for your Perufal, and not
for thofe I intended to divert with my melancholy
g50 Stories.

Yes, faid he, I would have you continue your
Penmanfhip by all means; and I affure you, in the
Mind I am in, I will not ask you for any after thefe;
except any thing very extraordinary occurs. And
g55 I have, added he, another thing to tell you, That
if you fend for thofe from your Father, and let me
read them, I may very probably give them all
back again to you. And fo I defire you will do
it.

Pamela, third extract (continued)

HE broke the Seal instantly, and open'd them. So much for your *Omen!* reply'd he. I am sorry for it, said I, very seriously; and was walking away. Whither now? said he. I was going in, Sir, that you might have Time to read them, if you thought fit. He put them into his Pocket, and said, You have *more* than these. Yes, Sir; but all they contain, *you* know as well as *I.*——But I don't know, said he, the Light you put Things in, and so give them me, if you have not a mind to be search'd.

SIR, said I, I can't stay, if you won't forbear that ugly Word.——Give me then no Reason for it. Where are the other Papers? Why then, unkind Sir, if it must be so, here they are. And so I gave him out of my Pocket the second Parcel, seal'd up, as the former, with this Superscription; *From the naughty Articles, down, thro' sad Attempts, to* Thursday *the 42d Day of my Imprisonment.* This is last *Thursday,* is it?——Yes, Sir; but now you *will* see what I write, I will find some other way to employ my Time: For I can neither write so free, nor with any Face, what must be for your Perusal, and not for those I intended to divert with my melancholy Stories.

YES, said he, I would have you continue your Penmanship by all means; and I assure you, in the Mind I am in, I will not ask you for any after these; except any thing very extraordinary occurs. And, I have another thing to tell you, added he: That if you send for those from your Father, and let me read them, I may very probably give them all back again to you. And so I desire you will do it.

He took the parcel, and broke the seal instantly. So much for your *omen!* reply'd he.——I am sorry for it, said I, very seriously; and was walking away.——Whither now? said he.——I was going in, sir, that you might read them (since you *will* read them) without interruption. He put them into his pocket, and said—You have *more* than these. I am sure you have. Tell me truth.—I have, sir, I own. But *you* know as well as *I* all that they contain.—But I don't know, said he, the light you represent things in. Give them to me, therefore, if you have not a mind that I should search for them myself.—Why then, unkind sir, if it must be so, here they are.

And so I gave him, out of my pocket, the second parcel, seal'd up, as the former, with this superscription; *From the wicked articles, down, thro' vile attempts, to* Thursday *the 42d day of my imprisonment.*—This is last Thursday, is it?—Yes, sir; but now that you seem determined to see every thing I write, I will find some other way to employ my time.

I would have you, said he, continue writing by all means; and I assure you, in the mind I am in, I will not ask you for any papers after these; except something very extraordinary happens. And if you send for those from your father, and let me read them, I may very probably give them all back again to you. I desire therefore that you will.

It can be seen that in the first extract of fifty-seven lines of the first edition (a1–a57), there are thirteen verbal variants in the octavo text (b1–b64). This is a higher proportion than the average for the whole of the first two volumes, but the changes are otherwise typical.[5] Their elevating tendency is obvious. Two of them correct Pamela's grammar (thinks/thought, a9/b11; was/were, a9/b12); and three more refine her phraseology (near an/near at an, a22/b25; these Men/Men, a47/b53; Lot is/Lot it is, a51/b58). Pamela's careless 'God bless me' becomes 'Heaven bless me' (a34/b38–9); the determination of her virtue is emphasized by the addition of 'I snatch'd my Hand from him' (a8/b9–10); and her distance from the fallen women she pities is indicated by the insertion of 'undone' (a49/b55). Three changes clarify the sense (hope/will add, a3/b3; will live/ought to live, a10/b13;[6] So it becomes/ Indeed it becomes the present Condition of, a55–6/b63). Finally there are two minor stylistic changes: the variation 'reply'd he' for 'said he' (a1/b1), and the deletion of Pamela's wordy 'Well, you see' (a13/b15). In addition to these verbal variants there are in the first extract twenty-three changes of spelling, punctuation, etc., between the first and the sixth editions, the most important of them being the italicization in b8, b20, b47, and b48.

In the second extract (16 lines in the first edition) there are 4 verbal variants and 4 changes of spelling, etc., in the octavo; and in the third extract (59 lines in the first edition) there are 6 verbal variants and 10 changes of spelling, etc., in the octavo.

Apart from detailed polishing, the main tendency of the changes made between the first edition and the octavo of 1742 was to enhance Pamela's virtues and accomplishments, beginning the process—later to be carried much further—of making her into a lady; though Richardson was careful never to deprive her completely of her linguistic vitality. The character of Mr. B remained one of almost unrelieved wickedness.[7]

The differences between the octavo and the final revision published in 1801 were much greater. Where the original narrative was reused it was tightened up by rephrasing and rearrangement. Compare for instance the fourth paragraph of the first extract in the octavo version (b41–b51) with the revision (c38–c45), in which every sentence has been slightly altered, but where the sense is unchanged and where most of Pamela's vivid phraseology (deriving from the first edition) is allowed to stand. Similarly, the last paragraph of the third extract (h56–h64/i31–i37) has been rewritten so as

---

[5] Eaves and Kimpel ('Richardson's revisions of *Pamela*', see p. 63 n. 1) found a total of 2,531 verbal variants between the first and the sixth editions of volumes 1 and 2, or an average of 3·7 verbal variants per page. Here there is an average of 8·7 verbal variants per page.

[6] Honest Pamela *is* living with Mr. B.

[7] At least in the text. He is idealized in the new plates, and some of the entries in the table of contents of the octavo appear to be slanted with the aim of rehabilitating him (note from Peter Sabor).

to leave scarcely a phrase unchanged, but without any alteration of the sense of the passage. But perhaps for Richardson the main purpose of the final revision was its improvement of the characters of Pamela and Mr. B.

The plot of *Pamela*, which had served as the vehicle for Richardson's first headlong inspiration, proved difficult to reconcile with his later urge to give the novel a stronger moral purpose. The very conviction carried by his original picture of Pamela was now something of an embarrassment: it was the picture of a lively and likeable but also common and self-seeking servant-girl, whose reward for the technical preservation of her 'virtue' was marriage to the libertine who had taken advantage of his position as her master to try to rape her. If Pamela's virtue was to be worth preserving, and if marriage to Mr. B. was to be its proper reward, then both characters had to be cleared of their grosser imperfections. Pamela should be one of nature's ladies, with grace and virtue inborn; while Mr. B. should have at least some of the standards of behaviour, as well as the position, of a gentleman. In these extracts we see Richardson continuing the elevation of Pamela and, more obviously, attempting to whitewash the character of Mr. B.

In the first extract, in the short second paragraph of the octavo (b14–b17), Pamela roundly calls Mr. B. a rake whose vice has taken him from bad to worse. In the revision (c11–c23), while Pamela still remarks that vicious people may easily go from bad to worse, the observation no longer applies to Mr. B. He is not called a rake; indeed, she says, he is not really wicked at all, only foolish—though of course he is not usually foolish, seeming so now only because of his natural contempt for her position. Then the association of Mr. B. with the grossly immoral Squire Martin (recounted in the third paragraph of the octavo, b34–b40) is deleted, along with Pamela's appeal to be sent out of 'this wicked House': the house of which she herself is to become mistress.

In the second extract, where the 1801 text is twice as long as the earlier versions, the character of Mrs. Jewkes is developed. This new material is in Richardson's liveliest manner (he never lost his gift for racy narrative, even if he suppressed it in re-drawing Pamela), but here his main purpose was to emphasize the wickedness of Mrs. Jewkes, allowing us to suppose that, if there is villainy about, it is more likely to derive from Mrs. Jewkes than from Mr. B. Finally, in the third extract, where the greatest change is the deletion of the whole second paragraph of the early versions (octavo, h5–h23), Richardson was concerned to avoid Pamela's reasonable conclusion that, if Mr. B. could read her reflections upon his vile treatment of her without being moved by them, he must have 'a very cruel and determin'd Heart'.

Thus there are three main versions of *Pamela*: the vivid first edition, with Pamela at her most natural but with crudities of tone and structure which

Richardson was later to reject; the early revisions (mostly of 1741-2, but with a few more added later) whereby minor alterations were made throughout, and Pamela's manners were refined; and the largely rewritten version published in 1801 in which Richardson used his mature technique to tackle the contradictions in the plot and to enhance its morality. What should be the principles for editing *Pamela* today?

Richardson's three versions of *Pamela* are so different from each other (the last one especially from the other two) that it will be apparent, first, that neither the first nor the intermediate version can be combined with the last version in a single edited text; and secondly that an editor's decision to follow one particular text, or to present more than one text in parallel, must be a critical, not a bibliographical, one. Copy-text cannot be chosen in the ordinary way, for the editor has got to choose between main versions of the work; and, since each main version exists in only one authoritative text (there being no surviving manuscripts or printed editions marked up for the compositor), the choice of copy-text is determined by the choice of version.

Since the question is a critical one, similar to questions such as whether to edit (or read) the first version of *Roderick Hudson* or the last, here is a critical answer. Having investigated Richardson's revisions of *Pamela*, Eaves and Kimpel concluded:

The 1801 revision merely goes further in the direction in which the other revisions were headed. It accomplishes what the second, fifth, and octavo editions set out to do, and (probably with those changes in the eighth duodecimo edition which were not included in the 1801) it best represents Richardson's final intention. If any single text is to be preferred to it, that text is the first edition, which has never been reprinted. Both are necessary to students of Richardson, and neither is readily accessible. A double-column *Pamela* containing the text of the first edition (with variants from the other duodecimos and the octavo) and the text of the 1801 edition (with the adoption of the few readings from the 1810 which clearly correct misprints in the 1801) would doubtless best serve the scholar. But though one eighteenth-century admirer said that "if all the Books in England were to be burnt, this Book, next the Bible, ought to be preserved,"* there is some doubt that it needs such extensive preservation. Both texts should be made available for anyone who wants to study *Pamela* in her country habit and in her country-gentry habit, but for anyone who simply wants to read *Pamela* for enjoyment, we believe that the text of the first edition should be the one reprinted. It is closer to the Pamela whom Richardson actually imagined, whereas all succeeding texts try to approach the Pamela he thought he should have imagined.[8]

* Knightley Chetwood to Richardson [*should read* Ralph Courteville], January 27, 1741, Forster MS XVI, 1, fol. 43.

[8] Eaves, T. C. D., and Kimpel, B. D., 'Richardson's revisions of *Pamela*', *Studies in bibliography*, xx, 1967, pp. 87–8.

Eaves and Kimpel followed their own advice and produced in 1971 an admirably accurate and uncluttered version of the first-edition text aimed at students and general readers.[9] This was followed in 1974 by a facsimile reprint of the 1801 text in four volumes, edited by M. F. Shugrue.[10] As a result, scholars, students, and general readers in America now have easy access to the two most important versions of Richardson's revolutionary first novel, in practice for the first time, since copies of the original editions are extremely rare.[11] Unfortunately, however, these American publications are not distributed in the United Kingdom, where the only available edition of *Pamela* remains the Everyman text of 1914, reset in 1962.[12] British readers are therefore limited (as they have been for decades) to the least appropriate, intermediate version of the work, in a text of hair-raising inaccuracy.

The last of the intermediate editions of *Pamela* that was amended by Richardson himself was the 'eighth' duodecimo edition dated 1762. The later eighteenth-century editions derived from it, as did some of the nineteenth-century editions; but there was also a considerable group of early nineteenth-century editions which, while they too derived ultimately from the 1762 edition, incorporated drastic textual change. This version of *Pamela* seems to have been prepared for Charles Cooke's 'Select novels', and to have appeared first *c.* 1810; there were at least five more editions of it up to 1825, the last of which was reissued in 1838.[13] Richardson's 1762 text was extensively cut, as much as a fifth of it being removed from some parts; while thousands of words were changed, and the punctuation was altered to include inverted commas for direct speech. It appears that the revision was made in order to refine and modernize the novel for early nineteenth-century readers; and that it was made without any authority.

Most unfortunately it was the Cooke version of *Pamela* that was used as copy for the Everyman edition of 1914. It may be that the anonymous Everyman editor chose it because it supplied the inverted commas conventional in Everyman reprints, and that he did not know that the words of the text had been interfered with. Whatever the reason, Messrs. Dent did not realize how bad their text was, and it was reset without alteration for the

[9] Houghton-Mifflin, New York.

[10] Garland Books, New York.

[11] The first edition of *Pamela* I was not reprinted until 1971 (the first edition of *Pamela* II has *never* been reprinted); and, although the 1801 edition was reprinted with corrections in 1810, and again, expurgated, as a Routledge 'yellow-back' in [1873], copies of all three editions are rare.

[12] Joseph Dent, London and New York. The Shakespeare Head edition of 1929, which reprinted the text of the sixth octavo edition, 1742, was an expensive library edition which did not have wide circulation.

[13] Cooke's stereotype edition of *c.* 1810 in the British Library is the earliest seen of this version, but it may have had predecessors. It was followed by at least eight other editions by various publishers, the last apparently being that of J. M'Gowan, London, *c.* 1825 (reissued 1838).

second Everyman edition, first published with an introduction by M. Kinkead-Weekes in 1962; which remained the only version of the novel available to British readers.

Here for comparison is the third of my extracts from *Pamela* in the 'eighth' edition text of 1762 (the last of the intermediate editions to be amended by Richardson, j1–j59), and in the Everyman text of 1962 (k1–k47) (see facing page).

The most obvious difference between the 1762 and Cooke–Everyman texts is the wholesale normalization of the punctuation of the revised version. On the whole this is unhelpful—the spatter of inverted commas impedes the flow of Pamela's narrative without making it much more comprehensible—and, since Richardson appears to have taken as much care with the emendation of the punctuation, etc., of the intermediate texts as he did with revising the words, it is also undesirable. But if the normaliza-tion of the punctuation is unfortunate, the unauthorized alteration of the words of the text is appalling. In the forty-seven lines of the Everyman setting three words are changed, while six separate words and two phrases totalling another seventeen words are omitted altogether; all these new readings being deliberate changes made to the text for Cooke's edition, long after Richardson last emended it.[14]

This extract happens to contain a large amount of variation, but the other two extracts discussed in this chapter (which, like this extract, were chosen at random as far as the Cooke–Everyman version was concerned) both show patterns of change in the revised versions which differ only in degree. In the first extract the forty-six lines of the Everyman setting contain two words changed, two words added, and two words omitted; and in the second extract two words are omitted in the thirteen Everyman lines.

Thus for the past half-century most British students and general readers of *Pamela* have had to use a text of the novel that differs grossly and mis-leadingly from any version authorized by Richardson.

[14] Although 'Penmanship' is changed to 'writing' in the authorized revision published in 1801 (i31) as well as in the unauthorized Cooke-Everyman text (j52/k42), this seems to be no more than an accidental coincidence.

He was going to speak; but I said, to drive him from thinking of any more, And I must beg you, Sir, to read the Matter favourably, if I have exceeded in any Liberties of my Pen.

j5 I think, said he, half-smiling, you may wonder at my Patience, that I can be so easy to read myself abused as I am by such a saucy Slut.——Sir, said I, I have wonder'd you should be so desirous to see my bold Stuff; and, for that very Reason, I have j10 thought it a very *good*, or a very *bad* Sign. What, said he, is your *good* Sign?—That it may have an Effect upon your Temper, at last, in my Favour, when you see me so sincere. Your *bad* Sign? j15 Why, that if you can read my Reflections and Observations upon your Treatment of me, with Tranquility, and not be mov'd, it is a Sign of a very cruel and determin'd Heart. Now, pray, Sir, don't be angry at my Boldness, in telling you so freely my j20 Thoughts. You may, perhaps, said he, be least mistaken, when you think of your bad Sign. God forbid! said I.

So I took out my Papers; and said, Here, Sir, they are. But if you please to return them, with- j25 out breaking the Seal, it will be very generous: And I will take it for a great Favour, and a good Omen.

He broke the Seal instantly, and open'd them: So much for your *Omen!* reply'd he. I am sorry j30 for it, said I, very seriously; and was walking away. Whither now? said he. I was going in, Sir, that you might have time to read them, if you thought fit. He put them into his Pocket, and said, You have *more* than these. Yes, Sir; but all they con- j35 tain, *you* know as well as *I.*—But I don't know, said he, the Light you put Things in; and so give them me, if you have not a mind to be search'd.

Sir, said I, I can't stay, if you won't forbear that ugly Word.——Give me then no Reason for it. j40 Where are the other Papers? Why, then, unkind Sir, if it must be so, here they are. And so I gave him, out of my Pocket, the second Parcel, seal'd up, as the former, with this Superscription; *From the naughty Articles, down, thro' sad Attempts, to* Thurs- j45 day *the 42d Day of my Imprisonment.* This is last *Thursday,* is it?—Yes, Sir; but now you *will* see what I write, I will find some other way to em- ploy my Time: For how can write I with any Face, what must be for your Perusal, and not for j50 those I intended to read my melancholy Sto- ries.

Yes, said he, I would have you continue your Penmanship, by all means; and I assure you, in the Mind I am in, I will not ask you for any after these; j55 except any-thing very extraordinary occurs. And I have another thing to tell you, added he: That if you send for those from your Father, and let me read them, I may, very probably, give them all back again to you. And so I desire you do it.

He was going to speak; but I said, to drive him from thinking of any more—" I must beg you, Sir, to read the matter favour- ably, if I have exceeded in any liberties of my pen."

k5 "I think," said he, half-smiling, "you may wonder at my patience, that I can be so easy to read myself abused as I am by such a saucy slut."—"Sir," said I, "I have wondered you should be so desirous to see my bold stuff; and, for that very reason, I have thought it a very *good* or a very *bad* sign."— k10 "What," said he, "is your *good* sign?"—"That it may have an effect upon your temper, at last, in my favour, when you see me so sincere."—"Your *bad* sign?"—"Why, that if you can read my reflections and observations upon your treatment of me, with tranquillity, and not be moved, it is a sign of a very k15 cruel and determined heart. Now, pray, Sir, don't be angry at my boldness, in telling you so freely my thoughts."—"You may, perhaps," said he, "be least mistaken, when you think of your bad sign."—"God forbid!" said I.

So I took out my papers, and said—"Here, Sir, they are. k20 But if you please to return them, without breaking the seal, it will be very generous: and I will take it as a great favour, and a good omen."

He broke the seal instantly, and opened them: "So much for your *omen!*" replied he. "I am sorry for it," said I, very k25 seriously; and was walking away. "Whither now?" said he. "I was going in, Sir, that you might have time to read them, if you thought fit." He put them into his pocket, and said—"You have *more* than these."—"Yes, Sir; but all they contain, *you* know as well as I."—"But I don't know," said k30 he, "the light you put things in: so give them me, if you have not a mind to be searched."

"Sir," said I, "I can't stay, if you won't forbear that ugly word"—"Give me then no reason for it. Where are the other papers?"—"Why, unkind Sir, if it must be so, here they are;" k35 and I gave him, out of my pocket, the second parcel, sealed up, as the former, with this superscription: "*From the naughty articles, down through sad attempts, to Thursday the 42nd day of my imprisonment.*"—"This is last Thursday, is it?"—"Yes, Sir; but now you *will* see what I write, I shall find some other k40 way to employ your time; for how can I write with any face, what must be for your perusal, and not for those I intended to read my melancholy stories?"

"Yes," said he, "I would have you continue your writing, by all means; and I will not ask you for any after these; k45 except any thing very extraordinary occurs. I have another thing to tell you," added he, "that if you send for those from your father, and let me read them, I may, very probably, give all back again to you."

Pamela, third extract·
 j1–j59: '8th' edn. 1762 (Univ. Lond. Lib.,
  YL.R.55.T(762), ii, pp. 27–8; ×0·79)
 k1–k47: 2nd Everyman edn., London 1962 (Trin.
  Coll. Cam., RR.043.RIC.1, i, pp. 211–12;
  ×0·65)

Verbal variants

	1762		Everyman
ja	And I must	k2	"I must
j25	take it for a	k20	take it as a
j35	and so give	k29	so give
j39	Why, then, unkind	k33	"Why, unkind
j40	And so I gave	k34	and I gave
j46	I will find	k38	I shall find
j52	Penmanship	k42	writing
j52–3	I assure you, in the Mind I am in,	k43	[omitted]
j54–5	And I have	k44	I have
j57	give them all	k46–7	give all
j58–9	And so I desire you will do it.	k47	[omitted]

EXAMPLE 4

Swift, *Directions to servants*, 1745

DEAN SWIFT[1] told Gay in 1731 that he had retired from Dublin to the country 'for the public good, having two great works in hand'; one was the set of dialogues known as *Polite conversation*; 'The other', Swift wrote, 'is of almost equal importance; I may call it the whole duty of servants, in about twenty several Stations from the Steward & waiting woman down to the Scullion & Pantry boy.'[2] The same two works were again referred to in a letter written the following year to Pope, when Swift said that both were 'begun above twenty-eight years ago' (i.e. before 1704), that *Polite conversation* was 'almost finished', but that *Directions to servants*—as it was eventually called—would 'require a long time to perfect'.[3] Two years later in 1734, in another letter to Pope, Swift said he was convinced that neither of these two books (or another which he also had in hand) would ever be finished, even though they wanted nothing but corrections; and as far as *Directions to servants* was concerned he was right.[4]

In 1738, having mislaid the manuscript, Swift wrote to his Dublin printer George Faulkner:

I believe you know that I had a Treatise, called, *Advice to Servants*, in two Volumes. The first was lost, but this Minute Mrs. *Ridgeway* brought it to me, having found it in some Papers in her Room; and truly, when I went to look for the second, I could not tell where to find it; if you happen to have it, I shall be glad; if not, the Messenger shall go to Mrs. *Whiteway*.[5]

---

[1] Swift is best approached through Irvin Ehrenpreis's *Swift: the man, his works, and the age*, 3 vols., Oxford 1962– . Herman Teerink's *A bibliography of the writings of Jonathan Swift*, 2nd edn., ed. Scouten, A. H., Philadelphia 1963, is comprehensive but difficult to use. The history of *Directions to servants* is summarized by Herbert Davis in his Shakespeare Head *Swift*, vol. xiii (*Directions to servants, and miscellaneous pieces 1733–1742*), Oxford 1959, pp. vii–xxiii, 209–20; this is similar to the account that Davis had previously given in the Festschrift for *Belle da Costa Greene*, Princeton 1954, pp. 433–44.

I was most fortunate in being able to discuss the development of this chapter with Mr. David Woolley.

[2] 28 Aug. 1731: Swift, J., *The correspondence of Jonathan Swift*, ed. Williams, H. 5 vols., Oxford 1963–5, iii, p. 493.

[3] 12 June 1732: Swift, *Correspondence*, iv, pp. 31–2.

[4] 1 Nov. 1734: Swift, *Correspondence*, iv, p. 262. *Polite conversation* was published as *A complete collection of genteel and ingenious conversation* in 1738; the other book which he had in hand was *The history of the four last years of the Queen*, posthumously published in 1758.

[5] 31 Aug. 1738: Swift, *Correspondence*, v, p. 121.

The outcome of this inquiry is not recorded, but Swift wrote again to Faulkner about his manuscript at the end of 1739:

> I cannot find a Manuscript I wrote, called *Directions* for *Servants*, which I thought was very useful, as well as humorous. I believe, you have both seen and read it; I wish you could give me some Intelligence of it, because my Memory is quite gone, therefore, let me know all you can conjecture about it.[6]

Poor Swift; his mind was going and, although the manuscript was soon found, he could do no more with it. In May 1740 Mrs. Whiteway wrote to Pope:

> A few years ago he [Swift] burnt most of his writings unprinted except a few loose papers, which are in my possession, and which I promise you, if I outlive him, shall never be made public without your approbation. There is one treatise in his own keeping, called Advice to Servants, very unfinished and incorrect, yet what is done of it, has so much humour, that it may appear as a posthumous work.[7]

Loss of memory turned to insanity in 1742. Two years later a manuscript of *Directions to servants* was listed amongst the 'Mss: found in the Dean's Study' as 'The Advice to Servants (A Copy) borrowed by ye Revd Dr King'.[8]

The Dean died at last on 19 October 1745. There were then at least three manuscript copies of *Directions to servants* in existence. These were (1) a holograph draft, corrected, of chapters i–iii, now at Trinity College, Cambridge (Rothschild MS);[9] (2) a scribal copy, with a few corrections by Swift, of about two-thirds of the text, lacking seven of the short chapters at the end, now at the Victoria and Albert Museum (Forster MS);[10] and (3) a manuscript of the whole text in Faulkner's possession (not incorporating the corrections made by Swift in the two surviving manuscripts) used for setting the first edition, now lost.[11]

George Faulkner[12]—one of the great printer-publishers of the mid

---

6 4 Dec. 1739: Swift, *Correspondence*, v, p. 172.

7 16 May 1740: Swift, *Correspondence*, v, p. 188.

8 Williams, II., *Dean Swift's library*, Cambridge 1932, pp. 25–6, 31–3.

9 Rothschild 2275. It had been found amongst the papers of Charles Agar, first Earl of Normanton (born Dublin 1736, Archbishop of Dublin 1801). It is described by Herbert Davis (see p. 80 n. 1).

10 MS. Forster 48.E.39. It had been in the possession of Swift's relatives Deane and Theophilus Swift before Forster had it. It is described by Herbert Davis (see p. 80 n. 1).

11 Its characteristics are deduced from the text of the first printed edition; it could have been a copy made for Faulkner during the period between the letters from Swift to Faulkner of 31 August 1738 and 4 December 1739 (transcribed above).

Faulkner sent Bowyer and Hitch a text of 'Advice to Servants' on 1 October 1745 as copy for the London edition, and this could have been a transcript of Faulkner's manuscript; but it is much more likely to have been proofs or sheets of Faulkner's edition (Faulkner to Bowyer, 1 Oct. 1745; Swift, *Correspondence*, Ball's edition, vi, 1914, pp. 223–4).

12 The best biographical account of Faulkner is the article by W. P. Courtney in *DNB*; he was printer and publisher in Dublin from 1724 to 1775. See also Ward, R. E., *Prince of Dublin publishers: the letters of George Faulkner*, Lexington 1972.

eighteenth century, comparable in professional ability with his contemporaries William Bowyer II and Samuel Richardson—had begun to print the first edition of *Directions to servants* a few weeks before Swift's death. He claimed in the Preface to have 'the Original', possibly meaning Swift's holograph but more likely an authorized scribal copy, in his custody;[13] and he said later that the book was published in accordance with the Dean's instructions: 'The *Directions to Servants* he [Swift] ordered to be published before his last Illness, in the Way of a Pamphlet: This, with several *original Poems* he gave the Printer [Faulkner] in his Life Time.'[14]

The result was a faithful version of the fragmented, incomplete text of the work—Faulkner was an admirably conscientious editor, both here and in his subsequent editions—which was published in November 1745 (*1745A*).[15] A second edition, scarcely changed, appeared simultaneously in London with the imprint of Dodsley and Cooper (*1745B*).[16] A number of details were altered for the text of the *Directions* included in Faulkner's first posthumous edition of Swift's *Works* (*1746*).[17] The last edition to have independent authority was in Faulkner's duodecimo edition of the *Works* (*1751*), for which he used the text of *1746* with the incorporation of Swift's last corrections.[18]

The following diagram shows what appears to be the main line of descent of the text of *Directions to servants*, although it is possible that there were intermediate manuscripts other than the three that we are sure of:

---

[13] First edition (see n. 15), p. [1].

[14] First posthumous collection (see n. 17), viii, 'The preface by the Dublin bookseller', p. [2].

[15] Swift, J., *Directions to servants*, Dublin, by G. Faulkner, 1745; Teerink, H., *A bibliography of the writings of Jonathan Swift*, 2nd edn., ed. Scouten, A. H., Philadelphia 1963 (hereafter Teerink), 787. Faulkner wrote to Bowyer on 1 October 1745 'Fix your day of publication, and I will wait until you are ready, that we may both come out on the same day. I think the middle of November will do very well . . .' (Swift, *Correspondence*, Ball's edn., vi, 1914, p. 223). The book was advertised in Faulkner's *Dublin journal* for 23–26 Nov. 1745.

[16] Swift, J., *Directions to servants*, London, for R. Dodsley and M. Cooper, 1745 (Teerink 785). Other partners in the publication were Bowyer and C. Hitch (Swift, *Correspondence*, Ball's edn., vi, 1914, pp. 223–4).

[17] Swift, J., *Works*, viii, Dublin, by and for G. Faulkner, 1746 (Teerink 44).

[18] Swift, J., *Works*, viii, Dublin, by G. Faulkner, 1751 (Teerink 51A(7)). Faulkner also used a corrected text of *1746* for the octavo *Works* in which the *Directions* were again dated 1751 (Teerink 45A(3)); but the 1751 octavo has no independent authority.

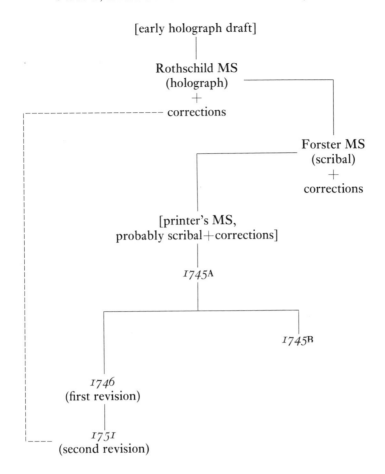

[early holograph draft]

Rothschild MS
(holograph)
+
corrections

Forster MS
(scribal)
+
corrections

[printer's MS,
probably scribal+corrections]

*1745*A

*1745*B

1746
(first revision)

1751
(second revision)

Before making a detailed comparison of the different versions of an extract from the text, we should look briefly at their general characteristics. The *Rothschild MS*, first, must have been copied from an early holograph draft because it includes copying errors (for instance in a22 of the extract, below). It was copied out by Swift in a foolscap quarto notebook made of half sheets of the writing paper he was using for letters in the mid-1720s, and it was probably not started before then.[19] It contains only the first three chapters of the work, and it may have been part of one of the two 'volumes' referred to by Swift in 1738.[20] It has both early alterations by Swift which were copied into the two other manuscripts, and later ones which were not (details of some of these alterations are given on p. 85).

---

[19] H. Davis in the Shakespeare Head *Swift* (see p. 80 n. 1), vol. xiii, pp. xi–xii.
[20] See above, p. 80.

The *Forster MS* was copied by an amanuensis, probably from the Rothschild MS in 1738–9. It is much longer than what survives of the Rothschild MS, containing about two-thirds of the text that appeared in the printed editions. It was a fairly faithful transcript with no more than ordinary copying errors, but with some intentional rearrangement and a small number of corrections in Swift's hand. It may have been the 'Copy' borrowed by Dr. King and found in the Dean's study in 1744.[21]

The characteristics and extent of the missing *printer's MS* may be deduced from the text of the first edition of 1745. It repeated most (but not all) of the copying errors in the Forster MS, from which it seems likely to have been copied, perhaps by the same scribe in 1738–9. It included further material not in the Forster MS, and it appears to have been corrected (by Swift?), but it did not incorporate the corrections made by Swift to the Forster MS, or the final alterations he made to the Rothschild MS. It is possible that this manuscript (or perhaps the Forster MS, which now has no cover sheet) was headed 'Advice' rather than 'Directions' to Servants.[22]

As to the printed texts, the first edition, *1745A*, had a 'Postscript' of two paragraphs on p. ²79 'left out by Mistake' from the Cook's chapter; these paragraphs were later incorporated in various places in the texts of *1745B*, *1746*, and *1751*. There were no other important textual differences between *1745A* and *1745B*. In the text of *1746*, however, there was some revision of grammatical detail, seemingly without manuscript authority. Finally, for the text of *1751* somebody—presumably Faulkner—took the text of *1746* and inserted in it Swift's final corrections from the Rothschild MS, using apparently those parts of the manuscript which are now missing as well as those which survive.[23]

Here, then, for comparison are the last thirty-nine lines of the Cook's

---

[21] See above, p. 81.

[22] The title 'Advice to servants' is used in Swift's letter to Faulkner of 31 Aug. 1738 (see p. 80 n. 5); in Mrs. Whiteway's letter to Pope of 16 May 1740 (see p. 81 n. 7); in the inventory entry of 1744 (see p. 81 n. 8); and in Faulkner's letter to Bowyer of 1 Oct. 1745 (see p. 81 n. 11). Swift referred to the work as 'Directions for Servants' in his letter to Faulkner of 4 Dec. 1739 (see p. 81 n. 6). The incomplete Rothschild MS was headed 'Directions to Poor Servants', the 'Poor' then being struck out.

[23] The reason for supposing that Faulkner checked the text for *1751* against the parts of the Rothschild MS which are now missing as well as against those which survive is this: a considerable number of corrections appeared in the parts of *1751* not covered by the surviving Rothschild MS which can be seen to have manuscript authority because they are also found in the Forster MS; but Faulkner did not take them from the Forster MS because *1751* does not incorporate Swift's own emendations to the Forster MS, which Faulkner would certainly have used if he had seen them; therefore Faulkner was using another manuscript, and the only likely candidate is the missing part of the Rothschild MS.

Faulkner may also have seen, but did not use, Swift's fragmentary draft Preface for *Directions to servants*, which was once attached to one of the manuscripts—it is not clear which one—and was copied for Sir Walter Scott by Theophilus Swift early in the nineteenth century; see Scott's *Works of Swift*, i, Edinburgh 1814, pp. 439–40 n.

chapter in the Rothschild MS, followed by the parallel passages in the Forster MS and in the four printed texts we have been discussing (see pp. 86-9, 91-4).

The thirty-nine lines of the Rothschild MS are divided into nine paragraphs on pp. 22-3. Page 22 ended originally with line a24, the 'in' beneath the 'And' at the end of the line being the catchword for the next page; but a note indicating that something was to be added was then written at the bottom of the page and marked with a cross (a25). Crosses also marked paragraphs 2 and 8, probably as a reminder that they were to be moved elsewhere. Swift's alterations are in four groups: five emendations during transcription of probable copying errors (a19, a22, a26, a27,[24] a39); three changes of wording during transcription (a28, a33, a36); three changes of wording after transcription but before the Forster MS was copied (a10, a14, a18);[25] and three changes of wording after the Forster MS was copied (a18^2, a24, a30).

The Forster MS follows the form of the Rothschild MS, except that the note about extra material to come (a25) has been mistaken for part of the text of paragraph 7 and has been interpolated between the first two words of 'And in the same manner' (a24-6/b32-4). Paragraphs 2 and 8 now have specific marginal directions for their removal; and there is a marginal 'Q^r' at b2 to inquire whether the word 'Cook' (which is obviously wrong, the chapter being addressed to the Cook) should not read 'Butler'. There are eleven verbal variants between the Rothschild MS and the Forster MS: four of them appear to be copying errors (were/was, a13/b17; kitchin/Kitchen's, a22/b29; hath/has, a24/b32; good/[omitted], a24/b32); four more result from the Forster MS scribe following the uncorrected state of the Rothschild MS (for/and, a18/b23; because/for, a24/b31; have/let, a27/b35;[26] When/if, a30/b38); two are new corrections (is is/[no repetition], a9-10/b13; wriggle/wriggling, a25/b33);[27] and the eleventh is 'hath' in b3, apparently altered from the 'has' copied from a2. The scribe has also introduced a few of his own spellings, and has thoroughly revised the punctuation and capitalization.

(*continued on p.* 90)

---

[24] It would appear that the phrase in the early holograph draft that Swift was copying was 'let half the bole of it be worn out'. Swift wrote down 'have' by mistake for 'half'; and then, thinking that 'have' was the verb, he crossed out 'let' but omitted to cross out 'be'; which produced the reading 'let have the bole of it be worn out'. This was plainly wrong, so the Forster MS scribe used the cancelled word and wrote 'let the bole of it be worn out' (b35). The phrase was probably corrected in the printer's MS; *1745A* reads 'let half the Bole of it be worn out' (c35-6).

[25] Originally a18 probably began 'as well bred gentry'. The 'as' was then crossed out, 'and' being written in above it. Finally 'and' was crossed out, and 'for' was written over the cancelled 'as'.

[26] See n. 24.

[27] It appears that the Forster MS scribe was puzzled by the 'wriggle it' of the Rothschild MS, and left a blank, and that 'wriggling it' was written in later.

When you roast a breast of Veal, remember your Sweet-heart the Cook, loves
a Sweet-bread. therefore set it aside till evening. You can say, the Cat or the dog has
run away with it, or you found it tainted, or fly-blown; and besides, it looks as
well on the table without the Sweet-bread as with it.

It is a very great using to put a Cook, who is a thorow servant to a
pudding work. for example; what Cook of Spirit, would lose her time in
picking larks, wheat-ears, and other small birds, therefore if you cannot get
the maids or the young Misses to assist you, een make short work, and either
singe or flay them. There is no great loss in the Skins, and the flesh is
is just the same

When you make the company wait long for dinner, and the meat be
overdone, which is generally the case, you may lawfully lay the fault on
your Lady, who hurryed you so to send up dinner, that you were forced to
send it up overdone too much boyld and roasted.

When you are in hast to take down your dishes, tip them in such a
manner, that a dozen will fall together upon the dresser just ready for y.e. hand.
To save time and trouble, cut your apples and Onyons with the same knife.
well bred gentry love the tast of an onyon in every thing they eat.
Dash Luvy three or four pounds of butter together with your hands
then dash it against the wall just over the dresser. so as to have it ready
to put by pieces, as you have occasion for it.

If you have a silver Sauce-pan for the kitchin use, let me advise you to
batter it well, and keep it always black; This will be for your masters
honor, it shews there hath been constant good house-keeping. And
Make room for the Sauspan by wriggling it on the coals &c   in

COOK.

in the same manner. If you are allowed a large Silver spoon for
the kitchen, have the bole of it be worn out with continual
scraping and stirring, and often say merrily, this Spoon owes my
master no service.

better hurrible of give your self no trouble; for it will serve
to quicken the fire, or if you are allowed the kitchen stuff that you know where to
put it.

When you send up a mess of broth, water-gruel, or the like
to your Master in a morning, do not forget with your thumb and two
fingers to put salt on the side of the plate. for if you make use of
a spoon or the end of a knife, there may be danger that the salt
would fall, and that would be a sign of ill luck. Onely remember to
lick your thumb and fingers clean before you offer to touch the salt

Rothschild MS (Trin. Coll. Cam. Rothschild 2275, pp. 22–3; ×0·74)

p. 22] When you roast a breast of Veal, remember your Sweet-heart the Cook, loves
a Sweet-bread, therefore set it a side till evening. You can say, the Cat or the dog has
run away with it, or you found it tainted, or fly-blown; and besides, it looks as
well on the table without the Sweet-bread as with it. } Par. 1

a5 × It is a very great injury to put a Cook, who is a thorow Servant to ～
piddling work, for example, what Cook of Spirit, would lose her time in ～
picking larks, wheat-ears, and other small birds; therefore if you cannot get
the maids or the young Misses to assist you, e'en make short work, and either
singe or flay them. There is no great loss in the skins, and the flesh is
a10 ~~never the worse~~ is just the same } Par. 2

When you make the company wait long for dinner, and the meat be
overdone, which is generally the case, you may lawfully lay the fault on
your Lady, who hurryed you so to send up dinner, that you were forced to
send it up ~~overdone~~ . too much boyld and roasted. } Par. 3

a15 When you are in hast to take down your dishes, tip them in such a ～
manner, that a dozen will fall together upon the dresser just ready for yʳ hand. } Par. 4

To save time and trouble, ~~y~~ cut your apples and Onyons with the same knife,
~~and~~
for well bred gentry love the tast of an onyon in every thing they eat. } Par. 5

~~Dash~~ Lump three or four pounds of butter together with your hands, ～
a20 then dash it against the wall just over the dresser, so as to have it ready
to pull, by pieces, as you have occasion for it. } Par. 6

have a
If you ₍ₐ₎ silver sawce-pan for the kitchin use, let me advise you to ～
batter it well, and keep it always black; [t]This will be for your masters
because
honor, ~~for~~ ₍ₐ₎ it shows there hath been constant good house-keeping. And

a25 × Make room for the sawcpan by wriggle it on the coals &c   in [catchword] } Par. 7

p. 23] in the same manner, if you are allowed a large ~~Kite~~ Silver spoon for
the kitchen, ~~let~~ have the bole of it be worn out with continuall ～
scraping and stirring, and often say merrily, this spoon ~~has done~~
Qu owes my Master no service.
When
a30 Before × ~~If~~ your butter turns to oyl, give your self no trouble; for it will serve
to quicken the fire, or if you are allowed the kitchen-stuff you know where to
put it. } Par. 8

When you send up a mess of broth, ~~milk~~ water-gruel, or the like
to your Master in a morning, do not forget with your thumb and two
a35 fingers to put salt on the side of the plate, for if you make use of
~~the~~ a Spoon or the end of a knife, there may be danger that the salt
would fall, and that would be a sign of ill luck. Onely remember to
~~lik~~ lick your thumb and fingers clean, before you offer to touch the salt. } Par. 9

Transcript of p. 86

[88]

When you roast a Breast of Veal, remember your
Sweet-heart the Butler loves a Sweetbread; then set
it aside till Evening: You can say the Cat or the Dog has
run away with it, or you found it tainted, or Flyblown;
And besides, it looks as well on the Table without the
Sweetbread as with it.

It is a very great Injury to put a Cook, who is a
thorow Servant, to fiddling Work; for example, what
Cook of Spirit, would loose her Time in picking Larks,
Wheatears, and other Small Birds; therefore if you can
not get the maids, or the young Misses to assist you, een
make short Work, and either singe or flay them. There is
no great Loss in the Skins, and the Flesh is just the same.

When you make the Company wait long for Dinner,
and the meat be overdone, which is generally the Case, you
may lawfully lay the fault on your Lady, who hurried you
so to send up Dinner, that you were forced to send it up
too much boyled and roasted.

When you are in haste to take down your Dishes, tip
them in such a Manner, that a dozen will fall together
upon the Dresser just ready for your Hand.

To save time and Trouble, cut your Apples and Onions
with the Same Knife, and well bred Gentry love the Taste
of an Onion in every thing they eat.

Lump three or four Pounds of Butter together with
your Hands, then dash it agst the Wall just over the
Dresser, so as to have it ready to pull by pieces as you have
Occasion for it.

If you have a Silver Saucepan for the Kitchen, use
let me advise you to batter it well, and keep it always
black, this will be for your Masters Honor, for it shews
there has been constant House-keeping: And make room
for the Saucepan by wrigging it on the Coals &c.

In the Same manner, if you are allowed a Large Silver
Spoon for the Kitchen, let the bole of it be worn out
with continual Scraping and Stirring, and often say merrily,
this Spoon owes my Master no Service.

If your Butter turns to Oyl give yourself no Trouble
for it will serve to quicken the Fire, or if you are allowed
the Kitchen stuff you know where to put it.

When you send up a Mess of Broth, Water-gruel
or the like to your Master in a Morning, do not forget
your Thumb and two fingers to put Salt on the Side of
the Plate, for if you make use of a Spoon or the end
of a Knife, there may be Danger that the Salt would fall,
and that would be a Sign of ill Luck. Only remember to
lick your Thumb and fingers clean, before you offer to
touch the Salt.

Forster MS (Victoria and Albert Museum, MS. Forster 48.E.39, fos. 32ᵃ, 33ᵃ; ×0·40)

p. 32]

When you roast a Breast of Veal, remember your
Butler

Q.^r Sweet-heart the Cook, loves a Sweet-bread; There fore, set
it aside till Evening: You can say, the Cat or the Dog hasth
run away with it, or you found it tainted; or fly-blown;
b5 And besides, it looks as well on the Table without the
Sweet-bread as wth it

Par. 1

It is a very great Injury to put a Cook, who is a
thorow servant, to fiddling Work; for example, what
Cook of Spirit, would loose her Time in picking Larks,
b10 Wheat-ears, and other small Birds; therefore if you can
not get the Maids, or the young Misses to assist you, e'en
make short Work, and either singe or flay them. There is
no great Loss in the Skins, and the Flesh is just the same

Par. 2

When you make the Company wait long for Dinner,
b15 and the Meat be overdone, which is generaly the Case, you
may lawfully lay the Fault on your Lady, who hurried you
so to send up Dinner, that you was forced to send it up
too much boyled and roasted.

Par. 3

p. 33]
b20 When you are in heast to take down your Dishes, tip
them in such a Manner, that a dozen will fall together
upon the Dresser just ready for your Hand.

Par. 4

To save time and Trouble, cut your Apples and Onions
wth the same Knife, and well bred Gentry love the Taste
of an Onion in every thing they eat.

Par. 5

b25 Lump three or four Pounds of Butter together w^th
your Hands, then dash it ag.^t the Wall just over the
Dresser, so as to have it ready to pull by pieces as you have
Occasion for it.

Par. 6

If you have a Silver Sauce-pan for the Kitchen's use
b30 let me advise you to batter it well, and keep it always
black, this will be for your Masters Honor, for it shews
there has been constant House-keeping: And make room
for the Sauce-pan by wriggling it on the Coals &c.
In the same Manner, if you are allowed a large Silver
b35 Spoon for the Kitchen, let the bole of it be worn out
wth continual scraping and stirring, and often say merrily
this Spoon owes my Master no Service.

Par. 7

If your Butter turns to Oyle give yourself no Trouble:
for it will serve to quicken the Fire, or if you are allowed
b40 the Kitchen stuff you know where to put it.

Par. 8

When you send up a Mess of Broth, Water-gruel,
or the like to your Master in a Morning, do not forget w^th
your Thumb and two Fingers to put Salt on the side of
the Plate, for if you make use of a Spoon or the end
b45 of a Knife, there may be Danger that the Salt would fall,
and that would be a Signe of ill Luck. Only remember to
lick your Thumb and Fingers clean, before you offer to
touch the Salt

Par. 9

This before page 28

This before page 30 ×

Transcript of p. 88

In *1745A*, set from a printer's MS which probably derived from the Forster MS, paragraphs 2 and 8 of the manuscripts have been moved elsewhere;[28] the original paragraph 7 is now split in two, the break coming after the interpolated phrase, at c33-4; and two new paragraphs belonging to the chapter are added at the end of the book (c49-c65). Two copying errors have been transmitted from the Forster MS (was, b17/c12; has, b32/c30); but, since the printer's MS has not survived, the origin of most of the new readings is doubtful. Two of them look like copying errors (on/at, b5/c6; on/upon, b16/c11). The suggested amendment of 'Cook' to 'Butler' is incorporated (b2/c2); and c4 reads 'has', not the altered 'hath' of b3. The other changes from the Forster MS readings suggest that the printer's MS had itself been corrected, perhaps by Swift: 'Kitchen's' is changed back to 'Kitchen' (b29/c27-8); the omitted 'good' is reintroduced (b32/c31); 'let the bole' becomes 'let half the Bole' (b35/c35-6);[29] and 'it' is substituted for 'the Sweet-bread' (b5-6/c6).[30] The printer has normalized the spelling, capitalization, and punctuation.

The London edition, *1745B*, was set from proofs or sheets of *1745A*, which it follows very closely not only in words but also in spelling, punctuation, etc. The only substantial change is the insertion of the two paragraphs from the Postscript of *1745A* into the body of the Cook's chapter, the first appearing on p. 42 (before the beginning of the extract), and the second being placed after the second paragraph of the extract (d14-d23). There is one verbal variant in the extract between *1745A* and *1745B* (would/will, c45/d55), which is probably a copying error.

Faulkner's second edition of *1746* was set from a corrected copy of his first edition, *1745A*. The two extra paragraphs are now placed at the end of the chapter (e49-e65); and a general revision of the third person singular indicative from the -s to the -th form has been attempted (loves/loveth, c2/e2; has/hath, c4/e4; looks/looketh, c6/e6; tastes, tasteth, c49/e49; smells/smelleth, c54/e54; miscarries/miscarrieth, c56/e56). The other verbal variant in the extract (till/until, c3/e3), and some of the alterations to the punctuation (c9-10/e9-10) and italicization (c37-8/e37-8) also appear to be deliberate corrections. There is no known manuscript authority for any of these changes.

For his last corrected edition of *Directions to servants*, *1751*, Faulkner appears to have used the Rothschild MS to make a careful revision of the text of *1746*. In the extract the two additional paragraphs are now placed rather absurdly in the middle of the original paragraph 7 (f28-f41); this makes more nonsense than ever of the phrase 'And in the same manner',

(continued on p. 95)

[28] To pp. 19 and 22 respectively (with some alteration).
[29] See p. 85 n. 24.   [30] This last one may be a mistake, not a deliberate correction.

When you roaſt a Breaſt of Veal, remember your Sweet-heart the Butler loves a Sweet-bread; therefore ſet it aſide till Evening: You can ſay, the Cat or the Dog has run away with it, or you found it tainted, or fly-blown; and beſides, it looks as well at the Table without it as with it.

When you make the Company wait long for Dinner and the Meat be overdone, which is gen rally the Caſe, you may lawfully lay the Fault upon your Lady, who hurried you ſo to ſend up Dinner, that you was forced to ſend it up too much boiled and roaſted.

When you are in haſte to take down your Diſhes, tip them in ſuch a manner, that a Doven will fall together upon the Dreſſer, juſt ready for your Hand.

To ſave Time and Trouble, cut your Apples and Onions with the ſame Knife; and well-bred Gentry love the Taſte of an Onion in every thing they eat.

Lump three or four Pounds of Butter together with your Hands, then daſh it againſt the Wall juſt over the Dreſſer, ſo as to have it ready to pull by Pieces as you have occaſion for it.

If you have a Silver Saucepan for the Kitchen Uſe, let me adviſe you to batter it well, and keep it always black; this will be for your Maſter's Honour, for it ſhews there has been conſtant good Houſekeeping: And make room for the Saucepan by wriggling it on the Coals, &c.

In the ſame Manner, if you are allowed a large Silver Spoon for the Kitchen, let half the Bole of it be worn out with continual ſcraping and ſtirring, and often ſay merrily, This Spoon owes my Maſter no Service.

When you ſend up a Meſs of Broth, Water-gruel, or the like, to your Maſter in a Morning, do not forget with your Thumb and two Fingers to put Salt on the Side of the Plate; for if you make uſe of a Spoon, or the End of a Knife, there may be Danger that the Salt would fall, and that would be a Sign of ill Luck. Only remember to lick your Thumb and Fingers clean, before you offer to touch the Salt.

POSTSCRIPT.

The following Paragraphs belong to the Cook, but were left out by Miſtake.

If your Butter, when it is melted, taſtes of Braſs, it is your Maſter's Fault, who will not allow you a Silver Sauce-pan; beſides, the leſs of it will go further, and new tinning is very chargeable: If you have a Silver Sauce-pan, and the Butter ſmells of Smoak, lay the Fault upon the Coals.

If your Dinner miſcarries in almoſt every Diſh, how could you help it: You were teized by the Footmen coming into the Kitchen; and, to prove it true, take Occaſion to be angry, and throw a Ladle-full of Broth on one or two of their Liveries; beſides, *Friday* and *Childermas-day* are two croſs Days in the Week, and it is impoſſible to have good Luck on either of them; therefore on thoſe two Days you have a lawful Excuſe.

*1745*A (Swift, J., *Directions to servants*, Dublin, by G. Faulkner, 1745, pp. ²24-6, ²79; Trin. Coll. Cam. Rothschild 2178; ×0·61)

When you roaſt a Breaſt of Veal, remember your Sweet-heart the Butler loves a Sweetbread; therefore ſet it aſide till Evening: You can ſay, the Cat or the Dog has run away with it, or you found it tainted, or fly-blown; and beſides, it looks as well at the Table without it as with it.

When you make the Company wait long for Dinner and the Meat be overdone, which is generally the Caſe, you may lawfully lay the Fault upon your Lady, who hurried you ſo to ſend up Dinner, that you was forced to ſend it up too much boiled and roaſted.

If your Dinner miſcarries in almoſt every Diſh, how could you help it? You were teized by the Footmen coming into the Kitchen; and, to prove it true, take Occaſion to be angry, and throw a Ladle-full of Broth on one or two of their Liveries; beſides, *Friday* and *Childermas-day* are too croſs Days in the Week, and it is impoſſible to have good Luck on either of them; therefore on thoſe two Days you have a lawful Excuſe.

When you are in haſte to take down your Diſhes, tip them in ſuch a manner, that a Dozen will fall together upon the Dreſſer, juſt ready for your Hand.

To ſave Time and Trouble, cut your Apples and Onions with the ſame Knife; and well-bred Gentry love the Taſte of an Onion in every thing they eat.

Lump three or four Pounds of Butter together with your Hands, then daſh it againſt the Wall juſt over the Dreſſer, ſo as to have it ready to pull by Pieces as you have occaſion for it.

If you have a Silver Saucepan for the Kitchen Uſe, let me adviſe you to batter it well, and keep it always black; this will be for your Maſter's Honour, for it ſhews there has been conſtant good Houſekeeping: And make room for the Saucepan by wriggling it on the Coals, &c.

In the ſame Manner, if you are allowed a large Silver Spoon for the Kitchen, let half the Bole of it be worn out with continual ſcraping and ſtirring and often ſay merrily, This Spoon owes my Maſter no Service.

When you ſend up a Meſs of Broth, Watergruel, or the like, to your Maſter in a Morning, do not forget with your Thumb and two Fingers to put Salt on the Side of the Plate; for if you make uſe of a Spoon, or the End of a Knife, there may be Danger that the Salt would fall, and that will be a Sign of ill Luck. Only remember to lick your Thumb and Fingers clean, before you offer to touch the Salt.

*1745*B (Swift, J., *Directions to servants*, London, for R. Dodsley and M. Cooper, 1745, pp. 44-6; Univ. Lib. Cam. Williams 301; ×0·61)

When you roaft a Breaft of Veal, remember
your Sweet-heart the Butler loveth a Sweet-
bread; therefore fet it afide until Evening: You
can fay, the Cat or the Dog hath run away with
it, or you found it tainted, or fly-blown; and
befides, it looketh as well at the Table without
it as with it.

When you make the Company wait long for
Dinner, and the Meat be overdone, (which is
generally the Cafe) you may lawfully lay the
Fault upon your Lady, who hurried you fo to
fend up Dinner, that you was forced to fend it
up too much boiled and roafted.

When you are in hafte to take down your
Difhes, tip them in fuch a manner, that a Dozen will fall together upon the Drefer, juft
ready for your Hand.

To fave Time and Trouble, cut your Apples
and Onions with the fame Knife; and well-bred
Gentry love the Tafte of an Onion in every
thing they eat.

Lump three or four Pounds of Butter together with your Hands, then dafh it againft the
Wall juft over the Drefer, fo as to have it
ready to pull by Pieces as you have occafion for
it.

If you have a Silver Saucepan for the Kitchen
Ufe, let me advife you to batter it well, and
keep it always black; this will be for your
Mafter's Honour, for it fhews there has been
conftant good Houfekeeping: And make room
for the Saucepan by wriggling it on the Coals,
&c.

In the fame Manner, if you are allowed a
large Silver Spoon for the Kitchen, let half the
Bowl of it be worn out with continual fcraping
and ftirring, and often fay merrily, *This Spoon
owes my Mafter no Service.*

When you fend up a Mefs of Broth, Water-
gruel, or the like, to your Mafter in a Morning, do not forget with your Thumb and two
Fingers to put Salt on the Side of the Plate;
for if you make ufe of a Spoon, or the End
of a Knife, there may be Danger that the Salt
would fall, and that would be a Sign of ill
Luck. Only remember to lick your Thumb
and Fingers clean, before you offer to touch
the Salt.

If your Butter, when it is melted, tafteth of
Brafs, it is your Mafter's Fault, who will not
allow you a Silver Sauce-pan; befides, the lefs
of it will go further, and new tinning is very
chargeable: If you have a Silver Sauce-pan,
and the Butter fmelleth of Smoak, lay the Fault
upon the Coals.

If your Dinner mifcarrieth in almoft every
Difh, how could you help it: You were teized
by the Footmen coming into the Kitchen;
and, to prove it true, take Occafion to be angry, and throw a Ladle-full of Broth on one
or two of their Liveries; befides, *Friday* and
Childermas-day are two crofs Days in the Week,
and it is impoffible to have good Luck on either of them; therefore on thofe two Days
you have a lawful Excufe.

1746 (Swift, J., *Works*, viii, Dublin, by and for G. Faulkner, 1746, pp. '24–6'; Univ. Lib. Cam.
Hib. 7.751.31; × 0·61)

When you roaſt a Breaſt of Veal, remember your Sweet-heart the Butler loveth a Sweet-bread; therefore ſet it aſide until Evening: You can ſay, the Cat or the Dog hath run away with it, or you found it tainted, or fly-blown; and beſides, it looketh as well on the Table without the Sweet-bread as with it.

When you make the Company wait long for Dinner, and the Meat be overdone, which is generally the Caſe, you may lawfully lay the Fault upon your Lady, who hurried you ſo to ſend up Dinner, that you were forced to ſend it up too much boiled and roaſted.

When you are in haſte to take down your Diſhes, tip them in ſuch a manner, that a Dozen will fall together upon the Dreſſer, juſt ready for your Hand.

To ſave Time and Trouble, cut your Apples and Onions with the ſame Knife; for well-bred Gentry love the Taſte of an Onion in every Thing they eat.

Lump three or four Pounds of Butter together with your Hands, then daſh it againſt the Wall juſt over the Dreſſer, ſo as to have it ready to pull by Pieces as you have Occaſion for it.

If you have a Silver Saucepan for the Kitchen Uſe, let me adviſe you to batter it well, and keep it always black; this will be for your Maſter's Honour, becauſe it ſhews there hath been conſtant good Houſekeeping: And make room for the Saucepan by wriggling it on the Coals, &c.

If your Butter when it is melted, taſteth of Braſs, it is your Maſter's Fault, who will not allow you a Silver Sauce-pan; beſides, the leſs of it will go further, and new tinning was very chargeable. If you have a Silver Sauce-pan, and the Butter ſmelleth of Smoak, lay the Fault upon the Coals.

If your Dinner miſcarrieth in almoſt every Diſh, how could you help it? You were teized by the Footmen coming into the Kitchen; and, to prove it true, take Occaſion to be angry, and throw a Ladle-full of Broth on one or two of their Liveries; beſides, *Friday* and *Childermas* Day, are two croſs Days in the Week, and it is impoſſible to have good Luck on either of them, therefore on thoſe two Days you have a lawful Excuſe.

In the ſame Manner, if you are allowed a large Silver Spoon for the Kitchen, let half the Bole of it be worn out with continual ſcraping and ſtirring; and often ſay merrily, This Spoon oweth my Maſter no Service.

When you ſend up a Meſs of Broth, Water-gruel, or the like, to your Maſter in a Morning, do not forget with your Thumb and two Fingers to put Salt on the Side of the Plate; for, if you make uſe of a Spoon, or the End of a Knife, there may be Danger that the Salt would fall, and that would be a Sign of ill Luck. Only remember to lick your Thumb and Fingers clean, before you offer to touch the Salt.

1751 (Swift, J., *Works*, viii, Dublin, by G. Faulkner, 1751, pp. '26-8'; Univ. Lib. Cam. Williams 32; ×0·92)

which was intended to link the remarks about the silver saucepan to those about the silver spoon. But most of the new readings restore the text to what Swift wrote in the Rothschild MS (at/on, e6/f5; it/the Sweet-bread, e7/f6; was/were, e12/f10; and/for, e19/f16; for/because, e30/f24; has/hath, e30/f25). There is one further -s/-th change (*owes*/oweth, e38/f45); and a verbal alteration in the first additional paragraph (is/was, e52/f31) which looks like a mistake.[31] The changes to the punctuation, etc., of *1746* were for the most part rejected.

It is clear from all this that Faulkner was not only the printer and publisher of the incomplete, posthumous *Directions to servants*, but was also its editor in our sense. The manuscript he had in 1745 was seriously defective, but Faulkner judged it best to print it as it stood 'that there may appear no Daubing or Patch-Work by other Hands';[32] and there was in fact very little alteration made to the text of the first edition beyond the usual normalization of the spelling, punctuation, etc. For his next edition an attempt was made to smooth the text by regularizing Swift's erratic use of certain grammatical forms. For his last revision Faulkner used a holograph manuscript that had been corrected by Swift to bring the printed text into line with the author's last recorded intentions. As printer and publisher Faulkner wanted to produce a book that would sell; but as editor he wanted to offer a text that was as complete, as authentic, and as faithful to Swift's intentions as he could make it.

A modern editor of *Directions to servants* may modify these aims. He may not wish, as Faulkner did, that Swift had finished the book, for the incomplete text has a bite that might not have survived the dilution of its simple central idea. He may not want to smooth away textual inconsistency, but may welcome the opportunity to approach Swift by way of the mechanics of his writing. And, while he will try to produce a fair and useful representation of the work, he will not hope for a 'definitive' text, for finality is precluded by the ambiguity of the evidence.

There is a modern critical text of *Directions to servants* (Herbert Davis's edition of 1959), but it is not entirely satisfactory[33] and the question of editing the work is worth reconsidering. The potential readership is a wide one, including general readers as well as specialists. Only specialists will need much textual apparatus—as we have seen, the textual situation is an untidy one, and other readers are unlikely to want to follow it in detail— but all readers should be offered a basic text of the work that is as complete, as authentic, and as faithful to Swift's intentions as possible.

The most promising basis for an edited text is Faulkner's final revised

---

[31] Faulkner's octavo edition of 1751, which also derived from *1746* (see p. 82 n. 18), reads 'is', not 'was'.   [32] *1745*A, p. [i].   [33] See p. 98 n. 37.

version of *1751*, even though we have a holograph manuscript for half the book, and a complete first-edition text. Certainly for the part of the book that is not covered by the Rothschild holograph—which is all except chapters i–iii—the *1751* text is the best surviving version of the words. Faulkner seems to have had access to the missing part of the Rothschild MS as well as to the part which survives, and to have used it for checking and mending the whole text in preparation for his final revision, so that *1751* is the only text of this part to incorporate the evidence of Swift's corrected draft.[34] It does not of course reproduce his spelling, punctuation, etc., but there is no good authority for the details of this part of the text: the Forster MS is a transcript which did not follow the spelling and punctuation of Swift's holograph, and all Faulkner's texts derived from what was probably a similar transcript.

If *1751* were chosen as copy-text for an edition of this half of the text, it would be emended by the entry of the few corrections that Swift made to the Forster MS (which Faulkner did not use); and possibly by the cancellation of the emendations which appeared in *1746* (changing -s to -th forms, etc.) for which Faulkner is not known to have had manuscript authority.[35] The spelling, punctuation, etc., which appears to have had some revision for *1751* at the same time as the words,[36] would not be altered.

For the other half of the book, chapters i–iii, we have the evidence of Swift's holograph manuscript, the Rothschild MS. This manuscript would not make an entire copy-text for an edition even of these three chapters, for it represents a relatively primitive state of the text, and it is besides disorganized and incomplete within itself (Faulkner apparently derived the arrangement of parts of his printed text from authoritative memoranda which are now lost). For the same reasons as before, therefore, *1751* would make a satisfactory copy-text for the first three chapters, the words being similarly emended with reference to the Forster MS and *1746*. Here, however, the editor might decide to take the spelling and punctuation for chapters i–iii from the Rothschild MS, using it as an additional copy-text for the parts that we have in Swift's holograph. This would result in some slight inconsistency, but scarcely enough to trouble even a fastidious reader, who would have the compensating advantage of being able to read at least part of the work with Swift's own characteristic spelling and punctuation; a reasonable compromise in the case of a book that was not prepared for the press or proof-read by the author. Here is our extract edited in this way:

[34] See p. 84 n. 23.

[35] Since we have not got the evidence of the Rothschild MS for this part of the book, we cannot be quite sure that it was not the source for the *1746* emendations; but the rest of the Rothschild MS and the whole of the Forster MS suggest strongly that it was not.

[36] Compare, for instance, e9–10/f8–9; e37–8/f44–6; e57/f35; etc.

When you roast a breast of Veal, remember your Sweet-heart the
Butler, loves a Sweet-bread, therefore set it a side till evening.
You can say, the Cat or the Dog has run away with it, or you found
it tainted, or fly-blown; and besides, it looks as well on the
g5 table without the Sweet-bread as with it.

When you make the company wait long for dinner, and the meat be
overdone, which is generally the case, you may lawfully lay the
fault on your Lady, who hurryed you so to send up dinner, that you
were forced to send it up too much boyld and roasted.
g10 When you are in hast to take down your dishes, tip them in such
a manner, that a dozen will fall together upon the dresser just
ready for your hand.

To save time and trouble, cut your apples and Onyons with the
same knife, for well bred gentry love the tast of an onyon in every
g15 thing they eat.

Lump three or four pounds of butter together with your hands,
then dash it against the wall just over the dresser, so as to have it
ready to pull, by pieces, as you have occasion for it.

If you have a silver sawce-pan for the kitchin use, let me advise
g20 you to batter it well, and keep it always black; This will be for
your masters honor, because it shows there hath been constant good
house-keeping. [Note: 'Make room for the sawcpan by wriggle it on
the coals &c'] And in the same manner, if you are allowed a large
Silver spoon for the kitchen, let half the bole of it be worn out
g25 with continuall scraping and stirring; and often say merrily, this
spoon owes my Master no service.

When you send up a mess of broth, water-gruel, or the like to
your Master in a morning, do not forget with your thumb and two
fingers to put salt on the side of the plate, for if you make use of
g30 a spoon or the end of a knife, there may be danger that the salt
would fall, and that would be a sign of ill luck. Onely remember
to lick your thumb and fingers clean, before you offer to touch
the salt.

If your Butter when it is melted, tastes of Brass, it is your
g35 Master's Fault, who will not allow you a Silver Sauce-pan; besides,
the less of it will go further, and new tinning is very chargeable.
If you have a Silver Sauce-pan, and the Butter smells of Smoak, lay
the Fault upon the Coals.

If your Dinner miscarries in almost every Dish, how could you
g40 help it? You were teized by the Footmen coming into the Kitchen;
and, to prove it true, take Occasion to be angry, and throw a Ladle-
full of Broth on one or two of their Liveries; besides, *Friday* and
Childermas Day, are two cross Days in the Week, and it is impossible
to have good Luck on either of them, therefore on those two Days
g45 you have a lawful Excuse.

The general arrangement of the text is that of *1751*, with verbal amendments from the earlier texts, and with the spelling, punctuation, etc., of all but the last two paragraphs taken from the Rothschild MS. There is no obvious place for the two 'Postscript' paragraphs in the body of the Cook's chapter, so they are both placed at the end of it (as they were in *1746*). The seventh paragraph of the Rothschild MS is reconstituted as the sixth paragraph of the edited text, and the reminder to put in a passage about wriggling the saucepan on the coals is separated from the text and entered as a note in brackets. Two readings not in the Rothschild MS are adopted: 'Butler', f2/g2, and 'let half the Bole', f43/g24. Five main-text readings not in the Rothschild MS are rejected: 'loveth', f2/g2; 'until', f3/g2; 'hath', f4/g3; 'looketh', f5/g4; 'upon', f9/g8. Five Postscript readings not in *1745*A are also rejected: 'oweth', f45/g26; 'tasteth', f28/g34; 'was', f31/g36'; 'smelleth', f32/g37; 'miscarrieth', f34/g39.[37]

[37] The details of this version of the extract produce a noticeably different effect from Herbert Davis's 1959 edition of the passage (see p. 80 n. 1), for which he followed a conventional course in choosing as copy-text the earliest printed edition in the ancestral series, i.e. *1745*A. Davis's version also differs from mine in incorporating the reminder note (g23-4) in the text, and in adopting the reading 'have the Bole of it' (g24) from the Rothschild MS. His textual notes, though comprehensive, are not easy to follow. Here is a transcript of Davis's text and notes:

When you roast a Breast of Veal, remember your Sweet-heart the Butler loves a Sweet-bread; therefore set it aside till Evening: You can say, the Cat or the Dog has run away with it, or you found it tainted, or fly-blown; and besides, it looks as well on the Table without the Sweet-bread as with it.

5   When you make the Company wait long for Dinner, and the Meat be overdone (which is generally the Case) you may lawfully lay the Fault on your Lady, who hurried you so to send up Dinner, that you were forced to send it up too much boiled and roasted.

When you are in haste to take down your Dishes, tip them in such a manner, that a Dozen will fall together upon the Dresser, just ready for your Hand.

10   To save Time and Trouble, cut your Apples and Onions with the same Knife, for well-bred Gentry love the Taste of an Onion in every thing they eat.

Lump three or four Pounds of Butter together with your Hands, then dash it against the Wall just over the Dresser, so as to have it ready to pull by Pieces as you have occasion for it.

If you have a Silver Saucepan for the Kitchen Use, let me advise you to batter it well, and keep it always black; make room for the Saucepan by wriggling it on the Coals, &c: This will be for your

15   Master's Honour, because it shews there has been constant good Housekeeping: And in the same manner, if you are allowed a large Silver Spoon for the Kitchen, have the Bole of it be worn out with continual scraping and stirring, and often say merrily, This Spoon owes my Master no Service.

When you send up a Mess of Broth, Water-gruel, or the like, to your Master in a Morning, do not forget with your Thumb and two Fingers to put Salt on the Side of the Plate; for if you make use

20   of a Spoon, or the End of a Knife, there may be Danger that the Salt would fall, and that would be a Sign of ill Luck. Only remember to lick your Thumb and Fingers clean, before you offer to touch the Salt.

If your Butter, when it is melted, tastes of Brass, it is your Master's Fault, who will not allow you a Silver Sauce-pan; besides, the less of it will go further, and new tinning is very chargeable: If you

25   have a Silver Sauce-pan, and the Butter smells of Smoak, lay the Fault upon the Coals.

If your Dinner miscarries in almost every Dish, how could you help it: You were teized by the Footmen coming into the Kitchen; and, to prove it true, take Occasion to be angry, and throw a Ladle-full of Broth on one or two of their Liveries; besides, *Friday* and *Childermas-day* are two cross Days in the Week, and it is impossible to have good Luck on either of them; therefore on those two Days you have

30   a lawful Excuse.

The textual apparatus should as always be kept to a minimum. Even a non-specialist edition will of course have an introductory note explaining the textual background, but in a situation of such complexity it would not be appropriate to record and explain every departure from the copy-text. Here only one textual note would be needed, to explain the bracketed reminder at g22–3.

Even in a specialist edition the treatment of the spelling, punctuation, etc., and of the *1746* emendations, would only occasionally require particular annotation, and could for the most part be dealt with in the textual introduction. Individual textual notes, however, would record other departures from *1751*, and also important variants from other authoritative texts (especially the Rothschild MS). Thus the textual footnotes for a version of the extract edited for specialists might be given as follows:

g2	Butler	RMS, Cook; FMS, Cook Q^r Butler; *1745*A→*1751*, Butler
g8	on	RMS, FMS, on; *1745*A→*1751*, upon

Davis's textual notes

3	as well on . . . without the Sweetbread S, A, 51	as well at . . . without it 45, 46, L

(*Here follows in* S *and* A *the passage which was already used on* p. 11. *Marginal note in* A: This before page 28.)

5	on your S, A	upon your 45, &c.
6	were forced S, 51	was forced A, 45 &c.
	too much boiled and roasted Sc, &c.	overdone S

(*Second supplementary passage inserted here in* L. *See below*, ll. 14–15.)

9	for Sc, 51	and S, A &c.
14–15	black; make room for the Saucepan by wriggling it on the Coals &c.: This . . . Housekeeping: And in S	make room . . . Coals &c. *added at the foot of the page* S *and marked* X. *It has been wrongly inserted at the end of the sentence in* A, 45 &c.

(*In* 51, *this passage is changed further by inserting the two paragraphs* (*not in* S *or* A) *first printed at the end of the book as a* 'Postscript' *in* 45, *with the note:* The following paragraphs belong to the Cook, but were left out by mistake. *More appropriate places were found to insert them in* L; *they were simply placed at the end in* 46 *and that has been done here. See below*, p. [33, ll. 5 ff.].)

16	have the Bole Sc	let the bole S, A; let half the Bole 45, 51; Bowl 46
17	This Spoon owes Sc	This Spoon has done S
18	Water-gruel Sc	milk S

Key to Davis's textual notes

S	RMS
Sc	Swift's corrections in RMS
A	FMS
Ac	corrections in FMS
45	*1745*A
L	*1745*B
46	*1746*
51	*1751*

g9	too much boyld and roasted.	RMS, ~~overdone.~~ too much boyld and roasted.
g16	Lump	RMS, ~~Dash~~ Lump
g19–26	[paragraph]	reconstituted from RMS; in *1745A→1751* it is divided into two, with the second paragraph beginning at 'In the same Manner'
g21	because	RMS, ~~for~~ because
g22–3	[bracketed note]	a reminder, written at the foot of the page in RMS, that a passage was to be added here
g24	Silver	RMS, ~~Kite~~ Silver
g24	let half the bole of it be	RMS, ~~let~~ have the bole of it be; FMS, let the bole of it be; *1745A→1751*, let half the Bole of it be
g26	spoon owes	RMS, spoon ~~has done~~ owes
g34–45	[paragraphs]	added as a 'Postscript . . . left out by Mistake' at the end of *1745A*; in *1745B* and *1751* placed in the body of the chapter; in *1746* placed at the end of the chapter
g36	is	*1745A→1746*, is; *1751*, was

EXAMPLE 5

Scott, *The Heart of Mid-Lothian*, 1818

NO novelist of the first rank ever wrote more easily than did Walter Scott.[1] A young lawyer who saw Scott's 'confounded hand' at work through an Edinburgh window one summer evening was much upset by its speed and assurance:

> Since we sat down . . . I have been watching it—it fascinates my eye—it never stops—page after page is finished and thrown on that heap of MS., and still it goes on unwearied—and so it will be till candles are brought in, and God knows how long after that. It is the same every night—I can't stand the sight of it when I am not at my books.[2]

But for all the abundance of his genius, when he poured out the Waverley novels with 'an energy and fertility of mind which make the feat one of the most remarkable recorded in literary history',[3] Scott was a conscious craftsman. He corrected his work, in proof as well as in manuscript, and even in the adversity of his last years he added to the texts of the novels for the collected edition.

In 1818, however, when he wrote *The Heart of Mid-Lothian*, Scott was at the happy and successful mid-point of his career. 'At this moment', wrote Lockhart,

> his position, take it for all in all, was, I am inclined to believe, what no other man had ever won for himself by the pen alone. His works were the daily food, not

---

[1] Lockhart, J. G., *Memoirs of the life of Sir Walter Scott, Bart.*, 2nd edn., 10 vols., Edinburgh 1839 (hereafter Lockhart, *Life*) is the indispensable first-hand account. There is a perceptive short life by Leslie Stephen in *DNB*; and a heavy-weight standard life by Edgar Johnson (*Sir Walter Scott, the great unknown*, 2 vols., London 1970) which corrects and amplifies Lockhart, taking account of much new evidence. See also Scott's *Letters* (ed. Grierson, H. J. C. *et al.*, 12 vols., London 1932-7), and *Journal* (ed. Anderson, W. E. K., Oxford 1972).

Scott's manuscripts are surveyed in Dyson, G., 'The manuscripts and proof sheets of Scott's Waverley novels', *Edinburgh Bibliographical Society transactions*, iv (1955-6), pp. 15-42; and Bell, A., 'Scott manuscripts in Edinburgh libraries', *Scott bicentenary essays*, ed. Bell, A., Edinburgh 1973, pp. 147-59.

On Scott's techniques as a novelist, see Lascelles, M., 'Scott and the art of revision', *Notions and facts*, Oxford 1972, pp. 213-29 (concerns *Redgauntlet*); Wood, G. A. M., 'The manuscripts and proof sheets of *Redgauntlet*', *Scott bicentenary essays*, ed. Bell, A., Edinburgh 1973, pp. 160-75; *idem*, 'Scott's continuing revision: the printed texts of "Redgauntlet"', *The Bibliothek*, vi, 1973, pp. 121-32.

I am extremely grateful to Brian Jenkins of Cambridge University Library, who has been working for some years on an edition of *The Heart of Mid-Lothian*, for his generosity in sharing his knowledge and experience of this text with me.

[2] Lockhart, *Life*, iv, pp. 172-3. Although dated 1814 by Lockhart, this episode probably took place early in 1818, when Scott was at work on *The Heart of Mid-Lothian* (Edgar Johnson, *Scott*, i, p. lxiv, n. 82). [3] Leslie Stephen in *DNB*, li, pp. 90-1.

only of his countrymen, but of all educated Europe. His society was courted by whatever England could show of eminence. Station, power, wealth, beauty, and genius, strove with each other in every demonstration of respect and worship— and, a few political fanatics and envious poetasters apart, wherever he appeared in town or in country, whoever had Scotch blood in him, "gentle or simple," felt it move more rapidly through his veins when he was in the presence of Scott. To descend to what many looked on as higher things, he considered himself, and was considered by all about him, as rapidly consolidating a large fortune:—the annual profits of his novels alone had, for several years, been not less than £10,000: his domains were daily increased—his castle was rising—and perhaps few doubted that ere long he might receive from the just favour of his Prince some distinction in the way of external rank, such as had seldom before been dreamt of as the possible consequence of a mere literary celebrity.[4]

Scott completed *Rob Roy*, his sixth novel, in December 1817, and it was published on the thirty-first. Indefatigably he set to work at once on its successor—in addition to his continuing activities as lawyer, businessman, and laird—and *The Heart of Mid-Lothian* was finished around the beginning of July 1818.[5] Published in four volumes as the Second Series of 'Tales of my landlord, by Jedediah Cleishbotham of Gandercleugh' the new novel was as great a popular success as any of its predecessors; and, although some of the early reviewers had reservations about it, it has remained one of the most admired of the whole series.

The transmission of the texts of Scott's novels was affected not only by his huge productivity but also by the fact that he was determined not to be known publicly as their author. His normal practice at this time (which he followed in writing *The Heart of Mid-Lothian*) was to begin the day with a stint of writing the current novel on the rectos of leaves of writing paper measuring about 26·5 cm × 19 cm;[6] and he entered corrections and additions, usually the same day, on the blank versos of the preceding leaves.[7] Each completed recto contained 500–600 words in Scott's small, fluent hand, and he would normally write three or four pages a day. His manuscript looked very neat, but it was not in fact at all easy to read.

As soon as it was finished each stint of manuscript was sent off to James

---

[4] Lockhart, *Life*, v, pp. 316–17.

[5] Lockhart (*Life*, v, p. 357) says that *The Heart of Mid-Lothian* was published before the end of June 1818; but it appears from a letter written by Scott to Terry on 11 July 1818 (*Letters*, v, p. 169) that the fourth volume was not then available to Scott except in proof.

[6] The paper was probably writing demy quarto, and Alan Bell of the National Library of Scotland has suggested that Scott was using bifolia (i.e. half sheets folded once), variously quired; but the tight sewing and binding of the manuscript now prevent investigation.

[7] Scott, like Trollope, preferred to write the daily stint of his current novel before breakfast, but when in a hurry to get on he would return to the task later in the day, as when Lockhart's friend saw Scott's 'confounded hand' at work that evening in 1818 (see p. 101 n. 2).

Ballantyne, the managing director of the Edinburgh printing firm of which Scott himself was the major partner, to be set in type. But, since Scott's handwriting might be familiar to employees and visitors at Ballantyne's, the manuscripts of his novels could not be sent to the composing room without the risk of disclosing the author's identity. Therefore they were copied out by an amanuensis, and the transcripts were used by the compositors. The copying was usually done at this time by James Ballantyne's gadabout brother John.[8]

The text having been set in type from the transcript, page proofs were pulled in eight-leaf sections containing about 2,800 words in the sixteen pages, rather more than Scott's usual daily stint. Although none survive, first proofs must have been read for typographical blemishes (turned letters, etc.); and then author's proofs were pulled and first scrutinized by James Ballantyne for textual anomalies. A good many author's proofs of the Waverley novels survive[9] and show considerable normalization and correction of Scott's manuscripts; but, since none of the intermediate transcripts used by the compositor have been found, we cannot tell how much of this alteration was introduced by the amanuensis and how much by the compositor; probably both of them were involved. In the proofs, at any rate, James Ballantyne suggested a considerable number of further alterations, and an author's proof with Ballantyne's annotations (together with a spare proof) was sent to Scott. Scott read it without reference to his manuscript, which was not always returned to him with the proofs;[10] he attended to most of Ballantyne's suggestions, and he made a yet larger number of spontaneous alterations himself, deliberately using proof-correction as a stage in the process of composition. Again these proofs corrected in Scott's hand could not be used in the printing-house without the risk of compromising his anonymity, so James Ballantyne would copy out Scott's corrections on to a spare proof for the use of the compositor. The author's proof was generally followed by two or three author's revises, which were treated in the same way.

[8] Although John Ballantyne was probably the chief copyist of the Waverley novels until his death in 1820, he may not have been the only one; see Wood, G. A. M. in *Scott bicentenary essays*, ed. Bell, A., Edinburgh 1973, pp. 164–5 (where Wood confuses the names of John Ballantyne, the MS. copyist, and James Ballantyne, the proof copyist).

There are *DNB* articles on both James and John Ballantyne.

[9] Gillian Dyson (1955–6, see p. 101 n. 1) was able to locate author's proofs, mostly fragmentary, of 15 of the 26 Waverley novels, and knew that proofs of 4 others had been in existence around 1900. She was also able to locate complete or nearly complete author's manuscripts of 16 of the 26 novels; partial or fragmentary manuscripts of 6 more; and knew of the survival into the twentieth century of at least fragmentary manuscripts of the other 4.

[10] On p. 334 of the author's proof of *The Heart of Mid-Lothian* (see p. 105 n. 16), where the amanuensis or the compositor (we cannot say which) had made an egregious mistake in a Latin tag, Scott wrote: 'you must always return my own ms where latin occurs—O I have it—but.'

When the final proofs had been passed, the sheets of the first edition were printed off one by one; so that, although publication did not take place until the printing of the whole book had been completed, the earlier sheets were printed off before Scott wrote the later ones. The first edition was normally followed by new impressions from standing type and by new editions printed from new settings of type. Few of these later impressions and editions were corrected or revised by Scott, although many of them contained textual variants introduced for the most part by James Ballantyne. 'Pray take great notice of inaccuracies in the Novels', Scott wrote to James Ballantyne in 1820. 'There are very very many—some mine, I dare say, but at all events you may and ought to correct. If you would call on William Erskine . . . he would point out some of them.'[11]

Late in his life, when he was in severe financial difficulties, Scott collaborated with his publisher Robert Cadell[12] in the production of a collected edition of all the Waverley novels; nicknamed the 'magnum opus', it was to have new illustrations, introductions and notes, and revised texts. Scott spent most of his spare time from 1828 to 1830 in annotation and in carrying out an extensive but rather patchy revision of the texts of his earlier novels. For this textual revision Scott used interleaved copies of the octavo editions, though exactly which editions is not always clear; the present whereabouts of his interleaved set, which was described in 1930 and was still in existence in 1939, is unknown.[13] Scott's interleaved and corrected set of the novels was not used, however, as copy for the 'magnum opus'; on account, probably, of his very shaky handwriting—for his anonymity was now given up—his alterations were transcribed from the interleaved copy into another set of octavo editions which was sent to the printer; and it appears that in the case of some of the novels Scott's interleaved copies were not of the same editions as the copies into which his alterations were transcribed for the printer. The 'magnum opus' was the last edition of the Waverley novels to be corrected by Scott; and, of the published editions of most of the novels, it is the first and 'magnum opus' editions which have the greatest textual authority.[14]

[11] *Letters*, vi, p. 160. Erskine was one of Scott's most intimate friends.
[12] *The Heart of Mid-Lothian*, like most of the earlier Waverley novels, was first published by Archibald Constable, whose junior partner was Robert Cadell (see *DNB* for their biographies). Constable crashed in 1826, whereupon Cadell took over as Scott's publisher. The collapse of Constable's brought down Ballantyne's, which resulted in Scott's own financial ruin.
[13] The forty-one interleaved volumes annotated by Scott remained with Cadell until 1851, when they were acquired (along with the copyrights of the Waverley novels) by the publishers A. & C. Black. In about 1930 the Blacks sold them to J. H. Isaac of New York who, as 'Temple Scott', described them in *Sir Walter Scott's 'magnum opus'*, New York 1930. By 1939 they were in the possession of the New York bookseller J. F. Drake. They were then sold and have not been heard of since.
[14] A. & C. Black claimed to have collated the texts of their Centenary (1871) and Dryburgh (1892–4) editions of the Waverley novels with Scott's interleaved copy, which was then in their possession; but these editions add little to the authority of the 'magnum opus'.

This general description of the composition and publication of the Waverley novels applies to *The Heart of Mid-Lothian* in particular, for which the surviving textual evidence is typical. In this case we have all but four leaves of Scott's original manuscript;[15] sixteen pages of author's proof, annotated by James Ballantyne, and corrected and revised by Scott;[16] the first edition of 1818 and three further issues of the first edition called the 'second', 'third', and 'fourth' editions;[17] five further editions dated 1819, 1821, 1822, 1823, and 1825;[18] and the 'magnum opus' of 1830,[19] which appears to have been set from a copy of the 1819 octavo edition into which Scott's alterations had been transcribed from an interleaved copy of the 1822 octavo.[20] But we have not got the transcript of the author's manuscript which was used for setting the first edition; any more author's proofs or revises for the first edition; any proofs or revises for the first edition with James Ballantyne's transcripts of Scott's proof corrections; the interleaved copy, probably of the 1822 octavo, used by Scott in preparing the text for the 'magnum opus';[21] the copy of the 1819 octavo into which these revisions were transcribed for setting the 'magnum opus'; or any proofs for the 'magnum opus'.

The descent of the main texts of *The Heart of Mid-Lothian* appears to have been as shown in the diagram on page 106. The essential relationship between these texts was a fairly simple one. The only surviving texts which Scott himself wrote or revised were (1) Scott's holograph MS; (2) the sixteen pages of corrected and revised page-proof for *1818*; (3) *1818*, the first edition; and (4) *1830*, the 'magnum opus'. Of these, *1818* and its proofs descended from the MS through a lost transcript; and *1830* descended from *1818* through a copy of *1819* (the second edition, set from *1818*) into which Scott's revisions had been transcribed. There is no evidence that Scott

---

[15] MS: the complete manuscript less five leaves is in the National Library of Scotland (MS. 1548); one leaf is in the South African Public Library, Cape Town.

[16] Yale University Library, Scott MSS. These sixteen pages of author's proofs, numbered 315–16, 319–30, 333–4, seem once to have been part of a ten- or twelve-leaf section. They have as a wrapper unmarked revises of pp. 314 and 315, which do not vary textually from the same pages in the first edition of 1818.

[17] *1818*: *Tales of my landlord, second series, collected and arranged by Jedediah Cleishbotham*, 4 vols., 8o, Edinburgh 1818. The 'second', 'third', and 'fourth' editions dated 1818 seem all to be sheets of *1818* with cancel title-pages; and there was also an issue of the *1818* sheets with an 1821 title-page.

[18] *1819*: vols. ix–x of *Novels and tales by the author of Waverley*, 12 vols., lge. 8o, Edinburgh 1819.
   1821: vols. xi–xiv of *Novels and tales by the author of Waverley*, 16 vols., 12o, Edinburgh 1821.
   1822: vols. ix–x of *Novels and tales by the author of Waverley*, 12 vols., lge. 8o, Edinburgh 1821–2.
   1823: vols. ix–x of *Novels and tales by the author of Waverley*, 12 vols., 18o, Edinburgh 1823.
   1825: vols. xi–xiv of *Novels and tales by the author of Waverley*, 16 vols., 12o, Edinburgh 1825.

[19] *1830*: vols. xi–xiii of *Waverley novels*, 41 vols., 12o, Edinburgh 1829–33.

[20] 'Temple Scott' (see p. 104 n. 13), p. 21, says that Scott's interleaved copy was dated 1822; and the textual peculiarities of *1830* show that it was set from a copy of *1819*.

[21] See p. 104 n. 13.

was responsible for the textual variation in any of the other surviving versions.

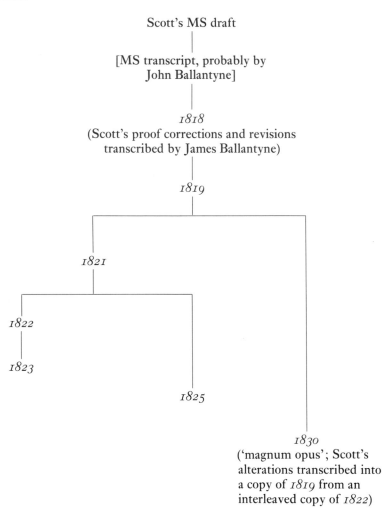

Scott's MS draft

[MS transcript, probably by
John Ballantyne]

1818
(Scott's proof corrections and revisions
transcribed by James Ballantyne)

1819

1821

1822

1823

1825

1830
('magnum opus'; Scott's
alterations transcribed into
a copy of *1819* from an
interleaved copy of *1822*)

We will therefore consider an extract from *The Heart of Mid-Lothian* in these four authoritative texts. The passage chosen for analysis is the contents of the recto of fo. 89 of the MS, part of the dialogue in which the wretched Mr. Deans discusses Effie's predicament with his other daughter Jeanie, and with Reuben Butler, the Laird of Dumbiedikes, and the amateur lawyer Saddletree (who does most of the talking). We have a revised proof, and the passage then comes towards the end of vol. i of *1818* and of vol. xi of *1830* (see pp. 108–13).

Folio 89 of MS (pp. 108–9) is typical of Scott's manuscripts at the height of his career as a novelist. At first glance the neatness of the hand seems to promise clarity, but in fact many of the letter forms are ambiguous, and it is not easy to read. The spelling is fairly consistent, with clear indications of the dialect forms intended, though on occasion Scott was careless about the spelling of proper names. The punctuation is light and erratic. Scott liked to fill his pages right up—this one contains 542 words—and it was probably for this reason that he did not employ the usual method of paragraphing direct speech. He rarely used ordinary paragraphs either, but sometimes wrote 'NL' (for 'new line'). Considering that this was a quickly written first draft there are not many verbal mistakes. There is a word missing after 'do' in a2; the third word in a4 is obscure, but appears to be 'sand'; the word 'say' in a29 should read 'sae' or 'so'; and 'woman' has been written by mistake for 'moment' in a36.

This page and the rest of the stint to which it belonged was then copied out by the amanuensis, whose transcript has not survived, and set in type from the transcript. The proof of this setting that was sent to Scott (pp. 110–11) varied considerably from the manuscript. It would seem likely that the major changes—the rectification of Scott's verbal mistakes and other alterations of words—were made by the amanuensis, but that the extensive normalization of the details of the text may have been carried out either by the amanuensis or by the compositor—or by both of them.

To deal first with the verbal variants, Scott's obvious mistakes were all attended to: 'naething;' was supplied in b3, and 'stand' in place of 'sand' in b6; 'say' in a29 is corrected to 'sae' in b49, and 'woman' in a36 to 'moment' in b61. Apart from these corrections, the word 'doubtless', a3, is omitted from b5; 'ilk' in a6 becomes 'ilka' in b10; 'whullying', clearly written in a19, is set as 'whiggling' in b33; 'only' is added in b42, and 'matter' in b54. It seems unlikely that Scott was responsible for initiating any of this second group of verbal alterations, although he changed only one of them in proof, correcting 'whiggling', b33, to 'whillying' (an alternative spelling of his manuscript 'whullying'). Probably 'doubtless' was omitted by mistake but missed by Scott because he did not read proof against copy; while the change to 'ilka' and the addition of 'only' and 'matter' may have been attempts at stylistic improvement by the amanuensis which Scott accepted, whether knowingly or not.

At the same time wholesale normalization of the details of the text had taken place. Many new punctuation marks were supplied (47 new commas and 30 other marks), as were the 11 new paragraph indents; while 7 of Scott's punctuation marks were changed for different ones. There were 12 changes of spelling, 8 of capitalization, 6 of contraction; and a word

(*continued on p.* 114)

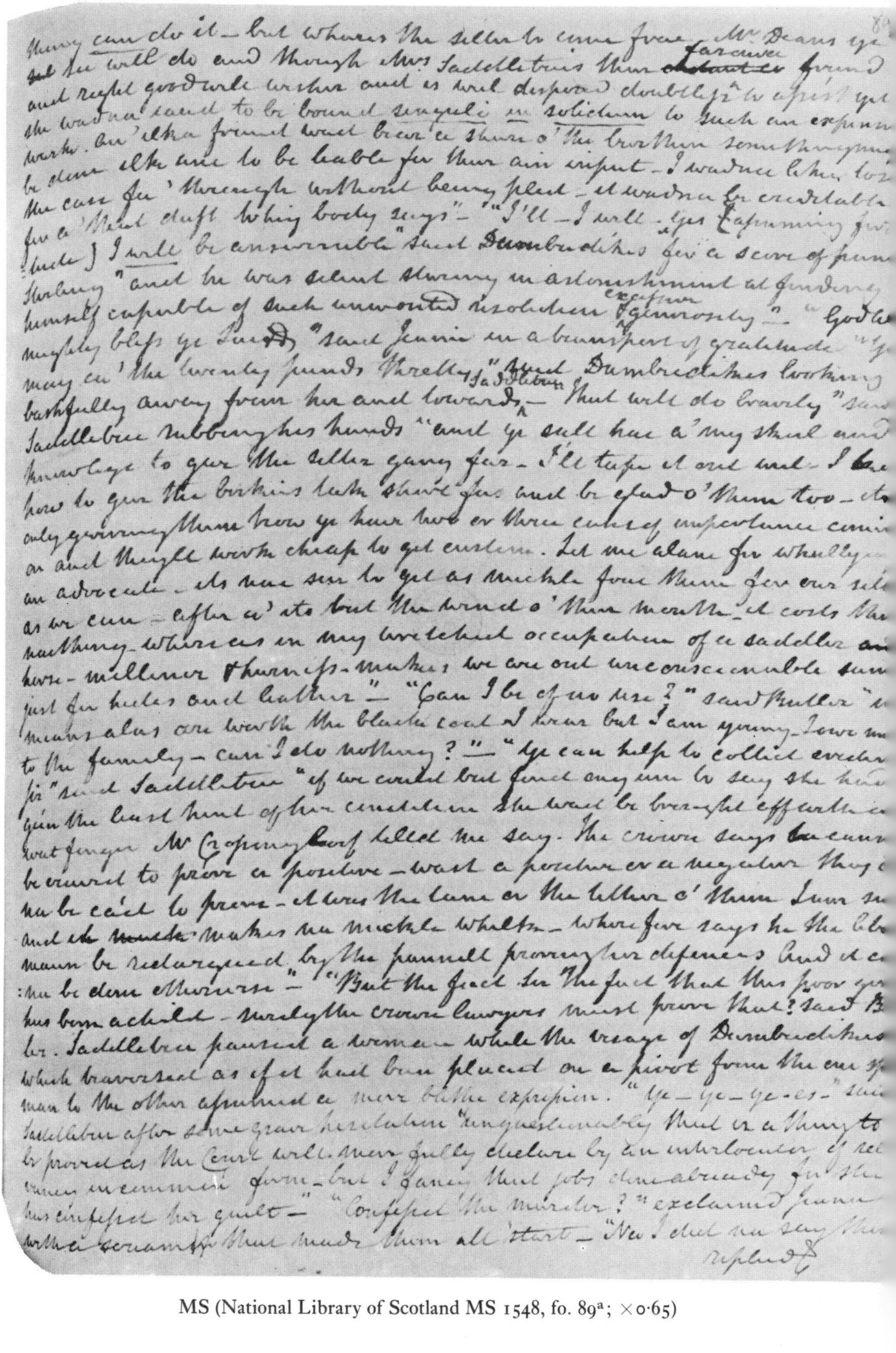

thing *can* do it—but whares the siller to come frae—Mr Deans ye
                                          farawa
~~sil~~ see will do and though Mrs Saddletree's their ~~distant a~~ friend
and right good well wisher and is weel disposed doubtless to assist yet
she wadna sand to be bound *singuli in solidum* to such an expensive
a5   wark. An' ilka friend wad bear a share o' the burthen something might
be done ilk ane to be liable for their ain input—I wadna like to see
the case fa' through without being pled—it wadna be creditable
for a' that daft Whig body says"—"I'll—I will—yes (assuming forti
-tude) I *will* be answerable" said Dumbiedikes "for a score of punds
a10   Sterling" and he was silent staring in astonishment at finding
                                          excessive
himself capable of such unwonted resolution & ^ generosity"—"God Al
mighty bless ye Laird" said Jeanie in a transport of gratitude "Ye
may ca' the twenty punds thretty" said Dumbiedikes looking
                                  Saddletree
bashfully away from her and towards ^ —"That will do bravely" said
a15   Saddletree rubbing his hands "and ye sall hae a' my skeel and
knowledge to gar the siller gang far—I'll tape it out weel—I ken
how to gar the birkies tak short fees and be glad o' them too—its
only garring them trow ye have two or three cases of importance coming
on and theyll work cheap to get custom. Let me alane for whullying
a20   an advocate—its nae sin to get as muckle frae them for our siller
as we can—after a' its but the wind o' their mouth—it costs them
naething—whereas in my wretched occupation of a saddler ~~and~~
horse-milliner & harness-maker: we are out unconscionable sums
just for hides and leather"—"Can I be of no use?" said Butler "my
a25   means alas are worth the black coat I wear but I am young—I owe much
to the family—can I do nothing?"—"Ye can help to collect evidence
Sir" said Saddletree "if we could but find ony ane to say she had
gi'en the least hint of her condition she wad be brought aff with a
wat finger Mr Crossmyloof telld me say. The crown says he canna
a30   be craved to prove a positive—wast a positive or a negative they cod
na be ca'd to prove—it was the tane or the tither o' them I am sure
and it ~~muck~~ makes na muckle whilk—wherefore says he the libell
maun be redargued by the pannell proving her defences And it can
-na be done otherwise"—"But the fact Sir The fact that this poor girl
a35   has born a child—surely the crown lawyers must prove that?" said But
ler. Saddletree paused a woman while the visage of Dumbiedikes
which traversed as if it had been placed on a pivot from the one spokes
man to the other assumed a more blithe expression. "Ye—ye—ye—es—" said
Saddletree after some grave hesitation "unquestionably that is a thing to
a40   be proved as the Court will more fully declare by an interlocutor of relevancy in common form—but I fancy that jobs done already for she
has confessed her guilt"—"Confessed the murder?" exclaimed Jeanie
with a scream~~in~~ that made them all start—"Na I did na say that
                                          replied

Transcript of p. 108

liament-house, if any thing *can* do it; but whare's the siller to come frae? Mr Deans, ye see, will do naething; and though Mrs Saddletree's their far-awa friend, and right good weel-wisher, and is weel disposed to assist, yet she wadna stand to be bound *singuli in solidum* to such an expensive wark. An' ilka friend wad bear a share o' the burthen, something might be dune— ilka ane to be liable for their ain input—I

like to

d

(p. 326)

wadna like to see the case fa' through without being pled—it wadna be creditable, for a' that daft whig body says."

"I'll—I will—yes," (assuming fortitude,) "I will be answerable," said Dumbiedikes, "for a score of punds sterling,"—and he was silent, staring in astonishment at finding himself capable of such unwonted resolution and excessive generosity.

"God Almighty bless ye, Laird!" said Jeanie in a transport of gratitude.

"Ye may ca' the twenty punds thretty," said Dumbiedikes, looking bashfully away from her and towards Saddletree.

"That will do bravely," said Saddletree, rubbing his hands; "and ye sall hae a' my skill and knowledge to gar the siller gang far—I'll tape it out weel—I ken how to gar the birkies tak short fees, and be glad o' them too—it's only garring them trow ye have twa or three cases of importance coming on, and they'll work cheap to get custom. Let me alane for whilgeling an advocate;—it's nae sin to get as muckle frae

flying

them for our siller as we can—after a', it's but the wind o' their mouth—it costs them naething; whereas, in my wretched occupation of a saddler, horse-milliner, and harness-maker, we are out unconscionable sums just for hides and leather."

(p. 327)

barkend

Page proof for *1818* (Yale University Library, Scott MSS; pp. 325–7; ×0·66)

"Can I be of no use?" said Butler. "My means, alas! are only worth the black coat I wear, but I am young—I owe much to the family—Can I do nothing?"

b45 "Ye can help to collect evidence, sir," said Saddletree ; "if we could but find ony ane to say she had gi'en the least hint o' her condition, she wad be brought off with a wet finger—Mr Crossmyloof tell'd me sae.

b50 The crown, says he, canna be craved to prove a positive—was't a positive or a negative they couldna be ca'd to prove ?—it was the tane or the tither o' them, I am sure, and it makes na muckle matter whilk.

b55 Wherefore, says he, the libel maun be redargued by the pannel proving her defences. And it canna be done otherwise."

"But the fact, sir, the fact that this poor

"argued Butler"

girl has born a child; surely the crown   (p. 328)
b60 lawyers must prove that ?" said Butler.

Saddletree paused a moment, while the visage of Dumbiedikes, which traversed, as if it had been placed on a pivot, from the one spokesman to the other, assumed a
b65 more blithe expression.

"Ye—ye—ye—es," said Saddletree, after some grave hesitation ; "unquestionably that is a thing to be proved, as the Court will more fully declare by an inter-
b70 locutor of relevancy in common form ; but I fancy that job's done already, for she has confessed her guilt."

"Confessed the murder?" exclaimed Jeanie, with a scream that made them all
b75 start.

"No, I didna say that," replied Bar-

Page proof for *1818*, continued (Yale University Library, Scott MSS; pp. 327–8; ×0·66)

Verbal variants

	manuscript		page proof
a2	do and	b3	do naething; and
a3	disposed doubtless to	b5	disposed to
a4	wadna sand [?]	b6	wadna stand
a6	ilk ane	b10	ilka ane
a19	whullying	b33	whiggling
a25	are worth	b42	are only worth
a29	say	b49	sae
a32	muckle whilk	b54	muckle matter whilk
a36	woman	b61	moment

liament-house, if ony thing *can* do it; but whare's the siller to come frae? Mr Deans, ye see, will do naething; and though Mrs Saddletree's their far-awa friend, and right c5 gude weel-wisher, and is weel disposed to assist, yet she wadna like to stand to be bound *singuli in solidum* to such an expensive wark. An' ilka friend wad bear a share o' the burthen, something might be dune—c10 ilka ane to be liable for their ain input—I wadna like to see the case fa' through without being pled—it wadna be creditable, for a' that daft whig body says."

"I'll—I will—yes," (assuming fortitude,)
c15 "I will be answerable," said Dumbiedikes, "for a score of punds sterling,"—and he was silent, staring in astonishment at finding himself capable of such unwonted resolution and excessive generosity.
c20 "God Almighty bless ye, Laird!" said Jeanie in a transport of gratitude.

"Ye may ca' the twenty punds thretty," said Dumbiedikes, looking bashfully away from her and towards Saddletree.
c25 "That will do bravely," said Saddletree, rubbing his hands; "and ye sall hae a' my skill and knowledge to gar the siller gang far—I'll tape it out weel—I ken how to gar the birkies tak short fees, and be glad o'
c30 them too—it's only garring them trow ye hae twa or three cases of importance coming on, and they'll work cheap to get custom. Let me alane for whillying an advocate;—it's nae sin to get as muckle frae
c35 them for our siller as we can—after a', it's but the wind o' their mouth—it costs them naething; whereas, in my wretched occupation of a saddler, horse-milliner, and harness-maker, we are out unconscionable sums
c40 just for barkened hides and leather."

"Can I be of no use?" said Butler. "My means, alas! are only worth the black coat I wear; but I am young—I owe much to the family—Can I do nothing?"
c45 "Ye can help to collect evidence, sir," said Saddletree; "if we could but find ony ane to say she had gi'en the least hint o' her condition, she wad be brought aff wi' a wat finger—Mr Crossmyloof tell'd me sae.
c50 The crown, says he, canna be craved to prove a positive—was't a positive or a negative they couldna be ca'd to prove?—it was the tane or the tither o' them, I am sure, and it maksna muckle matter whilk.
c55 Wherefore, says he, the libel maun be redargued by the pannel proving her defences. And it canna be done otherwise."

"But the fact, sir," argued Butler, "the fact that this poor girl has born a child;
c60 surely the crown lawyers must prove that?" said Butler.

Saddletree paused a moment, while the visage of Dumbiedikes, which traversed, as if it had been placed on a pivot, from the
c65 one spokesman to the other, assumed a more blithe expression.

"Ye—ye—ye—es," said Saddletree, after some grave hesitation; "unquestionably that is a thing to be proved, as the
c70 Court will more fully declare by an interlocutor of relevancy in common form; but I fancy that job's done already, for she has confessed her guilt."

"Confessed the murder?" exclaimed
c75 Jeanie, with a scream that made them all start.

"No, I didna say that," replied Bar-

1818 (Scott, W., *Tales of my landlord, second series: The Heart of Mid-Lothian*, Edinburgh 1818, i, pp. 326-30; Univ. Lib. Cam., Lib.8.81.10; ×0·63)

Variants
There are no verbal variants between the page proof and *1818* other than those marked in the proof for correction; but the following non-verbal variants may be noted:

	page proof		*1818*
b5	good	c5	gude
b15	will [underlined]	c15	will [not in italic]
b43	wear, but	c43	wear; but
b48	off	c48	aff
b49	wet	c49	wat
b54	makes na	c54	maksna

thing *can* do it; but whare's the siller to come frae? Mr Deans, ye see, will do naething; and though Mrs Saddletree's their far-awa friend, and right good weel-wisher, and is weel disposed to assist, yet she wadna like to stand to be bound *singuli in solidum* to such an expensive wark. An ilka friend wad bear a share o' the burden, something might be dune—ilka ane to be liable for their ain input—I wadna like to see the case fa' through without being pled—it wadna be creditable, for a' that daft whig body says."

"I'll—I will—yes," (assuming fortitude,) "I will be answerable," said Dumbiedikes, "for a score of punds sterling."—And he was silent, staring in astonishment at finding himself capable of such unwonted resolution and excessive generosity.

"God Almighty bless ye, Laird!" said Jeanie, in a transport of gratitude.

"Ye may ca' the twenty punds thretty," said Dumbiedikes, looking bashfully away from her, and towards Saddletree.

"That will do bravely," said Saddletree, rubbing his hands; "and ye sall hae a' my skill and knowledge to gar the siller gang far—I'll tape it out weel—I ken how to gar the birkies tak short fees, and be glad o' them too—it's only garring them trow ye hae twa or three cases of importance coming on, and they'll work cheap to get custom. Let me alane for whillywhaing an advocate:—it's nae sin to get as muckle frae them for our siller as we can—after a', it's but the wind o' their mouth—it costs them naething; whereas, in my wretched occupation of a saddler, horse-milliner, and harness-maker, we are out unconscionable sums just for barkened hides and leather."

"Can I be of no use?" said Butler. "My means, alas! are only worth the black coat I wear; but I am young—I owe much to the family—Can I do nothing?"

"Ye can help to collect evidence, sir," said Saddletree; "if we could but find ony ane to say she had gien the least hint o' her condition, she wad be brought aff wi' a wat finger—Mr Crossmyloof tell'd me sae. The crown, says he, canna be craved to prove a positive—was't a positive or a negative they couldna be ca'd to prove?—it was the tane or the tither o' them, I am sure, and it maksna muckle matter whilk. Wherefore, says he, the libel maun be redargued by the panel proving her defences. And it canna be done otherwise."

"But the fact, sir," argued Butler, "the fact that this poor girl has borne a child; surely the crown lawyers must prove that?" said Butler.

Saddletree paused a moment, while the visage of Dumbiedikes, which traversed, as if it had been placed on a pivot, from the one spokesman to the other, assumed a more blithe expression.

"Ye—ye—ye—es," said Saddletree, after some grave hesitation; "unquestionably that is a thing to be proved, as the court will more fully declare by an interlocutor of relevancy in common form· but I fancy that job's done already, for she has confessed her guilt."

"Confessed the murder?" exclaimed Jeanie, with a scream that made them all start.

"No, I didna say that," replied Bartoline. "But

1830 (Scott, W., *Waverley novels* (*The Heart of Mid-Lothian*), Edinburgh 1829–33, xi (1830), pp. 384–6; Trin. Coll. Cam. 210.c.83.42; ×0·70)

Verbal variant

	1818		1830
c33	whillying	d29	whillywhaing

underlined in the manuscript for italicization was set in roman type. Thus 122 non-verbal alterations were made in copying and setting 542 words (43 lines and a catchword) of Scott's manuscript.

Scott's normal habit in revising a proof was to alter the words but not as a rule the details of the text, and to do so without reference to his manuscript.[22] Here, as well as correcting 'whiggling' to 'whillying', he altered 'stand' (which had been supplied at b6 by the amanuensis or the compositor) to read 'like to stand'; he (or possibly James Ballantyne) underlined 'will' in b15 for italics, which had also been underlined in the MS; and he added the word 'barkened' in b40. The other addition, '"argued Butler"' in b58, was tautological, for Scott failed to notice that overleaf on p. 328 of the proof the speech ended with 'said Butler'; consequently *1818* and all subsequent editions printed both 'argued Butler' and 'said Butler'.

Apart from underlining 'will', Scott made no changes to the 123 non-verbal variants between MS and the page proof. There can be no doubt that he was aware that his text had been repunctuated and otherwise normalized, and that he was content with the result. It must not be supposed that Scott did not *care* about the spelling and other details of his published texts; on the contrary, he wanted them to be correct, but he wanted someone else to be responsible for making them so. But although he characteristically left the revision of the details of the text to others, he sometimes became actively interested in spellings which indicated dialect forms, and it was probably Scott, not Ballantyne, who (in a revise proof) changed 'good' to 'gude' (b5/c5), 'of' to 'aff' (b48/c48), 'wet' to 'wat' (b49/c49), and 'makes na' to 'maksna' (b54/c54); on the other hand 'skill' (b27), which had been normalized from the MS spelling 'skeel' (a15), was not emended. There was only one other change at this stage: 'wear, but' emended to 'wear; but' (b43/c43).

Nearly all the changes marked in the author's proof were incorporated in the first edition, *1818*, the only exception in the extract being the neglect to set 'will' in italics in c15. The second edition, *1819*, was a reasonably faithful reprint of the first. In the extract the two editions are verbally identical, and the only non-verbal variants are 'well' for 'weel' (c28) and 'court' for 'Court' (c70). A larger number of variants (including, elsewhere, some verbal changes) were introduced when *1821* was set from *1819*, but there is no reason to suppose that Scott was responsible for them; and these variants from *1821* were repeated in *1822*, *1823*, and *1825*. They were not repeated in *1830*, the 'magnum opus' edition, which was set from a copy of *1819* into which Scott's additions and corrections had been transcribed

[22] Although he did not read proof against copy as he went along, Scott liked to have his MS. available so that he could refer to it in case of difficulty; see p. 103 n. 10 above, and *Letters*, xi, p. 209 (to Robert Cadell, 14 June 1829); ibid., xi, p. 233 (to James Ballantyne, 27 Aug. 1829).

from his interleaved copy of *1822*, and which had also undergone a thorough revision of its spelling, punctuation, etc.

In revising the text of his interleaved copy for the 'magnum opus' Scott appears to have done no more than to alter a word or a sentence here and there, leaving many pages at a time unaltered. Since his interleaved copy cannot now be found, the precise extent of his revision is unknown; but it is at least improbable that Scott undertook for the 'magnum opus' the detailed revision of the spelling, punctuation, and other details of the text that he had hitherto left to others.

There is one verbal difference in the extract between the text of *1818/ 1819* and that of *1830*, and it looks like an emendation by Scott; 'whillying' (c33, meaning 'cheating') is changed to 'whillywhaing' (d29, meaning 'wheedling'). The non-verbal differences between these texts, on the other hand, follow a pattern of normalization which is unlikely to be his:

	1818/1819		*1830*
c5	gude	d4	good
c8	An'	d6	An
c9	burthen	d7	burden
c16	sterling,"—and	d14	sterling."—And
c21	Jeanie	d17	Jeanie,
c24	her	d20	her,
c28	weel (*1818*), well (*1819*)	d25	weel
c34	advocate;	d29	advocate:
c47	gi'en	d42	gien
c56	pannel	d49	panel
c59	born	d52	borne
c70	Court (*1818*), court (*1819*)	d60	court

The changes that were made here are typical of the 'magnum opus' text, but not of Scott's own practice. His personal spellings have been replaced by more conventional ones; commas and other stops have been added; and apostrophes used as marks of elision have been deleted.

Scott's main interest in getting out the 'magnum opus' was to make money in order to meet his huge financial obligations. Besides this he was glad of the opportunity to add notes and introductions to the novels. But revising their texts came a poor third, as the discontinuity of his verbal revisions indicates; still less can he have been interested in revising details such as spelling and punctuation, with which he had never previously concerned himself. No doubt he could have considered these details—his letters and journal of 1829–30 refer to correcting proofs of the new notes, and he is likely to have been sent proofs of the text as well—but, overworked and in failing health as he was at this time, he cannot be supposed to have read proofs of the text of *1830* with attention to detail, if indeed he read them at all.

The five intermediate editions of *The Heart of Mid-Lothian* (*1819*, *1821*, *1822*, *1823*, and *1825*) include some textual variation, but it does not appear to be authoritative. Collation of these texts with each other, and with *1818* and *1830*, reveals little that is of textual interest. In our brief extract three verbal variants appeared—one in *1821* and two in *1822*—which were all copying errors;[23] and there was the usual crop of minor variants. Elsewhere in these intermediate editions there were a few deliberate emendations, but these appear to have been the work of James Ballantyne, who was always apt to meddle, not of Scott. Scott's interleaved and corrected copy of *1822* is also in existence somewhere and, if it could be found, it should answer a number of questions about the authority of *1830*; but for the moment we have to do without it.[24]

What the editor of *The Heart of Mid-Lothian* has got, therefore, is a holograph draft of the novel that was to be altered verbally by Scott and in detail by the amanuensis and the compositor. He then has the first edition, *1818*, together with a fragment of author's proof, in which Scott carefully revised the words (often on the advice of James Ballantyne) and accepted the normalization of his spelling, punctuation, etc. Finally there is the 'magnum opus' text, *1830*, for which Scott revised occasional words and provided extensive new notes, but where he was not concerned with the further normalization of the details.

It is immediately clear that the edited text must be an eclectic one. The author's manuscript does not represent the completed work but is itself a stage in its composition, incomplete in words and defective in punctuation. It will prove essential to the editor in providing words that were mistaken by the amanuensis, or by the compositor of *1818*, and which were not afterwards rectified by Scott, but it would make an unsatisfactory copy-text because so much of the detail would have to be altered or supplied. The manuscript does of course give us Scott's own approximate punctuation, not the careful, normalized forms of the printed texts (and it might be possible to retain Scott's own punctuation by emending a printed copy-text). Yet Scott expected others to punctuate his work; and he actively accepted the first-edition punctuation by refining it in proof. It is arguable, moreover, not only that Scott probably approved of the first-edition punctuation of *The Heart of Mid-Lothian*, but also that it is the most successful pointing of the text that is available to us: better than Scott's light, erratic punctuation, and likely to be better than an editorial attempt to repoint the manuscript. So *1818* is proposed as copy-text.

---

[23] In *1821* 'from the one' (c64–5) was altered to read 'from one'; and in *1822* '*singuli*' (c7) was altered to read '*singula*', and 'of relevancy' (c71) to read 'in relevancy'. The *1821* variant was repeated in *1822*, *1823*, and *1825*; the *1822* variants were repeated in *1823*.   [24] See p. 104 n. 13.

In this case the editor would also have to consult *1830*, the 'magnum opus', which—although it would not do as copy-text because of the un-authoritative revision of its details—is the only available authority for Scott's last verbal revisions, and for his additional notes and introduction.

The edited text would therefore be based on *1818*, with verbal (and occasionally other) corrections from manuscript and from *1830*. In this case the emendations to the *1818* text of our extract might be as follows:

c5	*for* disposed to	*read* disposed doubtless to	[MS]
c10	*for* ilka ane	*read* ilk ane	[MS]
c27	*for* skill	*read* skeel	[MS]
c33	*for* whillying	*read* whillywhaing	[*1830*]
c61	*delete* said Butler.		[proof]

The editor has to decide, finally, how much textual apparatus to provide and where to put it. He must at least record all the verbal variants in the texts with which Scott himself was concerned, and also any other important variation between the copy-text and the edited text. On the other hand he may not think it necessary to record the much more extensive variation in the punctuation, paragraphing, etc., of these texts, but may feel that their character can be adequately conveyed by the inclusion of facsimiles of extracts. It would be helpful to provide a register of the hyphenated line-endings in the edition, with an indication of whether they should be hyphenated in quotation.

If Scott's genius for story-telling is to be allowed to run free—as it should be, even in a critical edition—his pages must not be encumbered by the evidence of the editor's labours. It is a good rule for the editors of novels in which narrative is more important than linguistic detail that all the apparatus should be placed in an appendix at the end. It need not be extensive here; and an edition of *The Heart of Mid-Lothian* prepared in this way could—variously bound in hard and paper covers—serve the needs not only of specialists but of students and general readers as well.

EXAMPLE 6

Tennyson, 'Œnone', 1833

TENNYSON began to write his poem about the desertion of the nymph Œnone by Paris in the late summer of 1830, when he was just twenty-one.[1] The first draft was made near Cauterets in the French Pyrenees, where he had gone with Arthur Hallam in a vain attempt to promote a revolution in Spain. The spectacular scenery of cataracts tumbling down deep gorges from the snow-topped mountains affected him profoundly, and the new poem (like others that were soon to follow it)[2] was partly inspired by its grandeur. But 'Œnone' had another inspiration as well: classical literature, and especially the *Eclogues* of Virgil and the *Idylls* of Theocritus.[3] The strength of the poem, indeed, was to lie in Tennyson's use of his verbal and rhythmic skill to set a classical pastoral in a romantic landscape, for the narrative itself was weak in drama and characterization.

The early drafts of 'Œnone' were followed by publication in Tennyson's *Poems* dated 1833.[4] The book was a disastrous failure; and the savage attacks of its critics, followed during 1833 by the death of his beloved Arthur Hallam, plunged Tennyson into the unhappiest decade of his life. Yet for all the pain of these years—partly because of it, indeed—Tennyson used the time to reconsider his early poems and to improve them by revision. When 'Œnone' reappeared in his next collection, the two-volume *Poems* of 1842,[5] it was a much better poem, both in content and in sound. Tennyson had done more than touch it up: much of it was actually rewritten in a series of intermediate drafts. This was essentially the final version of 'Œnone' but, being

[1] The best life of Tennyson is Sir Charles Tennyson's *Alfred Tennyson*, London 1949; and the *Poems* should be consulted in Christopher Ricks's monumental edition (London 1969), to be discussed hereafter. The only bibliography is T. J. Wise's unreliable *A bibliography of the writings of Alfred, Lord Tennyson*, 2 vols., London 1908.

For the early reviews of the poems, see *Tennyson, the critical heritage*, ed. Jump, J. D., London 1967. More recent criticism relevant to 'Œnone' and its development includes Pyre, J. F. A., *The formation of Tennyson's style*, Madison 1921; Turner, P., 'Some ancient light on Tennyson's Œnone', *Journal of English and Germanic philology*, lxi (1962), pp. 57–72; Baum, P. F., *Tennyson sixty years after*, Hamden 1963; and Ricks, C., *Tennyson*, London 1972.

Tennyson's working methods are described in Paden, W. D., 'A note on the variants of *In memoriam* and *Lucretius*', *The Library*, viii (1953), pp. 259–73; Shannon, E. F., 'The proofs of *Gareth and Lynette* in the Widener Collection', *PBSA*, xli (1947), pp. 321–40; and Shannon, E. F., 'The history of a poem: Tennyson's *Ode on the death of the Duke of Wellington*', *Studies in bibliography*, xiii (1960), pp. 149–77.

[2] Especially 'The lotos-eaters', 'Mariana in the south', and 'The palace of art'.

[3] Paul Turner makes the point that 'Œnone' is 'a distillation, not of life, but of literature' (n. 1 above at p. 57). This is certainly true of the narrative; but the setting of the poem was taken from the real Pyrenees, not from a literary landscape.

[4] Wise, *editiones principes*, 7; hereafter *1833*.   [5] Wise, *editiones principes*, 12; hereafter *1842*.

inclined to tinker with his work in later editions, Tennyson changed a handful of readings in the *Poems* of 1843, in the *Works* of 1882, and in the *Poems* of 1883. No further changes were made after the publication of the 1883 text,[6] but Tennyson's own textual and explanatory notes were published in 1907, after his death.[7]

The surviving evidence for the development of the text of 'Œnone' comprises eight manuscript drafts and three published versions, as follows:

1. Holograph draft in Trinity notebook T23, fos. 21^b–20^a;[8] 69 lines;[9] [1830–2].
2. MS. transcript (probably by John Allen)[10] in Trinity MS. R.7.50, fos. 60^a–63^a; 242 lines; [1830–2].
3. *1833* (pp. 51–64), published December 1832; 256 lines.
4. Copy of *1833* in the Fitzwilliam Museum, Cambridge, with MS. corrections by Tennyson; given by Tennyson to J. M. Heath before the spring of 1837.

Five successive holograph drafts in Trinity notebook T26:

5. fo. 1^a; 37 lines.
6. fos. 2^a–4^b; 282 lines.[11]
7. fo. 27^a; 15 lines.
8. fo. 28^a; 11 lines.
9. fos. 28^b–29^a; 90 lines.[12]
   The T26 drafts are apparently in the order of composition, but 6 was corrected between the composition of 8 and 9; [1837–42].

10. *1842* (pp. 118–31), published May 1842; 264 lines.
11. *1883* (pp. 197–212), published 1883; 264 lines.
    Tennyson's notes to this final published version were printed by Hallam Tennyson in the Eversley edition of Tennyson's *Works* (vol. i, London 1907, pp. 358–63).

Some of the stages in the development of the text of 'Œnone' are missing—notably the printer's copy and the author's proofs for *1833* and *1842*—but the evidence which survives gives a clear picture of how the poem progressed. We can see what happened by following Tennyson through the successive versions of the first thirty-two lines.

---

[6] Wise, *editiones principes*, 21; hereafter *1883*.

[7] Wise, collected editions, 21, vol. i, pp. 358–61 (the Eversley edition).

[8] Most of the Tennyson notebooks in the Library of Trinity College, Cambridge, were presented in 1924 by Hallam Tennyson. Until 1969 the Trinity manuscripts might not be copied or published.

[9] The line counts in this summary include repetitions and deletions.

[10] John Allen, 1810–86, friend of Tennyson, Thackeray, and others.

[11] Many leaves were torn and cut from this volume, mostly by Tennyson himself. One of them, which probably followed the present fo. 2, is now at the Henry E. Huntington Library, California (MS. 19501); it contains a further 80 lines of 6.

[12] There is also a false start for 9 at the end of 8 on fo. 28^a, reading 'ŒNONE. | There lies a vale in'.

Œnone.

—

There is a dale in Ida lovelier
Than any in old Ionia, beautiful
With many an emerald slope of sunny sward
Down to the loud glenriver which hath worn
5] A path thro' steepdown granitewalls o'ercrept
With thick & flowerful trailers down below
Afar between the cedarshadowy dell
Far-off & high above the Godbuilt wall
And many a snowbright pillared range divine
10] Aloft upon a subtleshadowed crag
Clearlined & dark against darkblue sky
The windy citadel of Ilion shone
The crown & strength of Ilion. Hither came
~~beautiful~~ wandering
15] Darksouled Œnone weeping & forlorn
Of Paris once her playmate. Round her neck
Her neck all marblewhite & marblecold
Floated her hair or seemed to float in rest
She leaning on a vinentwined stone
20] Sang to the stillness till the mountain shadow
Sloped downward to her seat from the upper cliff

O mother Ida, manyfountained Ida
Dear mother Ida hearken ere I die.
The lizard with his shadow on the rock
25] Sleeps like a shadow & the scarletwinged
Cicala in the noonday leapeth not
Along the waterrounded graniterock
The purple flower droops: the golden bee
Is lilycradled: I alone awake
30] My eyes are full of tears, my heart
My heart is breaking & my eyes are dim
And I am all aweary of my life.

1 See p. 119 (Trin. Coll. Cam., T23, fos. 21ᵇ-21ᵃ; ×0·78)

Œnone.

There is a dale in Ida lovelier
Than any in old Ionia, beautiful
With many an emerald slope of sunny sward
Down to the loud glenriver which hath worn
5]   A path thro' steepdown granitewalls o'ercrept
       thick &
With ~~many a~~ flowerful trailers down below.
Afar between the cedarshadowy dell
Far-off & high above the Godbuilt wall
And many a snowbrightpillared range divine
10]   Aloft many a subtleshadowed crag
Clearlined & dark against darkblue sky
The windy citadel of Ilion shone
The crown & strength of Ilion. Hither came
~~Beautiful browed Œnone wandering~~
          wandering
15]   Darksouled Œnone ~~weeping~~ & forlorn
Of Paris once her playmate. Round her neck
Her neck all marblewhite & marblecold
Floated her hair or seemed to float in rest
She leaning on a vineentwinèd stone
20]   Sang to the stillness till the mountain shadow[?]
Sloped downward to her seat from the upper cliff [?]
O mother Ida, manyfountained Ida
Dear mother Ida hearken ere I die.
The lizard with his shadow on yᵉ rock
25]   Sleeps like a shadow & yᵉ scarletwinged
Cicala in the noonday leapeth not
Along the waterrounded graniterock
The purple flower droops: yᵉ golden bee
Is lilycradled: I alone awake
30]   My eyes are full of tears, my heart of love
My heart is breaking & my eyes are dim
And I am all aweary of my life.

Transcript of p. 120

Œnone .   A rough sketch -   √ 60

There is a dale in Ida lovelier
Than any in old Ionia, beautiful
With many an emerald slope of sunny sward
Down to the loud glenriver, which hath worn
5] A path thro' steep down granite walls decrepit
With thick & flowerful trailers down below -
Afar between the cedar shadowy dell
Far off & high above the godbuilt wall
And many a snow bright pillared range divine
10] Aloft upon a subtle shadowed crag
Clearlined, & dark against the dark blue sky
The windy citadel of Ilion shone -
The crown & strength of Troas. Hither came
Dark souled Œnone wandering, forlorn
15] Of Paris once her playmate. Round her neck
Her neck all marble white & marble cold
Floated her hair or seemed to float in rest -
She leaning on a vine entwined stone
Sang to the stillness till the mountain shadow
20] Sloped down ward to her seat from the upper cliff -

O mother Ida, many fountained Ida
Dear mother Ida hearken ere I die -
The lizard with his shadow on the stone
Sleeps like a shadow & the scarlet winged
25] Cicala in the noonday leapeth not
Along the water-mended granite rock
The purple flower droops. the golden bee
Is lily cradled : I alone awake.
My eyes are full of tears my heart of love
30] My heart is breaking & my eyes are dim
And I am all aweary of my life -

2 See p. 119 (Trin. Coll. Cam., MS. R.7.50, fo. 60ᵃ; ×1·0)

Œnone   .   A rough sketch—

There is a dale in Ida lovelier
Than any in old Ionia, beautiful
With many an emerald slope of sunny sward
Down to the loud glenriver, which hath worn
5] A path thro' steep down granite walls o'ercrept
With thick & flowerful trailers down below—
Afar between the cedar shadowy dell
Far off & high above the God built wall
And many a snow bright pillared range divine
10] Aloft upon a subtle shadowed crag
Clearlined, & dark against the dark blue sky
The windy citadel of Ilion shone—
The crown & strength of Troas. Hither came
Dark souled Œnone wandering, forlorn
15] Of Paris once her playmate. Round her neck
Her neck all marble white & marble cold
Floated her hair or seemed to float in rest—
She leaning on a vine entwined stone
Sang to the stillness till the mountain shadow
20] Sloped down ward to her seat from the upper cliff—

O mother Ida, many fountained Ida
Dear mother Ida hearken ere I die—
The lizard with his shadow on the stone
Sleeps like a shadow & the scarlet-winged
25] Cicala in the noonday leapeth not
Along the water rounded granite rock
The purple flower droops. the golden bee
Is lily cradled: I alone awake.
My eyes are full of tears my heart of love
30] My heart is breaking & my eyes are dim
And I am all aweary of my life—

Transcript of p. 122

ŒNONE.

THERE is a dale in Ida, lovelier
Than any in old Ionia, beautiful
With emerald slopes of sunny sward, that lean
Above the loud glenriver, which hath worn
5]   A path thro' steepdown granite walls below
Mantled with flowering tendriltwine. In front
The cedarshadowy valleys open wide.
Far-seen, high over all the Godbuilt wall
And many a snowycolumned range divine,
10]   Mounted with awful sculptures—men and Gods,
The work of Gods—bright on the darkblue sky
The windy citadel of Ilion
Shone, like the crown of Troas. Hither came
Mournful Œnone wandering forlorn

15]   Of Paris, once her playmate. Round her neck,
Her neck all marblewhite and marblecold,
Floated her hair or seemed to float in rest.
She, leaning on a vine-entwinèd stone,
Sang to the stillness, till the mountain-shadow
20]   Sloped downward to her seat from the upper cliff.

    " O mother Ida, manyfountained Ida,
Dear mother Ida, hearken ere I die.
The grasshopper is silent in the grass,
The lizard with his shadow on the stone
25]   Sleeps like a shadow, and the scarletwinged*
Cicala in the noonday leapeth not
Along the water-rounded granite-rock
The purple flower droops: the golden bee
Is lilycradled: I alone awake.
30]   My eyes are full of tears, my heart of love,
My heart is breaking and my eyes are dim,
And I am all aweary of my life.

   * In the Pyrenees, where part of this poem was written, I saw a
very beautiful species of Cicala, which had scarlet wings spotted with
black. Probably nothing of the kind exists in Mount Ida.

3 *1833* (Trin. Coll. Cam. Adv. d.11.25, pp. 51-2; ×0·77)

ŒNONE.

———

THERE is a dale in Ida, lovelier
of the dale'
Than any ~~in~~ old Ionian ~~beautiful~~
Most beautiful with sunny
(made) With emerald slopes ~~of sunny sward~~, that lean

Above the loud glenriver, which hath worn

5] A path thro' ~~steepdown~~ *curving* granite walls below
&. all at once
Mantled with flower~~ing~~ ~~tendrilicame~~. In front

The cedarshadowy valleys open wide.
Thro' these
~~Farseen~~, high over all the ~~Godbuilt wall~~ *crowned towers*

And many a snowycolumned range divine,

10] Mounted with awful sculptures—men and Gods,

The work of Gods—bright on the darkblue sky

The windy citadel of Ilion
rise far.
Sh~~one~~. ~~like~~ the crown of Troas. Hither came

Mournful Œnone wandering forlorn

15] Of Paris, once her playmate. Round her neck,

Her neck all marblewhite and marblecold,

Floated her hair or seemed to float in rest.

She, leaning on a vine-entwinèd stone,

Sang to the stillness, till the mountain-shadow

20] Sloped downward to her seat from the upper cliff.

" O mother Ida, manyfountained Ida,

Dear mother Ida, hearken ere I die.

The grasshopper is silent in the grass,

The lizard with his shadow on the stone
garrulous
Sleeps like a shadow, and the ~~scarlet-winged~~*
25] *Cicala ceaseth now to twist the hake*
~~Cicala in the noonday leapeth not~~
with thick dry clamour chafed from griding wings
~~Along the water-rounded granite-rock'~~

The purple flower droops: the golden bee

Is lilycradled: I alone awake.

30] My eyes are full of tears, my heart of love,

My heart is breaking and my eyes are dim,

And I am all aweary of my life.

* In the Pyrenees, where part of this poem was written, I saw a
very beautiful species of Cicala, which had scarlet wings spotted with
black. Probably nothing of the kind exists in Mount Ida.

4 Tennyson's corrections to *1833*, pp. 51–2 (Fitzwilliam Museum, Cambridge; ×0·77)

There is a dale in Ida lovelier
Than any dale among Ionian hills.
There slants the mountains meadowy base to Leen
Above the long glen-river, while he wears
5] A pathway, load with various waterfalls,
Thro' curves of ivied granite; &, in front,
The shadowed valleys, opening wide, reveal
Ilion, & Simois, & the summer sea,
Troas, & Ilion's windy citadel,
10] The crown of Troas. Hither came at noon
Dark-eyed Onone, wandering forlorn
Of Paris once her playmate. Round her neck
Floated her hair, or seemed to float in rest.
She leaning on a fragment twined with vine
15] Sang to the stillness, till the mountain-eve
Sloped downward to her seat from the upper cliff.

  O mother Ida, many-fountained Ida.
Dear mother Ida, harken ere I die.
The grasshopper is silent in the grass.
20] The lizard with his shadow on the stone
Rests like a shadow & the garrulous
Cicala sleeps: the flowers droop: the bees
Are lily-cradled: I alone awake.
My eyes are full of tears, my heart of love
25] My heart is breaking & my eyes are dim
And I am all aweary of my life.

5 See p. 119 (Trin. Coll. Cam., T26, fo. 1ᵃ; ×1·16)

There is a dale in Ida lovelier
Than any dale among Ionian hills.
There slants the mountains meadowy base to lean
Above the long glen-river, while he wears
5]   A pathway, loud with various waterfalls,
Thro' curves of ivied granite; &, in front,
The shadowed valleys, opening wide, reveal
Ilion, & Simoïs, & the summer sea,
Troas, & Ilion's windy citadel,
10] The crown of Troas. Hither came at noon
Dark-eyed Œnone, wandering forlorn
Of Paris once her playmate. Round her neck
Floated her hair, or seemed to float in rest.
She leaning on a fragment twined with vine
15] Sang to the stillness, till the mountain-eve
Sloped downward to her seat from the upper cliff.
      O mother Ida, many-fountained Ida.
Dear mother Ida, harken ere I die.
The grasshopper is silent in the grass.
20] The lizard with his shadow on the stone
Rests like a shadow & the garrulous
Cicala sleeps: the flowers droop: the bees
Are lily-cradled: I alone awake.
My eyes are full of tears, my heart of love
25] My heart is breaking & my eyes are dim
And I am all aweary of my life.

Transcript of p. 126

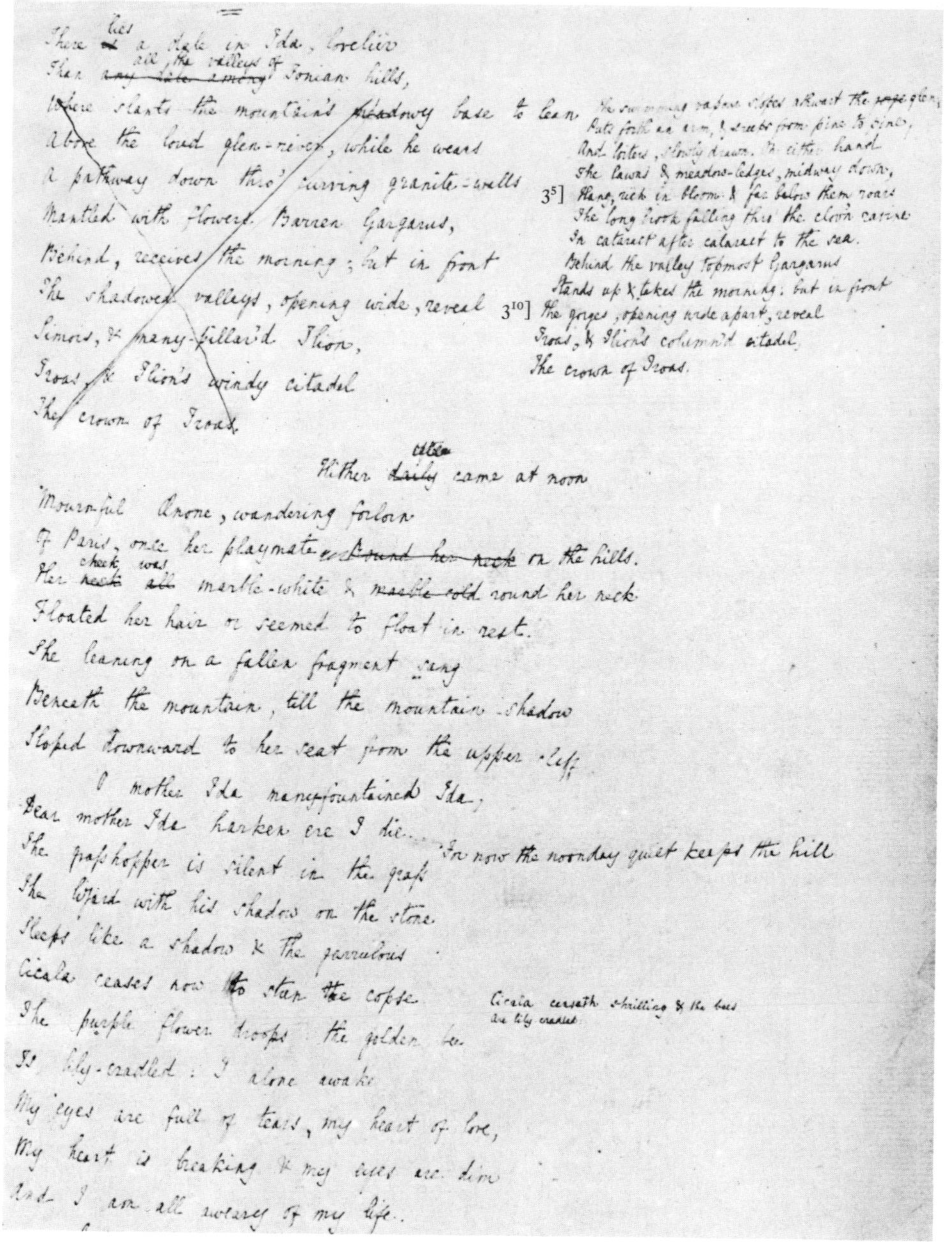

There lies a vale in Ida, lovelier
Than all the valleys of Ionian hills,
Where slants the mountain's meadowy base to lean
Above the loud glen-river, while he wears
5]   A pathway down thro' curving granite-walls
Mantled with flowers. Barren Gargarus
Behind, receives the morning; but in front
The shadowed valleys, opening wide, reveal
Ilion, & many-pillar'd Ilion,
10]   Troas & Ilion's windy citadel
The crown of Troas.

The marginal revision (right column):

The swimming vapour slopes athwart the glen,
Puts forth an arm, & creeps from pine to pine,
And loiters, slowly drawn. On either hand
The lawns & meadow-ledges midway down
35]   Hang, rich in bloom & far below them roars
The long brook falling thro' the cloven ravine
In cataract after cataract to the sea.
Behind the valley topmost Gargarus
Stands up & takes the morning: but in front
310] The gorge, opening wide apart, reveal
Troas, & Ilion's column'd citadel
The crown of Troas.

Hither came at noon
Mournful Œnone, wandering forlorn
Of Paris, once her playmate on the hills.
Her cheek was
Her neck all marble-white & marble-cold round her neck
15]   Floated her hair or seemed to float in rest.
She leaning on a fallen fragment sang
Beneath the mountain, till the mountain-shadow
Sloped downward to her seat from the upper cliff.

O mother Ida manyfountained Ida,
20]   Dear mother Ida harken ere I die.
The grasshopper is silent in the grass   For now the noonday quiet keeps the hill
The lizard with his shadow on the stone
Sleeps like a shadow & the garrulous
25]   Cicala ceases now to stun the copse
The purple flower droops the golden bee   Cicala ceaseth shrilling & the bee
Is lily-cradled: I alone awake   is lily cradled
My eyes are full of tears, my heart of love,
My heart is breaking & my eyes are dim
30]   And I am all weary of my life.

6 See p. 119 (Trin. Coll. Cam., T26, fo. 2^a; ×0·71)

lies ==
There is a dale in Ida, lovelier
    all the valleys of
Than any dale among Ionian hills,
Where slants the mountain's meadowy base to lean
Above the loud glen-rivers, while he wears
5] A pathway down thro' curving granite-walls
Mantled with flowers. Barren Gargarus,
Behind, receives the morning; but in front
The shadowed valleys, opening wide, reveal
Simois, & many-pillar'd Ilion,
10] Troas, & Ilion's windy citadel
The crown of Troas.

      glen,
The swimming vapour slopes athwart the gorge
Puts forth an arm, & creeps from pine to pine,
And loiters, slowly drawn. On either hand
The lawns & meadow-ledges, midway down,
3^5] Hang, rich in bloom: & far below them roars
The long brook falling thro' the clov'n ravine
In cataract after cataract to the sea.
Behind the valley topmost Gargarus
Stands up & takes the morning: but in front
3^{10}] The gorges, opening wide apart, reveal
Troas, & Ilion's column'd citadel,
The crown of Troas.

      often
Hither daily came at noon
Mournful Œnone, wandering forlorn
Of Paris, once her playmate. Round her neck on the hills.
    cheek was
Her neck all marble-white & marble-cold round her neck
15] Floated her hair or seemed to float in rest.
She leaning on a fallen fragment sang
Beneath the mountain, till the mountain-shadow
Sloped downward to her seat from the upper cliff.
    O mother Ida many-fountained Ida,
20] Dear mother Ida harken ere I die.
      For now the noonday quiet keeps the hill
The grasshopper is silent in the grass
The lizard with his shadow on the stone
Sleeps like a shadow & the garrulous
25] Cicala ceases now to stun the corpse.   Cicala ceaseth shrilling & the
The purple flower droops: the golden bee   bees are lily-cradled:
Is lily-cradled: I alone awake
My eyes are full of tears, my heart of love,
My heart is breaking & my eyes are dim
30] And I am all aweary of my life.

Transcript of p. 128

```
There is a dale in Ida, known to few,
But none is lovelier in Ionian hills.
For there on either side the mountain slants
To meadow-bases rich in flowers, & there
5]   Thro' all the clov'n ravine, in gulfs & grots,
Pouring innumerable waterfalls,
The long brook foams by many a knoll of pine.
Behind it darkens Gargarus but in front
The wooded gorges, opening wide, reveal
10]  Scamander wed with Simois, Hellespont,
Troas, & Ilion's column'd citadel
The crown of Troas.
                    Hither came at noon
Mournful Œnone wandering forlorn
Of Paris, once her playmate. Round her neck
15]  Floated
```

7 See p. 119 (Trin. Coll. Cam., T26, fo. 27[a]; ×1·0)

```
There lies a vale in Ida, lovelier
Than other vallies in Ionian hills.
For there the mountain slants on either hand
To meadow-bases rich with flowers, & there
5]   The long brook lapses thro' the clov'n ravine
In cataract after cataract to the sea.
Behind him darkens Gargarus; but in front
The gorges opening wide apart reveal
Scamander & the Simois, Hellespont
10]  Troas, & Ilion's columned citadel
The crown of Troas.
```

8 See p. 119 (Trin. Coll. Cam., T26, fo. 28[a]; ×1·0)

=

There is a dale in Ida, known to few,
But none is lovelier in Ionian hills.
For there on either side the mountain slants
To meadow-bases rich in flowers, & there
5] Thro' all the clov'n ravine, in gulfs & grots,
Pouring innumerable waterfalls,
The long brook foams by many a knoll of pine.
Behind it darkens Gargarus but in front
The wooded gorges, opening wide, reveal
10] Scamander wed with Simoïs, Hellespont,
Troas, & Ilion's column'd citadel
The crown of Troas.
                                    Hither came at noon
Mournful Œnone wandering forlorn
Of Paris, once her playmate. Round her neck
15] Floated

Transcript of no. 7 opposite

=

There lies a vale in Ida, lovelier .
Than other vallies in Ionian hills.
For there the mountain slants on either hand
To meadow-bases rich with flowers, & there
5] The long brook lapses thro' the clov'n ravine
In cataract after cataract to the sea.
Behind him darkens Gargarus; but in front
The gorges opening wide apart reveal
Scamander & the Simois, Hellespont
10] Troas, & Ilion's columned citadel
The crown of Troas.

Transcript of no. 8 opposite

OENONE

There lies a vale in Ida, lovelier
Than all the valleys of Ionian hills.
The swimming vapour slopes athwart the glen,
Puts forth an arm, & creeps from pine to pine,
5] And loiters, passing by. To left & right
The lawns & meadow-ledges midway down
Hang rich in flowers; & far below resounds
The long brook falling thro' the cloven ravine
In cataract after cataract to the sea.
10] Behind the valley topmost Gargarus
Stands up and takes the morning: but in front
The gorges, opening wide apart, reveal
Troas & Ilion's columned citadel,
The crown of Troas.

      Hither came at noon
Mournful Oenone wandering forlorn
Of Paris once her playmate on the hills.
Her cheek was marble-pale & round her neck
Floated her hair, or seemed to float in rest.
20] She leaning on a fragment twined with vine
Sang to the stillness, till the mountain-shade
Fell round her, darkening down from the upper cliff.
      Oh mother Ida, many-fountain'd Ida,
Dear mother Ida, harken ere I die.
25] The grasshopper is silent in the grass:
The lizard with his shadow on the stone
Rests like a shadow & the garrulous
Cicala ceaseth yet to hurt the hake:
The purple flower droops: the golden bee
30] Are lily-cradled: I alone awake
My eyes are full of tears: my heart of love:
My heart is breaking & my eyes are dim
And I am all aweary of my life.

9 See p. 119 (Trin. Coll. Cam., T26, fo. 28ᵇ; ×0·85)

ŒNONE.

———

There lies a vale in Ida, lovelier
Than all the valleys of Ionian hills.
The swimming vapour slopes athwart the glen,
Puts forth an arm, & creeps from pine to pine,
5] And lingers, passing by. To left & right
The lawns & meadow-ledges midway down
Hang rich in flowers; & far below resounds
The long brook falling thro' the clov'n ravine
In cataract after cataract to the sea
10] He comes from Gargarus: barren Gargarus
Behind, receives the morning: but in front
The gorges, opening wide apart, reveal
Scamander & the Simois, Hellespont,
Troas & Ilion's columned citadel
15] The crown of Troas.
      Hither came at noon
Mournful Œnone wandering forlorn
Of Paris once her playmate on the hills.
Her cheek was marble-pale & round her neck
Floated her hair, or seemed to float in rest.
20] She leaning on a fragment twined with vine
Sang to the stillness, till the mountain-shade
Fell round her, darkening down from the upper cliff.
  Oh mother Ida; many fountain'd Ida,
Dear mother Ida harken ere I die
25] The grasshopper is silent in the grass:
The lizard with his shadow on the stone
Rests like a shadow & the garrulous
Cicala ceaseth yet to burst the brake:
The purple flower droops: the golden bees
30] Are lily-cradled: I alone awake
My eyes are full of tears: my heart of love:
My heart is breaking & my eyes are dim
And I am all aweary of my life.

Transcript of p. 132

ŒNONE.

THERE lies a vale in Ida, lovelier
Than all the valleys of Ionian hills.
The swimming vapour slopes athwart the glen,
Puts forth an arm, and creeps from pine to pine,
5]   And loiters, slowly drawn.   On either hand
The lawns and meadow-ledges midway down
Hang rich in flowers, and far below them roars
The long brook falling thro' the clov'n ravine
In cataract after cataract to the sea.
10]   Behind the valley topmost Gargarus
Stands up and takes the morning : but in front
The gorges, opening wide apart, reveal
Troas and Ilion's column'd citadel,
The crown of Troas.

                    Hither came at noon
15]   Mournful Œnone, wandering forlorn
Of Paris, once her playmate on the hills.
Her cheek had lost the rose, and round her neck
Floated her hair or seem'd to float in rest.
She, leaning on a fragment twined with vine,
20]   Sang to the stillness, till the mountain-shade
Sloped downward to her seat from the upper cliff.

    " O mother Ida, many-fountain'd Ida,
Dear mother Ida, harken ere I die.
For now the noonday quiet holds the hill :
25]   The grasshopper is silent in the grass :
The lizard, with his shadow on the stone,
Rests like a shadow, and the cicala sleeps.
The purple flowers droop : the golden bee
Is lily-cradled : I alone awake.
30]   My eyes are full of tears, my heart of love,
My heart is breaking, and my eyes are dim,
And I am all aweary of my life.

10 *1842* (Trin. Coll. Cam., G.18.9, pp. 118-19; ×0·83)

ŒNONE.

THERE lies a vale in Ida, lovelier
Than all the valleys of Ionian hills.
The swimming vapour slopes athwart the glen,
Puts forth an arm, and creeps from pine to pine,
5]   And loiters, slowly drawn.   On either hand
The lawns and meadow-ledges midway down
Hang rich in flowers, and far below them roars
The long brook falling thro' the clov'n ravine
In cataract after cataract to the sea.
10]   Behind the valley topmost Gargarus
Stands up and takes the morning : but in front
The gorges, opening wide apart, reveal
Troas and Ilion's column'd citadel,
The crown of Troas.

                    Hither came at noon
15]   Mournful Œnone, wandering forlorn
Of Paris, once her playmate on the hills.
Her cheek had lost the rose, and round her neck
Floated her hair or seem'd to float in rest.
She, leaning on a fragment twined with vine,
20]   Sang to the stillness, till the mountain-shade
Sloped downward to her seat from the upper cliff.

   ' O mother Ida, many-fountain'd Ida,
Dear mother Ida, harken ere I die.
For ñow the noonday quiet holds the hill :
25]   The grasshopper is silent in the grass :
The lizard, with his shadow on the stone,
Rests like a shadow, and the winds are dead.
The purple flower droops : the golden bee
Is lily-cradled : I alone awake.
30]   My eyes are full of tears, my heart of love,
My heart is breaking, and my eyes are dim,
And I am all aweary of my life.

11 *1883* (Univ. Lib. Cam., XIX.54.127, pp. 197–8; ×0·92)

1, the holograph draft which is the earliest surviving version of 'Œnone', shows that the main structural elements of the poem—the introductory scene-setting followed by Œnone's first-person narrative, the 'mother Ida' refrain, the romantic landscape, and the classical references—were all decided at an early stage. This manuscript was a working draft which Tennyson continued to alter, changing a phrase in line 6 and cancelling line 14 (with a consequent alteration in line 15). The last five lines had already reached their final form and were not afterwards altered.

2, Allen's transcript, is textually close to **1**, but was not copied directly from it. 'Ilion' (line 13) has been changed to 'Troas', and 'rock' (line 24/23) to 'stone', both alterations becoming permanent parts of the text. The punctuation appears to be Allen's, not Tennyson's.

3, the first published version, is considerably altered from **1** and **2**, perhaps in the missing printer's copy and author's proof. Most of the changes are in the scene-setting of lines 3–13; line 23 is new. In line 12 Tennyson changed the rhythm of the word 'Ilion' (he was later to change it back again); and he added a footnote about the cicala of lines 24–5.

4, the corrected copy of *1833* which Tennyson gave to J. M. Heath between 1833 and 1837, shows the poet's early dissatisfaction with the first published version. But though many alterations were proposed here, they were less thorough-going than what was to come in the later drafts. Here Tennyson tinkered with the scenery at the beginning, and rewrote the cicala passage (which continued to trouble him to the last); the footnote was deleted.[13]

5–9, the five successive holograph drafts in the Trinity notebook of *c.* 1837–42, show Tennyson's steady progress towards the second published version of 1842. Their arrangement is at first confusing, because after writing **8** he returned to **6** to try out some further alterations, which were then incorporated in **9**. His meticulous search for the perfect balance of tone and rhythm can be followed in detail. Sometimes he tried out a new line and then discarded it again for the original one (as for instance in the development of what became lines 19–21 in *1842*). Gargarus appeared in **6** and was retained; Scamander and Simoïs were added in **7** and **5** but were dropped in the reworking of **6**. Various epithets were tried out for the noise the sleeping cicala made when it was awake: it was garrulous (from **4**), it

---

[13] An incomplete copy of *1833* annotated by Tennyson has recently been found amongst uncatalogued material at the Tennyson Research Centre at Lincoln which contains the version of 'Œnone' sent to Heath, but at a slightly earlier stage of revision. The alterations made by Tennyson to the extract in this Lincoln copy of *1833* were the same as those made for **4**, except that he first revised lines 2 and 3 to read:

> Than any dale in old Ionia,
> With slanting lawns of sunny sward, that lean

(Information from Susan Shatto.)

stunned, and shrilled, and burst the brake; eventually it merely slept. The crucial rewording which converted the first two lines of *1833* to the much better opening of *1842* began in **8** and was completed in the reworking of **6**.

10, the second published version of 1842, is the triumphant outcome of the five preceding drafts. In general it follows **9**, but there were some notable changes, especially in the Gargarus and cicala passages, perhaps made in the printer's copy and author's proof. The sense of the poem is still essentially what it was from the beginning, but Tennyson has transformed it into a magical evocation of an ancient wrong by simplifying the words and strengthening the rhythms, so that the lines so laboriously achieved now seem simply inevitable. The reading 'flowers droop' in line 28 was, according to Tennyson's later note, a misprint for 'flower droops', the reading of **9**.[14]

11 is the final version of the extract in *1883*, in which the second half of line 27 was changed from 'and the cicala sleeps' to 'and the winds are dead'; and the 'misprint' in line 28 was corrected.[15] This text was reprinted without further alteration in the annotated Eversley edition of Tennyson's *Works*, 1907.

The annotations in the Eversley editions were collected by the poet's son Hallam Tennyson, who was its editor. Here are the notes which refer to 'Œnone' as a whole, and to particular points in the first thirty-two lines (see next page). Most of them are Tennyson's, but there are bracketed additions by Hallam Tennyson.

Thus the documentary evidence for the development of 'Œnone' is sufficiently clear and copious, as indeed it is for many of Tennyson's other major poems. The main problem for an editor of these poems is to decide how much of the mass of evidence he should try to present in an edition.

As is usually the case with printed poetry from the early eighteenth century onwards, there will seldom be any need for the editor to correct the published texts, for Tennyson has done it already. As we have seen, the *1842* text of 'Œnone' was the result of long and careful refinement; Tennyson took care with its spelling and punctuation;[16] and even when he came to revise it more than forty years later he made only one substantial alteration to the extract.[17]

---

[14] Was it really a misprint? The reading of **5** was 'flowers droop'.

[15] There was also a purely typographical change (which first appeared in the Crown edition of 1878) from double to single inverted commas in line 22.

[16] 'Never since Milton has a poet been so fastidiously scrupulous about the minutiae of expression and language, . . . about spelling, . . . about the use of small or capital letters, about punctuation. . . . These editions teem with variants, and so restlessly, one might almost say morbidly, indefatigable was Tennyson in correction, that till an edition, even though there be no indication on the title page that it is anything more than a reprint, is inspected, there is no security that the text has not been altered.' (J. Churton Collins's edition of *In Memoriam, The Princess, and Maud*, 1902, pp. v–vi.)

[17] In line 27.

ŒNONE. Married to Paris, and afterwards deserted by him for Helen. The sequel of the tale is poorly given in Quintus Calaber.

[See *The Death of Œnone*, vol. ix, p. 288. My father visited the Pyrenees with Arthur Hallam in 1830. From this time forward the lonely Pyrenean peaks, the mountains with "their streaks of virgin snow," like the Maladetta, mountain "lawns and meadow-ledges midway down," and the "long brook falling thro' the clov'n ravine," were a continual source of inspiration. He wrote part of *Œnone* in the valley of Cauteretz. His sojourn there was also commemorated one-and-thirty years afterward in "All along the valley." *Œnone* was first published in 1832, but was republished in 1842 with considerable alterations.—ED.]

I had an idiotic hatred of hyphens in those days, but though I printed such words as "glénríver," "téndriltwíne" I always gave them in reading their full two accents. Coleridge thought because of these hyphened words that I could not scan. He said that I ought to write in a regular metre in order that I might learn what metre was—not knowing that in earliest youth I had written hundreds of lines in the regular Popian measure. I remember my father (who was himself something of a poet and wrote very regular metre) saying to me when in my early teens, "Don't write always such exact metre—break it now and then to avoid monotony." . . .

line 1. *Ida*. On the south of Troas.

line 10. *Gargara* or *Gargaron*. The highest part of Mt. Ida.

> Ipsa suas mirantur Gargara messes.
>
> *Georg*. i. 103.

line 16. *Paris, once her playmate on the hills*. [See Apollodorus, iii. 12, etc.—ED.]

lines 22, 23. This sort of refrain:

> *O mother Ida, many-fountain'd Ida,*
> *Dear mother Ida, harken ere I die*

is found in Theocritus. For "many-fountain'd" cf. *Il*. viii. 47:

> Ἴδην δ' ἵκανε πολυπίδακα, μητέρα θηρῶν

and elsewhere in the *Iliad*.

line 24.

> *For now the noonday quiet holds the hill.*
>
> μεσαμβρινὴ δ' εἶχ' ὄρος ἡσυχία.
>
> Callimachus, *Lavacrum Palladis*, 72.

line 27. *and the winds are dead*. Altered from the original reading of 1842, "and the cicala sleeps." In these lines describing a perfect stillness, I did not like the jump, "Rests like a shadow—and the cicala sleeps." Moreover, in the heat of noon the cicala is generally at its loudest, though I have read that, in extreme heat, it is silent. Some one (I forget who) found them silent at noon on the slopes of Etna.

In the Pyrenees, where part of this poem was written, I saw a very beautiful species of cicala, which had scarlet wings spotted with black. Probably nothing of the kind exists in Mount Ida.

line 28. *flower droops*. "Flowers droop" in the original edition of 1842 was a misprint for "flower droops."

line 30.

> *My eyes are full of tears, my heart of love.*

This line, that any child might have written, is not, as some writers say, taken from Shakespeare:

"Mine eyes are full of tears, my heart of grief."
                  2 Henry VI. II. iii. 17.[18]

[18] The Eversley edition of Tennyson's *Works*, i (London 1907), pp. 358–61.

There can be no doubt that the *1883* text of 'Œnone' precisely represents the author's final intentions.

A plain-text edition of Tennyson's poems, therefore, would simply reprint without alteration or normalization the final published versions that were revised, corrected, and authorized by Tennyson (unless there was reason in a particular case to prefer another version).

However, the earlier published versions of the more considerable of Tennyson's poems are often of great interest: they illustrate the development of his art, and they are what his original audience read. Thus the editor of something fuller than a plain-text Tennyson might decide as a next stage to give the variants from the earlier published versions as footnotes, or to print the earlier and later versions in parallel. For 'Œnone' this would mean printing *1842* or *1883* and giving the *1833* variants.

Where Tennyson actually published substantially different versions of his poems (as was the case for many of the poems that appeared both in *1833* and in *1842*) such a comparison will satisfy most students, and a good many Tennyson specialists as well. It is the published versions of these poems that matter as works of art and as documents of their time, and the variation between them tells us about the development of Tennyson's powers; the manuscript drafts are working sketches, means towards poetic ends, and it is perhaps unnecessary to publish all of the two pre-*1833* and six pre-*1842* drafts of 'Œnone'. The interest of these drafts can be adequately conveyed to most students of Tennyson by means of extracts, while those few specialists who need access to all of them will have no difficulty in obtaining microfilms.

But manuscript drafts also survive for a larger group of Tennyson's poems that were published in what were substantially single versions, sometimes with minor variation in later editions. Here the editor will probably want to print some of them for a wider audience, for these drafts are usually the only evidence we have of a poem's development, and they can be of great importance to the understanding of Tennyson's art. 'One day there will be an edition of Tennyson which records all MS variants', wrote Christopher Ricks; and added 'in ten large volumes?'[19] He may be right. If so the result will be both forbidding and costly, and we are lucky meanwhile to have his own scholarly yet attractive edition of Tennyson's poems, which includes all the printed variants and many variant manuscript readings as well.

This is the great edition of the *Poems* which appeared as one of Longman's Annotated English Poets in 1969. It is an astonishing *tour de force*, giving a good clear text, learned yet immediately useful headnotes to each poem, and a sensible selection of explanatory footnotes. The variants are mostly

[19] Tennyson, A., *Poems*, ed. Ricks, C., London 1969, p. xviii.

from the early published versions, although manuscript variants are given as well if it seemed worth it.

Here is Ricks's version of the first thirty-two lines of 'Œnone', together with his headnote to the whole poem:

---

164 Œnone

Published *1832*, much revised for *1842*. The changes are well discussed by P. F. Baum (*Tennyson Sixty Years After*, 1948, pp. 75–82). T. began such changes soon after *1832*, as is clear from the copy presented to J. M. Heath (*Fitzwilliam Museum*), which has various intermediate alterations in the opening lines and elsewhere. T. wrote to Spedding in 1835 of 'my old poems, most of which I have so corrected (particularly *Œnone*) as to make them much less imperfect' (*Mem.* i 145). It was written 1830–32; the scenery was suggested by the Pyrenees, where according to T. part of it was written, summer 1830. T.'s note observes that Œnone was 'married to Paris, and afterwards deserted by him for Helen. The sequel of the tale is poorly given in Quintus Calaber' (which T. was to adapt in *The Death of Œnone*, p. 1427). The sources and classical allusions – in particular Ovid's *Heroides* and Theocritus – have been comprehensively discussed by P. Turner *JEGP* lxi (1962) 57–72), who subsumes previous commentators and on whom the following notes draw extensively. D. Bush (*Mythology and the Romantic Tradition*, 1937, p. 204) describes the poem as an epyllion, or minor epic, in the manner of Theocritus. Some variants are selected from *Huntington MS* (HM 19501), ll. 54–124. The early version in *T.Nbk 23* (1830; it may not be quoted) is much briefer, and omits e.g. ll. 52–84. T. says: 'I had an idiotic hatred of hyphens in those days, but though I printed such words as "glénríver," "téndriltwine" I always gave them in reading their full two accents. Coleridge thought because of these hyphened words that I could not scan.'

There lies a vale in Ida, lovelier
Than all the valleys of Ionian hills.
The swimming vapour slopes athwart the glen,
Puts forth an arm, and creeps from pine to pine,
5   And loiters, slowly drawn. On either hand
The lawns and meadow-ledges midway down
Hang rich in flowers, and far below them roars
The long brook falling through the cloven ravine
In cataract after cataract to the sea.
10 Behind the valley topmost Gargarus
Stands up and takes the morning: but in front
The gorges, opening wide apart, reveal
Troas and Ilion's columned citadel,
The crown of Troas.
                    Hither came at noon
15 Mournful Œnone, wandering forlorn
Of Paris, once her playmate on the hills.
Her cheek had lost the rose, and round her neck
Floated her hair or seemed to float in rest.
She, leaning on a fragment twined with vine,
20 Sang to the stillness, till the mountain-shade
Sloped downward to her seat from the upper cliff.

'O mother Ida, many-fountained Ida,
Dear mother Ida, harken ere I die.
For now the noonday quiet holds the hill:
25 The grasshopper is silent in the grass:
The lizard, with his shadow on the stone,
Rests like a shadow, and the winds are dead.
The purple flower droops: the golden bee
Is lily-cradled: I alone awake.
30 My eyes are full of tears, my heart of love,
My heart is breaking, and my eyes are dim,
And I am all aweary of my life.

¶ 164.1–14] *1842*;   There is a dale in Ida, lovelier
                            Than any in old Ionia, beautiful
                            With emerald slopes of sunny sward, that lean
                            Above the loud glenriver, which hath worn
                            A path through steepdown granite walls below
                            Mantled with flowering tendriltwine. In front
                            The cedarshadowy valleys open wide.
                            Far-seen, high over all the Godbuilt wall
                            And many a snowycolumned range divine,
                            Mounted with awful sculptures – men and Gods,
                            The work of Gods – bright on the darkblue sky
                            The windy citadel of Ilion
                            Shone, like the crown of Troas. Hither came *1832*
1. *Ida*: the mountain on the south of the Troas. Paris describes the scene of the Judgment: *Est locus in mediis nemorosae vallibus Idae* … (Ovid, *Heroides* xvi 53–8). T.'s opening paragraphs follow the pastoral love-lament: hopeless lover, loved one, setting.
10. *Gargarus*: 'the highest part of Mount Ida'; T. compares Virgil's *Georgics* i 103: *Ipsa suas mirantur Gargara messes*.
16–17] *1842*; … playmate. Round her neck, / Her neck all marblewhite and marblecold, *1832*.   *forlorn of*: Spenserian and Miltonic.
17–18. P. Turner suggests that this associates Œnone ominously with Cassandra: *diffusis comis* (*Heroides* v 114); and with Dido: *aut videt aut vidisse putat* (*Aeneid* vi 454).
19. *fragment . . . vine*] *1842*; vine-entwinèd stone *1832*.
20. *-shade*] *1842*; -shadow *1832*.
20–1. As in Virgil's *Eclogues* i 83: *maioresque cadunt altis de montibus umbrae*.
22. T. remarks that 'this sort of refrain is found in Theocritus'.   *mother*: because of Theocritus ix 15; in the source of 'many-fountained' (*Iliad* xiv 283), Ida is 'mother of wild beasts'; hence the pard and panther later. *ere I die*: a traditional feature of the pastoral love-poem.
24] *1842*; not *1832*. In Eversley, T. quotes Callimachus, *Lavacrum Palladis* 72: μεσαμβρινὴ δ'εἶχ' ὅρος ἡσυχία ('and noontide quiet held all the hill'). And yet when John Churton Collins originally suggested this, T. wrote in the margin: 'not known to me' (*Cornhill*, Jan. 1880, *Lincoln*).
25–9. Based on Virgil's *Eclogues* ii 8–13, where *cicadis* suggested the cicala of *1832*. The antithesis, *rests/awake*, is from Theocritus iii 38–9; and the lizard, from vii 21–3. Alongside John Churton Collins's suggestion of Theocritus, T. wrote: 'from nature in the south of France' (*Cornhill*, Jan. 1880, *Lincoln*).
27] *1883*;   Sleeps like a shadow, and the scarletwinged
                   Cicala in the noonday leapeth not
                   Along the water-rounded granite-rock. *1832*;
Rests like a shadow, and the cicala sleeps *1842–82*. T. says: 'In these lines describing a perfect stillness, I did not like the jump, "Rests like a shadow – and the cicala sleeps". Moreover, in the heat of noon the cicala is generally at its loudest, though I have read that, in extreme heat, it is silent. Some one (I forget who) found them silent at noon on the slopes of Etna.' *1832* note: 'In the Pyrenees, where part of this poem was written, I saw a very beautiful species of Cicala, which had scarlet wings spotted with black. Probably nothing of the kind exists in Mount Ida.' T. emended J. M. Heath's copy of *1832* (*Fitzwilliam Museum*) to:
                   . . . and the garrulous
                   Cicala ceaseth now to burst the brake
                   With thick dry clamour chafed from griding wings.
28. *flower droops*] *1832*, *1883*; flowers droop *1842–82* ('*misprint*', T.).
30. T. denied the influence of *2 Henry VI* II iii 17: 'Mine eyes are full of tears, my heart of grief'.

Tennyson, *Works*, ed. Ricks, C. (London 1969), pp. 384–7 (×0·65)

Inevitably in so enormous a work—it runs to 1,870 close-packed pages—there are details which another editor might have handled differently. It is regrettable, for instance, that Ricks followed the convention of the Longman series and normalized some of Tennyson's spellings (including spellings in quotations from the manuscripts), an unfortunate and unnecessary interference with textual details to which the poet had given careful thought. Also unfortunate—though in no way Ricks's fault—was the fact that the Trinity manuscripts were not allowed to be copied at the time when his edition was being prepared.[20]

Taken as a whole, however, the scale and success of Ricks's Tennyson must command awed respect. His edition is excellent; and its excellence is the most telling argument against the need for anything more elaborate.

---

[20] Ricks says in his Preface that the Trinity manuscripts were presented to the College 'in 1924, by Hallam Tennyson, on conditions which the college interprets as forbidding copying or quotation in perpetuity' (p. xix); and goes on to imply criticism of the College for not meeting the wishes of the poet's descendants and lifting the restrictions. But in fact the conditions on which the College had accepted the manuscripts in 1924 were unambiguous: they clearly forbade copying or quotation in perpetuity, and there is no other way of interpreting them. The only thing that the College authorities could do about it was to repudiate the conditions and allow copying and quotation in spite of them; which, after long and painful debate, they did in 1969—too late, alas, for Ricks.

EXAMPLE 7

Dickens, *David Copperfield*, 1850

MUCH editorial effort has been directed since the mid 1960s towards the work of the major English and American novelists of the nineteenth century, most of it in America under the sponsorship of the Center for Editions of American Authors; here in Britain the Clarendon editions of Dickens and the Brontës are in progress, and there is to be a Cambridge critical edition of Lawrence. Various theoretical and practical problems have arisen in the course of all this work but, although they have been widely discussed, they have not yet been solved to everyone's satisfaction.[1] This example and the three that follow it are designed to illustrate some of these problems; and we start with *David Copperfield*, a part-issue novel of the mid century.[2]

Most of Dickens's major novels were published in shilling Numbers on the last day of each month. *David Copperfield* was typical in being made up of 18 parts of 32 octavo pages, each totalling about 20,000 words, plus a final 'double' Number of 48 pages. There were also two plates included in each part—Dickens considered the illustrations to his novels important adjuncts to the text—and in addition a frontispiece and engraved title-page in the double Number.

Dickens wrote the book part by part, and was seldom more than a week or two ahead of the mid-month deadline. The task of filling each Number with the right number of words could seem Procrustean, while his practice of writing the novel during publication meant both that the beginning of the story could not be reconsidered in the light of its ending, and that publication might be interrupted at any time by illness or accident. Yet for Dickens these disadvantages were outweighed by the value

[1] See Example 9, and the references given in p. 183 n. 1.

[2] The number of books and articles about Dickens is huge, but many of them are trivial. There is no comprehensive bibliography; the best biography is Edgar Johnson's *Dickens: his tragedy and triumph*, 2 vols., New York 1952. An edition of the *Letters* by M. House and G. Storey is in progress.

Serious work on the textual bibliography of Dickens began with Butt, J., and Tillotson, K., *Dickens at work*, London 1957, a pioneering study that has been supplemented by the introductions to the successive volumes of the Clarendon Dickens: *Oliver Twist* (ed. Tillotson, K., 1966); *The mystery of Edwin Drood* (ed. Cardwell, M., 1972); and *Dombey and Son* (ed. Horsman, A., 1974).

The editor of the forthcoming Clarendon *David Copperfield* is Miss Nina Burgis, to whom I am again most grateful for help and advice.

of the mutual relationship that developed with his readers as each part appeared, whereby their reactions influenced and encouraged him as the tale unfolded.

Dickens prefaced the manuscript of each part of *David Copperfield* with a 'Number plan', a combined synopsis and notesheet which was normally started before the Number was written and was then added to during and after the main work of composition. There was only one manuscript draft, which was written out on sheets of post quarto writing paper[3]—Dickens called them 'slips'[4]—at the normal rate of two or three sheets a day; and about thirty sheets of this manuscript were required to fill the thirty-two printed pages of the monthly Number. Dickens wrote a small, neat, and fairly legible hand, but he impaired both the appearance and the legibility of his manuscripts by revising each sentence as he went along, often blotting out whole phrases and adding replacements in a tiny script in the narrow spaces between the lines. He also went back afterwards to make further changes.

Difficult as it was to read, Dickens intended this first and last draft to be a precise instruction to the compositors who were to set it in type. The exact position for each interlinear correction was marked with a caret, punctuation and paragraphing was provided, and there were few mistakes or ambiguities (other than those caused by the cramped script of the interlineations).

Dickens usually got the manuscript of each number finished by the twentieth of the month, and sent it without further editing to Bradbury and Evans, who both printed and published the book. Here the compositors, skilled men experienced in Dickens's manuscripts, would take a leaf apiece for setting in type; or sometimes even half a leaf, cutting the whole leaf across the middle so that two of them could set it simultaneously.[5] The compositors transcribed this difficult copy with great accuracy, normalizing the details in the usual way; but its sheer illegibility did sometimes lead to verbal errors. Indeed it is curious that Dickens, who must have been aware of some of these mistakes and of the reason for them, did not think it worth

---

[2] They measured about 22·5 × 18·75 cm

[4] This can be confusing since type in long galleys might be proofed on pieces of paper which were called 'slips', whence the term 'slip proof' as a synonym for 'galley proof'.

[5] In the extract from the manuscript of *David Copperfield* which is reproduced below (pp. 148-9) it can be seen that leaf '9' was cut across between lines 19 and 20, the reference '9*' being written at the end of line 20 to show where the lower half of the leaf belonged when the manuscript was reassembled for proof-reading. As a rule the leaves of this manuscript were divided between paragraphs so that the type set by the two compositors could easily be fitted together. Here, however, the cut came in the middle of a sentence, and it may be that in this case it was not made until the compositor who started setting the leaf had got to the ends of lines a19/b26, which happened to coincide. On the other hand it may be that the leaf was divided as usual in advance of setting by two compositors, and that a few lines of type were run over later to make their two stints match.

while to increase the legibility of his manuscripts by using a little more paper.[6]

The first Number of *David Copperfield* was set and proofed in galley, but the rest went directly into page.[7] Author's proofs, probably accompanied by the manuscript, were sent to Dickens; and there were also author's revises for at least some of the Numbers. The corrected pages were usually stereotyped straight away, and plates were used for printing both the individual parts and the single-volume issues that appeared from 1850; but occasional variation suggests that the type pages were used alongside plates for printing some of the individual parts. All these impressions of the original setting constituted the first edition (*1850*A).

A three-volume edition, meanwhile, had been set for Tauchnitz from corrected proofs of *1850*A sent to Leipzig for the purpose (*1850*B); and the work was set a third time for part-issue in America, Numbers I and II from proofs, the rest from the English parts (eleven parts published by John Wiley and nine by G. P. Putnam, New York 1849–50; *1850*C). Dickens did not make additional revisions specially for *1850*B or *1850*C.

There were then three London editions published by Chapman and Hall: the two-column Cheap Edition (*1858*), set from an impression of *1850*A; and two editions set from *1858*, the Library Edition (*1859*) and the Charles Dickens Edition (*1867*). It was claimed by the publishers that the texts of *1858* and *1859* were 'carefully revised' by the author, and a similar revision of *1867* was implied; but in each case the textual changes were few and trivial and, although Dickens may have made one or two alterations to these texts, it is clear that he himself did not revise them systematically.[8] There were a number of reprints from the plates of *1858*, *1859*, and *1867*. No later edition of *David Copperfield* has any independent textual authority.

---

[6] In fact as time went on Dickens's handwriting became smaller and more illegible; by the time he got to *Edwin Drood* he was down from 30 to 27 leaves of manuscript for a 32-page Number.

[7] On galley and page, see *NIB*, pp. 194–5; and above, p. 143 n. 4.

[8] On the Cheap, Library, and Charles Dickens editions, see the Clarendon Dickens *Oliver Twist* (see p. 142 n. 2), pp. xxviii–xxx, liii–liv; *Dombey and Son*, pp. vii, xxxvi–xxxviii.

The relationship of the first six editions was as follows:

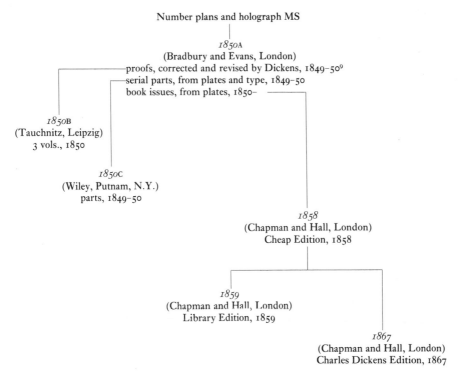

Number plans and holograph MS

*1850*A
(Bradbury and Evans, London)
proofs, corrected and revised by Dickens, 1849-50[9]
serial parts, from plates and type, 1849-50
book issues, from plates, 1850-

*1850*B
(Tauchnitz, Leipzig)
3 vols., 1850

*1850*C
(Wiley, Putnam, N.Y.)
parts, 1849-50

1858
(Chapman and Hall, London)
Cheap Edition, 1858

1859
(Chapman and Hall, London)
Library Edition, 1859

1867
(Chapman and Hall, London)
Charles Dickens Edition, 1867

The development of the text of *David Copperfield* was in no way abnormal. Dickens planned and wrote his manuscript month by month; the printer set it in type with a few transcription errors and a modest amount of normalization; Dickens corrected and revised the proofs with careful attention to their details but without reference to the manuscript; the book was published first in parts and then in volume form from the original setting of type; and there were five further settings of the novel in Dickens's lifetime which resulted in the usual deterioration of the text, and which were at most very scantily corrected by the author. While not all serial novelists cared for the risks and the excitements of keeping one jump ahead of the printer, Dickens's course in writing *David Copperfield* was otherwise a perfectly ordinary one, which was followed in its essentials by most of his fellow professionals.

The main editorial task, that of getting the words of the text right, is seldom a difficult one in the case of *David Copperfield*. We have the Number

---

[9] The set of proofs with Dickens's first corrections that was sent to Leipzig as copy for the Tauchnitz edition cannot have been the set marked by Dickens himself, but would have been a second set with his corrections transcribed on to it.

plans and the manuscript complete;[10] the author's proof and some of the author's revises;[11] and all the printed editions.[12] Collation reveals the variation between these texts, and usually the reason for it, so that emendation of verbal errors poses few problems. Difficulties can arise, however, where Dickens passed in proof compositors' alterations that were not obviously wrong; and where he did notice that there was a mistake in the proof but, failing to consult his manuscript, corrected it with a reading that differed from that of the original text.

Here to illustrate these points is an extract from the text of *David Copperfield*. It comes from Chapter 4 in Number II, in which David describes his miserable life with the Murdstones, and is given as it appears in the manuscript, the author's proofs, and the first edition (see pp. 148-51).

To consider first the verbal variants between these versions, there were four changes between the manuscript and the author's proof.

  (1) a6   there is
      b8   there's

Here the compositor has given Miss Murdstone a more colloquial, and perhaps a less menacing, turn of phrase. Dickens passed the alteration in proof, but it is very possible that he did not notice it, and the editor might decide to revert to the manuscript reading.

  (2) a15-16 My father had left in a little room upstairs to which I had access (for it adjoined my own) a small collection of books which nobody in our house ever troubled.

      b19-21   My father had left a small collection of books in a little room up stairs, to which I had access (for it adjoined my own) which nobody in our house ever troubled.

In this case the compositor understandably mistook the order of Dickens's interlineations, so that the proof text seems to say that it was the little room, not the collection of books, which nobody ever troubled. Dickens saw that something was wrong with the proof, and attempted to mend it by adding 'and' at the beginning of the final clause of the sentence, so that it referred unambiguously to the room, not the books; and he also added 'else' to the same clause, since David himself obviously went into the room. Thus the final form of the sentence in *1850*A was:

  c20-2   My father had left a small collection of books in a little room up-stairs, to which I had access (for it adjoined my own) and which nobody else in our house ever troubled.

Here the editor is in more of a quandary. The best reading is probably

---

[10] Victoria and Albert Museum MS. Forster 47.A.23-6.
[11] Victoria and Albert Museum MS. Forster 48.B.14.   [12] See *NIB*, pp. 384-91.

that of the manuscript, for it makes more sense to suppose that it was the collection of books which nobody troubled than that it was the room in which they were kept. But Dickens authorized the altered version by tidying it up with corrections, and there is no way of being sure that he did not consciously prefer it. Personally I would print the manuscript text, but not without misgivings.

(3) a24 blameless
    b34 brainless

This is a transcription error caused by the compositor misreading a tiny, cramped interlinear alteration in the manuscript. Dickens, seeing that it was wrong, proof-corrected 'brainless' to 'harmless'. This was not the original reading, which Dickens is unlikely to have altered if it had not been wrongly set in type. Yet both words were written by Dickens, neither is notably better than the other in the context, and we do not know which of them he preferred.[13] It is suggested that one of them should be chosen for the edited text, not because it was Dickens's first thought or his last, but because the editor prefers it on critical grounds.

(4)   a30 dignity from
     b41-2 dignity, and from

The compositor seems to have mistaken the tail of a 'g' in the line above (in 'being', a29) for an ampersand following the interlinear 'dignity'. Dickens saw that the 'and' was an erroneous addition, and deleted it in proof; it stays out, of course.

Besides these four verbal variants between the manuscript and the author's proof, there was one verbal variant between a manuscript correction in the author's proof and the published text of *1850A*:

(5) b15 (correction): months,
    c16   months or more,

This addition strongly suggests that there was a further revised proof, now missing, between the surviving author's proof and the published *1850A*. If so, and if (as would seem likely) this was an author's revise, the addition was made by Dickens and would be accepted.

Next we can consider the problem of choosing the most satisfactory copy-text for an edition of *David Copperfield*; and it is soon apparent that there are only two possibilities to choose from: MS and *1850A*.[14] As our extract

(*continued on p.* 152)

---

[13] There is the possibility that, since 'brainless' is similar in form to 'blameless', it reminded Dickens of what he had originally written; and that, if so, 'harmless' was deliberately chosen in preference to 'blameless'.

[14] '*1850A*' refers to all the states of the first setting of *David Copperfield* in type before and after proof-correction, whether or not they now survive.

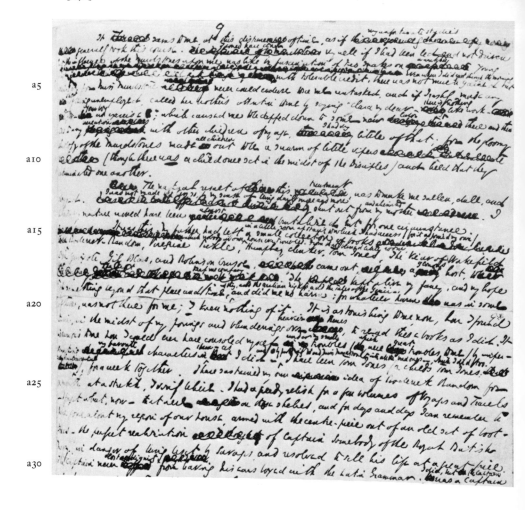

Dickens's MS (Victoria and Albert Museum MS. Forster 47.A.23, fo. 59ª; ×0·71)

[a1] It seems to me, at this distance of time, as if my unfortunate studies [a2] generally took this course. I could have done very well if I had been led and not driven [a3] but the influence of the Murdstones upon me was like the fascination of two snakes on a wretched young [a4] bird. Even when I did get through the morning with tolerable credit, there was not much gained but [a5] dinner, for Miss Murdstone never could endure to see me untasked, and if I rashly made any [a6] show of being unemployed, called her brother's attention to me by saying "Clara my dear—there is nothing like work—[a7] give your boy an exercise;" which caused me to be clapped down to some new labor there and then. [a8] As to any recreation with other children of my age, I had very little of that; for the gloomy [a9] theology of the Murdstones made all children out to be a swarm of little vipers [a10] (though there *was* a child once set in the midst of the Disciples) and held that they [a11] contaminated one another.

[a12] The natural result of this treatment, was to make me sullen, dull, and [a13] dogged. I was not made the less so, by my sense of being daily more and more shut out and alienated from my mother. I [a14] believe my nature would have been almost brutalized but for one circumstance.

[a15] It was this. My father had left in a little room upstairs to which I had access (for it adjoined my own) a small collection of books [a16] which nobody in our house ever troubled. From that blessed little room, Roderick Random, Peregrine Pickle, Humphrey Clinker, Tom Jones, The Vicar of Wakefield [a17] Don Quixote, Gil Blas, and Robinson Crusoe, came out, a glorious host, to [a18] keep me company. They kept alive my fancy, and my hope [a19] of something beyond that place and / time,—they, and the Arabian Nights, and the Tales of the Genii—, and did me no harm; for whatever harm was in some [a20] of them, was not there for me; *I* knew nothing of it. It is astonishing to me, now, how I found 9* [a21] time, in the midst of my porings and blunderings over heavier themes, to read these books as I did. It [a22] is curious to me how I could ever have consoled myself under my small troubles (which were great troubles to me) by imper-[a23]sonating my favorite characters in them—as I did—and by putting M^r and Miss Murdstone into all the bad ones— which I did too. I have been Tom Jones (a child's Tom Jones: [a24] a blameless creature), for a week together. I have sustained my own idea of Roderick Random for [a25] a month at a stretch, I verily believe. I had a greedy relish for a few volumes of Voyages and Travels [a26]—I forget what, now—that were on those shelves, and for days and days I can remember to [a27] have gone about my region of our house, armed with the centre-piece out of an old set of boot-[a28]trees—the perfect realization of Captain Somebody of the Royal British [a29] Navy, in danger of being beset by Savages, and resolved to sell his life at a great price. [a30] The Captain never lost dignity from having his ears boxed with the Latin Grammar. I did, but the Captain was a Captain

Transcript of p. 148, omitting deletions—which are mostly illegible—and with insertions placed in accordance with Dickens's indications

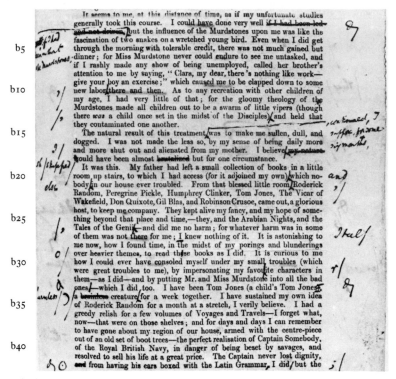

[150]

It seems to me, at this distance of time, as if my unfortunate studies generally took this course. I could have done very well if I had been led and not driven, but the influence of the Murdstones upon me was like the fascination of two snakes on a wretched young bird. Even when I did get through the morning with tolerable credit, there was not much gained but dinner; for Miss Murdstone never could endure to see me untasked, and if I rashly made any show of being unemployed, called her brother's attention to me by saying, " Clara, my dear, there's nothing like work— give your boy an exercise;" which caused me to be clapped down to some new labor there and then. As to any recreation with other children of my age, I had very little of that; for the gloomy theology of the Murdstones made all children out to be a swarm of little vipers (though there was a child once set in the midst of the Disciples) and held that they contaminated one another.

The natural result of this treatment was to make me sullen, dull, and dogged. I was not made the less so, by my sense of being daily more and more shut out and alienated from my mother. I believe my nature would have been almost bewildered but for one circumstance.

It was this. My father had left a small collection of books in a little room up stairs, to which I had access (for it adjoined my own) which nobody in our house ever troubled. From that blessed little room Roderick Random, Peregrine Pickle, Humphrey Clinker, Tom Jones, The Vicar of Wakefield, Don Quixote, Gil Blas, and Robinson Crusoe, came out, a glorious host, to keep me company. They kept alive my fancy, and my hope of something beyond that place and time,—they, and the Arabian Nights, and the Tales of the Genii—and did me no harm; for whatever harm was in some of them was not there for me; I knew nothing of it. It is astonishing to me now, how I found time, in the midst of my porings and blunderings over heavier themes, to read these books as I did. It is curious to me how I could ever have consoled myself under my small troubles (which were great troubles to me), by impersonating my favourite characters in them—as I did—and by putting Mr. and Miss Murdstone into all the bad ones—which I did, too. I have been Tom Jones (a child's Tom Jones, a blameless creature) for a week together. I have sustained my own idea of Roderick Random for a month at a stretch, I verily believe. I had a greedy relish for a few volumes of Voyages and Travels—I forget what, now—that were on those shelves; and for days and days I can remember to have gone about my region of our house, armed with the centre-piece out of an old set of boot trees—the perfect realisation of Captain Somebody, of the Royal British Navy, in danger of being beset by savages, and resolved to sell his life at a great price. The Captain never lost dignity, and from having his ears boxed with the Latin Grammar, I did; but the

Author's proof (Victoria and Albert Museum MS. Forster 48.B.14–14A, fol. 109^a; ×0·68)

Variants

	Manuscript		Author's proof
a2	driven	b3	driven,
a5	dinner,	b6	dinner;
a6	saying "Clara my dear—there is	b8	saying, "Clara, my dear, there's
a12	treatment	b15	treatment
a15-16	left in a little room upstairs to which I had access (for it adjoined my own) a small collection of books which	b19-20	left a small collection of books in a little room up stairs, to which I had access (for it adjoined my own) which
a16	room,	b21	room
a16	Wakefield	b23	Wakefield,
a19	Genii—,	b26	Genii—
a20	them,	b27	them
a20	*I*	b27	I
a20	me,	b28	me
a22	me)	b31	me),
a23	favorite	b31	favouite
a23	M^r	b32	Mr.
a23	ones—	b33	ones,—
a23-4	Jones: a blameless creature),	b33-4	Jones), a brainless creature
a26	shelves,	b37	shelves;
a27-8	boot-trees	b39	boot trees
a28	realization	b39	realisation
a28	Somebody	b39	Somebody,
a29	Savages	b40	savages
a30	dignity from	b41-2	dignity, and from
a30	Grammar.	b42	Grammar,

It seems to me, at this distance of time, as if my unfortunate studies
generally took this course. I could have done very well if I had been without
the Murdstones; but the influence of the Murdstones upon me was like the
fascination of two snakes on a wretched young bird. Even when I did get
through the morning with tolerable credit, there was not much gained but
dinner; for Miss Murdstone never could endure to see me untasked, and
if I rashly made any show of being unemployed, called her brother's
attention to me by saying, "Clara, my dear, there 's nothing like work—
give your boy an exercise;" which caused me to be clapped down to some
new labor, there and then. As to any recreation with other children of
my age, I had very little of that; for the gloomy theology of the
Murdstones made all children out to be a swarm of little vipers (though
there *was* a child once set in the midst of the Disciples), and held that
they contaminated one another.

The natural result of this treatment, continued, I suppose, for some six
months or more, was to make me sullen, dull, and dogged. I was not
made the less so, by my sense of being daily more and more shut out and
alienated from my mother. I believe I should have been almost stupified
but for one circumstance.

It was this. My father had left a small collection of books in a little room
up-stairs, to which I had access (for it adjoined my own) and which nobody
else in our house ever troubled. From that blessed little room, Roderick
Random, Peregrine Pickle, Humphrey Clinker, Tom Jones, The Vicar of
Wakefield, Don Quixote, Gil Blas, and Robinson Crusoe, came out, a glorious
host, to keep me company. They kept alive my fancy, and my hope of something beyond that place and time,—they, and the Arabian Nights, and the
Tales of the Genii,—and did me no harm; for whatever harm was in some
of them was not there for me; *I* knew nothing of it. It is astonishing to
me now, how I found time, in the midst of my porings and blunderings
over heavier themes, to read those books as I did. It is curious to me
how I could ever have consoled myself under my small troubles (which
were great troubles to me), by impersonating my favorite characters in
them—as I did—and by putting Mr. and Miss Murdstone into all the bad
ones—which I did too. I have been Tom Jones (a child's Tom Jones,
a harmless creature) for a week together. I have sustained my own idea
of Roderick Random for a month at a stretch, I verily believe. I had a
greedy relish for a few volumes of Voyages and Travels—I forget what,
now—that were on those shelves; and for days and days I can remember
to have gone about my region of our house, armed with the centre-piece
out of an old set of boot-trees—the perfect realisation of Captain Somebody,
of the Royal British Navy, in danger of being beset by savages, and
resolved to sell his life at a great price. The Captain never lost dignity,
from having his ears boxed with the Latin Grammar. I did; but the

1850A (Cambridge Univ. Lib. CCC.14.2, p. 41; a copy bound from parts; ×0·68)

Variants (other than those marked as proof corrections)

	Author's proof		1850A
b15	[correction] months,	c16	months or more,
b20	up stairs	c21	up-stairs
b31	[correction] favourite	c32	favorite
b39	boot trees	c40	boot-trees

indicates, Dickens's manuscript was not always easy to read, but it was nevertheless carefully written, meticulously amended, and for most part adequately punctuated. Provided that his later corrections and revisions are taken into account it offers a usable basis for an edited text. Likewise *1850*A, the first-edition text, was carefully transcribed and lightly normalized by the printers, and was then considered in detail by Dickens and further amended. Provided that the variants in the manuscript and proofs are taken into account, it too offers a usable basis for an edited text. The later editions from *1850*B onwards have no independent authority; they are no more than degraded derivatives of *1850*A, and should not be used as the basis for an edition.

In practice the choice between these two potential copy-texts is between their two sets of details (punctuation, spelling, etc.), because editorial emendation should result in the words of the edited text being the same whichever is chosen. Since both the potential copy-texts are satisfactory representations of the work as a whole—there was only one main text of the novel—and since both of them have sets of details that could be used in an edited text, the editor goes on to ask whether either of the two sets of details can be said to come closer than the other to fulfilling Dickens's own intentions for the novel? And which of them would be preferred by users of the edition for critical or other reasons?

It is clear that Dickens's first intentions for the details of the text of *David Copperfield* are represented by those of the manuscript. But although he must have known from experience that his details would be altered by the compositors, he did not prevent these alterations from being carried out—as he surely could have done if he had made his wishes known in advance—but accepted and refined them, and passed them for publication; so that his final intentions for the published text are represented by *1850*A.[15] Nevertheless it may be supposed that, if the compositors of *1850*A had (however uncharacteristically) copied the details of the manuscript without normalization, Dickens would have accepted the result, and that the manuscript details, not the normalized ones, would have entered the finally intended text. They would not have entered it without correction and most probably revision, however; and, since we cannot know how Dickens would have altered them in proof, it is not easy to say that the manuscript details as they stand are closer to his final intentions for the text than the details of *1850*A which he actually passed for publication.

[15] Strictly speaking by the final author's proof of *1850*A with his corrections. However, this author's revise, although it did exist, has now mostly disappeared, and Dickens's final intentions for the published text would appear to be better represented by the published version of *1850*A itself than by the first author's proof (which does survive).

This leaves the question of whether the readers of a critical edition of
David Copperfield today would prefer to have a text with its details based
on those of Dickens's own manuscript, speculatively emended by the editor;
or whether they would prefer to have the version that was read by Dickens's
original audiences, with its details based on the compositors' normalization
of the manuscript, emended by Dickens. The reasons for preferring one or
the other will usually be critical (though they are occasionally historical or
even reverential); in any case no rule or rationale is going to give the answer.[16]
The editor has to decide for himself and, whichever copy-text he chooses,
he is not going to please everybody.

On the other hand nobody should be seriously displeased by his choice,
for the variants that are governed by the choice of copy-text are of small
importance here. In our extract of 43 printed lines there are only 15 details
which might be changed as a result of editing it from one copy-text rather
than from the other. There might be 11 changes of punctuation, 2 of spelling,
1 of capitalization, and 1 of contraction. None of them would affect the meaning or the tone of Dickens's story in more than a trivial way; and of course if
the editor were worried about the effect of any of them he could emend it.

These are the possible changes:[17]

MS line/ 1850A line	MS copy-text	1850A copy-text
a5/c6	dinner,	dinner;
a6/c8	saying "Clara my dear—	saying, "Clara, my dear,
a15/c21	upstairs to	up-stairs, to
a20/c28	them, was	them was
a20/c29	me, now	me now
a22/c32	me)	me),
a23/c33	M^r	Mr.
a26/c38	shelves,	shelves;
a28/c40	realization	realisation
a28/c40	Somebody	Somebody,
a28/c41	Savages	savages
a30/c42-3	dignity from	dignity, from

[16] G. T. Tanselle argues (*Studies in the novel*, vii, 1975, pp. 344–50) that the editors of the first three
volumes of the Clarendon Dickens should have chosen manuscript copy-texts in accordance with
Greg's 'Rationale of copy-text'. Actually Greg had nothing to say about the problems of editing
nineteenth-century novels: his 'Rationale' was concerned with the problems of editing Renaissance
works of which the authors' manuscripts have not survived and in the printing and reprinting of which
the authors took little part. (See also pp. 190–1 below.)

[17] This is not of course a list of all the variants between MS and *1850A*, but only of the differences
that would probably result from altering the choice of copy-text. In either case the editor will no doubt
incorporate in his final text the alterations made by Dickens himself (e.g. there is no comma after 'labor'
in MS line 7, but it was added by Dickens in proof); and will accept the compositor's emendations of
undoubted MS errors (e.g. the insertion of the missing comma after 'Wakefield' at the end of MS line 16).

The effect of these possible changes may be gauged by reading through the *1850A* text of the extract (p. 151) and imagining how it would seem if these details were introduced from the manuscript.

To see how *David Copperfield* might actually be edited we can turn to the first few volumes of the Clarendon Dickens.[18] *David Copperfield* has not yet appeared in the series, but *Dombey and Son* (to which *Copperfield* is textually similar) was published in Alan Horsman's edition in 1974.[19] *Dombey and Son* also appeared first in parts (1846-8), and later in the Cheap, Library, and Charles Dickens editions; and again we have the Number plans, the complete manuscript, and most of the author's proofs and revises.[20]

Horsman uses the first edition of *Dombey and Son* as copy-text, with verbal amendments from the manuscript. The normalized details of the printed text are allowed to stand; and the surviving inconsistencies of detail are largely regularized. The verbal variants between the manuscript and the printed versions are given as footnotes to the text, as are a number of passages cut from the proof by Dickens because the amount he had written would not fit into the 32-page parts. This record of variants does not normally cover non-verbal details, or obvious slips, or Dickens's deletions from the manuscript (which were mostly so heavily scored out as to be completely illegible). The editor's supplementary apparatus includes an introductory account of the composition of the novel; the texts of the preface to the later editions, of the Number plans, and of the descriptive headings added to the Charles Dickens Edition of 1867; and essays on the text prepared for Dickens's Readings, and on the illustrations. The illustrations themselves are all crisply reproduced, and there is a facsimile of the printed wrapper of one of the part issues.

The Clarendon *Dombey and Son* is (like its predecessors *Oliver Twist*, 1966, and *The mystery of Edwin Drood*, 1972) an estimable edition, providing much the most satisfactory version of the novel ever to have appeared. The verbal errors of the first edition and the corruptions of its successors are convincingly emended; the passages which Dickens deleted merely for lack of space are given as footnotes. The editorial and textual apparatus is learned, and attractively presented.

A few questions remain. The use of footnotes for recording textual variants is a distracting nuisance in the text of a novel—which ought above all to be readable—and it might have been better to present as footnotes only the passages cut from the proofs, and to remove the other variants to an appendix.

---

[18] See p. 142 n. 2. The editorial principles of the series are summarized in the preface to the Clarendon *Oliver Twist*, 1966.

[19] Dickens, C., *Dombey and Son*, ed. Horsman, A., Oxford 1974.

[20] The pre-publication documents are in the Forster collection at the Victoria and Albert Museum.

A relatively minor omission from the apparatus is that there is no register of the words hyphenated at the ends of the lines of the edition, to show how they should be given in quotation.

Horsman followed the practice of the series in taking the first edition as copy-text. This was no doubt the right choice—the manuscript would have required too much speculative emendation—but the case for it could have been more clearly made. Horsman also followed the practice of the series in regularizing the inconsistent spelling, capitalization, hyphenation, etc., of the copy-text. The Clarendon editors do not explain clearly why they believe that inconsistency of detail should be eliminated; it is simply taken for granted that inconsistency must be wrong.[21] It is true of course that editors and printers, in the nineteenth century as well as in the twentieth, commonly preferred regularity of detail in printed texts, but it is equally true that many authors, including Dickens, did not care about it one way or the other. Dickens, indeed, would even introduce inconsistency of punctuation or capitalization, especially for rhetorical reasons. When Forster was 'editing' Numbers I and II of *Dombey and Son* on Dickens's behalf, he

requests the printer, near the end of chapter vi, to 'Observe some consistency in these Sirs—Let them be uniformly small or caps', or near the beginning of chapter xxx asks, 'Had not this better be the usual spelling? Mary-le-bone?' The printer's query about a comma before a vocative—'Should there not be a comma here, and in like cases?'—is answered 'Yes' by Forster, though Dickens himself sometimes takes out such commas where they are in conflict with the way he hears a piece of conversation (and wishes it to be read).[22]

In cases such as this it would plainly be wrong for us to normalize Dickens's inconsistency of punctuation. But even where his inconsistency was apparently careless, there is much to be said for leaving it alone where it does not interfere with the meaning of the text. It was the way he wrote; why change it to satisfy the expectations of modern readers?

---

[21] This is not to suggest that the Clarendon editors believe in *normalizing* the details of the text; but they do seek consistency. Thus Alan Horsman comments on the spelling of *Dombey and Son*: 'Where 48 [the printed copy-text] shows variants like *parlor* and *parlour*, *shew* and *show*, the one which preponderates has been used. Dickens does not change spelling in proof, so that the inference is fair that he approved of the printer's attempts to regularize'; and on capitalization: 'It is not consistent in either MS or 48 and Dickens does not always accept, as he does with spelling, what is in the proof. Some of his decisions, either to leave the proof alone or not, give inconsistent results . . . here the predominant form in the MS must be restored throughout the text' (*Dombey and Son*, Clarendon edition, p. xli).

[22] *Dombey and Son*, Clarendon edition, p. xlvi.

EXAMPLE 8

Thackeray, *Henry Esmond*, 1852

THACKERAY began to write *Henry Esmond* in the late autumn of 1851, immediately after the emotional crisis of his break with Jane Brookfield—with whom he had been in love—and her husband; and it was finished and revised by the end of May 1852.[1] Hitherto Thackeray had been a dilatory author who did not give himself time to be meticulous, but now he was encouraged to publish in volume form, not in monthly parts, in order to increase his control over the work as a whole.[2] He worked hard at the background research, and he revised the greater part of the completed manuscript before it was set in type. On the other hand he was disinclined to recast what had once been written down. When a change in the direction of the story made an earlier passage anomalous he would often improvise a justification for the anomaly rather than go back and rectify it; and it seems to have been largely a first draft that went to the printer to be set in type.

The manuscript (which survives in the library of Trinity College, Cambridge)[3] is a patchwork affair, just over half of it being written out by Thackeray, and the rest by his daughter Anne and his secretary Eyre Crowe. It consisted of about 940 leaves of post octavo writing paper, some of them embossed with the emblems of the Athenaeum Club, etc. For the most part they were written on one side only, and all but the few leaves that are now missing are mounted in two large albums.

The three 'Books' of *Henry Esmond* are of approximately equal length. Thackeray himself wrote out 88 per cent of Book I, mostly using his neat upright hand, but occasionally changing to his sloping script; while, of the rest of the manuscript of the first Book, 7 per cent is in Anne Thackeray's

---

[1] For the background see G. N. Ray's biography *Thackeray: the uses of adversity, 1811-1846*, and *The age of wisdom, 1847-1863*, London 1955, 1958 (which largely supersedes Professor Ray's *The buried life*, Oxford 1952); and Thackeray's *Letters*, ed. Ray, G. N., 4 vols., Cambridge, Mass., 1945-6. There is no full bibliography.

Thackeray's working methods are investigated by J. A. Sutherland in *Thackeray at work*, London 1974; but it seems likely that new findings will emerge from the work now in progress in America on a critical edition of Thackeray's works, for which *Esmond* will be edited by Edgar F. Harden (see p. 177 n. 14). I am most grateful for Dr. Harden's advice about the problems of editing *Esmond*.

[2] The encouragement given to Thackeray by his publisher is described by J. A. Sutherland in *Victorian novelists and publishers*, London 1976, ch. 4.

[3] MS. O.17.21-2. It was given to the College in 1888 by Leslie Stephen, whose first wife was Thackeray's younger daughter.

large spiky writing, and 5 per cent in Eyre Crowe's fluent hand.[4] Thackeray left more of Books II and III to his amanuenses, writing out only 42 per cent and 38 per cent of them respectively. Anne Thackeray wrote 18 per cent of the manuscript of Book II and 2 per cent of that of Book III; while Eyre Crowe's contribution increased to 40 per cent of Book II and 60 per cent of Book III. In all, 57 per cent of the manuscript was written out by Thackeray, 34 per cent by Crowe, and 9 per cent by Anne Thackeray.

It would appear from numerous false starts that most of the passages written out by Anne Thackeray and Eyre Crowe were dictated to them by Thackeray (as indeed they later affirmed to have been the case);[5] but a few of their passages may have been copied from written drafts, and of course Thackeray may himself have been dictating to them from notes or earlier versions. In any case most of the manuscript appears to have been the first and only draft of the work.[6] Some substantial revisions were patched in, mostly in Book I, but there does not seem to have been much rewriting. Thackeray read over most of the manuscript, and made a number of inter-linear corrections, but obvious mistakes show that some passages were not even cursorily revised.

The detailed presentation of the manuscript text differed according to which of the three wrote it out. Thackeray's own punctuation was light and sporadic, and he seems deliberately to have left the compositors to make up its deficiencies (subject to his attention to the proofs); when writing dialogue, for instance, he would begin with an inverted comma, but would leave later speeches unmarked. He capitalized more heavily than printers of the period, but his spelling was largely conventional, and he paragraphed deliberately. He seems, moreover, to have had a clear idea of what the printed text would look like, specifying break lines and drop capitals.

The passages written out by Anne Thackeray were also well paragraphed, but her spelling was shaky and her punctuation negligible; while she often omitted to cross out a first attempt at a sentence when Thackeray changed his mind and began it again. It seems as if Anne took down her father's words with mechanical accuracy; and that he dictated the paragraphs to her but not the punctuation marks (or of course the spelling).

Eyre Crowe's passages are much the best presented of the three. They are well spelt and adequately punctuated, and the false starts are mostly crossed out; but, since it appears from Anne Thackeray's passages that Thackeray

---

[4] For the main handwritings, see pp. 160, 170, 174. The percentages are calculated not from the number of manuscript pages but from the number of words written by each of the three scribes.

[5] Leslie Stephen to Montague Butler, quoting Anne Thackeray, 13 Apr. 1888 (Trin. Coll. Cam. Add. MS. a.225[95]); Crowe, E., *With Thackeray in America*, London 1893, pp. 3–5.

[6] As Anne Thackeray said many years after the event (Trin. Coll. Cam. Add. MS. a.225[95]).

did not dictate the punctuation, the full punctuation of Crowe's passages is likely to be Crowe's, not Thackeray's.

This heterogeneous manuscript was turned into a strange-looking book. Instead of setting it in the normal typographical style of the mid-nineteenth century, the printing firm of Bradbury and Evans (who printed *Esmond* for Smith, Elder) acquired an eighteenth-century type-face, complete with long ſ, and produced three small, heavily leaded volumes of deliberately anachronistic appearance: the visual equivalent of Thackeray's pastiche eighteenth-century prose.[7] There were to be no illustrations.

Collation of the manuscript with the first edition shows a relatively small amount of verbal change between them other than the correction of the main muddles in the manuscript (mostly undeleted false starts), and the addition of chapter rubrics and of descriptive headlines to the recto pages; there was also wholesale revision and normalization of the punctuation, etc. The individual verbal changes and the additions were presumably made by Thackeray, but it seems likely that the muddles were rectified by the printer, and almost certain that the normalization was carried out by the compositors (whose names were written on the manuscript at the beginnings of their stints). The reason for supposing that the false starts, etc., were amended by the printer and not by Thackeray is that the printer marked on the manuscript the points at which each new sheet began, and that these marks were still in the right places for the beginnings of the sheets as they were finally printed. This suggests both that the type was originally set and proofed in page, not in galley; and that any amendment which disturbed more than a few words of the text was not made as a result of proof correction, but earlier on, when the type was first set.[8]

The first edition of *Esmond* was published in its three pastiche volumes at the end of October 1852 (*1852*). The Tauchnitz and New York editions (set from sheets of the London edition) were also dated 1852;[9] and there was a 'second' London edition dated 1853, reset in the style of the first with a few

---

[7] The type used was Caslon's Pica No. 2, originally cut in 1741-2, and probably recast in a small fount specially for this book. Eyre Crowe suggests that the speed at which the job went through was limited by the small supply of this type (*With Thackeray in America*, London 1893, p. 7). The same type was used for the second edition of *Esmond*, 1853.

[8] Since the main purpose of marking the manuscript with the sheet divisions was to enable the proof-reader to relate the page proof to the copy, there would have been no point in doing it if there had been intervening proofs in galley; while extensive alterations to the page proofs would have resulted in the shifting of the final sheet divisions.

There are sheet division marks at a41 (p. 162) and g30 (p. 174). Each of them marks the final sheet division, although the page number 97 at a41 was altered to 121 to accommodate the twenty-four pages of preface that were added during the setting of volume i.

[9] The Tauchnitz edition (Leipzig 1852) reprinted *1852* without much alteration or normalization; but the Harper edition (New York 1852) was heavily normalized to accord with the Harper house style.

minor revisions of the punctuation, etc., almost certainly unauthoritative.[10] The only other edition to appear in Thackeray's lifetime was the one-volume cheap edition of 1858 (*1858*), set from the second edition of 1853 but containing a few verbal alterations for which he may have been responsible, and in which he deleted a passage of twenty-six lines; there was also further normalization of excess commas, etc., some new copying errors, and the suppression of a number of page headings as the result of using smaller type and a fuller page.[11]

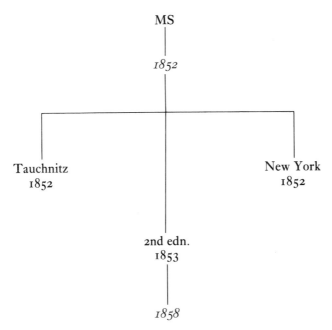

MS

1852

Tauchnitz   New York
1852   1852

2nd edn.
1853

1858

For a more detailed consideration of the text we will take extracts from the manuscript written by each of the three scribes, and follow their development in *1852* and *1858*; beginning with a passage written out by Thackeray himself at the start of Book I, Chapter VI, in which the soldiers come to search Castlewood.

---

[10] In the three extracts from the text examined in this chapter, which totalled 137 lines (just over five pages) of *1852*, the only variants introduced in 1853 were four changes of punctuation, all of which appear to be casual compositors' normalization. It is most unlikely that Thackeray revised the text for the second edition; he received copies of *1852* just as he was on the point of leaving London for America, and he was still in America when 1853 was published. (For three of the four changes see the captions to p. 167 and p. 173.)

[11] See the captions to p. 167, p. 173, and p. 176 (*1858*). The twenty-six lines were deleted from pp. 308-9 of vol. ii of *1852*. T. C. and W. Snow's edition of *Esmond* (2nd edn., Oxford 1915, p. 464) gives examples of verbal errors that entered the text in *1858*.

The morning after their departure the Countess herself announced to H. Esm
                                                    also
that she intended to make a journey — the Coach was ready & her trunks
packed and my lady was to set forth before noon — but she spent always
so much time before her looking glass that I do believe there was the real
reason why she was not ready to move much before noon. Half an hour
before this time however, Tob Lockwood came running from the village &
said that a lawyer three officers and twenty a form and twenty soldiers
were marching up there — and one of the officers and a half dozen of
the men went to ~~the~~ Dr. Tusher's: whilst the remainder came up to
Castlewood — ~~a couple~~

Her ladyship was dressed in a dark damask with a cloth coat
                                                              over
ready to go away, and the orders to the coachman had actually been
given, when this news was brought her.
                my lady
At first ~~she~~ was for flying like Mary Queen of Scots (whom she fancied
she bore a resemblance in beauty) and stroking her scraggy neck
said — they will that Isabel of Castlewood is equal to her fate. But her
            gentlewoman
~~waiting woman~~ ~~too~~ Victoire persuaded her that her best course was
                              was
~~to bide it~~; as she could not fly, to receive the troops as though she suspected
nothing, and that her chamber was the best place wherein to await them.
So her black Japan casket wh. Harry was to carry to the Coach was taken
back to her ladyships Chamber — whither the maid and mistress retired.
                        came out presently bedding
Victoire ~~before~~ ~~unfounded~~ the page ~~that~~ was to say her ladyship
was ill, confined to her bed with the rheumatism.
By this time the soldiers had reached Castlewood. H. Esmond saw them

Cap. VI   4̶8̶   58—1

The morning after their departure the Countess herself announced to H. Esm
　　　　　　　　　　　　　also
ond that she intended to make a journey—the coach was ready & her trunks
packed and my lady was to set forth before noon—but she spent always
so much time before her looking glass that I do believe this was the rea
a5　son why she was not ready to move much before noon. Half an hour
before this time however, Job Lockwood came running from the village &
said that a lawyer three officers and twenty or four and twenty soldiers
were marching up thence—and one of the officers and a half dozen of
the men went off to M̶r̶ D̶r̶ Tusher's: whilst the remainder came up to
a10　Castlewood.—a̶ ̶c̶o̶u̶p̶l̶e̶　　　　　　　　　　　　　over
　　Her ladyship was dressed in a dark damask with a cloth coat
ready to go away, and the orders to the coachman had actually been
given, when this news was brought to her
　　　　　　my lady　　　　　　　　　　　　King
　　At first s̶h̶e̶ was for dying like Mary Queen of Scots (to whom she fancied
a15　she bore a resemblance in beauty) and stroking her scraggy neck
said—'They will find Isabel of Castlewood is equal to her fate.' B̶u̶t̶ her
　　gentlewoman　　　　　　　　　　　prudent
w̶a̶i̶t̶i̶n̶g̶ ̶w̶o̶m̶a̶n̶ ̶I̶s̶a̶ Victoire persuaded her that her b̶e̶s̶t̶ course was
　　　　　　　　　　　　　　　was
t̶o̶ ̶b̶e̶ ̶i̶l̶l̶ as she could not fly, to receive the troops as though she suspected
nothing, and that her chamber was the best place wherein to await them.
a20　So her black Japan casket w̶h̶ Harry was to carry to the coach was taken
back to her ladyships chamber—whither the maid and mistress retired.
　　　　　　came out presently bidding
Victoire l̶e̶f̶t̶ ̶a̶n̶ ̶i̶n̶j̶u̶n̶c̶t̶i̶o̶n̶ ̶w̶i̶t̶h̶ the page t̶h̶a̶t̶ ̶h̶e̶ was t̶o̶ say her ladyship
was ill, confined to her bed with the rheumatism.
　　By this time the soldiers had reached Castlewood. H.Esmond saw them

Transcript of p. 160

from the window of the tapestry parlor – a couple of sentinels were
posted at the gate – ~~and who looked in~~ a half dozen more walked towards
the stable; and some others preceded by their commander and a man in
black a lawyer probably were ~~led~~ conducted by the one of the servants to the stair
leading up to the part of the house which my lord & lady inhabited.

The Captain a handsome kind man and the lawyer came to the anti
room, to the tapestry parlour, and where there was nobody but young H
Emmond the page – ~~Humbo~~

Tell your mistress, little man, says the Captain kindly that we must
speak to her.

My mistress is ill abed said the page.

What complaint has she? asked the Captain.

The boy said the rheumatism.

Rheumatism! that's a sad complaint continues the good natured
Captain – and the coach is in the yard to fetch the doctor, I suppose?

~~I don't~~ I don't know says the boy.

And how long has her ladyship been ill?

I don't know says the boy.

When did my lord go away? [Yesterday night.

With Father Holt? [With Mr. Holt.

And which way did they travel? asks the lawyer [They ~~left behind~~ travelled without me says the page.

I must see Lady Castlewood. I have orders that nobody goes in to her
ladyship – she is sick says the page – but at this moment Victoire came out.
Hush! says she and not knowing that any one was near – what's the
~~matter says she~~ Is this gentleman the doctor?

Stuff – we must see Lady Castlewood says the lawyer – pushing by.
The curtains of her ladyship's room were down; and the chamber dark

MS (Trin. Coll. Cam., MS. O.17.21, 58-2) Thackeray's hand (×1·0)

49   58—2

a25 from the window of the tapestry parlor—a couple of centinels were
posted at the gate—~~another looked li~~ a half dozen more walked towards
the stable; and some others preceded by their commander and a man in
                              conducted
black—a lawyer probably were ~~led~~ by ~~the~~ one of the servants to the stair
leading up to the part of the house which my lord & lady inhabited.
   So   through
a30   The Captain a handsome kind man and the lawyer came ~~to~~ the ante
room, to the tapestry parlour, and where now was nobody but young H
Esmond the page—~~that ha~~
    Tell your mistress, little man, says the Captain kindly that we must
speak to her.
a35   My mistress is ill abed said the page.
    What complaint has she ? asked the Captain.
    The boy said the rheumatism.
    Rheumatism ! thats a sad complaint continues the good natured
Captain—and the coach is in the yard to fetch the Doctor, I suppose ?
        I dont
a40   ~~How ca~~ know says the boy.
    | And how long has her ladyship been ill ?   97H
    I dont know says the boy.
    When did my lord go away ?   [Yesterday night.
    With Father Holt ?   [With Mr Holt.
            asks the lawyer   travelled without me
a45   And wh way did they travel ?   [They ~~left me behind~~ says the page.
    We must see Lady Castlewood. I have orders that nobody goes in to her
ladyship—she is sick says the page—but at this moment Victoire came out.
                              —and
Hush ! says she ‸ as if not knowing that any one was near—What's this
noise ? says she, Is this gentleman the Doctor ?
                                        lawyer
a50 Stuff—we must see Lady Castlewood says the ~~Captain~~—pushing by.
    The curtains of her ladyships room were down, and the chamber dark

Transcript of p. 162

and she was in bed with a night.head and propped up by her pillows looking ——— her ghastly because of the red w^c was still on her cheeks and w^c she could not afford to forego.

a55 !s that the Doctor? She said.

There is no use with —— deception Madam the Captain said —my duty is to

—— my duty Madam Captain Westbury (for so he was named) said is to arrest the person of Thomas Earl of Castlewood, a non-juring Peer — of Robert Tusher Vicar of Castlewood, and Henry Holt, known under various

a60 other names and ————, a Jesuit Priest who officiated as Chaplain here in the late King's time, and is now at the head of the conspiracy w^c was about to break out in this County against the authority of —— King William & Queen Mary — and my orders are to search the house for a65 papers —— conspiracy —— may be found here — your ladyship will please to give me your keys, and —— it will be as well for yourself that you should help us, in every way in our search —

MS (Trin. Coll. Cam., MS. O.17.21, 58-3, 58-4) Thackeray's hand (×1·0)

5̶0̶   58—3

and she was in bed with a night-head and propped up by her pillows
looking none the less ghastly because of the red w^h was still on her cheeks
and w^h she could not afford to forego.

a55   Is that the Doctor ? she said.

     There is no use wit⟨h this⟩ deception Madam the Captain said. My
duty is to

5̶1̶   58—4

    M̶y̶   -Westbury said

    My duty Madam Captain E̶a̶s̶t̶b̶u̶r̶y̶ (for so he was named) s̶a̶i̶d̶ is to
                         Viscount

arrest the person of Thomas E̶a̶r̶l̶ ̶o̶f̶ Castlewood, a non-juring Peer—of

a60 Robert Tusher Vicar of Castlewood, and Henry Holt, known under various
                   designations

other names and q̶u̶a̶l̶i̶t̶i̶e̶s̶, a Jesuit Priest who officiated as Chaplain

here in the late King's time, and is now at the head of the conspiracy w^h
                                      their Majesties

was about to break out in this county against the authority of o̶u̶r̶ ̶L̶o̶r̶d̶

King William & Queen Mary—and my orders are to search the house for

such   or traces of the   as   Your ladyship

a65 ˄ papers w̶^h̶ ̶v̶e̶r̶y̶ ̶l̶i̶k̶e̶l̶y̶ conspiracy w^h may be found here—Y̶o̶u̶ will please
to give me your keys, and t̶a̶ it will be as well for yourself that you
should help us, in every way in our search.

Transcript of p. 164

CHAPTER VI.

THE ISSUE OF THE PLOTS.—THE DEATH OF THOMAS, THIRD VISCOUNT OF CASTLEWOOD: AND THE IMPRISONMENT OF HIS VISCOUNTESS.

AT first my lady was for dying like Mary, Queen of Scots (to whom she fancied she bore a resemblance in beauty), and, stroking her scraggy neck, said, "They will find Isabel of b5 Castlewood is equal to her fate." Her gentlewoman, Victoire, persuaded her that her prudent course was, as she could not fly, to receive the troops as though she suspected nothing, and that her chamber was the best place wherein to await them. So b10 her black Japan casket which Harry was to carry to the coach was taken back to her ladyship's chamber, whither the maid and mistress retired. Victoire came out presently, bidding the page to say her ladyship was ill, confined to her bed b15 with the rheumatism.

By this time the soldiers had reached Castlewood. Harry Esmond saw them from the window of the tapestry parlour; a couple of sentinels were posted at the gate—a half-dozen b20 more walked towards the stable; and some others, preceded by their commander, and a man in black, a lawyer probably, were conducted by one of the servants to the stair leading up to the part of the house which my lord and lady b25 inhabited.

So the Captain, a handsome kind man, and the lawyer, came through the ante-room, to the tapestry parlour, and where now was nobody but young Harry Esmond, the page.

b30 "Tell your mistress, little man," says the Captain, kindly, "that we must speak to her."

"My mistress is ill a-bed," said the page.

"What complaint has she?" asked the Captain.

b35 The boy said "the rheumatism!"

"Rheumatism! that's a sad complaint," continues the good-natured Captain; "and the coach is in the yard to fetch the Doctor, I suppose?"

b40 "I don't know," says the boy.

"And how long has her ladyship been ill?"

"I don't know," says the boy.

"When did my lord go away?"

"Yesterday night."

b45 "With Father Holt?"

"With Mr. Holt."

"And which way did they travel?" asks the lawyer.

"They travelled without me," says the page.

b50 "We must see Lady Castlewood."

"I have orders that nobody goes in to her ladyship—she is sick," says the page; but at this moment Victoire came out. "Hush!" says she; and, as if not knowing that any one b55 was near, "What's this noise?" says she, "Is this gentleman the Doctor?"

"Stuff! we must see Lady Castlewood," says the lawyer pushing by.

The curtains of her ladyship's room were b60 down, and the chamber dark, and she was in bed with a night-cap on her head, and propped up by her pillows, looking none the less ghastly because of the red which was still on her cheeks, and which she could not afford to forego.

b65 "Is that the Doctor?" she said.

"There is no use with this deception, Madam," Captain Westbury said (for so he was named). "My duty is to arrest the person of Thomas, Viscount Castlewood, a non-juring peer b70 —of Robert Tusher, Vicar of Castlewood, and Henry Holt, known under various other names and designations, a Jesuit-priest, who officiated as chaplain here in the late king's time, and is now at the head of the conspiracy which was about to b75 break out in this country against the authority of their Majesties King William and Queen Mary— and my orders are to search the house for such papers or traces of the conspiracy as may be found here. Your ladyship will please to give me b80 your keys, and it will be as well for yourself that you should help us, in every way, in our search."

1852 (Thackeray, W. M., *Henry Esmond*, 3 vols., London 1852; i, pp. 119–22; Trin. Coll. Cam. G.13.41–3; ×0·55)

Verbal variants
  Manuscript

1852
  [chapter rubric added]

	Manuscript		1852
a18	fly, was to	b7	fly, to
a22	page was say	b13–14	page to say
a24	H.	b17	Harry
a31	H	b29	Harry
		b40/41	[page heading added (but not reproduced here)] *The soldiers at Castlewood.*
a52	night-head	b61	night-cap on her head,
a56–8	Madam the Captain said. My duty is to My duty Madam Captain Westbury said (for so he was named) is to	b67–8	Madam," Captain Westbury said (for so he was named). "My duty is to
a63	county	b75	country

CHAPTER VI.

THE ISSUE OF THE PLOTS.—THE DEATH OF THOMAS, THIRD VISCOUNT OF
CASTLEWOOD; AND THE IMPRISONMENT OF HIS VISCOUNTESS.

c5 AT first my lady was for dying like Mary, Queen of Scots (to
whom she fancied she bore a resemblance in beauty), and, stroking
her scraggy neck, said,"They will find Isabel of Castlewood is equal
to her fate." Her gentlewoman, Victoire, persuaded her that her
prudent course was, as she could not fly, to receive the troops as
though she suspected nothing, and that her chamber was the best
place wherein to await them. So her black Japan casket which
Harry was to carry to the coach was taken back to her ladyship's
chamber, whither the maid and mistress retired. Victoire came
c10 out presently, bidding the page to say her ladyship was ill, confined
to her bed with the rheumatism.

By this time the soldiers had reached Castlewood. Harry Esmond saw them from the window of the tapestry parlour; a couple
of sentinels were posted at the gate—a half-dozen more walked to-
c15 wards the stable; and some others, preceded by their commander,
and a man in black, a lawyer probably, were conducted by one of
the servants to the stair leading up to the part of the house which
my lord and lady inhabited.

So the Captain, a handsome kind man, and the lawyer, came
c20 through the anteroom to the tapestry parlour, and where now was
nobody but young Harry Esmond, the page.

"Tell your mistress, little man," says the Captain, kindly, "that
we must speak to her."

"My mistress is ill a-bed," said the page.
c25 "What complaint has she?" asked the Captain.

The boy said, "the rheumatism!"

"Rheumatism! that's a sad complaint," continues the good-
natured Captain; "and the coach is in the yard to fetch the
Doctor, I suppose?"

c30 "I don't know," says the boy.

"And how long has her ladyship been ill?"

"I don't know," says the boy.

"When did my lord go away?"

"Yesterday night."

c35 "With Father Holt?"

"With Mr. Holt."

"And which way did they travel?" asks the lawyer.

"They travelled without me," says the page.

"We must see Lady Castlewood."

c40 "I have orders that nobody goes in to her ladyship—she is sick,"
says the page; but at this moment Victoire came out. "Hush!"
says she; and, as if not knowing that any one was near, "What's
this noise?" says she, "Is this gentleman the Doctor?"

"Stuff! we must see Lady Castlewood," says the lawyer, push-
c45 ing by.

The curtains of her ladyship's room were down, and the chamber
dark, and she was in bed with a nightcap on her head, and propped
up by her pillows, looking none the less ghastly because of the red
which was still on her cheeks, and which she could not afford to
c50 forego.

"Is that the Doctor?" she said.

"There is no use with this deception, Madam," Captain Westbury
c55 said (for so he was named). "My duty is to arrest the person of
Thomas, Viscount Castlewood, a nonjuring peer—of Robert Tusher,
Vicar of Castlewood—and Henry Holt, known under various other
names and designations, a Jesuit Priest, who officiated as chaplain
here in the late king's time, and is now at the head of the conspiracy which was about to break out in this country against the authority of their Majesties King William and Queen Mary—and my
c60 orders are to search the house for such papers or traces of the conspiracy as may be found here. Your ladyship will please to give
me your keys, and it will be as well for yourself that you should
help us, in every way, in our search."

1858 (Thackeray, W. M., *Henry Esmond*, London 1858, pp. 46–8; Univ. Lib. Cam. LO.78.18; ×0·54)

Variants

		1852			*1858*
	rubric	CASTLEWOOD:		rubric	CASTLEWOOD;[12]
	b27	ante-room, to		c20	anteroom to
	b35	said "the		c26	said, "the[12]
	b58	lawyer pushing		c44	lawyer, pushing
	b61	night-cap		c47	nightcap
	b69	non-juring		c54	nonjuring
	b70	Castlewood, and		c55	Castlewood—and
	b72	Jesuit-priest		c56	Jesuit Priest

[12] These two variants first appeared in 1853, from which *1858* was set.

The manuscript of this first extract, which is in Thackeray's neat upright hand, is an illustration of the kind of problem that printers had to solve in the days before publishers' copy-editing. It begins with a false start of thirteen lines which Thackeray deleted, abbreviated, and placed at the end of the preceding chapter. The compositor, whose name was King, therefore began setting at a14, and it was almost certainly he who was responsible for normalizing the details of the text, and in particular for supplying what was virtually a new punctuation in place of the lean and frequently defective pointing of the manuscript. This new punctuation was so heavy that it may even have been intended as a pastiche of eighteenth-century pointing, to go with the pastiche prose style and the pastiche typography; and it may be noted in this connection that, when the details of the whole book were further normalized for the revised edition of 1858, the punctuation was on balance slightly reduced in weight, so that it conformed more closely to nineteenth-century usage.

Since the proofs have not survived, we cannot be sure who was responsible for the verbal variants between the manuscript and *1852* (see p. 166); but it is likely that the compositor or composing-room overseer dealt with the minor muddles in a18 and a22 of the manuscript, and perhaps also with the more serious confusion of a56–8; and expanded 'H' in a24 and a31. On the other hand only Thackeray could have corrected the composition (or copying) error 'night-head' (a52), and it would also have been Thackeray who supplied the chapter rubric and the heading for page 121 of *1852*. Finally 'country' (*1852*, b75) looks like a compositor's copying error for 'county' (MS, a63) which nobody spotted in proof.

No new verbal variants were introduced in the *1858* setting of this extract, but there were a few minor alterations of detail (see p. 167).

Next we can consider two shorter passages, dictated by Thackeray to Anne Thackeray and Eyre Crowe respectively (see pp. 169–76). The details of the passage written out by Anne Thackeray, which is from Book I, Chapter IV, are obviously different from those of Eyre Crowe's passage from Book III, Chapter VIII. As can be seen from the false starts (d32–3 and g26–7), both extracts were taken from dictation, but whereas Anne Thackeray's passage is virtually unpointed, Eyre Crowe supplied a careful punctuation, most of which was copied by the compositor. There were also differences of revision between the two passages. The false start taken down by Anne Thackeray was not deleted in the manuscript, and it would seem that Thackeray himself did not so much as read this passage over before it went to the printer. The false start recorded by Eyre Crowe, on the other hand, was crossed out; and Thackeray later corrected the whole passage in his own hand.

As he was going in at the gate
by w.^h the coach had just rolled
another cry begins – of no popery
–no Papists, My Lord ~~another~~
~~back~~ turns round & faces
them once more.
God save the King says he at
the highest pitch of ~~h~~ his
voice – who dares abuse the
Kings religion – You you d—d
Psalm singing cobbler as
sure as I'm a magistrate of

this county I'll commit you – the
fellow shrank back & my Lord
retreated with all the honours
of the day. But when the little
flurry caused by the scene
was over & the flush passed
off his face, he relapsed into
his usual ~~yawning~~ languor
trifled with ^his^ ~~the~~ little dog &
yawned when my Lady spoke
to him Plummer
This mob was one of many

d5

d10

d15

d20

MS (Trin. Coll. Cam. MS. O.17.21, 40g, 40h) Anne Thackeray's hand (×0·72)

d25 thousands that were going about
the country at that time.
huzzaing for the acquittal
of the 7 bishops who had been
tried just then & about whom
d30 little Harry Esmond at that

time knew scarce any thing. It
was assizes and a meeting
for here was a great meeting
of the gentry, at the Bell &
d35 My Lord's people had their new
liveries on & Harry a little
suit of blue and silver which
he wore upon occasions of state
and the gentlefolks came round
d40 and talked to My Lord, &
a Judge in a red gown
that turned a very great
personage especially complimented him and my Lady.
d45 who was mighty grand Harry

MS (Trin. Coll. Cam. MS. O.17.21, 40h, 40i) Anne Thackeray's hand (×0·72)

As he was going in at the gate
by w.ʰ the coach had just rolled
another cry begins—of no popery—
—no Papists, My Lord ~~dashes~~
d5 ~~back~~ turns round & faces
them once more.
God save the King says he at
the highest pitch of ~~M~~ his
voice—who dares abuse the
d10 Kings religion—You you d-d
Psalm singing cobbler as
sure as Im a magistrate of

40h
this county I'll commit you—the
fellow shrank back & my Lord
d15 retreated with all the honours
of the day. But when the little
flurry caused by the scene
was over & the flush passed
off his face, he relapsed into
d20 his usual ~~yawning~~ languor
his
trifled with ~~a~~ little dog &
yawned when my Lady spoke
to him   Plummer
This mob was one of many
d25 thousands that were going about
the country at that time
uz
~~Hee~~zaying for the acquittal
of the 7 Bishops who had been
tried just then & about whom
d30 little Harry Esmond at that

40i
time knew scarce any thing. It
   Assizes
was ~~Sessions~~ and a meeting
for there was a great meeting
of the gentry, at the Bell &
d35 My Lord's people had their new
liveries on & Harry a little
suit of blue and silver which
he wore upon occasions of state
and the gentlefolks came round
    talked to
d40 and ~~complimented~~ My Lord, &
a Judge in a red gown
that seemed a very great
personnage especially complimented him and My Lady,
d45 who was mighty grand Harry

Transcript of pp. 169-70

As he was going in at the gate, through which the coach had juſt rolled, another cry begins, of " No Popery—no Papiſts !" my lord turns round and faces them once more.

e5 " God ſave the King ! " ſays he at the higheſt pitch of his voice. " Who dares abuſe the King's religion? You, you d——d pſalm-ſinging cobbler, as ſure as I'm a magiſtrate of this county, I'll commit you." The fellow e10 ſhrunk back, and my lord retreated with all the honours of the day. But when the little flurry cauſed by the ſcene was over, and the fluſh paſſed off his face, he relapſed into his uſual languor, trifled with his little dog and yawned e15 when my lady ſpoke to him.

This mob was one of many thouſands that were going about the country at that time, huzzaing for the acquittal of the ſeven biſhops who had been tried juſt then, and about whom e20 little Harry Eſmond at that time knew ſcarce anything. It was aſſizes at Hexton, and there ·was a great meeting of the gentry at the Bell ; and my lord's people had their new liveries on, and Harry a little ſuit of blue and e25 ſilver, which he wore upon occaſions of ſtate ; and the gentlefolks came round and talked to my lord ; and a judge in a red gown, who ſeemed a very great perſonage, eſpecially complimented him and my lady, who was mighty grand.

1852 (Thackeray, W. M., *Henry Osmond*, 3 vols., London 1852 ; i, pp. 92–3 ; Trin. Coll. Cam. G.13.41–3 ; × 0·97)

Verbal variants

	Manuscript		*1852*
d2	by wʰ	e1	through which
d14	shrank	e10	shrunk
		e20/21	[page heading added (but not repro-duced here)] *The Assize Ball.*
d32–3	Assizes and a meeting for there	e21	assizes at Hexton and there
d42	that seemed	e27	who seemed

As he was going in at the gate, through which the coach had just rolled, another cry begins, of "No Popery—no Papists!" my lord turns round and faces them once more.

"God save the King!" says he at the highest pitch of his voice. "Who dares abuse the King's religion? You, you d——d psalm-singing cobbler, as sure as I'm a magistrate of this county I'll commit you!" The fellow shrunk back, and my lord retreated with all the honours of the day. But when the little flurry caused by the scene was over, and the flush passed off his face, he relapsed into his usual languor, trifled with his little dog, and yawned when my lady spoke to him.

This mob was one of many thousands that were going about the country at that time, huzzaing for the acquittal of the seven bishops who had been tried just then, and about whom little Harry Esmond at that time knew scarce any thing. It was assizes at Hexton, and there was a great meeting of the gentry at the Bell; and my lord's people had their new liveries on, and Harry a little suit of blue and silver, which he wore upon occasions of state; and the gentlefolks came round and talked to my lord: and a judge in a red gown, who seemed a very great personage, especially complimented him and my lady, who was mighty grand. Harry remembers her train borne

f5

f10

f15

f20

1858 (Thackeray, W. M., *Henry Esmond*, London 1858, pp. 33–4; Univ. Lib. Cam. LO.78.18; × 1·0)

Variants

	1852		*1858*
e9	county, I'll	f6	county I'll
e9	you."	f7	you!"
e14	dog and	f10	dog, and
e21	anything	f15	any thing
e27	lord;	f19	lord:[13]

[13] This variant first appeared in 1853, from which *1858* was set.

g5

g10

g15

g20

g25

g30

now near twenty years ago. His Grace
opened to him when he found that
Mr. Esmond was one of Webb's brave
regiment, that had once been His
Grace's own. He was the sword and
buckler indeed of the Stuart cause:
there was no stain on his shield,
except the bar across it, that w^h
Marlborough's sister left him. Had
Berwick been his father's heir, James
the Third had assuredly sat on the English throne; he
c^d dare, endure, strike, speak, be silent.
The fire and genius, perhaps, he had
not (that were given to men but)
except these, he had some of the best
qualities of a leader; his grace knew Esmond;
father, and history: and hinted at his
illegitimacy in such a way as made
the Col. half think he was aware of
the particulars of that story. But
Esmond did not choose to enter on it
nor did the Duke press him. Mr. Esmond
said, 'no doubt he should come by his
right; if ever greater people came by
theirs.'

What confirmed Esmond in
his notion that the Duke of Berwick
knew of his case was that when the
Colonel went to pay his duty at S^t G^s
Her Majesty once addressed him by the title of
Marquis. He took the Queen the dutiful

MS (Trin. Coll. Cam. MS. O.17.22, ²231, ²232) Eyre Crowe's hand, with interlinear corrections by
Thackeray in lines 2, 8, 11, 14, 22, 32; the parentheses in line 14 also probably added by Thackeray
(×0·72)

231

now near twenty years ago. His Grace

            that

opened to him when he found ~~who~~

Mr. Esmond was one of Webb's brave

regiment, that had once been His

g5   Grace's own. He was the sword and

buckler in deed of the Stuart cause:

there was no stain on his shield,

except the bar across it, ~~that~~ w.^h

Marlborough's sister left him. Had

g10   Berwick been his father's heir, James

              assuredly the English

the Third had sat on ~~his~~ throne. He

c.^d dare, endure, strike, speak, be silent.

The fire and genius, perhaps, he had

                baser

not, (that were given to ~~lower~~ men,) but

g15   except these, he had some of the best

             His Grace

qualities of a leader. ~~He~~ knew Esmond's

father, and history; and hinted at his

illegitimacy in such a way as made

the Col half think he was aware of

g20   the particulars of that story. But

Esmond did not choose to enter on it

         the Duke

nor did ~~His Grace~~ press him. Mr. Esmond

said, 'No doubt he should come by his

right; if ever greater people came by

g25   their's?'

  ~~Monsieur Simon paid his duty at~~

~~St Germains~~   Rickes   232

  What confirmed Esmond in

          O

his notion that the Duke of Berwick

      193 ——

g30   knew of his case was that | when the

Colonel went to pay his duty at St Germains,

                addressed him by the title of

Her Majesty once ~~called Monsieur-le-~~

Marquis. He took the Queen the dutiful

Transcript of p. 174

now near twenty years ago. His Grace opened to him when he found that Mr. Eſmond was one of Webb's brave regiment, that had once been his Grace's own. He was the ſword and buckler indeed of the Stuart cauſe: there was no ſtain on his ſhield, except the bar acroſs it, which Marlborough's ſiſter left him. Had Berwick been his father's heir, James the Third had aſſuredly ſat on the Engliſh throne. He could dare, endure, ſtrike, ſpeak, be ſilent. The fire and genius, perhaps, he had not (that were given to baſer men), but except theſe, he had ſome of the beſt qualities of a leader. His Grace knew Eſmond's father and hiſtory; and hinted at the latter in ſuch a way as made the Colonel to think he was aware of the particulars of that ſtory. But Eſmond did not chooſe to enter on it, nor did the Duke preſs him. Mr. Eſmond said, "No doubt he ſhould come by his name, if ever greater people came by theirs."

What confirmed Eſmond in his notion that the Duke of Berwick knew of his caſe was, that when the Colonel went to pay his duty at St. Germains, her Majeſty once addreſſed him by the title of Marquis. He took the Queen the dutiful remembrances of her goddaughter,

1852

who had visited Castlewood now near twenty years ago. His Grace opened to him when he found that Mr. Esmond was one of Webb's brave regiment, that had once been his Grace's own. He was the sword and buckler indeed of the Stuart cause: there was no stain on his shield except the bar across it, which Marlborough's sister left him. Had Berwick been his father's heir, James the Third had assuredly sat on the English throne. He could dare, endure, strike, speak, be silent. The fire and genius, perhaps, he had not (that were given to baser men), but except these he had some of the best qualities of a leader. His Grace knew Esmond's father and history; and hinted at the latter in such a way as made the Colonel to think he was aware of the particulars of that story. But Esmond did not choose to enter on it, nor did the Duke press him. Mr. Esmond said, "No doubt he should come by his name if ever greater people came by theirs."

What confirmed Esmond in his notion that the Duke of Berwick knew of his case was, that when the Colonel went to pay his duty at St. Germains, her Majesty once addressed him by the title of Marquis. He took the Queen the dutiful remembrances

1858

1852 (Thackeray, W. M., *Henry Esmond*, 3 vols., London 1852; iii, pp. 192–3; Trin. Coll. Cam. G.13.41–3; ×0·59)

Verbal variants

	Manuscript		*1852*
g17–18	his illegitimacy	h15	the latter
g19	the Col half think	h15–16	the Colonel to think
g24	right;	h19	name,
		h22/3	[page heading added (but not reproduced here)] *At St. Germains.*

1858 (Thackeray, W. M., *Henry Esmond*, London 1858, pp. 400–1; Univ. Lib. Cam. LO.78.18; ×0·61)

Variants

	1852		*1858*
h6	shield, except	i5	shield except
h12	these, he	i9	these he
h19–20	name, if	i14–15	name if

Some of the verbal variation between the manuscript of these extracts and *1852* is evidence of alterations made in proof, probably by Thackeray: see e21 and perhaps also e1, e10, and e27; and h15–16, and h19. But, as with the first extract, there were no verbal variants between the *1852* and *1858* versions of these passages, only amendments of detail (including the deletion of five commas).

To summarize the evidence for the text of *Esmond*: we have, first, the sole original manuscript which also served as printer's copy, some of it in Thackeray's hand, some of it written from his dictation by amanuenses. It is substantially complete, but much of it was left unrevised by Thackeray; its punctuation, moreover, is seriously defective in the parts written out by Thackeray, largely absent in the parts written out by Anne Thackeray, and present but probably unauthoritative in the parts written out by Eyre Crowe. Next we have the first edition, *1852*, which was read and corrected in proof by Thackeray; it includes some new copying errors and its punctuation, although complete and self-consistent, appears to have been supplied largely by the compositors and by Eyre Crowe. Finally there is *1858*, the only reprint to have been revised by Thackeray. It includes a few authoritative amendments, a few new copying errors, and a good deal of further normalization for which Thackeray was probably not responsible.

Esmond has often been edited—its use in examinations has led to the publication of an unusually large number of annotated texts—but it is only recently that active consideration has been given to the production of a critical text.[14] The editors of the students' editions, who have been chiefly concerned to provide criticism and explanation, have been content to reprint *1858* or one of its descendants, often with further normalization of the details. This has not led to much harm for, apart from a little authorized revision, *1858* does not differ greatly from *1852*; but the editor of a critical text is likely to reject *1858* as copy-text on account of its probably unauthorized normalization of the details of *1852*, and to consider instead the two earlier versions: the first edition and the manuscript.

There is a clear case for choosing *1852*, the first printed version, as copy-text for an edition: it is complete, its details are self-consistent, it was accepted and at least tacitly approved by Thackeray, and it was read by his original audience. Yet the choice of copy-text is essentially the choice of a set of details for the edited text, and *1852* has the disadvantage that most of its details, including punctuation, were not Thackeray's but were supplied

---

[14] An edition is now being prepared by Edgar F. Harden for inclusion in *The complete works of William Makepeace Thackeray* (general editor Peter L. Shillingsburg) to be published by Faust, Columbia, S.C.

by his collaborators, the amanuenses and the compositors; and we do not know how—or even if—he amended them in proof.

What then of using the manuscript as copy-text for an edition? Certainly it would be a more adventurous choice. For the most part its details are not good enough to use in an edition, it does not represent Thackeray's final intentions for the form of the novel, and it is not the form in which the book was originally read; but on the other hand it is more or less complete, and it does include *some* of Thackeray's own punctuation. Since the details of *1852*, although usable, were mostly not supplied by Thackeray, the editor might think it better to take the manuscript with all its defects and to supply the punctuation and other details himself: to become, in effect, Thackeray's collaborator in place of those who supplied the details of *1852*. In this case he would follow the details of the parts of the manuscript written out by Thackeray so far as they were usable, but would otherwise introduce a new system of punctuation, etc., based on Thackeray's normal practice elsewhere, taking into account any *1852* details that seemed likely to have been introduced by Thackeray in proof. Thus he would make good the defects of Thackeray's holograph, and would very largely replace the details of the passages written out by Anne Thackeray and Eyre Crowe.

This is the radical course that Edgar F. Harden, the editor of the forthcoming critical edition of *Esmond*, is proposing to take. He will not please everybody; the suppression of the details of *1852*—accepted by Thackeray, read by his original audience, and possibly intended as eighteenth-century pastiche—is not easy to accept; yet by liberating Thackeray's prose from their constraint Harden may enable the author to speak more clearly to his readers.

Whether this is the right course to take is essentially a critical question; and, to show how it might work in practice, here are our three extracts edited afresh from the manuscript by Edgar Harden.[15]

---

[15] I am most grateful to Dr. Harden for editing the texts of the extracts for this chapter.

At first my lady was for dying like Mary Queen of Scots (to whom
she fancied she bore a resemblance in beauty) and stroking her scraggy
neck said—"They will find Isabel of Castlewood is equal to her fate."
Her gentlewoman, Victoire, persuaded her that her prudent course, as she
j5 could not fly, was to receive the troops as though she suspected nothing,
and that her chamber was the best place wherein to await them. So her
black Japan casket which Harry was to carry to the coach was taken back
to her ladyship's chamber—whither the maid and mistress retired.
Victoire came out presently, bidding the page say her ladyship was
j10 ill, confined to her bed with the rheumatism.

By this time the soldiers had reached Castlewood. Harry Esmond saw
them from the window of the tapestry parlor—a couple of centinels were
posted at the gate; a half dozen more walked towards the stable; and some
others preceded by their commander and a man in black—a lawyer probably—
j15 were conducted by one of the servants to the stair leading up to the part
of the house which my lord and lady inhabited.

So the Captain, a handsome kind man, and the lawyer came through the
ante-room, to the tapestry parlour, and where now was nobody but young
Harry Esmond, the page.
j20 "Tell your mistress, little man," says the Captain kindly, "that we
must speak to her."

"My mistress is ill abed," said the page.

"What complaint has she?" asked the Captain.

The boy said, "the rheumatism!"
j25 "Rheumatism! that's a sad complaint," continues the good-natured
Captain—"and the coach is in the yard to fetch the Doctor, I suppose?"

"I don't know," says the boy.

"And how long has her ladyship been ill?"

"I don't know," says the boy.
j30 "When did my lord go away?"

"Yesterday night."

"With Father Holt?"

"With Mr. Holt."

"And which way did they travel?" asks the lawyer.
j35 "They travelled without me," says the page.

"We must see Lady Castlewood."

"I have orders that nobody goes in to her ladyship—she is sick,"
says the page—but at this moment Victoire came out. "Hush!" says she—
and as if not knowing that any one was near—"What's this noise?" says
j40 she, "Is this gentleman the Doctor?"

"Stuff! we must see Lady Castlewood," says the lawyer—pushing by.

The curtains of her ladyship's room were down, and the chamber dark,
and she was in bed with a night-cap on her head and propped up by her
pillows, looking none the less ghastly because of the red which was still
j45 on her cheeks and which she could not afford to forego.

"Is that the Doctor?" she said.

"There is no use with this deception, Madam," Captain Westbury said
(for so he was named). "My duty is to arrest the person of Thomas,
Viscount Castlewood, a non-juring Peer—of Robert Tusher, Vicar of

The first extract edited from the manuscript (cf. a14-60)

j50 Castlewood, and Henry Holt, known under various other names and
designations, a Jesuit Priest who officiated as Chaplain here in the late
King's time, and is now at the head of the conspiracy which was about to
break out in this county against the authority of their Majesties King
William and Queen Mary—and my orders are to search the house for such
j55 papers or traces of the conspiracy as may be found here—Your ladyship
will please to give me your keys, and it will be as well for yourself
that you should help us, in every way in our search."

The first extract edited from the manuscript (cf. a60–67)

As he was going in at the gate through which the coach had just
rolled another cry begins—of "No Popery—no Papists!" My lord turns
round and faces them once more.
"God save the King!" says he at the highest pitch of his voice.
k5 "Who dares abuse the King's religion? You, you d——d psalm-singing
cobbler—as sure as I'm a magistrate of this county I'll commit you."
The fellow shrank back and my lord retreated with all the honours of the
day. But when the little flurry caused by the scene was over and the
flush passed off his face, he relapsed into his usual languor, trifled
k10 with his little dog and yawned when my lady spoke to him.
This mob was one of many thousands that were going about the country
at that time huzzaying for the acquittal of the seven bishops who had
been tried just then and about whom little Harry Esmond at that time
knew scarce any thing. It was assizes at Hexton and there was a great
k15 meeting of the gentry at the Bell; and my lord's people had their new
liveries on and Harry a little suit of blue and silver which he wore upon
occasions of state; and the gentlefolks came round and talked to my lord;
and a judge in a red gown who seemed a very great personage especially
complimented him and my lady, who was mighty grand.

The second extract edited from the manuscript (cf. d1–45)

now near twenty years ago. His Grace opened to him when he found that
Mr. Esmond was one of Webb's brave regiment, that had once been his
Grace's own. He was the sword and buckler indeed of the Stuart cause;
there was no stain on his shield except the bar across it which
l5 Marlborough's sister left him. Had Berwick been his father's heir, James
the Third had assuredly sat on the English throne. He could dare,
endure, strike, speak, be silent. The fire and genius, perhaps, he had
not (that were given to baser men), but except these, he had some of the
best qualities of a leader. His Grace knew Esmond's father, and history;
l10 and hinted at the latter in such a way as made the Colonel to think he
was aware of the particulars of that story. But Esmond did not choose
to enter on it, nor did the Duke press him. Mr. Esmond said no doubt he
should come by his name, if ever greater people came by theirs.
What confirmed Esmond in his notion that the Duke of Berwick knew
l15 of his case was that when the Colonel went to pay his duty at St. Germains,
her Majesty once addressed him by the title of Marquis. He took the Queen
the dutiful

The third extract edited from the manuscript (cf. g1–33)

The words of the edited text will be largely the same whichever copy-text is used. Variant readings from *1852* will be preferred to manuscript readings where, as is usually the case, they appear to have resulted from necessary compositorial emendation or from authoritative proof-revision. This would apply to all the verbal variants between the manuscript and *1852* in these extracts, except that 'country' in the *1852* text of the first extract (b75) appears to be a copying error for 'county' (a63); and that in the *1852* text of the second extract it is not clear whether 'through' (e1/d2), 'shrunk' (e10/d14), and 'who' (e27/d42) were unauthorized alterations or proof-revisions by Thackeray. In his edition of the passages Harden rejects 'country' (j53) and 'shrunk' (k7), but accepts 'through' (k1) and 'who' (k18) as likely to be authoritative.

Elsewhere the editor will encounter careless slips made by Thackeray which were not corrected in the printed texts. For instance the village called Hexton in the second extract (*1852*, e21) is called Hexham in Book III; similarly the conspirator Lowick (Book I) becomes Lodwick (Book III), and so on. Although editors have been inclined to smile on these vagaries and to let them stand, and although it is undesirable to emend inconsistency merely for the sake of regularity, these mistakes are not so innocuous as irregularities of spelling, etc., which do not affect the meaning. A reader might well suppose that Hexton is one place and Hexham another; and if the editor expects his text to be read with close attention he may think it right to emend blunders that could be misleading.

Two matters of presentation will give the editor of *Esmond* pause. First he will want to include the descriptive page headings of *1852*, which were probably added in proof by Thackeray. The pages of the edited text are most unlikely to parallel those of *1852*, however, and the headings will have to be given elsewhere than at the tops of the pages. This can be done either as shoulder notes opposite the places in the text where recto pages of *1852* began or, less usefully, in an appendix.[16] Secondly, there is the question of whether to imitate the pastiche typography of the first edition. Although the typography of *1852* was certainly intended to convey a period flavour to its readers, these machine-printed volumes do not nowadays look like a hand-printed eighteenth-century novel. At best, therefore, a modern pastiche would be imitating an imitation; and this would probably not serve any useful purpose.

The textual apparatus is unlikely to pose new problems; but critical and explanatory notes are to be included in the forthcoming critical edition of

---

[16] The editors of the Clarendon Dickens have collected the page headings in appendices; but they have the justification that the headings were not part of the original editions but were added (in most cases) for the Charles Dickens Edition of 1867.

Esmond, and call for brief comment even though they are not a central concern of this book. Here is the paragraph which introduces the notes to John Sutherland's Penguin edition:

The pernicious respectability of the historical novel for school study and examination has rendered *Henry Esmond* the most edited and annotated of Thackeray's novels. Dryasdust commentary can, however, spoil a work much of whose charm is a brilliant, but often very thin, period veneer. It is no service to Thackeray or his reader to show the author blatantly lifting from his sources, to emphasize in the reading of it the *pastiche* of the style or to offer incidental historical essays. Thackeray did not believe with George Eliot that carelessness was 'a mortal sin in authorship', consequently there are a lot of small errors and discrepancies—hair is in one place brown, another fair; Walcote is near to Winchester and then Wells; non-jurors attend court, etc. The absorbed reader ignores these, but it is easy to assume a spurious editorial ascendancy. Notes are therefore offered; where the reference may be obscure; where Thackeray assumes a greater historical literacy in his reader than can reasonably be expected (though sometimes undeniably Thackeray wants to blind him); where there are significant errors or where interesting insight into working methods and opinion is given.[17]

This is indeed apposite; and, although the editor of *Esmond*—as of any other work of English literature—will certainly be troubled by the insoluble problem of how far to go in providing explanations for readers of widely different educational, cultural, and national backgrounds, there is really no more to be said.

[17] Thackeray, W. M., *Henry Esmond*, Harmondsworth 1970, p. 514.

EXAMPLE 9

Hawthorne, *The marble faun*, 1860

NOWHERE is the debate on editorial principles livelier, nowhere has disagreement between textual bibliographers been more pungently expressed, than where it concerns the editions sponsored by the Center for Editions of American Authors (the CEAA). The CEAA is a Committee of the Modern Language Association of America set up in 1963 to encourage the responsible editing of American authors, dispensing grants from the National Endowment for the Humanities, and approving the results with a 'seal'. The Center has been concerned with editions of the novels of Crane, Hawthorne, Howells, Melville, Simms, and Mark Twain, each one a vast and costly enterprise supported by a particular university and university press; and, although the Center is likely to become less effective as a result of the withdrawal of its funds in circumstances of economic recession, the influence of the editions it has sponsored—now numbering more than a hundred—is far-reaching.[1]

The central editorial principle of the CEAA is that an eclectic 'clear text' should be established according to Greg's theory of copy-text, adapted to nineteenth-century textual situations, and should be supported by an apparatus of detailed evidence.[2] Another main principle of the Center is that the investigation of the textual evidence should be so thoroughly carried out

---

[1] Since this was written the CEAA has been replaced by the Center for Scholarly Editions (CSE), which is likewise a committee of the MLA. The aims and accomplishments of the CEAA (which was originally called the Center for American Editions—the name was changed in 1967) are surveyed in Bruccoli, M. J., 'A few missing words', *PMLA*, lxxxvi, 1971, pp. 587-9; Bruccoli, M. J., and others, *Statement of editorial principles and procedures: a working manual for editing nineteenth-century American texts*, revised edn., New York 1972 (the original edition was prepared by W. M. Gibson and others, [New York] 1967); and Tanselle, G. T., 'Problems and accomplishments in the editing of the novel', *Studies in the novel*, vii, 1975, pp. 323-60.

The publications in the debate on the work of the CEAA up to 1972 are listed in the *Statement of editorial principles* (pp. 17-25), and there are further references in Tanselle's 'Problems and accomplishments'. The most recent, and perhaps the best, contribution is Tom Davis's 'The CEAA and modern textual editing', *The Library*, xxxii, 1977, pp. 61-74. See also Freehafer, J., 'Greg's theory of copy-text and the textual criticism in the CEAA editions', *Studies in the novel*, vii, 1975, pp. 375-88, and the 'Forum' on the CEAA which follows Freehafer's article (pp. 389-406); Tanselle, G. T., 'Greg's theory of copy-text and the editing of American literature', *Studies in bibliography*, xxviii, 1975, pp. 167-229; and the references given in p. 3 n. 5 (Peckham and Tanselle) and p. 184 n. 5 (Bowers and Freehafer).

[2] *Statement of editorial principles* (see n. 1 above), chs. 3 and 4.

and so fully recorded that the apparatus will be 'definitive', by which it is meant that it will not be necessary for the investigation to be repeated in the foreseeable future.[3]

The textual bibliographer at the centre of this debate has been Fredson Bowers, the scholar who more than any other has been responsible for establishing the editorial principles adopted by the CEAA, and who is himself the most distinguished of the CEAA editors. Amongst other works Bowers edited the Ohio 'Centenary' edition of Hawthorne's *The marble faun* (1968), which he believed to be a classic case of the use of demonstrable evidence in a scientific manner for the solution of difficult editorial problems.[4] It is indeed a central CEAA text, and it will serve as a demonstration not so much (as with the other examples) of the various ways in which a work of literature might be edited, as of the actual strengths and weaknesses of a typical CEAA edition.

The marble faun, Hawthorne's last major work of fiction, was first drafted from July to December 1858 during a family tour of Italy, and was rewritten in a revised version from July to November 1859, after the Hawthornes had returned to England.[5] The holograph manuscript of the revised version went to the printer to be set in type, Hawthorne corrected the proofs, and the first edition was published in London in three volumes at the end of February 1860 (*1860*A).[6] Sheets of this printing, meanwhile, had been sent to America, and the first American edition, set from *1860*A with a few deliberate alterations, was published in two volumes in Boston about a week after the English edition (*1860*B). In England the novel was called *Transformation*; the American title (which Hawthorne himself preferred) was *The marble faun*.

The reception of the book was mixed, and almost immediately after publication Hawthorne wrote an afterword to explain its ending; this was added as a 'Postscript' to the second printing of *1860*A and—with a slightly altered text—as a 'Conclusion' to the fourth printing of *1860*B. There was a Tauchnitz edition in 1860 (set from sheets of the second printing of *1860*A), and second and third English editions in 1860 and 1861. In America,

---

[3] Bruccoli, 'A few missing words' (see p. 183 n. 1), p. 587; Bowers, *Two lectures* (see n. 4 below), pp. 25–7.

[4] Hinman, C., and Bowers, F., *Two lectures on editing*, Columbus 1969, pp. 55, 57. Bowers's lecture, 'Practical texts and definitive editions' (*Two lectures*, pp. 21–70), is the best exposition of his views on editing nineteenth-century American novels.

[5] The background to the writing of *The marble faun* is well summarized in the Centenary edition, Columbus 1968, pp. xix–xliv; see also *Hawthorne: the critical heritage*, ed. Crowley, J. D., London 1970.

The major articles on the Centenary *Marble faun* are Bowers's 'Practical texts and definitive editions' (see n. 4 above), and Freehafer, J., 'The *Marble faun* and the editing of nineteenth-century texts', *Studies in the novel*, ii, 1970, pp. 487–503.

[6] For the bibliographical details of the early printed editions, see the Centenary edition, pp. xlv–lii.

although there were several further printings of *1860*B from plates in 1860, 1864, and 1865, the book was not reset until 1876, after Hawthorne's death.

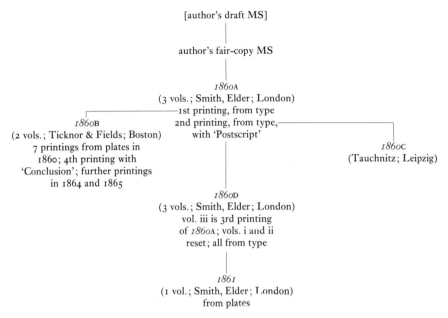

[author's draft MS]

author's fair-copy MS

*1860*A
(3 vols.; Smith, Elder; London)
1st printing, from type
2nd printing, from type, with 'Postscript'

*1860*B
(2 vols.; Ticknor & Fields; Boston)
7 printings from plates in 1860; 4th printing with 'Conclusion'; further printings in 1864 and 1865

*1860*C
(Tauchnitz; Leipzig)

*1860*D
(3 vols.; Smith, Elder; London)
vol. iii is 3rd printing of *1860*A; vols. i and ii reset; all from type

1861
(1 vol.; Smith, Elder; London)
from plates

The first draft of *The marble faun* has not survived, but the revised draft made by Hawthorne in 1859, which was used as copy by the printer, was given by Hawthorne to his English friend H. A. Bright, and was presented to the British Museum by Bright's daughter in 1936.[7] The proofs are lost, so the only other early documentary evidence for the text are the various printed editions of 1860 and 1861. Of these *1860*A, the first edition set from the surviving manuscript, is much the most important; all the other printed texts derived from it, although there were some deliberate alterations in *1860*B, the first American edition.

Hawthorne's holograph fair copy of *The marble faun*, which is thus of crucial importance for the establishment of the text, was legibly written on half sheets of paper folded once to make post quarto bifolia. The compositors, whose names were written on the manuscript at the beginnings of their stints, had no great difficulty in transcribing it. There are a few verbal differences between the manuscript and *1860*A which appear to be copying errors, and a larger number which appear to be the result of deliberate revision in proof. The compositors normalized the text freely, altering a good deal of the punctuation and making changes of capitalization and spelling.

---

[7] It is now British Library MS. Add. 44889-90.

Here as an example is fo. 125 of the manuscript, followed by the passage in *1860*A that was set from it:

> ...ble thraldom did it suggest! Free as she seemed
> to be — beggar as he looked — the nameless vagrant must
> be dragging the beautiful Miriam through the streets
> of Rome, fettered and shackled more cruelly than any
> captive queen of yore, following in an Emperor's
> triumph. And was it conceivable that she would have
> been thus enthralled, unless some great error — how great
> he dared not think — or some fatal weakness, had
> given this dark adversary a vantage-ground?
> "Hilda," said he abruptly, "who and what is Mir-
> iam? Pardon me; but, are you sure of her?"
> "Sure of her!" repeated Hilda, with an angry blush
> for her friend's sake. "I am sure that she is kind, good,
> and generous — a true and faithful friend, whom I
> love dearly, and who loves me as well! What more
> than this need I be sure of?"
> "And your delicate instincts say all this in her
> favour? — nothing against her?" continued the sculptor,
> without heeding the irritation of Hilda's tone. "These are
> my own impressions too. But she is such a mystery! We
> do not even know whether she is a countrywoman of
> ours, or an Englishwoman, or a German. There is An-
> glo Saxon blood in her veins, one would say, and a right Eng-
> lish accent on her tongue, but much that is not English
> breeding, nor American. Nowhere else but in Rome, and
> as an artist, could she hold a place in society, with-
> out giving some clue to her past life."
> "I love her dearly," said Hilda, still with displeas-
> ure in her tone, "and trust her most entirely."
> "My heart trusts her, at least — whatever my head may
> do," replied Kenyon; "and Rome is not like one of our
> New England villages, where we need the permission of

MS (British Library MS. Add. 44889, fo. 125ᵃ; ×0·63)

~~104~~ 125

rible thraldom did it suggest! Free as she seemed
to be—beggar as he looked—the nameless vagrant must
then
ᴧ be dragging the beautiful Miriam through the streets
of Rome, fettered and shackled more cruelly than any

a5 captive queen of yore, following in an Emperor's
triumph. And was it conceivable that she could have
been thus enthralled, unless some great error—how great,

~~Graydon~~ Kenyon
he ᴧ dared not think—or some fatal weakness, had
given this dark adversary a vantage-ground?

a10 "Hilda," said he abruptly, "who and what is Miriam? Pardon me; but, are you sure of her?"
"Sure of her!" repeated Hilda, with an angry blush
for her friend's sake. "I am sure that she is kind, good,
and generous—a true and faithful friend, whom I

a15 love dearly, and who loves me as well! What more
than this need I be sure of?"
"And your delicate instincts say all this in her
favour?—nothing against her?" continued the sculptor,
without heeding the irritation of Hilda's tone.—"These are

a20 my own impressions too. But she is such a mystery! We
do not even know whether she is a countrywoman of
ours, or an Englishwoman, or a German. There is An-
glo Saxon blood in her veins, one would say, and a right English accent on her tongue, but much that is not English

a25 breeding, nor American. Nowhere else but in Rome, and
as an artist, could she hold a place in society, without giving some clue to her past life."
"I love her dearly," said Hilda, still with displeasure in her tone, "and trust her most entirely."

a30 "My heart trusts her, at least —whatever my head may
Kenyon
do," rejoined ~~Graydon~~; "and Rome is not like one of our
we
New England villages, where ᴧ need the permission of

Transcript of p. 186

what a terrible thraldom did it suggest! Free as she seemed to be—beggar as he looked—the nameless vagrant must then be dragging the beautiful Miriam through the streets of Rome, fettered and shackled more cruelly than any captive queen of yore following in an emperor's triumph. And was it conceivable that she would have been thus enthralled unless some great error—how great Kenyon dared not think—or some fatal weakness had given this dark adversary a vantage-ground?

"Hilda," said he, abruptly, "who and what is Miriam? Pardon me; but are you sure of her?"

"Sure of her!" repeated Hilda, with an angry blush, for her friend's sake. "I am sure that she is kind, good, and generous; a true and faithful friend, whom I love dearly, and who loves me as well! What more than this need I be sure of?"

"And your delicate instincts say all this in her favour?—nothing against her?" continued the sculptor, without heeding the irritation of Hilda's tone. "These are my own impressions, too. But she is such a mystery! We do not even know whether she is a countrywoman of ours, or an Englishwoman, or a German. There is Anglo-Saxon blood in her veins, one would say, and a right English accent on her tongue, but much that is not English breeding, nor American. Nowhere else but in Rome, and as an artist, could she hold a place in society without giving some clue to her past life."

"I love her dearly," said Hilda, still with displeasure in her tone, "and trust her most entirely."

"My heart trusts her at least, whatever my head may do," replied Kenyon; "and Rome is not like one of our New England villages, where we need the permission of each individual neigh-

*1860*A (Hawthorne, N., *Transformation*, London 1860, i, pp. 191-2; Univ. Lib. Cam. Nov.1.10; ×0·62)

Variants	MS		*1860*A	
	a5	yore,	b6	yore
	a5	Emperor's	b6	emperor's
	a6	could	b7	would
	a7	enthralled,	b8	enthralled
	a7	great,	b8	great
	a8	weakness,	b9	weakness
	a10	he	b11	he,
	a11	but,	b12	but
	a12	blush	b14	blush,
	a14	generous—	b15	generous;
	a19	tone.—	b22	tone.
	a20	impressions	b22	impressions,
	a22-3	An-|glo Saxon	b26	Anglo-Saxon
	a26	society,	b30	society
	a30	her,	b35	her
	a30	least—	b35	least,
	a31	rejoined	b36	replied

There are two verbal variants between the manuscript and printed versions of the extract: 'could' in the manuscript becomes 'would' in *1860*A (a6/b7) and 'rejoined' becomes 'replied' (a31/b36). The fifteen non-verbal variants between the manuscript and *1860*A, which are typical of the book as a whole, comprise the deletion of seven commas and a dash, the addition of three commas and a hyphen, the substitution of two punctuation marks for others, and the alteration of one capital letter to lower case.

There were no changes in the extract between *1860*A and *1860*B.

Let us look, then, at the Centenary edition of *The marble faun*. At the heart of the edition is a plain text—it is the laudable aim of the CEAA to lease its edited texts inexpensively to reprint publishers[8]—which is based, in accordance with the principles of the series, on the manuscript, not on the first printed edition. The text is preceded by a short historical 'Introduction' by Claude M. Simpson, which describes the genesis and composition of the work, and a long 'Textual introduction' by Fredson Bowers, which explains and argues the case for the editorial procedures used. The lengthy textual apparatus which follows the plain text is in seven main parts: (1) 35 textual notes on particular readings; (2) a list of 688 editorial emendations to the copy-text; (3) a list of 190 verbal variants from the manuscript which appeared in the first printed edition but which were not incorporated in the edited version (on the other hand there is no corresponding list of non-verbal variants from the manuscript found in *1860*A but not incorporated in the edited version); (4) lists of line-end hyphenation in the edited version and in the manuscript; (5) a historical collation, recording the verbal variation between the early printed editions, and also all variation between *1860*A and *1860*B; (6) a list of 1,447 alterations made to the manuscript (mostly by Hawthorne) while it was being written out or soon afterwards; and (7) an analysis of the 145 compositorial stints into which the manuscript was divided for setting, which also serves as a concordance between the pages of the manuscript, the first printed edition, and the edited version. At the end of the apparatus the 'Editorial principles' of the series are reprinted from its earlier volumes; and a list of corrections made to the introduction and apparatus is added to the second printing (1971).

Assessment of the Centenary *Marble faun* must rest on the answers to three main questions. These are, first, has the textual evidence been thoroughly investigated, and have the results been adequately and accurately recorded? Is the edition in fact 'definitive' in the sense that the investigation need not be repeated in the foreseeable future? Secondly, is the edited version well founded: are the principles upon which it is based generally sound, and in this particular case efficacious? And thirdly, does the editor offer a convincing treatment of the text? Are his 688 emendations of the copy-text acceptable?

Collation of the holograph manuscript of *The marble faun* with the Centenary text and its apparatus, and with the early printed editions, shows a very high standard of accuracy in the edited version and in the records of variants, etc. This is of course what we should hope to be the case, and indeed what we should expect, since the early texts were each checked three times,

---

[8] Laudable but not necessarily attainable; for, rather than pay even the modest royalties asked by the CEAA, a publisher may prefer to reprint for nothing the unedited text of a work that is out of copyright.

comprehensively and expensively, by the editorial team. Yet mistakes can be made in collation by the hardest-working editors, and it is no small matter that this great quantity of detail has been noted and used with so little error.[9]

The records of variants, etc., in the textual apparatus are therefore reliable (if somewhat awkwardly divided) as far as they go; but they do not include a record of the non-verbal variation between the manuscript copy-text and the first printed edition, for some of which the author could have been responsible. The omission of this record means that the edition is not 'definitive' in the sense intended by the CEAA, for without it a future investigator of the text would have to do this part of the work again.[10] In any case this omission suppresses the evidence of the normalized punctuation, etc., of the first edition—accepted and perhaps refined by Hawthorne but not incorporated in the edited version—which is required for an assessment of the Centenary text. No doubt the inclusion of such a long list in the apparatus would have been difficult and expensive; but a solution to the problem might be to place it, together with the rest of the apparatus, in the form of microfiches in a pocket at the back of the volume.[11]

Next we consider the CEAA's central editorial principle, the establishment of an eclectic text according to Greg's theory of copy-text. Greg offers a procedure for choosing copy-texts for editions of Renaissance works which, he insists, is to be used with flexibility and critical discretion. (Taking it for granted that the author's manuscript has not survived and that the author himself was not much concerned with the printing and reprinting of his book, Greg recommends that the earliest in an ancestral series of printed texts shall normally be chosen as copy-text because it comes nearest to the author's 'original'.[12])

The application of Greg's theory by the CEAA to the editing of nineteenth- and twentieth-century works is both more comprehensive and less flexible than Greg's pragmatic approach, and it denies the editor much critical discretion in the choice of copy-text. The CEAA's *Statement of editorial*

---

[9] Total accuracy is of course impossible, even if annotated photo-reproductions are used. The editor cannot avoid all error himself, nor can he be in complete control of his printers. This Centenary edition is accurate enough for practical purposes; and the suggestion that CEAA collations are likely to be inaccurate because they are carried out by graduate students and by professors of literature poorly qualified for the task (Morse Peckham in *Studies in the novel*, vii, 1975, p. 402) is not borne out here.

[10] It is hardly likely that a future *editor* of Hawthorne would feel that he could rely on the collations, etc., of the Centenary editors, or of anyone other than himself; the 'investigator' postulated here would be someone other than an editor who needed detailed textual information for a study of Hawthorne's work.

[11] A similar conclusion was reached independently by Tom Davis (see p. 183 n. 1).

[12] Greg, W. W., *Collected papers*, Oxford 1966, pp. 374–91. See also the references in p. 183 n. 1; and, on Greg's 'substantives' and 'accidentals', p. 5 above.

principles says that the author's manuscript should be chosen as copy-text—or, if the manuscript is lost, then the version nearest to it—because the manuscript 'almost always' represents the author's intentions more closely than any later version.[13] Greg's theory was based on the reasonable assumption that the earlier printed versions of Renaissance texts were likely to be more authoritative in detail than the later ones; but the assumption underlying the CEAA's editorial principle is the very dubious one that, in the absence of evidence to the contrary, a nineteenth- or twentieth-century author 'intended' the manuscript rather than the printed version of his work. In fact, of course, such an author may have preferred the printed version, but without actually saying so.

In practice, as we have seen, the authors of nineteenth-century novels did not as a rule specifically approve or disapprove the normalization of the text that accompanied the transformation of their works from manuscript to print; we know that they accepted it, and usually that is all we know. The editor cannot normally say that this version or that comes closest to the author's intentions. All he can say is that this version is to be preferred to that on other—perhaps critical—grounds.

Sometimes (as other examples have shown) there are critical reasons for choosing an early printed version of a work as copy-text for an edition even though the author's final manuscript is available; but sometimes it is better to use the manuscript, and *The marble faun* is such a case. The details of Hawthorne's printer's-copy manuscript, and especially its excellent punctuation, are complete and well considered, and they convey the rhythm of the dialogue and the balance of Hawthorne's precise, parenthetical prose in a way that the mechanical details of the normalized printed texts do not: consider, for instance, how Hawthorne's style is blunted in the *1860*A version of the extract by the addition of three and the deletion of seven commas. So, in spite of the fact that Hawthorne accepted, and perhaps refined, the normalized details of the printed text, there is a good critical

---

[13] 'When an author's manuscript is preserved, this has paramount authority, of course' (Bowers, F. T., 'Some principles for scholarly editions of nineteenth-century American authors', *Studies in bibliography*, xvii, 1964, p. 226).

'. . . it is almost always true that the accidentals—and of course the vast majority of the words will be closest to the author's intent in a finished or fair-copy manuscript, if it exists, or, if not, in the proofs or first printing. For this reason, one of the earliest forms of the text will normally be chosen as copy-text. . . .

'If the sole form of the author's work is manuscript unpublished (or imperfectly published) during his lifetime, the manuscript becomes copy-text.

'Where both manuscript and printed edition are available, still the manuscript, if it is a finished or printer's-copy manuscript, normally becomes copy-text. . . .

'If the sole surviving forms of the author's work are printed . . . that form which stands closest to the missing final manuscript is normally chosen as copy-text.' (CEAA *Statement of editorial principles and procedures*, revised edn., 1972, pp. 4–6.)

case for basing an edition on the text of the final manuscript, which is that it offers the most convincing punctuation of the text. There is no need to introduce the assumption, which cannot be supported by evidence, that Hawthorne intended or would have preferred his own punctuation to that of the first edition, although the editorial principles of the series indicate that it was partly because of this assumption that the manuscript was chosen as copy-text for the Centenary edition of *The marble faun*.

The Centenary editor reproduces his manuscript copy-text with admirable accuracy, and with similar accuracy he reports his 688 editorial emendations. The remaining questions are whether these emendations are both necessary and right, and whether they are adequately supported by annotation.

About half of the 688 emendations of the copy-text incorporated in the Centenary text had first appeared in *1860*A. Most of them corrected obvious errors in the manuscript, while a few appear to have resulted from proof-revision by the author. It is plainly right that these *1860*A readings should be included in the edited version (although there is a lack of supporting annotation—surprising in an edition in which textual scholarship is so much in evidence—which obliges the reader to search for their origins in the lists of the apparatus).

Then there is a group of verbal variants between the manuscript and *1860*A which might have resulted either from Hawthorne's corrections in proof or from mistakes made by the compositors. The editor has approached them by counting the transcription errors made by each compositor in a control section of the text. (This was a part of the book which was sent to the American printers as uncorrected proofs of the English edition, and which was then proof-corrected by Hawthorne before the English edition was published.[14]) It was supposed that, if a doubtful variant appearing in another part of the text had been set by a compositor who made many mistakes in the control section, it was more likely to be an error (not an authoritative correction) than if it had been set by one who made few. While this supposition is likely to be true on average, it cannot properly be used to decide particular cases. The danger of doing so is illustrated in our extract, of which the *1860*A version was set by a compositor called Mintern who happened to be the man with the highest rate of error (in the control section) of all the compositors who worked on *The marble faun*. In *1860*A two words differed from the manuscript (a6/b7, a31/b36). One of them was written ambiguously in the manuscript, and it is likely enough that Mintern misread 'could' (p. 186, a6) as 'would' and that Hawthorne did not notice the change; the editor reasonably prints 'could'. But 'rejoined' was written reasonably clearly in the manuscript (p. 186, a31), and 'replied' is more

---

[14] Centenary edition, pp. cvff.; *Two lectures* (see p. 184 n. 4), pp. 56–7.

the hidden significance of Miriam's gesture—what a terrible thraldom did it suggest! Free as she seemed to be—beggar as he looked—the nameless vagrant must then be dragging the beautiful Miriam through the streets of Rome, fettered c5 and shackled more cruelly than any captive queen of yore, following in an Emperour's triumph. And was it conceivable that she could have been thus enthralled, unless some great errour—how great, Kenyon dared not think—or some fatal weakness, had given this dark adversary a vantage-ground?

c10 "Hilda," said he abruptly, "who and what is Miriam? Pardon me; but, are you sure of her?"

"Sure of her!" repeated Hilda, with an angry blush for her friend's sake. "I am sure that she is kind, good, and generous—a true and faithful friend, whom I love dearly, c15 and who loves me as well! What more than this need I be sure of?"

"And your delicate instincts say all this in her favour?— nothing against her?" continued the sculptor, without heeding the irritation of Hilda's tone.—"These are my own impressions c20 too. But she is such a mystery! We do not even know whether she is a countrywoman of ours, or an Englishwoman, or a German. There is Anglo-Saxon blood in her veins, one would say, and a right English accent on her tongue, but much that is not English breeding, nor American. Nowhere else but in c25 Rome, and as an artist, could she hold a place in society, without giving some clue to her past life."

"I love her dearly," said Hilda, still with displeasure in her tone, "and trust her most entirely."

"My heart trusts her, at least—whatever my head may do," c30 rejoined Kenyon; "and Rome is not like one of our New England villages, where we need the permission of each indi-

Centenary edition (Hawthorne, N., *The marble faun*, 2nd printing, Columbus 1971, pp. 108-9; Trin. Coll. Cam. RR.054.HAW.5; ×0·96)

Variants

	MS		Centenary
a5	Emperor's	c6	Emperour's
a7	error	c8	errour

likely to have been a proof-revision by Hawthorne than a mistake by Mintern. Nevertheless the editor prints 'rejoined', arguing:

Ordinarily a change like this from MS 'rejoined' to E1ª [= *1860*A] 'replied' would be imputed to the author. But the word is not very legible and could readily be confused by such a careless compositor as Mintern.[15]

Thus a general suspicion of Mintern's competence has led the editor to reject, on the doubtful ground that the manuscript reading is illegible, a particular emendation that he would otherwise have accepted.

Finally there is the considerable group of emendations in the Centenary text that were introduced by the editor. Apart from the officious correction of the prepositions in three Italian proper names, there is only one verbal emendation, and that one is wrong in a way that indicates a critical insensitivity to the meaning of Hawthorne's text. Hawthorne wrote:

And yet Donatello's heart was so fresh a fountain, that, had Miriam been more world-worn than she was, she might have found it exquisite to slake her thirst with the feelings that welled up and brimmed over from it. She was far, very far, from the dusty mediæval epoch, when some women have a taste for such refreshment.[16]

By 'the dusty mediæval epoch' Hawthorne referred of course to Miriam's middle age, from which she was as yet many years distant. In the Centenary edition 'have a taste' (which is the reading of the manuscript and of all the early printed editions) is emended to 'had a taste'—as if Hawthorne was referring not to Miriam's middle age but to the historical Middle Ages![17]

Most of the editorial emendations regularize details of the copy-text in an undesirable way. Hawthorne sporadically attempted to use English spellings for the benefit of the English compositors, sometimes spelling '-our' in place of the American '-or', etc. Here the editor has altered a large number of Hawthorne's '-or' forms to '-our', even when it was not normal English practice to do so, and has for instance spelt 'horrour' ten times when Hawthorne himself spelt 'horror' nine times out of the ten. (Similarly absurd are the emendations to 'Emperour's' and 'errour' in lines 6 and 8 of the Centenary version of the extract.) There is also much regularization of Hawthorne's capitalization, hyphenation, etc., which is not only unnecessary but also objectionable where such details convey meaning. For instance Hawthorne generally wrote 'Nature' where he intended personification and 'nature' where he did not, but in the Centenary text the word is regularized to 'Nature' throughout.[18]

---

[15] Centenary edition, p. 474.   [16] MS fo. 92; Centenary edition, p. 80.

[17] This emendation is not the subject of an editorial note.

[18] The Centenary editor could not see any system in Hawthorne's use of 'Nature' and 'nature' (Centenary edition, p. 471), but Professor Freehafer demonstrates Hawthorne's intentional distinction between the two forms (*Studies in the novel*, ii, 1970, pp. 496-7).

Most of these editorial emendations, very few of which are supported by textual notes, would have been better left unmade. Too much editing can be as bad as too little, and the Centenary text would have had greater critical value if the editor had done no more than transcribe the manuscript and emend it with all the verbal variants from *1860*A.

The CEAA and its editors have been noble in vision, rich in good intentions as well as in funds, indefatigable in industry, and scrupulous in accuracy. These qualities, and the features of the CEAA editions that derive from them, are applauded even by the CEAA's critics. Yet the whole great enterprise seems to have gone astray. CEAA editions are not and never can be 'definitive'; their main editorial principle is unsound yet inflexibly applied; and individual editions sealed by the Center can be grossly imperfect.

It would seem that editing—which is at least as much a part of literary criticism as of bibliography—cannot well be regimented, and that editors should always consider the why and the wherefore and the how of their work according to the circumstances and the needs of each individual case. Books of rules can prove delusive guides.

EXAMPLE 10

Hardy, *The woodlanders*, 1887

ALTHOUGH Hardy thought of himself as a poet and would refer to his fiction as 'mere journey work', it was a poet's precision and care for detail that went into their construction. Of all the authors whose techniques are examined in this book, the one who most resembled Hardy in craftsmanship was not another novelist but Milton. Like Milton's *Maske*, Hardy's *Woodlanders* was limited at first by the circumstances of its original production, and was completed only after repeated revision by its author over a period of years. Hardy put *The woodlanders* into final shape as a work of art by means of revision; and it is on this revision that any editorial investigation must focus.[1]

Hardy thought of writing a woodland story as early as the mid 1870s, but then put the idea aside until November 1885 when he returned to it in response to an invitation to contribute a novel to *Macmillan's magazine*. Once started he worked quickly: publication in monthly instalments began in May 1886, the manuscript was completed in February 1887, and the final instalment appeared in April 1887. As usual Hardy wrote carefully, and revised both manuscript and proofs as best he could; but, although he had written for serial publication before, the form was not well suited either to his craftsmanship or to the development of this particular story. It may be that the exigency of meeting monthly deadlines helped Hardy to get the novel written, but it also led to untidiness in the details of plot and phrasing. A tale, moreover, of the conflict between love and the laws of society was bound to be hobbled by serialization in a family magazine of the 1880s,

---

[1] For the background see Hardy, F. E., *The early life of Thomas Hardy* (to 1891), London 1928, and *The later years of Thomas Hardy* (to 1928), London 1930, which is in reality autobiography rather than biography. The main manuscript sources are the Thomas Hardy Collection at Dorset County Museum, Dorchester (hereafter DCM), and the Macmillan papers at the British Library. R. L. Purdy's *Thomas Hardy: a bibliographical study*, London 1954, is good as far as it goes (which is not much further than the first editions). See also *Thomas Hardy: the critical heritage*, ed. Cox, R. G., London 1970.

There are three outstanding studies of the text of *The woodlanders*, to which I am much indebted. Two are papers by Dale Kramer: 'Two "new" texts of Thomas Hardy's *The woodlanders*', *Studies in bibliography*, xx, 1967, pp. 135–50, and 'Revisions and vision: Thomas Hardy's *The woodlanders*', *Bulletin of the New York Public Library*, xxv, 1971, pp. 195–230, 248–82 (referred to hereafter as Kramer, 'New texts', and Kramer 'Revisions', respectively). The third study is an unpublished thesis by A. L. Manford: *Materials for an edition of Thomas Hardy's 'The woodlanders'* (University of Birmingham Faculty of Arts M.A. thesis, 1976; hereafter 'Manford'). I was also fortunate in being able to read Simon Gatrell's unpublished thesis on *Under the greenwood tree*.

where the censorship imposed by its readers prevented anything like plain speaking about sex.² This prompted further revision, and Hardy took advantage of four of the editions of *The woodlanders* which appeared during the next twenty-five years (the first two book editions, 1887, and editions of 1896 and 1912) to refine the details of the work and to say more plainly what he had previously been obliged to conceal; while his developing artistic judgement led him to alter at the same time some larger features of the work in order to give it greater unity.

The relationship between the main texts of *The woodlanders*—the manuscript, the English editions which were revised by Hardy, and two American editions which derived from the English magazine proofs³—is shown in the following diagram:

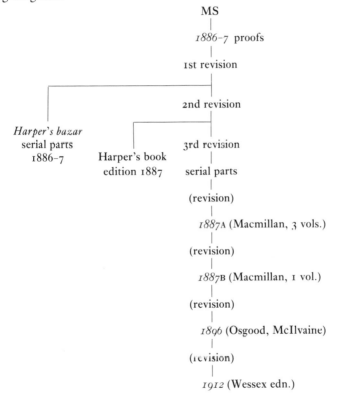

MS
|
1886–7 proofs
|
1st revision
|
2nd revision
|

Harper's bazar
serial parts
1886–7

Harper's book
edition 1887

3rd revision
|
serial parts
|
(revision)
|
*1887*A (Macmillan, 3 vols.)
|
(revision)
|
*1887*B (Macmillan, 1 vol.)
|
(revision)
|
1896 (Osgood, McIlvaine)
|
(revision)
|
1912 (Wessex edn.)

² Mowbray Morris, the editor of *Macmillan's magazine*, wrote to Hardy on 19 Sept. 1886 asking him not to bring Suke Damson 'to too open shame', explaining 'Already, in my short Editorial career, I have received a Round Robin concerning some offence against morality that had been smelled out in our pages! . . . Of course, it is very annoying to have to reckon for such asses: still, I can't help it; an Editor must be commercial as well as literary; and the magazine has scarcely so abundant a sale that I can afford to disregard any section of its readers.' (MS, DCM.)   ³ See Kramer, 'New texts'.

The diagram does not show all the separate editions of *The woodlanders* that were produced in Hardy's lifetime, or printings from plates of any edition; but it does include all the versions that were authoritatively revised.

The manuscript of *The woodlanders*, which is now at the Dorset County Museum,[4] was written on 498 sheets of post quarto writing paper. For the most part it is a fair copy, four-fifths of it written out by Hardy himself and the rest by his wife Emma (who may have written occasionally from Hardy's dictation);[5] and it was read over and revised by Hardy before being sent in batches to serve as the printer's copy for the monthly instalments in *1886-7* (*Macmillan's magazine*).[6] The handwriting of the manuscript is easily legible—though it is not always easy to tell Hardy's hand from his wife's—while its punctuation and other details are coherent and largely complete.

The manuscript was transcribed in type for the magazine instalments with few mistakes and only moderate normalization. We also know—because proofs of *1886-7* in different stages of revision were used as copy for the American magazine and first book settings respectively—that Hardy revised the proofs for *Macmillan's magazine* in three successive stages.[7]

Although the English magazine text of *The woodlanders* was revised by Hardy, he was dissatisfied with this bowdlerized version of the story, and he set about revising it further for the first English book edition (*1887*A)[8] while the serial parts were still in course of publication. He made the sexual relationships between his main characters more explicit—perhaps as explicit as it could be in the 1880s—Grace in particular being made to behave more seductively towards Giles, while Giles's character was refined; and he undertook a general revision of the language towards less artificial forms, including (as in each subsequent revision) a careful adjustment of the dialect used in direct speech.

The next revision—for the second book edition (*1887*B)[9]—was concerned more with detail than with major themes; but the character of Fitzpiers was made even less attractive; and Hardy, worried because some of his readers mistook the final reunion of Grace and Fitzpiers for a happy ending to the story, made Melbury express doubts about their future happiness.

Next came a more substantial revision made for the Osgood, McIlvaine

---

[4] A microfilm of the manuscript has been published by University Microfilms, Ltd.

[5] See Manford, ch. 2.

[6] *Macmillan's magazine*, liv, May–Oct. 1886; lv, Nov. 1886–Apr. 1887. Hardy was not constrained to write in instalments of equal length; the length of the instalments varied from three to five chapters, and from fifteen to twenty-two double-column pages.

[7] Kramer, 'New texts'.

[8] 3 vols., Macmillan & Co., London 1887.   [9] 1 vol., Macmillan & Co., London 1887.

edition of *1896*.[10] By this time Hardy seems to have felt that he could attack social mores with greater freedom. The relationships between the four main characters were detailed yet more frankly; slighting references to religious belief were introduced; Mrs. Charmond was made more obviously worldly; and Melbury's final doubts were more clearly expressed. Hardy also began to revise the geography of Wessex, but on this occasion he was not much concerned with minor detail.

Hardy's final revision, for Macmillan's Wessex edition (*1912*),[11] although it touched up some of the major themes (strengthening the treatment of Grace's desire for Giles, for instance), was more concerned with detail. In this case we can be sure it was Hardy himself who was attending to the details, since we have the actual printed copy from which *1912* was set,[12] in which he marked not only verbal changes but also extensive alterations to the punctuation.

It is impossible in a brief extract to include examples of every sort of change made in the six main layers of revision, stretching over a period of twenty-five years, or to give more than a rough idea of their scale, but the passage written on fo. 391 of the manuscript, which is entirely in Hardy's hand, is fairly typical. It is a passage from Chapter XXXIX, in which Grace—still thinking that she can be divorced from Fitzpiers—tempts Giles to kiss her (see pp. 200–1).

Hardy's care in preparing the manuscript copy is obvious. His revision of the text, shown by changes of pen (a12) to have been in at least two stages, involved details as well as words (dash added in a1). The punctuation was adequate, and the passage was reproduced with little change in *1886-7* (*Macmillan's Magazine*) (see p. 202).

Hardy's proof revision has resulted in two verbal changes (b4 and b4-5 of the serial text). There are also four changes of punctuation, one of spelling, and one of contraction, for some of which Hardy may have been responsible. The American texts, which were set from copies of the English magazine proofs at two successive stages of revision, can be helpful here. For instance, 'O—' in the manuscript (a12) appears as 'Oh,' not only in the English magazine text but also in both the American editions, and it seems

(continued on p. 203)

[10] Osgood, McIlvaine & Co., London 1896. Plates of this setting were later reprinted by Macmillan for the Uniform edition (1903–), Pocket edition (1906–), and—following revision—Scholars Library edition (1934–). See Manford, pp. 84, 121, and Appendix III.

[11] Macmillan & Co., London 1912. Reprinted 1920, 1931, 1949, 1955, 1958 (Library edition); 1967, 1971, 1972 (Greenwood edition); and in America 1915 (autograph edition), 1921 (Anniversary edition).

[12] This is a copy of the 1906 Macmillan printing of the *1896* Osgood, McIlvaine plates, marked up by Hardy and used by the *1912* compositors (Dorset County Museum, Hardy Collection I.A.5). There are also five leaves of page-proof for *1912* in DCM; see Manford, pp. 115-17. Hardy kept a 'study copy' of *1912* in which he later entered three more verbal revisions (Manford, pp. 118-19).

391

himself all this while, though he would have protected Grace's good
repute as the apple of his eye, was only a man; and in face of the agonizing
seductiveness shown by her, in her unenlightened school-girl simplicity about the laws
& ordinances, he betrayed a man's weakness. Since it was so — since it
had come to this, that Grace, deeming herself free to do it, was virtually
asking him to demonstrate that he loved her — since he could demonstrate
it only too truly — since life was short & love was strong — he gave way
to the temptation, notwithstanding that he perfectly well knew her to be
wedded inevocably to Fitzpiers. Indeed he cared for nothing past or
future, simply accepting the present & what it brought, desiring once in his life
to clasp in his arms her he had watched over & loved so long.
from his embrace, influenced

She started back suddenly by a sort of inspiration. O — I suppose",
she stammered, "that I am really free? — that this is right? Is there really a new law?
Father have been too sanguine in saying — cannot

He did not answer, & in a moment afterward Grace
burst into tears in spite of herself. "Oh, why does not my father come
home & explain", she sobbed, "and let me know clearly what I am! It is
too trying, this, to ask me to — and then to leave me so long in so vague a state that I do not
know what to do, & perhaps do wrong!"
Winterbourne felt like a very Cain, over & above his previous sorrow. How
her in not telling her what he knew. He turned aside; the feeling of
his cruelty mounted higher & higher. How could he have dreamt

MS of *The woodlanders* (fo. 391ᵃ, in Hardy's hand; Dorset County Museum; ×0·73)

391

himself all this while ∧ though he would have protected Grace's good
repute as the apple of his eye, was only a man; and in face of the agonizing
                                        school-girl
seductiveness shown by her, in her unenlightened ∧ simplicity about the laws
& ordinances, he betrayed a man's weakness. Since it was so—since it
a5   had come to this, that Grace, deeming herself free to do it, was virtually
asking him to demonstrate that he loved her—since he could demonstrate
it only too truly—since life was short & love was strong—he gave way
to the temptation, notwithstanding that he perfectly well knew her to be
wedded
~~bound~~ irrevocably to Fitzpiers. Indeed he cared for nothing past or
a10 future, simply accepting the present & what it brought, desiring once in his life
to clasp in his arms her he had watched over & loved so long. ~~as~~
                from his embrace, influenced, ~~by a half-prophetic fear~~.
She started back suddenly ∧ by a sort of inspiration. "O—I suppose,"
                                Is there really a new law?
she stammered, "that I am really free?—that this is right? ∧ ~~But can~~
        cannot
Father ∧ have been too sanguine in saying—"
                                afterwards
a15   He did not answer, & ~~in~~ a moment ~~the tribute was taken.~~ Grace
burst into tears in spite of herself. "Oh, why does not my father come
home & explain," she sobbed, "and let me know clearly what I am! It is
                to ask me to—and then
too trying, this, ∧ to leave me so long in so vague a state that I do not
know what to do, & perhaps do wrong!"
                        like a very Cain, over & above his previous sorrow. How
a20   Winterborne felt ~~a Cain-like guiltiness,~~ He had sinned against
her in not telling her what he knew. He turned aside; the feeling of
his cruelty ~~to her~~ mounted higher & higher. How could he have dreamt

Transcript of p. 200

antly against himself all this while—though he would have protected Grace's good repute as the apple of his eye, was a man; and, as Desdemona said, men are not gods. In face of the agonising seductiveness shown by her, in her unenlightened school-girl simplicity about the laws and ordinances, he betrayed a man's weakness. Since it was so—since it had come to this, that Grace, deeming herself free to do it, was virtually asking him to demonstrate that he loved her—since he could demonstrate it only too truly—since life was short and love was strong—he gave way to the temptation, notwithstanding that he perfectly well knew her to be wedded irrevocably to Fitzpiers. Indeed he cared for nothing past or future, simply accepting the present and what it brought, desiring once in his life to clasp in his arms her he had watched over and loved so long.

She started back suddenly from his embrace, influenced by a sort of inspiration. "Oh, I suppose," she stammered, "that I am really free?—that this is right? Is there *really* a new law? Father cannot have been too sanguine in saying——"

He did not answer, and a moment afterwards Grace burst into tears in spite of herself. "Oh, why does not my father come home and explain!" she sobbed, "and let me know clearly what I am! It is too trying, this, to ask me to—and then to leave me so long in so vague a state that I do not know what to do, and perhaps do wrong!"

Winterborne felt like a very Cain, over and above his previous sorrow. How he had sinned against her in not telling her what he knew! He turned aside: the feeling of his cruelty mounted higher and higher. How could he have dreamt of kissing her?

1886-7 (*Macmillan's magazine*, lv, 1887, pp. 314-15; Trin. Coll. Cam. 325.c.17.43; ×0·86)

Variants

	MS		*1886-7*
a2	was only a	b4	was a
a2	and in face	b4-5	and, as Desdemona said, men are not gods. In face
a2	agonizing	b6	agonising
a4 [etc.]	&	b8 [etc.]	and
a12	"O—I	b27	"Oh, I
a17	explain,	b35	explain!
a21	knew.	b45	knew!
a21	aside;	b46	aside:

likely that this is an example of normalization by the English printer which was copied by the Americans. But the word 'explain' (a17) is followed by a comma not only in the manuscript but also in both the American texts, and it is only in *1886–7* itself that the comma is replaced by an exclamation mark; and in this case it seems likely that the punctuation mark was altered by Hardy himself in a late proof[13] (see p. 202).

The only changes to the text of the extract in *1887*A (the first book edition, prepared while the publication of the serial parts was in progress and published just before the appearance of the last instalment) were the verbal amendment in c18, presumably made by Hardy, and the comma added in c16, perhaps also by Hardy (see p. 204).

In *1887*B (the second book edition, published six months after the first) the extract shows more extensive changes in three verbal alterations, each of which describes an aspect of the physical relationship between Giles and Grace. An exclamation mark, added in *1886–7*, is removed again from d30 (see p. 205).

One of the two verbal alterations to the extract made for *1896* again extends the description of Giles's embrace (e18–19); while the other points up his sense of guilt for what he is doing. The changes of detail could all have been made by Messrs. Osgood, McIlvaine, who were surely responsible for the change from double to single quotation marks; but the spelling 'agonizing' returns to Hardy's manuscript form, and Hardy used both 'O' and 'Oh' (manuscript a12 and a16) (see p. 206).

In marking up the copy of the 1906 printing of *1896* for use by the *1912* compositors (see p. 207), Hardy made only the two verbal alterations to the text of the extract (f18 and f19); but elsewhere in the marked-up copy he deleted more than 460 commas and made numerous other alterations to the punctuation, etc.[14]

In the Wessex edition of the extract, *1912*, there were no changes except for the two verbal alterations marked by Hardy in the copy, which keep Giles and Grace in even closer physical propinquity (see p. 209). Elsewhere, however, variants show that Hardy made further revisions to the proofs of *1912*.

Hardy's five main revisions of *The woodlanders* were undertaken in response to influences that were both external (relaxation of social constraints, readers' reactions) and internal (self-criticism, developing artistic

(continued on p. 207)

---

[13] *Harper's bazar*, xx, 1887, p. 147; Harper's first book edition, New York 1887, p. 288. The two verbal variants (b4 and b4–5 in *1886–7*) do not appear in *Harper's bazar* but had been added to the proof from which Harper's book edition was set. (I am most grateful to Terry Belanger, Robin Halwas, and William Matheson for help in investigating the American editions.)

[14] See Manford, pp. 111–12.

against himself all this while—though he would have protected Grace's good repute as the apple of his eye, was a man; and, as Desdemona said, men are not gods. In face c5 of the agonising seductiveness shown by her, in her unenlightened school-girl simplicity about the laws and ordinances, he betrayed a man's weakness. Since it was so—since it had come to this, that Grace, deeming herself c10 free to do it, was virtually asking him to demonstrate that he loved her—since he could demonstrate it only too truly—since life was short and love was strong—he gave

way to the temptation, notwithstanding that c15 he perfectly well knew her to be wedded irrevocably to Fitzpiers. Indeed, he cared for nothing past or future, simply accepting the present and what it brought, deciding once in his life to clasp in his arms her he c20 had watched over and loved so long.

She started back suddenly from his embrace, influenced by a sort of inspiration. "Oh, I suppose," she stammered, "that I am really free?—that this is right? Is there c25 *really* a new law? Father cannot have been too sanguine in saying——"

He did not answer, and a moment afterwards Grace burst into tears in spite of herself. "Oh, why does not my father come c30 home and explain!" she sobbed, "and let me know clearly what I am! It is too trying, this, to ask me to—and then to leave me so long in so vague a state that I do not know what to do, and perhaps do wrong!"

c35 Winterborne felt like a very Cain, over and above his previous sorrow. How he had sinned against her in not telling her what he knew! He turned aside: the feeling of his cruelty mounted higher and c40 higher. How could he have dreamt of

*1887*A (Hardy, T., *The woodlanders*, Macmillan & Co., London 1887, 3 vols.; vol. iii, pp. 119-21; Univ. Lib. Cam. Syn. 7.87.68; ×0·60)

Variants

	1886-7		*1887*A
b19	Indeed	c16	Indeed,
b21	desiring	c18	deciding

Winterborne, though fighting valiantly against himself all
this while—though he would have protected Grace's good
repute as the apple of his eye, was a man; and, as Desdemona said, men are not gods. In face of the agonising
d5 seductiveness shown by her, in her unenlightened school-
girl simplicity about the laws and ordinances, he betrayed a
man's weakness. Since it was so—since it had come to
this, that Grace, deeming herself free to do it, was virtually
asking him to demonstrate that he loved her—since he
d10 could demonstrate it only too truly—since life was short and
love was strong—he gave way to the temptation, notwithstanding that he perfectly well knew her to be wedded
irrevocably to Fitzpiers. Indeed, he cared for nothing past
or future, simply accepting the present and what it brought,
d15 deciding once in his life to clasp in his arms her he had
watched over and loved so long.

She started back suddenly from his long embrace, influenced by a sort of inspiration. "Oh, I suppose," she stammered, "that I am really free?—that this is right? Is there
d20 *really* a new law? Father cannot have been too sanguine
in saying——"

He did not answer, and a moment afterwards Grace burst
into tears in spite of herself. "Oh, why does not my father
come home and explain!" she sobbed upon his breast, "and
d25 let me know clearly what I am! It is too trying, this, to ask
me to—and then to leave me so long in so vague a state
that I do not know what to do, and perhaps do wrong!"

Winterborne felt like a very Cain, over and above his previous sorrow. How he had sinned against her in not telling her
d30 what he knew. He lifted her up and turned aside: the feeling
of his cruelty mounted higher and higher. How could he have
dreamt of kissing her? He could hardly refrain from tears.

*1887*B (Hardy, T., *The woodlanders*, Macmillan & Co., London 1887, 1 vol.; pp. 278–9; Dorset County
Museum; × 1·0)

Variants

	*1887*A		*1887*B
c21–2	his embrace	d17	his long embrace
c30	sobbed, "and	d24	sobbed upon his breast, "and
c38	knew!	d30	knew.
c38	He turned	d30	He lifted her up and turned

Winterborne, though fighting valiantly against himself all this while—though he would have protected Grace's good repute as the apple of his eye, was a man; and, as Desdemona said, men are not gods. In face e5 of the agonizing seductiveness shown by her, in her unenlightened school-girl simplicity about the laws and ordinances, he betrayed a man's weakness. Since it was so—since it had come to this, that Grace, deeming herself free to do it, was virtually asking him to demon-e10 strate that he loved her—since he could demonstrate it only too truly—since life was short and love was strong—he gave way to the temptation, notwithstanding that he perfectly well knew her to be wedded irrevocably to Fitzpiers. Indeed, he cared for nothing past or e15 future, simply accepting the present and what it brought, deciding once in his life to clasp in his arms her he had watched over and loved so long.

She started back suddenly from his long embrace and kiss, influenced by a sort of inspiration. 'O, I e20 suppose,' she stammered, 'that I am really free?— that this is right? Is there *really* a new law? Father cannot have been too sanguine in saying——'

He did not answer, and a moment afterwards Grace

burst into tears in spite of herself. 'O, why does e25 not my father come home and explain!' she sobbed upon his breast, 'and let me know clearly what I am! It is too trying, this, to ask me to—and then to leave me so long in so vague a state that I do not know what to do, and perhaps do wrong!'

e30 Winterborne felt like a very Cain, over and above his previous sorrow. How he had sinned against her in not telling her himself only knew. He lifted her up and turned aside: the feeling of his cruelty mounted higher and higher. How could he have dreamt of

1896 (Hardy, T., *The woodlanders*, Osgood, McIlvaine, London 1896, pp. 365–6; Univ. Lib. Cam. S718.d.89.55; × 1·0)

Variants

	*1887*B			*1896*	
d4	agonising		e5	agonizing	
d17	embrace		e18–19	embrace and kiss,	
d18 [etc.]	[double quotes]		e19 [etc.]	[single quotes]	
d18, 23	"Oh,		e19, 24	'O,	
d29–30	her what he knew.		e32	her himself only knew.	

Winterborne, though fighting valiantly against himself all this while—though he would have protected
Grace's good repute as the apple of his eye, was a man;
and, as Desdemona said, men are not gods. In face
of the agonizing seductiveness shown by her, in her
unenlightened school-girl simplicity about the laws and
ordinances, he betrayed a man's weakness. Since it
was so—since it had come to this, that Grace, deeming
herself free to do it, was virtually asking him to demonstrate that he loved her—since he could demonstrate
it only too truly—since life was short and love was
strong—he gave way to the temptation, notwithstanding
that he perfectly well knew her to be wedded irrevocably
to Fitzpiers. Indeed, he cared for nothing past or
future, simply accepting the present and what it brought,
deciding once in his life to clasp in his arms her he
had watched over and loved so long.

She ~~started back~~ *looked up* suddenly from his long embrace
and, kiss, influenced by a sort of inspiration. 'O, I *passionate*
suppose,' she stammered, 'that I am really free?—
that this is right? Is there *really* a new law? Father
cannot have been too sanguine in saying——'
He did not answer, and a moment afterwards Grace

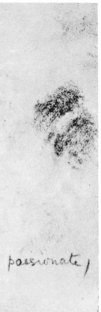

Part of p. 365 of *1896*, in the Macmillan printing of 1906, marked up by Hardy for use as printer's copy for *1912* (Dorset County Museum). No changes were marked for the rest of the extract on p. 366.

vision); and although they did not alter the novel fundamentally they strengthened and clarified it in ways that Hardy, at least, thought beneficial. The manuscript version of *The woodlanders* was already a considerable novel; but most readers would probably agree that the final, *1912*, version was a much better one, a major work of art resulting from Hardy's development of his original conception.

If so, it is the last not the first version of *The woodlanders* that an editor would aim to reproduce, at any rate in words, and practically all of Hardy's verbal emendations up to *1912* would be incorporated in an edition whatever was used as copy-text. The question of which set of details—and especially which punctuation—should be adopted as the basis of an edited text is a difficult one, however. It is the case that here (as in his other major novels) Hardy supplied the manuscript text with a deliberate, homogeneous punctuation which employed fewer commas and more dashes than his printers normally used, and that the printers then normalized many of these details in accordance with their ordinary practice and presumably without

Hardy's authority.[15] Yet Hardy's sporadic revision of *The woodlanders* over the next twenty-five years included much alteration of detail (such as the 460+ commas removed for *1912*), and the editor has the awkward problem of deciding whether he thinks it more likely that Hardy continued to prefer the punctuation and other details of the manuscript right up to 1912 and would even then have reinserted them in the printed text—presumably with some revision—if he had had the time and energy to do so; or whether it is more likely that he was eventually content with the details of the printed text and that, in revising them for *1912*, he actively accepted them. If the editor thinks the former, he will take the manuscript as copy-text for his edition (and with it the problem of how Hardy might have altered the manuscript punctuation, etc., if it had entered a printed version); if the latter, he will take *1912*.

Of course there are other possibilities. If for instance the editor thinks that Hardy would have reinserted the manuscript details in the magazine or early book texts of 1886-7 if he had had the opportunity to do so at the time, but that twenty-five years later he was content with his revision of the printed details; or if he feels that, not knowing Hardy's own view of the matter, there is not sufficient evidence of the author's intentions one way or the other, he may choose his copy-text for other reasons, such as a critical preference for one system of punctuation rather than another.

My own inclination is to the view that Hardy actively accepted the revised details of *1912*, and I would therefore choose *1912* (or the copy for it) as copy-text for an edition. But another editor might well think it right to follow Hardy's manuscript, and there is no doubt that the result would be worth while. This is a case in which there is no one right answer.[16]

For a reset edition based on *1912* the editor's choice would seem to lie between (1) taking the actual copy of the 1906 printing of *1896* which was marked up by Hardy and using it—as the *1912* compositors did—as copy-text for his edition, emending it where the variants in *1912* seemed to derive from Hardy's revisions in proof;[17] and (2) taking *1912* itself as copy-text, emending it where its variation from the marked-up copy of *1896* seemed not to have derived from Hardy's proof-revision. In either case the words and most of the details of the edited text should be the same; but there would be some small variation resulting from the choice of one copy-text rather

[15] Information from Simon Gatrell, who kindly enabled me to read part of his thesis on the text of *Under the greenwood tree*.

[16] Simon Gatrell, who is able to argue from a close acquaintance with a wide range of Hardy's texts, would base an edition of *The woodlanders* on Hardy's manuscript, not on a printed edition; he prefers the punctuation of the manuscript on critical grounds, and he considers that Hardy did no more than acquiesce passively in the printers' alterations.

[17] This is Manford's solution.

Winterborne, though fighting valiantly against himself all this while—though he would have protected Grace's good repute as the apple of his eye, was a man ; and, as Desdemona said, men are not gods.   In g5 face of the agonizing seductiveness shown by her, in her unenlightened school-girl simplicity about the laws and ordinances, he betrayed a man's weakness.   Since it was so—since it had come to this, that Grace, deeming herself free to do it, was virtually asking him g10 to demonstrate that he loved her—since he could demonstrate it only too truly—since life was short and love was strong—he gave way to the temptation, notwithstanding that he perfectly well knew her to be wedded irrevocably to Fitzpiers.   Indeed, he cared for g15 nothing past or future, simply accepting the present and what it brought, deciding once in his life to clasp in his arms her he had watched over and loved so long.

g20 She looked up suddenly from his long embrace and passionate kiss, influenced by a sort of inspiration. 'O, I suppose,' she stammered, 'that I am really free? —that this is right? Is there *really* a new law? Father cannot have been too sanguine in saying——'

g25 He did not answer, and a moment afterwards Grace burst into tears in spite of herself. 'O, why does not my father come home and explain!' she sobbed upon his breast, 'and let me know clearly what I am! It is too trying, this, to ask me to—and then to leave me so long in so vague a state that I do g30 not know what to do, and perhaps do wrong!'

Winterborne felt like a very Cain, over and above his previous sorrow. How he had sinned against her in not telling her himself only knew. He lifted her up and turned aside: the feeling of his cruelty mounted g35 higher and higher. How could he have dreamt of

1912 (Hardy, T., *The woodlanders*, Macmillan & Co., London 1912 (Wessex edition), p. 351; Girton Coll. Cam. 826.4H22; ×1·0)

Variants	*1896*		*1912*
	e, f18	She started back	g19	She looked up
	e, f19	and kiss,	g20	and passionate kiss,

(i.e. the two changes marked by Hardy in the copy for *1912*, and no others.)

than the other, because the editor might not be able to say whether some of the variation between them was more likely to have resulted from Hardy's proof-revision or from unauthorized alterations made by the *1912* printers; and in uncertain cases he would follow the chosen copy-text. Since Hardy was actively concerned with revising the textual details of *1912*, these indifferent variants might as plausibly be attributed to him as to the printers; and there would seem to be little to choose between basing an edited text on the copy of *1896* marked up by Hardy for setting *1912*, and basing it on *1912* itself.

But if *1912* could be used as copy-text for an edition of *The woodlanders*, do we need a reset edited version at all? What we are after is a reliable text of the last version of the novel—one that represents Hardy's final intentions, uncorrupted by interference or error—and we already have it: *1912*, the Wessex edition, revised in detail and proof-corrected by the author. If an editor were to use *1912* as copy-text for a new, reset edition of *The wood-landers* he could do no more than emend it in those few places where it appeared that unauthorized readings had been introduced by the printers of *1912* and had been missed by Hardy; while at the same time he would probably introduce a few new errors of his own.

It is true, alas, that *1912* is no longer in print[18]—its setting was last used by Macmillan's for the Greenwood edition of 1967–72—and also true that Macmillan's New Wessex edition of 1974–5 is textually unreliable.[19] There is nevertheless a simple solution to the problem of publishing a reliable critical text of *The woodlanders*: this is to incorporate the very few necessary emendations in a copy of the first impression of *1912*, and then to reproduce it by photolithography.[20] Not only would new copying errors be avoided, but the version could be produced at a small fraction of the cost of a reset critical text—a luxury which even universities and their publishers may not always be able to afford.

There would seem to be no such simple solution to the related problem of presenting a record of Hardy's revisions as an adjunct to a critical text,

[18] There is still available a 'book club' reprint published by Heron Books which derives ultimately from the *1912* setting.

[19] Manford (Appendix II) gives a disturbing list of thirty-seven variants between the text of the New Wessex edition and *1912*, of which no fewer than twelve are *verbal* errors made by the printer. Six of the rest are errors of punctuation, etc., made by the printer, and the remainder are changes of detail either made deliberately by the publisher for the New Wessex edition, or resulting from earlier changes made to the setting of the Greenwood edition (from which the New Wessex edition was set). The worst New Wessex text was the first, paperback impression dated 1974, and some of the errors were rectified for the hardback of 1975; but Manford says that his list was made from a single collation and may not be complete.

[20] The copy of *1912* could be emended by stripping type-set corrections into the text; or by printing, typing, or writing the corrections in the margins (as suggested by Morse Peckham, *Studies in the novel*, vii, 1975, pp. 402–4); or by a combination of these methods.

however reproduced. There is a case for presenting them, since they illuminate Hardy's intentions for *The woodlanders* and his development as an artist; yet the six layers of revision, changing and rechanging so many aspects of the text, include too much evidence of too many sorts for there to be any easy, economical way of setting it out and publishing it.

Parallel texts are easy to use and may be the best solution where there are only two—preferably brief—versions to be compared with each other; but where three or more versions of a lengthy book are involved, the expense of parallel texts cannot be justified unless both book and variants are of outstanding literary importance. It is arguable that a full knowledge of Joyce's revisions is essential to understanding *Ulysses*, and a case is made in the next chapter for producing a 'compact' parallel-text version of that book; but the same cannot be said of Hardy's revisions to *The woodlanders*, interesting as they are, and a parallel-text edition would be impossibly costly.

The synoptic method of presenting variants, whereby all of them are brought together into a single 'text' and identified by symbols or special type, is a possible one where (as with *Ulysses* again) they consist chiefly of additions to a basic text; but where the variants are substitutions rather than additions the synoptic method produces a version that is unreadable. Thus, to take simple examples,

(a17) . . . sobbed $_\wedge$ ^{e}upon his breast$^e_\wedge$, "and . . .

is a comprehensible way of indicating an addition;[21] but

(a21) . . . telling her [what he] $_\wedge$ ^{f}himself only^f $_\wedge$ knew[.][$_\wedge$^{c}!^{c}$_\wedge$]$_\wedge$^{e}.$^e_\wedge$ . . .

is a confusing way of saying that the phrase was changed from 'telling her what he knew' to 'telling her himself only knew', and that the final punctuation mark was changed from a full stop to an exclamation mark and then back to a full stop again. It is hard to see how confusion of this sort could be avoided in a synoptic presentation of substituted readings.

Hardy's revisions would therefore have to be recorded outside the critical text, either as footnotes (where they would be easy to refer to but would interfere with the impact of Hardy's story) or in appendices following the text. But a full record of *all* the variants in Hardy's six main revisions of *The woodlanders*, wherever it was printed, would be so dense and unreadable as to be virtually useless (except perhaps to the editor himself). To see that this is so it is only necessary to look at the five lists of variants appended to the reproductions of the printed versions of our brief extract,

---

[21] The convention used in these examples is that a caret and a superior letter (^{e} for *1887*B, ^{f} for *1896*, etc.) is placed at each end of an insertion to show its extent and origin; and that square brackets enclose words removed or replaced. Other symbols might be used in place of these ones, but the effect would be essentially similar.

and to visualize a sixth and longer list of revisions to the manuscript; and then to imagine what it would be like to try to use a combined version of all six lists in the absence of the reproductions, and to do so not just for one extract of less than a single page of *1912* but for the whole 444-page novel.

Therefore a compromise must be sought, probably one whereby some but not all of Hardy's revisions are recorded. One such compromise would be to print annotated reproductions of extracts from the text in all their successive versions (after the manner of the reproductions given here) for the sake of exemplifying the complete process of revision; and also to give a selection of variants from the whole book, chosen for their critical importance and general interest. An apparatus of this sort would be supplemented, finally, by a general account of Hardy's revisions along the lines of Dale Kramer's excellent 'Revisions and vision'.[22]

[22] See p. 196 n. 1.

EXAMPLE 11

Joyce, *Ulysses*, 1922

As early as 1906 James Joyce was thinking about writing a story called 'Ulysses', but he got no further than the title and the idea remained dormant until he decided sometime during the writing of *A portrait of the artist as a young man* in 1907-13 that his next book would be a Dublin Odyssey; and he withheld some of the material written for *A portrait* for use in the first sketches for *Ulysses*.[1] These were made in 1914, when Joyce was living, and more or less supporting his family, as a teacher of English in Trieste: heterodox, improvident, yet so certain of the quality and value of his art that he always commanded the self-discipline he needed to shape the movement and control the detail of the immense novel that was to occupy him for the next eight years.

During the first year, 1914-15, Joyce was also concerned with writing his play, *Exiles*, but from mid-1915 (when the Joyces moved to Zürich) he worked single-mindedly at *Ulysses*. When the war ended in 1918 he had completed nine episodes, and serial publication was under way in *The little review* of New York.[2] At this point *Ulysses* was ostensibly a fairly straight-

[1] The Joyce literature is large and learned, many hundreds of books and articles having been published about *Ulysses* alone. The essential introduction to the study of Joyce's texts is Richard Ellmann's fine but poorly indexed biography, *James Joyce*, Oxford 1959, 1966. The standard bibliography is Slocum, J. J., and Cahoon, H., *A bibliography of James Joyce*, London 1953; and there is a published *Catalogue* of Joyce's manuscripts and letters at the State University of New York at Buffalo by Spielberg, P., Buffalo 1962. The *Letters* themselves, 3 vols., ed. Gilbert, S., and Ellmann, R., London 1957-66, contain much important material.

Joyce's 'Ulysses' notesheets in the British Museum have been edited by P. F. Herring, Charlottesville 1972; and the Rosenbach MS of *Ulysses* has been published in facsimile, ed. Driver, C., 3 vols., London and Philadelphia 1975, including a reduced, annotated facsimile of the whole of the first edition of *Ulysses*, Paris 1922. There is a facsimile of *The little review*, including all the serial parts of *Ulysses* published 1918-20, New York 1967. There is a concordance (which refers to the first Random House edition, 1934): Hanley, M. L., *Word index to James Joyce's 'Ulysses'*, Madison 1937, etc.

Modern textual study of *Ulysses* begins with A. W. Litz's excellent *The art of James Joyce*, Oxford 1961, 1964. An important pioneering article on the problems of correcting the text of *Ulysses* is Dalton, J. P., 'The text of *Ulysses*' in *New light on Joyce*, Bloomington 1972 (written 1966). Much of the best detailed work on the text is contained in unpublished theses; references are given in Herring's edition of the *Notesheets* (see above), p. 5 n. Special mention must be made of M. L. Groden's Princeton dissertation 'The growth of James Joyce's *Ulysses*', 1975 (since published); and of the same author's '"Cyclops" in progress, 1919', *James Joyce quarterly*, xii, 1974-5, pp. 123-68.

I am especially grateful to Dr. Hans Walter Gabler for his help and advice.

[2] Publication in *The little review* ran from 'Telemachus' in March 1918 to part of 'Oxen of the Sun' in Sept./Dec. 1920. The 'Nestor', 'Proteus', and 'Hades' episodes, and part of 'Wandering rocks', were also published in *The Egoist* (from *Little review* texts), London, Jan.-Dec. 1919.

forward novel of character, a sequel to *A portrait* that seemed unusual chiefly in its extended use of interior monologue. But the later episodes, and especially those written after Joyce moved to Paris in 1920, relied increasingly for their effect on the schematic manipulation of language and symbol, and less on narrative and characterization. Serial publication was brought to an end by court order in 1920 and Joyce, whose concept of the work may have been changing as he wrote the last nine episodes, attempted to unify it for book publication by revising the earlier episodes, adding material in proof that linked them with what followed. *Ulysses* was finished— or at least Joyce stopped writing it—early in 1922, and it was published in Paris on 2 February, his fortieth birthday.

Ulysses was immediately recognized as a work of astonishing originality, but many even of its most enthusiastic early readers found it difficult to understand; while others were repelled by its explicit sexual and scato-logical references, with the result that full publication was delayed in America until 1934 and in England until 1936. Once it became generally available in the English-speaking world, however, understanding and appreciation increased until nowadays *Ulysses*—no longer a dirty book or even a really difficult one—has a huge and devoted readership, and tens of thousands of copies are sold every year to students and general readers. These are not, alas, good, reliable texts: every edition of *Ulysses* that has yet been published teems with errors that affect Joyce's meaning.[3]

The inadequacy of the text of this central work is not irremediable, for we have abundant evidence of its development: many of Joyce's early drafts and notesheets, a holograph fair copy, typed transcripts, and many of the revised proofs, as well as references in Joyce's correspondence and in the reminiscences of his friends. Few works of literature, indeed, are so well documented; and, although profuse documentation can itself pose an editorial problem, it does illuminate Joyce's art, and it does help the editor of *Ulysses* to produce a better text than has yet been seen.

Joyce drafted the episodes of *Ulysses* on the right-hand pages of flimsy exercise books, leaving the left-hand pages blank for later additions. Both in drafting and amending the text he drew on a huge collection of notes written first on separate slips of paper, and later transferred to large note-sheets, each note being crossed out in coloured pencil as it was used. The separate notes have not survived, but we have notesheets and drafts for most of the later episodes, and fragmentary drafts of some of the earlier

[3] J. P. Dalton (see p. 213 n. 1) estimates that the first edition of *Ulysses*, which is also the least faulty text, contains over 2,000 errors affecting the meaning; and that the additional errors accumulated in subsequent editions have put the total up to nearly 4,000. See also the Appendix to this chapter.

ones.[4] For the most part Joyce wrote *Ulysses* from beginning to end, episode by episode, but his preliminary work in 1914 may have included sketches for 'Eumaeus', all or part of the Telemachia, and 'Scylla and Charybdis'; and we know that he commonly worked on two or even three episodes at a time.[5]

Joyce next made a complete working manuscript of each episode which, after revision, could be typed out for the printer. He also wanted a fair-copy manuscript for sale to the American collector John Quinn (to whom he had previously sold the manuscript of *Exiles* and the proofs of *A portrait*). In some cases the working manuscript could be used by the typist and then sent off to Quinn; but in others, perhaps because the working manuscript was untidy, Joyce found it necessary to make a separate fair copy for Quinn, while keeping the working manuscript for the typists' use (see the diagram and notes on p. 218).[6] Quinn's copy, which was sent to New York in batches in 1920-1, survives as the 'Rosenbach MS'.[7]

Typing began with 'Telemachus' in November 1917 and ended with 'Ithaca'—completed after 'Penelope', the last episode—in October 1921. Three carbon copies were made of most of the typescripts.[8] Joyce revised all the copies of the typescripts soon after they were typed, and again later when they were to be used for setting the book edition, not always making the same amendments to all the copies. In a few cases second typescripts were made from the first.

Despite the amateurish appearance of much of their work, Joyce's typists made a tolerably good job of transcribing the Rosenbach MS, which was written in Joyce's fast correspondence hand; and there is no reason to suppose that they did less well with the working manuscript, which is likely to have been written in a similar hand (rather than the almost illegible scribble that Joyce used for writing rough notes, or the specially careful and legible script with which he amended typescripts and proofs).[9]

[4] See Herring's edition of the *Notesheets*, and Spielberg's *Catalogue* of the Buffalo manuscripts (see p. 213 n. 1).

[5] For the chronology of the composition and publishing of *Ulysses*, see Litz, A. W., *The art of James Joyce*, revised imp., Oxford 1964, pp. 141-5; and the table in Ellmann, R., *James Joyce*, revised imp., Oxford 1966, p. 456.

[6] The evidence is incomplete. Not only has the working manuscript disappeared, but there are no surviving typescripts for 'Telemachus' or 'Lotus eaters', only one page each for 'Nestor' and 'Proteus', and eight pages for 'Calypso'.

[7] Quinn sold it to A. S. W. Rosenbach in 1924, and it now belongs to the Rosenbach Foundation of Philadelphia, which published an excellent facsimile in 1976 (dated 1975); see p. 213 n. 1.

[8] See Spielberg's *Catalogue* (p. 213 n. 1), pp. 51 ff. Joyce appears to have asked for only two carbon copies of 'Telemachus' and 'Nestor', which may have been typed from the Rosenbach MS (Joyce, *Letters*, i, p. 108; ii, p. 413).

[9] For the handwriting of the Rosenbach MS, see p. 226; for Joyce's 'amendment' hand, see pp. 229-33.

Typescripts of the episodes up to 'Oxen of the Sun', with the first layer of revision, were sent to Ezra Pound in London, who edited and expurgated them before sending them on to New York for serialization in *The little review*. This set has disappeared, but we can tell from other copies of the typescripts that the *Little review* compositors were extremely careless, correcting few of the obvious errors in the typescripts and adding many new errors of their own. Joyce did not correct the proofs of the *Little review* instalments.

A second set of typescripts up to 'Oxen of the Sun' was considered by B. W. Huebsch for book publication in America, but no agreement was reached and the set was returned to Joyce in Paris in April 1921. Lastly another set of typescripts—or perhaps the same one—consisting of a mixture of top and carbon copies was further amended by Joyce for use as printers' copy for the book edition which was finally undertaken by Sylvia Beach of Shakespeare and Company, Paris, and printed by Maurice Darantière of Dijon in 1921-2. Most of the printers' typescripts, together with a few duplicate typescript pages in different states of revision, have survived and are now in the Lockwood Memorial Library of the State University of New York at Buffalo.[10]

None of Darantière's compositors knew English, but his foreman Maurice Hirschwald had a reading knowledge of the language.[11] Hirschwald quite properly corrected some of the more obvious mistakes made by typists and compositors, but he was also inclined to take unusual features of Joyce's prose for mistakes, and to 'correct' them as well.[12] Joyce used successive proofs of this printed transcript as part of the process of composition, making substantial alterations—mostly additions—to the text in order both to recast the earlier episodes and to bring the later ones to their final form.[13] Sylvia Beach had given orders that Joyce was to have as many proofs as he liked, regardless of expense;[14] and there were (for instance) three successive

[10] They are listed in Spielberg's *Catalogue* (see p. 213 n. 1), pp. 51 ff.

[11] Dalton, J. P., 'The text of *Ulysses*' (see p. 213 n. 1), pp. 108-9.

[12] In the extract below the unusual word 'toady' is amended in the typescript, probably by Hirschwald, to read 'today' (p. 228, l. 26); Joyce changed it back again in the first proof (p. 229, l. 18).

A more necessary—but still erroneous—emendation was attempted by the printer in the preceding sentence, where 'fogy' was set for the typist's mistranscription 'fo' for Joyce's MS 'fox' (p. 226, l. 8; p. 228, l. 25; p. 229, l. 18). Joyce first corrected this to 'fogey'; and then changed it to 'hunks' (p. 229, l. 18; p. 230, l. 21).

[13] See the extract below, where the MS had 144 words; the final TS 147; the first proof 195; the second proof 302; the third proof 370; the fourth proof 379; the fifth proof 462; and the final published text 464 words, which was thus more than three times as long as the manuscript draft.

Similarly the manuscript of 'Ithaca'—the last episode to be completed—contained 14,812 words, to which Joyce added 4,363 words in the typescripts and 3,246 words in the proofs; he also changed 348 words and deleted 79 words (Madtes, R. E., 'A textual and critical study of the "Ithaca" episode of James Joyce's *Ulysses*' (Columbia University Ph.D. dissertation, 1961, p. 61).

[14] Beach, S., *Shakespeare and Company*, London 1960, p. 68.

placard proofs (analogous to galley proofs)[15] of 'Aeolus', followed by three successive page proofs; and three or four *placard* proofs of 'Cyclops' followed by three, four, or five page proofs.[16] Many of these proofs have survived: there are marked sets of *placards* at Harvard, of page proofs at Buffalo, and of final page proofs at Austin, Texas; and others, mostly unmarked, in various private and public collections.[17]

The result of this long development, Shakespeare and Company's first book edition (*S1*), published in February 1922 in a first impression of 1,000 copies, was a professional piece of printing, less marred by errors than it might have been considering the inherent difficulty of Joyce's text and the complication of his massive additions to the proofs. There were still many errors that affected the meaning, but some of the more obvious ones were corrected in later impressions—altogether there were seven impressions of the first edition, from February 1922 to October 1925, after which the text was reset—by means of errata lists and amendments to the plates.[18]

This was as far as Joyce took the text of *Ulysses*, for he neither revised it further nor corrected the errors that accumulated in later editions. Its development so far may be shown diagrammatically (see overleaf).

Ulysses might be edited in a number of ways, but three particular approaches would be especially rewarding. The first would be to produce a plain, accurate text of the final form of the book, all the available editions being sadly defective. The second would be to edit the first half of *Ulysses*— say up to 'Scylla and Charybdis'[19]—in its first-draft form, before Joyce shifted the emphasis of his work away from narrative and character towards language and symbol. The third would be to illustrate the development of the text by making available the earlier drafts and versions, in order both to elucidate it and to illuminate Joyce's mind and art.

---

[15] Although he may have made them for his own use, Darantière did not send Joyce true galley (or slip) proofs of *Ulysses*. His *épreuves en placard* consisted of eight 'pages' of type printed broadside—i.e. not for folding—on a sheet of proofing paper; but they were not true pages, being without page numbers and being altered in length as Joyce amended the text. (A similar practice was known in British printing whereby true pages were proofed broadside before being proofed in folded sheets: see *The Library*, xxvi, 1976, pp. 114–15.) There is no term in English which precisely describes Darantière's *placards*, so the French word is used here.

Darantière's page proofs were the ordinary sort, being pages of constant length, complete with page numbers, imposed for proofing in folded sheets.

[16] Groden, M. L., 'The growth of James Joyce's *Ulysses*' (see p. 213 n. 1), pp. 133, 163–4.

[17] Darantière normally sent Joyce three sets of each proof stage; Joyce would amend one of them, leaving the other two sets largely unmarked.

[18] In the second impression (Oct. 1922) the plates of pp. 694–5 were altered to move a short passage that had been misplaced; and a list of 201 'Errata' was inserted. These errata were corrected in the plates for the fourth to seventh impressions (1924–5), but further mistakes were then discovered, and these same impressions had a list of 106 'Additional corrections' printed at the end.

[19] Although publication in *The little review* continued up to the first part of 'Oxen of the Sun', Joyce's approach to *Ulysses* became more noticeably experimental before this; hence the suggestion that an edition of the first-draft form of the novel should not go beyond 'Scylla and Charybdis'.

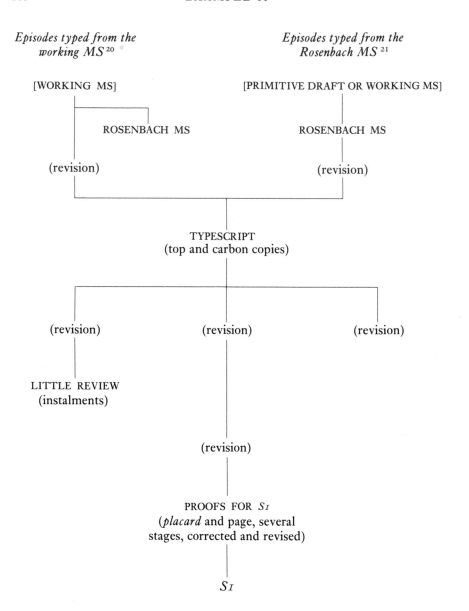

Episodes typed from the
working MS[20]

[WORKING MS]

ROSENBACH MS

(revision)

Episodes typed from the
Rosenbach MS[21]

[PRIMITIVE DRAFT OR WORKING MS]

ROSENBACH MS

(revision)

TYPESCRIPT
(top and carbon copies)

(revision)   (revision)   (revision)

LITTLE REVIEW
(instalments)

(revision)

PROOFS FOR *S1*
(*placard* and page, several
stages, corrected and revised)

S1

[20] Probably 'Calypso', part of 'Lotus eaters', 'Hades', 'Aeolus', 'Lestrygonians', 'Scylla and Charybdis', 'Sirens', 'Nausicaa', and 'Oxen of the Sun'.
[21] Probably 'Telemachus', 'Nestor', 'Proteus', part of 'Lotus eaters', 'Wandering rocks', and 'Cyclops'; the last three episodes ('Eumaeus', 'Penelope', 'Ithaca') also belong essentially to this group, although there were complications not shown here. 'Circe' appears to have had the Rosenbach MS in its line of descent, but there was also a scribal longhand copy from which the typescripts were made.

A newly edited plain text of *Ulysses* would be based on the first edition, *S1*. This edition, which Joyce saw through all its many proof stages, and which he was anxious to have corrected after publication,[22] was the culmination of his labour on the novel, the end towards which he had consciously worked. No earlier draft had been anywhere near complete; no later edition improved on or even matched the first for accuracy, for each one both accumulated the errors of its predecessors and introduced new errors of its own.[23]

But, although *S1* would be chosen as copy-text for an edition of *Ulysses* in its final form, the novel singularity of much of Joyce's prose, the importance that he attached to its slightest details, and the extent of his revision in typescript and proof, mean that the copy-text would have to be scrutinized with exceptional care. Not surprisingly *S1* does include a good many transmission variants, especially of the normalizing kind.

Joyce did what he could to correct the mistakes in both typescript and proof, but his sight was poor, the labour was immense, and so they slipped through. 'Since the completion of *Ulysses*', he wrote to Harriet Weaver on 6 November 1921, 'I feel more and more tired but I have to hold on till all the proofs are revised. I am extremely irritated by all those printer's errors.[24] Working as I do amid piles of notes at a table in a hotel I cannot possibly do this mechanical part with my wretched eye and a half. Are these to be perpetuated in future editions? I hope not.'[25]

The best way of spotting errors in the copy-text is to collate all the early versions that are available—first drafts, Rosenbach MS, typescripts, proofs—each one being compared with its immediate neighbours in the line of descent. Even this will not solve every problem. When a variant appears in a transcript, and we also have the draft from which that transcript was made, we may be able to see what caused it; but when we do not have the draft it may be uncertain whether the variant resulted from an error of transcription or from an emendation made by Joyce to the missing draft. Even when we have identified an unauthorized variant which Joyce did not correct, there is the question of whether he was aware of it; and, if not, whether he would have corrected it if he had been.

[22] Joyce, *Letters*, i, pp. 184, 187; iii, p. 86.
[23] The later editions of *Ulysses* are of little textual interest except as a classic case of textual deterioration; they are briefly surveyed in the appendix to this chapter.
[24] Presumably in those episodes that had already been printed off; but perhaps in the current proofs as well.
[25] Joyce, *Letters*, i, p. 176.

A few examples may make this clearer:

(1) 158.21/200.7:[26] When Mr. Bloom contemplates Mrs. Breen's dilapidated appearance in Westmoreland Street he thinks, according to the Rosenbach MS, 'And that dusty looking toque: three old cherries to take the harm out of it.' In the surviving typescript, however, this phrase reads 'And that dowdy toque, three old grapes to take the harm out of it.' The changes from 'dusty looking' to 'dowdy' and from 'cherries' to 'grapes', which cannot be supposed to be the result of transcription errors and which entered all the printed texts, show that the typescript was copied not from the Rosenbach MS but from another draft, now missing but presumably the revised working manuscript.[27] Here the editor would certainly follow the typescript, not the Rosenbach MS.

(2) 71.33/86.31: In Westland Row Mr. Bloom took off his hat to get out the card secreted in it; and then, in the Rosenbach MS, 'His right hand once more more slowly went over his brow and hair. Then he put on his hat again, relieved: and read again: choice blend, made of the finest Ceylon brands.' There is no surviving typescript of 'Lotus-eaters', but we can be sure that the phrase was copied accurately by the typist because it appears unchanged in *The little review*. But the eye of Darantière's compositor skipped what was probably one whole line of the typescript copy, so that in *S1* (and all subsequent editions) the passage reads 'His right hand once more more slowly went over again; choice blend, made of the finest Ceylon brands.' This is nonsense; and, since the omission is plainly a mistake even though Joyce passed it in proof, the editor would restore the missing words.

(3) 172.42/219.31: Joyce wrote in the Rosenbach MS that, when Boylan's name was mentioned in Davy Byrne's, 'A warm shock of air, heat of mustard, hanched on Mr. Bloom's heart.' For 'hanched' (which means 'snapped' or 'fastened its jaws') the typescript reads 'hauched' (which has no meaning); and, although we have not got the working manuscript from which 'Lestrygonians' was probably transcribed, this must surely be a transcription error, not a deliberate alteration by Joyce. The *Little review* and Darantière compositors copied 'hauched' from the typescript, which was passed in proof and entered the printed editions.[28] Joyce would scarcely have passed the change if he had noticed it; therefore the editor must suppose that he did not, and would print 'hanched'.

[26] References to the text of *Ulysses* are to pages and lines of *R2* (Random House, 2nd edn., 1961-) and *B2* (Bodley Head, 2nd edn., 1960-) respectively. Recent impressions of *R2* include references to the page divisions of *R1* (Random House, 1st edn., 1934-60), so that they can be used with Hanley's concordance (see p. 213 n. 1).

[27] See, similarly, the variants listed in the caption to p. 228.

[28] The *S1* reading 'hauched' is wrongly left unamended in vol. iii of the facsimile of the Rosenbach MS (*S1*, p. 164; see p. 213 n. 1); the word in the MS is clearly 'hanched'.

(4) 87.11/108.4: According to the Rosenbach MS, when Mr. Bloom entered the funeral carriage, 'He pulled the door to after him and slammed it twice till it shut tight.' The beginning of the typescript of 'Hades' (which was copied, probably, from the working manuscript, not from the Rosenbach MS) is lost, but it is clear that for 'twice' it read 'tight', for in both *The little review* and *S1* the sentence reads 'He pulled the door to after him and slammed it tight till it shut tight.' This may well be another transcription error by the typist which Joyce failed to notice and correct in proof; but we cannot be sure that the working manuscript from which the typescript was copied was not emended by Joyce so that 'tight' was repeated. Even if the editor thinks it likely that Joyce intended 'slammed it twice' rather than 'slammed it tight', he will give careful thought to the cancellation of an alteration which Joyce could have made and did pass in proof.

(5) 688.10/806.1: Answering the question 'How was a glyphic comparison made [etc.]?', Joyce wrote in the Rosenbach MS 'On the penultimate blank page of a book [etc.]'; then, by a marginal addition, he added 'By juxtaposition' at the beginning of the answer. The first typescript (probably made from the Rosenbach MS) is missing; the addition did not appear in the second typescript, and was not reinserted at any later stage. The editor, who cannot know whether 'By juxtaposition' was accidentally omitted from the first typescript or deleted from it by Joyce, would probably leave it out.

(6) 734.25-9/867.10-14: Bloom's 'final satisfaction', as he muses in bed at the end of the day is (in the Rosenbach MS, from which the first typescript was made) 'at the ubiquity . . . of adipose female hemispheres'. Joyce altered this by a marginal addition in the manuscript to read 'of adipose anterior and posterior female hemispheres', which is the reading of the typescripts and first proof. Then in the first proof Joyce deleted 'anterior and'; but, changing his mind again, he attempted to cancel the deletion by writing 'laissez' in the margin of the proof. The marginal instruction was ignored by the compositor, who removed 'anterior and'; they were not reinserted in the later proofs. The editor has to decide whether it is more likely that Joyce failed to notice that the words had gone, or more likely that he did notice but, changing his mind yet again, decided that he preferred to delete them after all. Again the editor would probably leave the phrase in its final form: 'of adipose posterior female hemispheres'.[29]

There remains the question of whether an edited plain text should have any textual apparatus. A brief textual introduction would be useful, but to include extensive textual notes would defeat the purpose of making the text of *Ulysses* not only accurately but easily available. The complications of the

---

[20] Examples (5) and (6) were noted in R. E. Madtes's outstanding dissertation on 'Ithaca' (see p. 216 n. 13), pp. 98–9, 95–6.

textual background are such that abbreviated notes would have little value; and it would surely be best to omit textual notes altogether. The textual evidence must nevertheless be made available somewhere; and we shall see, in discussing the third editorial project, what is currently being done about providing it.

The second project, meanwhile, was to edit the earlier part of *Ulysses* in its first-draft form, with the aim of making it possible both to appreciate Joyce's original approach to the book, and to see how he then altered the text to accord with the new approach of the later part. This requires, first, an accurate text of the first-draft version of the episodes up to 'Scylla and Charybdis', with the corrections Joyce made up to the end of 1918; and secondly a record of the sum of the changes Joyce made to these episodes in typescript and proof in 1920-1.

The edited text of the first-draft version would have to be based on the *Little review* instalments, for the surviving typescripts are seriously incomplete for the early episodes while the Rosenbach MS is outside the main line of descent of the text of most of the first half of the book.[30] The *Little review* text, however, is marred by errors and omissions, and would therefore be amended by reference to the surviving typescripts and the Rosenbach MS. The record of the later changes would of course derive from S_I.

There are various possible ways of presenting the amended first-draft text and of recording the later changes, those requiring complicated type-setting being the most expensive. Since the audience for such an edition would be limited, the most practical solution would be to print reduced facsimiles of the *Little review* and S_I texts in parallel, with footnote corrections to the *Little review* pages and rings drawn round the major changes in S_I.[31]

A page of 'Aeolus' as it appeared in *The little review* is edited in this way on pp. 224-5. The footnotes correct the errors of the *Little review* text, but do not record the readings of the Rosenbach MS where they differ from those of the typescripts made from the lost working manuscript. The ringed passages in the S_I text show how Joyce altered the passage by inserting cross-heads, references to wind, etc.

The third editorial project—to illustrate the development of *Ulysses* by making the pre-publication documents generally available—requires the presentation of a very large and complex mass of material. Taken together the surviving manuscript, typescript, and proof versions are several times as long as *Ulysses* itself, which is not a short book. Any such project would be expensive both in editorial effort and in production costs, and the first

[30] See p. 215 n. 7.

[31] Drawing rings round the changes in S_I is the method used for recording the differences between the manuscript and the *Little review* and book texts in vol. iii of the Rosenbach MS facsimile (see p. 213 n. 1).

question must therefore be whether there is a potential readership large enough to make the presentation of the documents worth while.

It is arguable that, in the unique case of *Ulysses*, the number of readers who would be interested in the pre-publication documents would in fact be considerable. In most prose fiction the meaning of the words (if they are rightly transcribed) is usually apparent without the need to consult the author's working papers; and the reproduction of the author's spelling and capitalization (if not of his punctuation) is seldom of crucial importance. For *Ulysses* the case is otherwise: satisfactory exegesis often depends on recourse to the readings of the early versions, while Joyce conveyed meaning by variations of spelling and capitalization. Those readers and students of *Ulysses* who care about its precise implications—and it is a work which stimulates particularity, so they are numerous—would often be glad to have access to the pre-publication material.

The scale of the problem may be indicated by means of an extract. Illustrated here are the surviving textual stages that led up to page 153 of the first edition, *S1* (160.18–161.19/202.24–204.6 in *R2/B2*), a passage from 'Lestrygonians' which describes part of Mr. Bloom's interior monologue between his meeting with Mrs. Breen and his arrival at the Burton. We have:

1. The Rosenbach MS (lines 3–23, 'Lestrygonians', p. 9)
   Fair-copied from a lost working MS; 133 words; interlinear addition of 11 words.
2. Typescript (lines 22–36, 'Lestrygonians', p. '100')
   Typed from the lost working MS at a later stage of revision; 147 words; MS. additions totalling 48 words.
3. First *placard* proof (lines 15–31, '*Placard 17*', p. |2])
   Set from the typescript; 195 words; MS. additions totalling 107 words.
4. Second *placard* proof (lines 15–39, '*Placard 17*', p. [2])
   The first *placard* proof amended; 302 words; MS. additions totalling 69 words.
5. First page proof (lines 36–7, 1–28, pp. 152–3)
   The second *placard* proof amended; 370 words; MS. addition of 9 words.
6. Second page proof (lines 1–30, p. 153)
   The first page proof amended; 379 words; MS. additions totalling 85 words.
7. Third page proof (lines 1–37, p. 153)
   The second page proof, amended; 462 words; MS. addition of 2 words
8. *S1*, 1922 (lines 1–37, p. 153)
   The third page proof, amended; 464 words.

— Just another spasm, Ned Lambert said .

— What is it? Mr. Bloom asked .

—̇ A recently discovered fragment of Cicero's, professor Mac-
Hugh answered with pomp of tone. *Our lovely land.*

5   — Whose land? Mr. Bloom said simply.

— Most pertinent question, the professor said between his
chews, with an accent on the whose.

— Dan Dawson's land, Mr. Dedalus said.

— Is it his speech last night? Mr. Bloom asked.

10   Ned Lambert nodded.

— But listen to this, he said.

The doorknob hit Mr. Bloom in the small of the back as the
door was pushed in.

— Excuse me, J . J. O'Molloy said, entering.

15   Mr. Bloom moved nimbly aside.

— I beg yours, he said.

— Good day, Jack.

— Come in. Come in.

— Good day.

20   — How are you, Dedalus?

— Well. And yourself?

J. J. O'Molloy shook his head.

Cleverest fellow at the junior bar he used to be. Decline,
poor chap. Touch and go with him.

25   — *Or again if we but climb the towering mountain peaks.*

— You're looking as fit as a fiddle.

— Is the editor to be seen? J. J. O'Molloy asked, looking
towards the inner door.

— Very much so, professor MacHugh said. To be seen and
30   heard. He's in his sanctum with Lenehan.

J. J. O'Molloy strolled to the sloping desk and began to turn
back the pink pages of the file.

Practice dwindling. Losing heart. Used to get good retainers from D. and T. Fitzgerald. Believe he does some literary work
35   for the *Express* with Gabriel Conroy. Well-read fellow. Myles
Crawford began on the *Independent.*. Funny the way they veer
about. Go for one another baldheaded in the papers and then hail
fellow well met the next moment.

— Ah, listen to this for God's sake. Ned Lambert pleaded. *Or*

7 chews. With (MS, TS)
35 Wellread (MS, TS)
39 God' sake (MS, TS)

Parallel-text presentation of the *Little review* and 1922 texts (*The little review*, v, Oct. 1918, p. 32, Tom
Stoppard, ×0·93; *S1*, 2nd imp., 1922, pp. 119–21, P.G., ×0·81)

— Just another spasm, Ned Lambert said.

— What is it ? Mr Bloom asked.

— A recently discovered fragment of Cicero's, professor Mac Hugh answered with pomp of tone. *Our lovely land.*

(SHORT BUT TO THE POINT)

— Whose land ? Mr Bloom said simply.

— Most pertinent question, the professor said between his chews. With an accent on the whose.

— Dan Dawson's land, Mr Dedalus said.

— Is it his speech last night ? Mr Bloom asked.

Ned Lambert nodded.

— But listen to this, he said.

The doorknob hit Mr Bloom in the small of the back as the door was pushed in.

— Excuse me, J. J. O'Molloy said, entering.

Mr Bloom moved nimbly aside.

— I beg yours, he said.

— Good day, Jack.

— Come in. Come in.

— Good day.

— How are you, Dedalus ?

— Well. And yourself ?

J. J. O'Molloy shook his head.

(SAD).

Cleverest fellow at the junior bar he used to be. Decline poor chap. That hectic flush spells finis for a man. Touch and go with him. What's in the wind, I wonder. Money worry.

— *Or again if we but climb the serried mountain peaks.*

— You're looking extra.

— Is the editor to be seen ? J. J. O'Molloy asked, looking towards the inner door.

— Very much so, professor MacHugh said. To be seen and heard. He's in his sanctum with Lenehan.

J. J. O'Molloy strolled to the sloping desk and began to turn back the pink pages of the file.

Practice dwindling. A mighthavebeen. Losing heart. Gambling. Debts of honour. Reaping the whirlwind. Used to get good retainers from D. and T. Fitzgerald. Their wigs to show their grey matter. Brains on their sleeve like the statue in Glasnevin. Believe he does some literary work for the *Express* with Gabriel Conroy. Wellread fellow. Myles Crawford began on the *Independent.* Funny the way those newspaper men veer about when they get wind of a new opening. Weathercocks. Hot and cold in the same breath. Wouldn't know which to believe. One story good till you hear the next. Go for one another baldheaded in the papers and then all blows over. Hailfellow well met the next moment.

— Ah, listen to this for God' sake, Ned Lambert pleaded. *Or again if we*

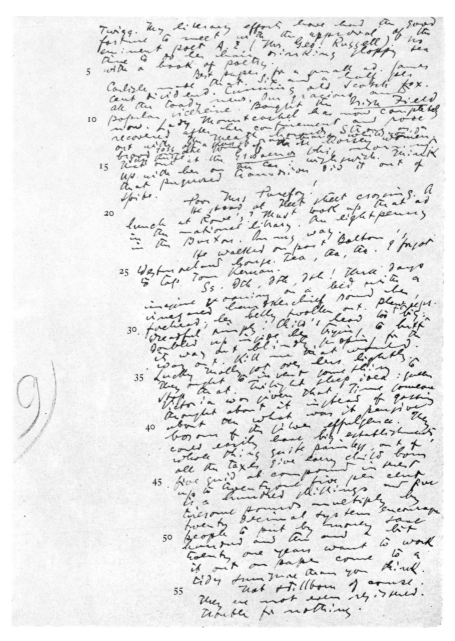

1 The Rosenbach MS of *Ulysses*, 'Lestrygonians', p. 9 (The Rosenbach Foundation, Philadelphia; × 0·72)

eminent poet A.E. (Mr Geo. Russell). No
time to do her hair drinking sloppy tea
5   with a book of poetry.
     Best paper for a small ad. James
Carlisle made that. Six and a half per
cent dividend. Cunning old Scotch fox.
All the toady news. Our gracious and
10 popular vicereine. Bought the Irish Field
now. Lady Mountcashel has now completely
recovered after her confinement and rode
out with the Meath hounds. Strong as a
     Toss off a glass of raw brandy while you'd
brood mare some of those horsey women. ᴧ
     say knife.
15 That one at the Grosvenor this morning.
Up with her on the car: wishswish. Think
that pugnosed tramdriver did it out of
spite.
     Poor Mrs Purefoy!
20   He stood at Fleet Street crossing. A
lunch at Rowe's? Must look up that ad
in the national library. An eightpenny
in the Burton. On my way.

Transcript of p. 226 lines 3–23

Like old times.He suffered her to overtake him without surprise
and thrust his dull grey beard towards her,his loose jaw wagging
as he spoke earnestly.
        Orf his chump.
        — Mr Bloom walked on again easily,seeing ahead of him,in
sunlight the tight skullpiece,the dangling stickumbrelladustcoat.
Going the two days.Watch him!Out he goes again.And that other
old mosey lunatic.Hard time she must have with him.
        U.P:up,I'll take my oath that's Alf Bergan or Richie
Goulding.Wrote it for a lark in the Scotch house I bet anything.
Round to Menton's office.His oyster eyes staring at the postcard
Be A feast for the gods.
        He passed the Irish Times.There might be other answers
lying there.At their lunch now.Clerk with the glasses there
doesn't know me.O,let them stay there.Enough bother wading through
forty four of them.Wanted smart lady typist to aid gentleman in
literary work.I called you naughty darling because I do not like
that other world.Please tell me what is the meaning .Please tell
me what perfume your wife.Tell me who made the world.The way
they spring those questions on you.And the other one Lizzie Twigg.
My literary efforts have had the good fortune to meet with the
approval of the eminent poet A.E.(Mr Geo Russell).No time to do
her hairdrinking sloppy tea with a book of poetry.
        Best paper by long chalks for a small ad.James Carlisle
made that.Six and a half per cent dividend.Cunning old Scotch fo
All the toady news.Our gracious and popular vicereine.Bought the
Irish Field now.Lady Mountcashel has quite recovered after her
confinement and rode out with the Meath hounds.Strong as a brood
mare some of those horsey women.Toss off a glass of brandy neat
while you'd say knife.That one at the Grosvenor this morning.Up
with her on the car:wishswish.Think that pugnosed driver did it
out of spite.
        Poor Mrs Purefoy!
        He stood at Fleet street crossing.A sixpenny at Rowe's?
Must look up that ad in the national library.An eightpenny in
the Burton.Better.On my way.
        He walked on past Bolton's Westmoreland house.Tea.Tea.
Tea.I forgot to tap Tom Kernan.
        Sss.Dth,dth,dth!Three days imagine groaning on a bed
with a vinegared handkerchief round her forehead,her belly
swollen out.Phew!Dreadful simply!Child's head too big:forceps.
Doubled up inside her trying to butt its way out blindly,groping
for the way out.Kill me that would.Lucky Molly got over hers
lightly.They ought to invent something to stop that.Twilight
sleep idea:queen Victoria was given that.Time someone thought
about it instead of gassing about the what was it the pensive
bosom of the silver effulgence?They could easily have big estab-
lishments whole thing quite painless out of all the taxes give
every child born five quid at compound interest up to
twentyone,five per cent is a hundred shillings and five tiresome
pounds,multiply by twenty decimal system encourage people to put
by money save hundred and ten and a bit twentyone year want to
work it out on paper come to a tidy sum more than you think.
        Not stillborn of course.They are not even registered
Trouble for nothing.
        How flat they look after all of a sudden!Peaceful eyes
Weight off their minds.Old Mrs Thornton was a jolly old soul.Snuffy
Dr Brady.People knocking them up at all hours.For God's sake,doctor
Wife in her throes.Then keep them waiting months for their
fee.No gratitude in people.

2 Typescript of *Ulysses*, 'Lestrygonians', p. '100'; carbon copy, used by Darantière for setting the
first *placard* (S.U.N.Y. at Buffalo, Lockwood Memorial Library, Poetry Collection, V.B.6; ×0·5)

The following variants between 1 and 2 probably resulted from Joyce's later revision of the lost
working MS from which 2 was set.

MS line/TS line	MS		TS
6/24		*adds*	by long chalks
11/27	now completely		quite
13–14/29	raw brandy		brandy neat
17/31	tramdriver		driver
21/34	lunch		sixpenny
23/36		*adds*	Better.

The *Little review* text of this passage was set from a copy of the typescript that was not annotated with
Joyce's later MS additions (i.e. 2 without the additions to lines 28 and 33).

⌐One way of getting on in the world.

tight skull piece, the dangling stick, umbrella, dust coat. Going the two days.
Watch him! Out he goes again. And that other old mosey lunatic. Hard time
she must have with him.

5 U. P : up. I'll take my oath that's Alf Bergan or Richie Goulding. Wrote
it for a lark in the Scotch house, I bet anything. Round to Menton's office. His
oyster eyes staring at the postcard. Be a feast for the gods.

He passed the *Irish Times*. There might be other answers lying there. At
their lunch now. Clerk with the glasses there doesn't know me. O, let them
10 stay there. Enough bother wading through forty four of them. Wanted smart
lady typist to aid gentleman in literary work. I called you naughty darling
because I do not like that other world. Please tell me what is the meaning.
Please tell me what perfume does your wife. Tell me who made the world. The
way they spring those questions on you. And the other one Lizzie Twigg. My
15 literary efforts have had the good fortune to meet with the approval of the
eminent poet A. E. (Mr Geo Russell). No time to do her hair drinking sloppy
tea with a book of poetry.

Best paper by long chalks for a small ad. James Carlisle made that. Six and
a half per cent dividend. Cunning old Scotch fogey. All the throaty news. Our
20 gracious and popular vicereine. Bought the *Irish Field* now. Lady Mountcashel has
quite recovered after her confinement and rode out with the Meath hounds.
Uneatable fox. Riding astride. No sidesaddle for her, not for Joe. First to the
meet and in at the death. Strong as a brood mare some of those horsey women.
Toss off a glass of brandy neat while you'd say knife. That one at the Gros-
25 venor this morning. Up with her on the car : wishswish. Think that pug nosed
driver did it out of spite.

Poor Mrs Purefoy! Methodist husband. Method in his madness. Saffron
bun and milk lunch in the educational dairy. Still his whiskers grew. Hardy
annuals he presents her in the Squallers. Poor thing!

30 He stood at Fleet street crossing. A sixpenny at Rowe's? Must look up
that ad in the national library. An eightpenny at Burton. Better. On my
way.

He walked on past Bolton's Westmoreland house. Tea. Tea. Tea. I forgot
to tap Tom Kernan.

35 Sss. Dth, dth, dth! Three days imagine groaning on a bed with a vinegared handkerchief round her forehead, her belly swollen out! Phew! Dreadful
simply! Child's head too big : forceps. Doubled up inside her trying to butt its
way out blindly, groping for the way out. Kill me that would. Lucky Molly

3 First placard proof of Ulysses, 'Placard 17', p. [2] (Harvard University, Houghton Library; X 0·68)

tight skullpiece, the dangling stick, umbrella, dust coat. Going the two days. Watch him! Out he goes again. One way of getting on in the world. And that other old mosey lunatic. Hard time she must have with him.

A in those duds.

U. P: up. I'll take my oath that's Alf Bergan or Richie Goulding. Wrote 5 it for a lark in the Scotch house, I bet anything. Round to Menton's office. His oyster eyes staring at the postcard. Be a feast for the gods.

He passed the *Irish Times*. There might be other answers lying there. At their lunch now. Clerk with the glasses there doesn't know me. O, let them stay there. Enough bother wading through forty four of them. Wanted smart 10 lady typist to aid gentleman in literary work. I called you naughty darling because I do not like that other world. Please tell me what is the meaning. Please tell me what perfume does your wife. Tell me who made the world. The way they spring those questions on you. And the other one Lizzie Twigg. My literary efforts have had the good fortune to meet with the approval of the 15 eminent poet A. E. (Mr Geo Russell). No time to do her hair drinking sloppy tea with a book of poetry.

hunks.

Best paper by long chalks for a small ad. Got the provinces now. Cook and general, exc cuisine, housemaid kept. Wanted live man for spirit counter. Resp. girl (R. C.) wishes to hear of post in fruit or pork shop. James Carlisle
L ft 2 T 20 made that. Six and a half per cent dividend. Made a big deal on Coates's shares. Ca' canny. Cunning old Scotch fogey. All the toady news. Our gracious and
M and X popular vicereine. Bought the *Irish Field* now. Lady Mountcashel has quite recovered after her confinement and rode out with the Ward Union staghounds at the enlargement yesterday at Rathoath. Uneatable fox. Pothunters too. Fear 25 injects juices make it tender enough for them. Riding astride. Sit her horse like a man. Weight carrying huntress. No sidesaddle or pillion for her, not for Joe. First to the meet and in at the death. Strong as a brood mare some of those horsey women. Toss off a glass of brandy neat while you'd say knife. That one at the Grosvenor this morning. Up with her on the car: wishswish. Think that 30 pug nosed driver did it out of spite. F

Poor Mrs Purefoy! Methodist husband. Method in his madness. Saffron bun and milk and soda lunch in the educational dairy. Eating with a stopwatch, thirtytwo chews to the minute. Still his muttonchop whiskers grew. Supposed to be well connected. Theodore's cousin in Dublin Castle. One tony relative 35 in every family. Hardy annuals he presents her in the squallers. Poor thing! Selfish those mare. Dog in the manger. with. T Ls

III t.t's

He stood at Fleet street crossing. Luncheon interval a sixpenny at Rowe's? Must look up that ad in the national library. An eightpenny in the Burton. Better. On my way.

40 He walked on past Bolton's Westmoreland house. Tea. Tea. Tea. I forgot to tap Tom Kernan.

clotheshorse. Her ears ought to have tingled for a few weeks after. Want to be a bull for her. Born courtesan. No nursery work for her, thanks

45 Sss. Dth, dth, dth! Three days imagine groaning on a bed with a vinegared handkerchief round her forehead, her belly swollen out! Phew! Dreadful simply! Child's head too big: forceps. Doubled up inside her trying to butt its way out blindly, groping for the way out. Kill me that would. Lucky Molly

R F who is this she was like? O yes! Mrs Miriam Dandrade that sold me her old wraps and black underclothes in the Shelbourne hotel. Divorced Spanish American. Didn't take a feather out of her my handling them. As if I was her

4 Second *placard* proof of *Ulysses*, 'Placard 17', p. [2] (Harvard University, Houghton Library; ×0·68)

The first two lines of the extract in the first page-proof are at the bottom of p. 152, whither they were transferred unaltered from the second *placard* proof (lines 15-16).

⌈Stonewall or fivebarre(
gate put her mount to it.
153

Best paper by long chalks for a small ad. Got the provinces now. Cook and general, exc cuisine, housemaid kept. Wanted live man for spirit counter. Resp. girl (R. C.) wishes to hear of post in fruit or pork shop. James Carlisle made that. Six and a half per cent dividend. Made a big deal on Coates's shares.
5 Ca' canny. Cunning old Scotch hunkys. All the toady news. Our gracious and popular vicereine. Bought the *Irish Field* now. Lady Mountcashel has quite recovered after her confinement and rode out with the Ward Union staghounds at the enlargement yesterday at Rathoath. Uneatable fox. Pothunters too. Fear injects juices make it tender enough for them. Riding astride. Sit her horse
10 like a man, Weightcarrying huntress. No sidesaddle or pillion for her, not for Joe. First to the meet and in at the death. Strong as a brood mare some of those horsey women. Toss off a glass of brandy neat while you'd say knife. That one at the Grosvenor this morning. Up with her on the car: wishswish! Think that pugnosed driver did it out of spite. Who is this she was like? O yes! Mrs
15 Miriam Dandrade that sold me her old wraps and black underclothes in the Shelbourne hotel. Divorced Spanish American. Didn't take a feather out of her my handling them. As if I was her clotheshorse. Her ears ought to have tingled for a few weeks after. Want to be a bull for her. Born courtesan. No nursery work for her, thanks.
20 Poor Mrs Purefoy! Methodist husband. Method in his madness. Saffron bun and milk and soda lunch in the educational dairy. Eating with a stopwatch, thirtytwo chews to the minute. Still his muttonchop whiskers grew. Supposed to be well connected. Theodore's cousin in Dublin Castle. One tony relative in every family. Hardy annuals he presents her with. The squallers. Poor thing!
25 Selfish thoset.t's are. Dog in the manger.
He stood at Fleet street crossing. Luncheon interval a sixpenny at Rowe's? Must look up that ad in the national library. An eightpenny in the Burton. Better. On my way.
He walked on past Bolton's Westmoreland house. Tea. Tea. Tea. I forgot
30 to tap Tom Kernan.
Sss. Dth, dth, dth! Three days imagine groaning on a bed with a vinegared handkerchief round her forehead, her belly swollen out! Phew! Dreadful simply! Child's head too big : forceps. Doubled up inside her trying to butt its way out blindly, groping for the way out. Kill me that would. Lucky Molly
35 got over hers lightly. They ought to invent something to stop that. Life with hard labour. Twilightsleep idea : queen Victoria was given that. Nine she had. A good layer. Old woman that lived in a shoe she had so many children.

5 First page proof of *Ulysses*, p. 153 (S.U.N.Y. at Buffalo, Lockwood Memorial Library, Poetry Collection, V.C.10a; ×0·65)

marching along
bareheaded

R ——————

A. Saw him out at the Three Jolly
Topers and his eldest boy carrying
one in a marketnet. 153

poet A. E. (Mr Geo Russell). No time to do her hair drinking sloppy tea with
a book of poetry.

Best paper by long chalks for a small ad. Got the provinces now. Cook
and general, exc cuisine, housemaid kept. Wanted live man for spirit counter.
5 Resp. girl (R. C.) wishes to hear of post in fruit or pork shop. James Carlisle
made that. Six and a half per cent dividend. Made a big deal on Coates's shares.
Ca' canny. Cunning old Scotch hunks. All the toady news. Our gracious and
popular vicereine. Bought the *Irish Field* now. Lady Mountcashel has quite
recovered after her confinement and rode out with the Ward Union staghounds
10 at the enlargement yesterday at Rathoath. Uneatable fox. Pothunters too. Fear
injects juices make it tender enough for them. Riding astride. Sit her horse
like a man. Weightcarrying huntress. No sidesaddle or pillion for her, not for
Joe. First to the meet and in at the death. Strong as a brood mare some of those
horsey women. Toss off a glass of brandy neat while you'd say knife. That one
15 at the Grosvenor this morning. Up with her on the car: wishwish. Stonewall
or fivebarred gate put her mount to it. Think that pugnosed driver did it out
of spite. Who is this she was like? O yes! Mrs Miriam Dandrade that sold
me her old wraps and black underclothes in the Shelbourne hotel. Divorced
20 Spanish American. Didn't take a feather out of her my handling them. As if
I was her clotheshorse. Her ears ought to have tingled for a few weeks after.
Want to be a bull for her. Born courtesan. No nursery work for her, thanks.
Poor Mrs Purefoy! Methodist husband. Method in his madness. Saffron
bun and milk and soda lunch in the educational dairy. Eating with a stopwatch,
25 thirtytwo chews to the minute. Still his muttonchop whiskers grew. Supposed
to be well connected. Theodore's cousin in Dublin Castle. One tony relative
in every family. Hardy annuals he presents her with. The squallers. Poor thing!
Selfish those t.t's are. Dog in the manger.

He stood at Fleet street crossing. Luncheon interval a sixpenny at Rowe's?
30 Must look up that ad in the national library. An eightpenny in the Burton.
Better. On my way.
He walked on past Bolton's Westmoreland house. Tea. Tea. Tea. I forgot
to tap Tom Kernan.
Sss. Dth, dth, dth! Three days imagine groaning on a bed with a vinegared handkerchief round her forehead, her belly swollen out! Phew! Dreadful
35 simply! Child's head too big : forceps. Doubled up inside her trying to butt its
way out blindly, groping for the way out. Kill me that would. Lucky Molly
got over hers lightly. They ought to invent something to stop that. Life with

Q. *Swagger*
around livery
stables.

M. *Then having*
to give the
breast year
after year
all hours of
the night.

H. *Only one*
lump of
sugar in
my tea, if
you please.

Π St

h 3

M

I. Saw her in the viceregal party when Stubbs the
park ranger got me in with Whelan of the
Express. Scavenging what the quality left.
High tea. Mayonnaise I poured on the
plums thinking it was custard.

6 Second page proof of *Ulysses*, p. 153 (S.U.N.Y. at Buffalo, Lockwood Memorial Library, Poetry
Collection, V.C.10b; ×0·65)

poet A. E. (Mr Geo Russell). No time to do her hair drinking sloppy tea with
a book of poetry.

   Best paper by long chalks for a small ad. Got the provinces now. Cook
and general, exc cuisine, housemaid kept. Wanted live man for spirit counter.
5 Resp. girl (R. C.) wishes to hear of post in fruit or pork shop. James Carlisle
made that. Six and a half per cent dividend. Made a big deal on Coates's shares.
Ca' canny. Cunning old Scotch hunks. All the toady news. Our gracious and
popular vicereine. Bought the *Irish Field* now. Lady Mountcashel has quite
recovered after her confinement and rode out with the Ward Union staghounds
10 at the enlargement yesterday at Rathoath. Uneatable fox. Pothunters too. Fear
injects juices make it tender enough for them. Riding astride. Sit her horse
like a man. Weightcarrying huntress. No sidesaddle or pillion for her, not for
Joe. First to the meet and in at the death. Strong as a brood mare some of those
horsey women. Swagger around livery stables. Toss off a glass of brandy neat
15 while you'd say knife. That one at the Grosvenor this morning. Up with her on
the car : wishswish. Stonewall or fivebarred gate put her mount to it. Think
that pugnosed driver did it out of spite. Who is this she was like? O yes!
Mrs Miriam Dandrade that sold me her old wraps and black underclothes in
the Shelbourne hotel. Divorced Spanish American. Didn't take a feather out
20 of her my handling them. As if I was her clotheshorse. Saw her in the
viceregal party when Stubbs the park ranger got me in with Whelan of the
Express. Scavenging what the quality left. High tea. Mayonnaise I poured on
the plums thinking it was custard. Her ears ought to have tingled for a few
weeks after. Want to be a bull for her. Born courtesan. No nursery work for
25 her, thanks.

   Poor Mrs Purefoy! Methodist husband. Method in his madness. Saffron
bun and milk and soda lunch in the educational dairy. Eating with a stopwatch,
thirtytwo chews to the minute. Still his muttonchop whiskers grew. Supposed
to be well connected. Theodore's cousin in Dublin Castle. One tony relative
30 in every family. Hardy annuals he presents her with. Saw him out at the Three
Jolly Topers marching along bareheaded and his eldest boy carrying one in
a marketnet. The squallers. Poor thing! Then having to give the breast year
all hours of the night. Selfish those t.t's are. Dog in the manger. Only one
lump of sugar in my tea, if you please.

35   He stood at Fleet street crossing. Luncheon interval a sixpenny at Rowe's?
Must look up that ad in the national library. An eightpenny in the Burton.
Better. On my way.

7 Third page proof of *Ulysses*, p. 153 (University of Texas, Humanities Research Center; ×0·68)

poet A. E. (Mr Geo Russell). No time to do her hair drinking sloppy tea with a book of poetry.

Best paper by long chalks for a small ad. Got the provinces now. Cook and general, exc cuisine, housemaid kept. Wanted live man for spirit counter.

5 Resp. girl (R. C.) wishes to hear of post in fruit or pork shop. James Carlisle made that. Six and a half percent dividend. Made a big deal on Coates's shares. Ca' canny. Cunning old Scotch hunks. All the toady news. Our gracious and popular vicereine. Bought the *Irish Field* now. Lady Mountcashel has quite recovered after her confinement and rode out with the Ward Union staghounds

10 at the enlargement yesterday at Rathoath. Uneatable fox. Pothunters too. Fear injects juices make it tender enough for them. Riding astride. Sit her horse like a man, Weightcarrying huntress. No sidesaddle or pillion for her, not for Joe. First to the meet and in at the death. Strong as a brood mare some of those horsey women. Swagger around livery stables. Toss off a glass of brandy neat

15 while you'd say knife. That one at the Grosvenor this morning. Up with her on the car : wishswish. Stonewall or fivebarred gate put her mount to it. Think that pugnosed driver did it out of spite. Who is this she was like? O yes! Mrs Miriam Dandrade that sold me her old wraps and black underclothes in the Shelbourne hotel. Divorced Spanish American. Didn't take a feather out

20 of her my handling them. As if I was her clotheshorse. Saw her in the viceregal party when Stubbs the park ranger got me in with Whelan of the *Express*. Scavening what the quality left. High tea. Mayonnaise I poured on the plums thinking it was custard. Her ears ought to have tingled for a few weeks after. Want to be a bull for her. Born courtesan. No nursery work for

25 her, thanks.

Poor Mrs Purefoy! Methodist husband. Method in his madness. Saffron bun and milk and soda lunch in the educational dairy. Eating with a stopwatch, thirtytwo chews to the minute. Still his muttonchop whiskers grew. Supposed to be well connected. Theodore's cousin in Dublin Castle. One tony relative

30 in every family. Hardy annuals he presents her with. Saw him out at the Three Jolly Topers marching along bareheaded and his eldest boy carrying one in a marketnet. The squallers. Poor thing! Then having to give the breast year after year all hours of the night. Selfish those t.t.'s are. Dog in the manger. Only one lump of sugar in my tea, if you please.

35 He stood at Fleet street crossing. Luncheon interval a sixpenny at Rowe's ? Must look up that ad in the national library. An eightpenny in the Burton. Better. On my way.

It is plain both that such extensive evidence of the development of the text of *Ulysses* will not be easy to comprehend, however it is presented, and that its presentation will be expensive in editorial effort, or in production costs—or in both. There are two main options open to an editor: either he can gather the evidence together and incorporate it in a single text with a synoptic apparatus; or he can present the evidence itself with relatively little interference. Both methods have their advantages and disadvantages, those of the one being approximately the reverse of those of the other.

A synoptic version would consist of a critical text (produced either by using S_I, the first edition, as copy-text and emending it, or by building up an ideal text from the pre-publication documents) which would be marked to show which of its constituent parts came from where. Such a genetic presentation is particularly appropriate for *Ulysses* because from the final draft stages onwards Joyce developed the book very largely by adding to the text; he seldom altered what he had written, and he very rarely deleted anything altogether.

The advantages of producing a synoptic version are that the editor, in considering all the evidence, can suppress inessentials (such as errors of transmission) in order to concentrate on authorial variation and the textual and critical conclusions that can be drawn from it. If the conflated textual strata are recorded along with the synoptic code on magnetic tape, individual versions—the emended plain text itself, for instance, or any transitory stage of the text such as the first-draft version—can be extracted mechanically for scrutiny or separate publication. A synopsis, moreover, although it will cost the editor much effort, will not be much more expensive to reproduce than an ordinary edition.

But this method also has disadvantages. Much of the evidence that the pre-publication documents contain will necessarily be omitted, but some of it may eventually elucidate Joyce's text in ways that have not yet been developed, and an editor would have to be able to see into the future to include now all that might be useful then. It is likely to be difficult, moreover, to produce a synoptic version of *Ulysses* that is not forbidding in appearance and laborious to use, a reference book rather than a guide to the growth of the whole novel.

There is now a project to produce a critical edition of *Ulysses* with a synoptic apparatus, whereby unobtrusive symbols will indicate the points at which particular readings entered—and occasionally left—the text, and to record editorial matter in footnotes. This can be an adequately comprehensible way of summarizing the genetic relationships of the constituent parts of the final text,[32] as is shown by the following version of our extract presented in the manner proposed for the editorial project being directed by Hans Walter Gabler.[33] The production of the synopsis is not the only aim of the project, and Dr. Gabler hopes that a critical plain text, and perhaps an intermediate version, will be extracted from it for separate publication.

Best paper +by long chalks+ for a small ad. ⌜¹Got the
provinces now. Cook and general, exc. cuisine, housemaid
kept. Wanted live man for spirit counter. Resp. girl (R.C.)
wishes to hear of post in fruit or pork shop.¹⌝ James
5   Carlisle made that. Six and a half per cent dividend. ⌜¹Made
a big deal on Coates's shares. Ca'canny.¹⌝ Cunning old Scotch
⌜⁰[fox] [²fogey]⁰⌝ ⌜²hunks²⌝. All the toady news. Our gracious
and popular vicercine. Bought the Irish Field now. Lady
Mountcashel has +[now completely] quite+ recovered after
10   her confinement and rode out with the ⌜¹[Meath hounds] Ward
Union staghounds at ˆthe enlargement yesterday atˆ Rathoath¹⌝.
⌜⁰Uneatable fox. ⌜¹Pothunters too. Fear injects juices make
it tender enough for them.¹⌝ ˆRiding astride.ˆ ⌜¹Sit her
horse like a man. Weightcarrying huntress.¹⌝ No sidesaddle
15   ⌜¹or pillion¹⌝ for her, not for Joe. First to the meet and
in at the death.⁰⌝ Strong as a brood mare some of those
horsey women. ⌜⁴Swagger around livery stables.⁴⌝ Toss off a
glass of [+raw] brandy +neat+ while you'd say knife. That
one at the ⌜⁰[Grosvenor] Grosvenor⁰⌝ this morning. Up with
20   her on the car: wishswish. ⌜³Stonewall or fivebarred gate
put her mount to it.³⌝ Think that pugnosed [+tram] driver did
it out of spite. ⌜²Who is this she was like? O yes! Mrs Miriam
Dandrade that sold me her old wraps and black underclothes in
the Shelbourne hotel. Divorced Spanish American. Didn't take
25   a feather out of her my handling them. As if I was her
clotheshorse. ⌜⁴Saw her in the viceregal party when Stubbs
the park ranger got me in with Whelan of the Express.
Scavenging what the quality left. High tea. Mayonnaise I
poured on the plums thinking it was custard.⁴⌝ Her ears
30   ought to have tingled for a few weeks after. Want to be a
bull for her. Born courtesan. No nursery work for her, thanks.²⌝
Poor Mrs Purefoy! ⌜⁰Methodist husband. Method in his madness.
Saffron bun and milk ⌜¹and soda¹⌝ lunch in the educational
dairy. ⌜¹Eating with a stopwatch, thirtytwo chews to the
35   minute.¹⌝ Still his ⌜¹muttonchop¹⌝ whiskers grew. ⌜¹Supposed
to be well connected. Theodore's cousin in Dublin Castle.

---

[32] More so, for instance, than the typographical system used in David Hayman's *A first-draft version of 'Finnegans Wake'*, Austin 1963, in which the successive versions are indicated by the use of different type-faces (italic, bold, etc.).

[33] I am most grateful to Dr. Gabler for providing this specimen and explanation of his work.

One tony relative in every family.⌐¹ Hardy annuals he presents
her with.⁰¹ ⌐⁴Saw him out at the Three Jolly Topers ^marching
along bareheaded^ and his eldest boy carrying one in a
40 marketnet.⁴¹ ⌐⁰[²Squallers] ⌐²The squallers²¹. Poor thing!⁰¹
⌐⁴Then having to give the breast year after year all hours
of the night.⁴¹ ⌐¹Selfish those t.t's are. Dog in the manger.¹¹
⌐⁴Only one lump of sugar in my tea, if you please.⁴¹
He stood at Fleet street crossing. ⌐¹Luncheon interval.¹¹
45 A ⁺[lunch] sixpenny⁺ at Rowe's? Must look up that ad in the
national library. An eightpenny ⌐⁰[in the] [¹with]⁰¹ ⌐¹in the¹¹
Burton. ⁺Better.⁺ On my way.

2 exc.] *overlay* P₁; ∼ₐ P₂ +
14 man. Weightcarrying] *overlay* P₁; ∼ₐ∼ P₂ +
44 interval.] *this ed.*; ∼ₐ *entry* P₁; P₂ +
45 A] MS, TS, P₁; a *transmissional* P₂ +, *following add. l.* 44

KEY

[. . .] deletions
⁺. . .⁺ changes from MS to TS
⌐⁰. . .⁰¹ authorial overlay in printer's copy
⌐¹. . .¹¹ authorial overlay in 1st *placard* (P₁)
⌐². . .²¹ authorial overlay in 2nd *placard* (P₂)
⌐³. . .³¹ authorial overlay in 1st page-proof (PP₃)
⌐⁴. . .⁴¹ authorial overlay in 2nd page-proof (PP₄)
^. . .^ additions within additions³⁴

The very different method of illustrating the development of *Ulysses* by
presenting the evidence itself has the great advantage of suppressing
nothing, but it asks more of the user, and it is usually costly to reproduce.
Full-size photographic reproductions of the evidence as it stands (such as
Garland Publishing's *James Joyce archive*, now in course of publication),

³⁴ Dr. Gabler gives the following explanation of his synoptic presentation:
'The textual substratum for the synoptical presentation of the textual development from final draft
to print is the final-draft working manuscript as handed to the typist. Being lost as a document, it is
critically established from the witnesses radiating from it, the Rosenbach Manuscript (MS) and the
typescript (TS). The TS represents a later textual state of the working manuscript than does the MS.
The textual augmentation unique to it is marked off between plus signs (⁺. . .⁺). In cases of textual
divergence between MS and TS, the MS variant is considered deleted in the working manuscript
and set between deletion brackets: [. . .]. MS deletions of readings unique to it and not linked to
MS–TS changes—i.e., pre-final-draft variants—are indicated with a minus sign inside the opening
deletion bracket. Interlinear and marginal additions in the MS are understood as part of the base text
of the working manuscript, and no note of their position in the MS is taken. (NB: where the TS
derives directly from the MS, its deletions are bracketed, and its interlinear or marginal additions
are given between plus signs. The few Sykes-type changes communicated by letter, etc., could be
dealt with by double-plusses.) Upon the establishment of the final-draft text, the TS copy used as
printer's copy and the several proofs are taken as textual witnesses *only* for the successive layers of
authorial revisions and additions they carry. These layers are numerically indexed. Corresponding
to the n number of proofs per episode, or sheet of the finished book, numbered 1 to n (with P for
'placard' and PP for 'page-proof', without break in the through numbering), the successive layers of
textual change are indexed 1 to n. The index number for the authorial overlay in the printer's-copy
typescript is 0. Superior carets indicate additions within additions.'

though they bring all the material together for the specialist in his own university library, are too expensive for individuals to own, and they give little help to non-specialists. The least that the ordinary student of *Ulysses* needs is to have the evidence presented in parallel.

Here again full-size photographic reproductions, and even transcripts, are likely to be impossibly expensive; but recent developments in 'compact' publishing may offer a solution. By this method, several pages of a bulky printed original such as a dictionary are reduced photographically and reproduced all together on one page of the compact edition; the scale of reduction depends on the type size of the original, but is typically in the range $\times 0.5$ to $\times 0.35$ of the original. In this way expensive multi-volume reference works are turned into compact editions at a fraction of the original size and cost, which require no more than a reading glass to make them easily legible.[35] Parallel texts, it is clear, could be similarly reduced, and the method is indeed particularly well suited to their study, since it enables the reader to make a direct comparison of several versions of a text on a single page.

The surviving versions of our extract, reduced to compact size, follow on pp. 240–3. Each such group of facsimiles (relating to a single page of *S1* and therefore duplicating some of the pre-publication documents in adjacent groups) could be reproduced either, as here, on several small pages of a compact parallel-text *Ulysses*, or on one large page the size of the compact *OED*.

Appendix

THE LATER EDITIONS OF *ULYSSES*

The only edition of which Joyce himself corrected the proofs was the first, *S1*, of 1922; and with the incorporation of the corrections given in the two lists of errata that accompanied the second and fourth impressions (1922 and 1924) it remains the least faulty of all the editions published so far. Since then each new edition has introduced new errors, and each has reprinted the accumulated errors of its ancestors. Some publishers have attempted, in later impressions, to purge their editions of newly added errors, but these attempts have not been very successful, and have not been extended to the errors inherited from previous editions.

---

[35] Halliwell-Phillipps's compact facsimile of the Shakespeare first folio appeared as long ago as 1876, reduced photolithographically $\times 0.56$; and there was a semi-compact volume-for-volume version of the 11th edition of the *Encyclopaedia Britannica* (New York 1910–11, $\times 0.73$). Recent compact editions have reduced not only the page size but also the number of volumes; for instance the British Museum *Catalogue of printed books* (1967, $\times 0.425$), *The Oxford English dictionary* (1971, $\times 0.5$), and *The dictionary of national biography* (1975, $\times 0.39$). The reduction of my specimen for a compact parallel-text *Ulysses* is approximately $\times 0.38$, except for the typescript, which is $\times 0.32$.

The line of descent of the main published editions of *Ulysses* was as follows:[36]

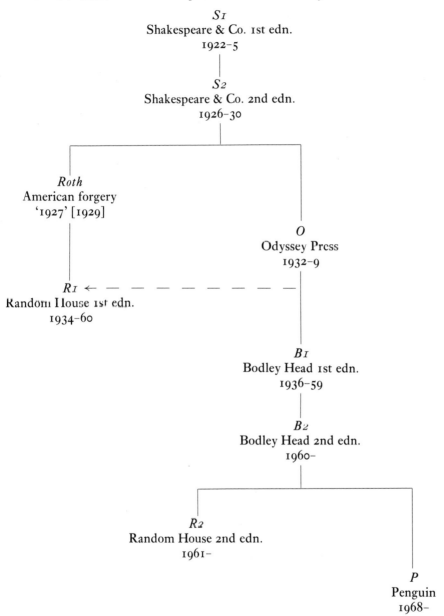

S1
Shakespeare & Co. 1st edn.
1922–5

S2
Shakespeare & Co. 2nd edn.
1926–30

Roth
American forgery
'1927' [1929]

O
Odyssey Press
1932–9

R1 ←
Random House 1st edn.
1934–60

B1
Bodley Head 1st edn.
1936–59

B2
Bodley Head 2nd edn.
1960–

R2
Random House 2nd edn.
1961–

P
Penguin
1968–

[36] There was also an edition with illustrations by Matisse put out by the Limited Editions Club in New York in 1935; it was set from the second Odyssey Press impression, 1933, and did not affect the text of main published editions.

The extract from 'Lestrygonians' reproduced as a compact parallel-text facsimile. (For references to the individual pages reproduced, see the captions to pp. 226–34.)

eminent poet A.E. (Mr Geo. Russell). No time to do her hair drinking sloppy tea with a book of poetry.

Best paper for a small ad. James Carlisle made that. Six and a half per cent dividend. Cunning old Scotch fox. All the toady news. Our gracious and popular vicereine. Bought the Irish Field now. Lady Mountcashel has now completely recovered after her confinement and rode out with the Meath hounds. Strong as a brood mare some of those horsey women. That knife of the Grosvenor this morning. Up with her on the car: wishwish. Think that pugnosed tramdriver did it out of spite.

Poor Mrs Purefoy!

He stood at Fleet street crossing. A lunch at Rowe's? Must look up that ad in the national library. An eightpenny in the Burton. On my way.

ROSENBACH MS (and own transcript)

FINAL TYPESCRIPT

SECOND *PLACARD*

FIRST *PLACARD*

153

Best paper by long chalks for a small ad. Got the provinces now. Cook and general, etc cuisine, housemaid kept. Wanted live man for spirit counter. Resp. girl (R.C.) wishes to hear of post, in fruit or pork shop. James Carlisle made that. Six and a half per cent dividend. Made a big deal on Coates's shares. Ca' canny. Cunning old Scotch hunks. All the toady news. Our gracious and popular vicereine. Bought the *Irish Field* now. Lady Mountcashel has quite recovered after her confinement and rode out with the Ward Union staghounds at the enlargement yesterday at Rathoath. Unstable fox. Foxhunters too. Fear injects juices make it tender enough for them. Riding astride. Sit her horse like a man, Weightcarrying huntress. No sidesaddle or pillion for her, not for Joe. First to the meet and in at the death. Strong as a brood mare some of those horsey women. Tons off a glass of brandy neat while you'd say knife. That one at the Grosvenor this morning. Up with her on the car: wishwish. Think that papoosed driver did it out of spite. Who is this she was like? O yes! Mrs Miriam Dandrade that sold me her old wraps and black underclothes in the Shelbourne hotel. Divorced Spanish American. Didn't take a feather out of her my handling them. As if I was her clotheshorse. Want to be a bull for her, thanks.

Poor Mrs Purefoy! Methodist husband. Method in his madness. Saffron bun and milk and soda lunch in the educational dairy. Eating with a stopwatch, thirtytwo chews to the minute. Still his muttonchop whiskers grew. Supposed to be well connected. Theodore's cousin in Dublin Castle. One tony relative in every family. Handy annuals he presents her with. The squallers. Poor thing! Selfish those t.t.'s are. Dog in the manger.

He stood at Fleet street crossing. Luncheon interval a sixpenny at Rowe's? Must look up that ad in the national library. An eightpenny in the Burton. Better. On my way.

He walked on past Bolton's Westmoreland house. Tea. Tea. Tea. I forgot to tap Tom Kernan.

Sss. Dth, dth, dth! Three days imagine groaning on a bed with a vinegared handkerchief round her forehead, her belly swollen out! Phew! Dreadful simply! Child's head too big: forceps. Doubled up inside her trying to butt its way out blindly, groping for the way out. Kill me that would. Lucky Molly got over hers lightly. They ought to invent something to stop that. Life with hard labour. Twilightsleep idea: queen Victoria was given that. Nine she had. A good layer. Old woman that lived in a shoe she had so many children.

FIRST PAGE PROOF

SECOND PAGE PROOF

153

poet A. E. (Mr Geo Russell). No time to do her hair drinking sloppy tea with a book of poetry.

Best paper by long chalks for a small ad. Got the provinces now. Cook and general, exc cuisine, housemaid kept. Wanted live man for spirit counter. Resp. girl (R. C.) wishes to hear of post in fruit or pork shop. James Carlisle made that. Six and a half per cent dividend. Made a big deal on Coates's shares. Ca' canny. Canning old Scotch hunks. All the toady news. Our gracious and popular vicereine. Bought the *Irish Field* now. Lady Mountcashel has quite recovered after her confinement and rode out with the Ward Union staghounds at the enlargement yesterday at Rathoath. Uneatable fox. Pothunters too. Fear injects juices make it tender enough for them. Riding astride. Sit her horse like a man. Weightcarrying huntress. No sidesaddle or pillion for her, not for Joe. First to the meet and in at the death. Strong as a brood mare some of those horsey women. Swagger around livery stables. Toss off a glass of brandy neat while you'd say knife. That one at the Grosvenor this morning. Up with her on the car : wishswish. Stonewall or fivebarred gate put her mount to it. Think that regpnosed driver did it out of spite. Who is this she was like ? O yes ! Mrs Miriam Dandrade that sold me her old wraps and black underclothes in the Shelbourne hotel. Divorced Spanish American. Didn't take a feather out of her my handling them. As if I was her clotheshorse. Saw her in the viceregal party when Stubbs the park ranger got me in with Whelan of the *Express*. Scavering what the quality left. High tea. Mayonnaise I poured on the plums thinking it was custard. Her ears ought to have tingled for a few weeks after. Want to be a bull for her. Born courtesan. No nursery work for her, thanks.

Poor Mrs Purefoy ! Methodist husband. Method in his madness. Saffron bun and milk and soda lunch in the educational dairy. Eating with a stopwatch, thirtytwo chews to the minute. Still his muttonchop whiskers grew. Supposed to be well connected. Theodore's cousin in Dublin Castle. One tony relative in every family. Hardy annuals he presents her with. Saw him out at the Three Jolly Topers marching along barehead and his eldest boy carrying one in a marketnet. The squallers. Poor thing ! Then having to give the breast year after year all hours of the night. Selfish those i t's are. Dog in the manger. Only one lump of sugar in my tea, if you please.

He stood at Fleet street crossing. Luncheon interval a sixpenny at Rowe's ? Must look up that ad in the national library. An eightpenny in the Burton. Better. On my way.

153

poet A. E. (Mr Geo Russell). No time to do her hair drinking sloppy tea with a book of poetry.

Best paper by long chalks for a small ad. Got the provinces now. Cook and general, exc cuisine, housemaid kept. Wanted live man for spirit counter. Resp. girl (R. C.) wishes to hear of post in fruit or pork shop. James Carlisle made that. Six and a half per cent dividend. Made a big deal on Coates's shares. Ca' canny. Canning old Scotch hunks. All the toady news. Our gracious and popular vicereine. Bought the *Irish Field* now. Lacy Mountcashel has quite recovered after her confinement and rode out with the Ward Union staghounds at the enlargement yesterday at Rathoath. Uneatable fox. Pothunters too. Fear injects juices make it tender enough for them. Riding astride. Sit her horse like a man. Weightcarrying huntress. No sidesaddle or pillion for her, not for Joe. First to the meet and in at the death. Strong as a brood mare some of those horsey women. Swagger around livery stables. Toss off a glass of brandy neat while you'd say knife. That one at the Grosvenor this morning. Up with her on the car : wishswish. Stonewall or fivebarred gate put her mount to it. Think that regpnosed driver did it out of spite. Who is this she was like ? O yes ! Mrs Miriam Dandrade that sold me her old wraps and black underclothes in the Shelbourne hotel. Divorced Spanish American. Didn't take a feather out o' her my handling them. As if I was her clotheshorse. Saw her in the viceregal party when Stubbs the park ranger got me in with Whelan of the *Express*. Scavering what the quality left. High tea. Mayonnaise I poured on the plums thinking it was custard. Her ears ought to have tingled for a few weeks after. Want to be a bull for her. Born courtesan. No nursery work for her, thanks.

Poor Mrs Purefoy ! Methodist husband. Method in his madness. Saffron bun and milk and soda lunch in the educational dairy. Eating with a stopwatch, thirtytwo chews to the minute. Still his muttonchop whiskers grew. Supposed to be well connected. Theodore's cousin in Dublin Castle. One tony relative in every family. Hardy annuals he presents her with. Saw him out at the Three Jolly Topers marching along barehead and his eldest boy carrying one in a marketnet. The squallers. Poor thing ! Then having to give the breast year after year all hours of the night. Selfish those i t's are. Dog in the manger. Only one lump of sugar in my tea, if you please.

He stood at Fleet street crossing. Luncheon interval a sixpenny at Rowe's ? Must look up that ad in the national library. An eightpenny in the Burton. Better. On my way.

THIRD PAGE PROOF

S_I

To comment on the individual editions after the first: the second Shakespeare and Company setting, $S2$, appeared in four impressions called the 'eighth' to the 'eleventh' printings, 1926–30. It attended to the errata lists from $S1$, but it introduced many new and serious errors. Dalton lists a dozen,[37] all of which are still reprinted in the current editions. Here is another: after the words 'Holland and' at 719.22/847.16 $S2$ omitted 'for Liverpool Underwriters' Association the cost of acquired rolling stock'; which has continued to be omitted from all subsequent editions.

The next edition to appear was *Roth*, a forgery which pretended to be the second (called the 'ninth') impression of $S2$; it was dated Paris 1927 but was actually printed for Samuel Roth in America in 1929. It was set, very badly, from $S2$, and it could be ignored if a copy of it had not, by mischance, been chosen for setting $R1$, the first authorized American edition published by Random House in 1934.[38] The early impressions of $R1$ were full of startling errors, such as (on the first page, at 3.39/2.10) '[Buck Mulligan] went over the parapet'; but some of the worst of them were corrected in later impressions, and $R1$ fortunately had no progeny.

Next in the main line of descent from $S2$ was the Odyssey Press edition, Hamburg 1932. Although it was claimed that O might 'be regarded as the definitive standard edition, as it has been specially revised, at the author's request, by Stuart Gilbert', it appears that Gilbert did little more than glance at the proofs.[39] The old $S2$ errors are included, together with several new ones, such as the notorious full stop in 'Stephen. Hand' at 426.22/558.29, which continues to make nonsense of a paragraph at the end of 'Oxen of the Sun'.

Since O was supposed to be the 'definitive standard edition', it was chosen as copy for the first authorized British edition, the Bodley Head setting of 1936. Besides repeating the errors of $S2$ and O, $B1$ added amongst many other new errors '*likes*' for '*lies*' at 599.13/695.26; this is a case of a fairly obvious new error that was not repeated in subsequent editions. But the eight new errors in $B1$ listed by Dalton were all repeated in subsequent editions.

So the line goes depressingly on. The second Bodley Head edition ($B2$) was set from $B1$ in 1960, and the second Random House edition ($R2$) was set from $B2$ in 1961; both repeated the same old mistakes, both introduced new errors of their own.[40] Finally the Penguin edition (P) was set from $B2$ in 1968, in which may be found gathered together the errors from $S2$, O, $B1$, and $B2$; and of course some new ones too, such as a misplaced cross-head, 'SHINDY IN WELLKNOWN RESTAURANT' (132.19/168.8).

---

[37] See p. 213 n. 1.

[38] $R1$ also includes readings that appear to derive from O.

[39] Communicated by Clive Hart, who had it from Gilbert. Like other editions O did of course correct some of the errors of its predecessors. In the extract, for instance, where Darantière's compositor set 'Scavening' by mistake for 'Scavenging' (p. 232, MS. addition to line 20; p. 233, line 22), Joyce failed to notice the error, which persisted through all the impressions of $S1$ and $S2$ until it was eventually corrected in O.

[40] Dalton, again, provides examples; see p. 213 n. 1.

EXAMPLE 12

Stoppard, *Travesties*, 1974

APART from Milton's *Maske* all the works of literature which have been discussed so far were intended primarily for communication as printed and published books; and, although *A maske* was originally intended for performance, it was not an ordinary play written for the theatre. But now as a final example we have a play written by an experienced professional playwright for the London stage, a work which was completed and realized in 1974 not as a book to be read but as a series of performances to be experienced at the Aldwych Theatre. The choice of a modern example has made it possible both to consider the text of the play as it was actually performed, and to consult the author himself about his intentions.[1]

Any work of literature (and also incidentally any work of learning) which is intended to be communicated primarily by spoken performance rather than by a written text characteristically goes through three textual stages. There is first the script, the written version of what was originally intended to be said. Secondly there is the performance text, what is actually said in one or more performances. And thirdly there is the reading text, the version subsequently published by author or editor as a record of what might or should have been said. Anyone who has written a lecture, has delivered it, and has published it, will recognize these three textual stages; and they are especially apparent in plays, in which the second stage, the performance text, is developed not by the author alone but by the director and the actors as well.

Tom Stoppard's *Travesties*, which was successfully produced in London in 1974 and again in 1975, and then went to New York, was published in book form early in 1975, between the two London productions.[2] The play is a dazzling intellectual romp on the theme of the mutual relationship between artist and society, which in Stoppard's hands is both wonderfully funny and first-rate theatre.

Tom Stoppard drafted the script of *Travesties* in 1973-4. His usual method of writing dialogue for a play is to draft and redraft each speech, or

---

[1] I am immensely grateful to Tom Stoppard for his tolerant—and I think amused—co-operation in the writing of this chapter. He lent me his own annotated copy of the script of *Travesties* and allowed me to reproduce it, he discussed the development of the text with me, and he commented on a number of specific differences between versions of his play.　　　　[2] Stoppard, T., *Travesties*, London 1975.

even each sentence, as he goes along, refining the text as he composes it. By the time he reaches the last line of the play, which has by now been rewritten many times, he considers the text to be complete and finished, although as we shall see further modification is sure to take place in rehearsal. When the script of *Travesties* had got to this point, it was fair-copied by a typewriting agency which specializes in scripts, was photocopied for the Royal Shakespeare Company, and went into rehearsal.

Stoppard attended rehearsals, joining the director and the cast in working out a performance text for the play, basing it of course on the script but incorporating a number of alterations both major and minor. During rehearsals Stoppard marked his own copy of the script in blue pencil for possible cuts (not all of which were adopted) and in red for points to be made to the actors, and he jotted down notes for other changes in the margins and on the backs of the sheets. He himself began with clear ideas of how each sentence should be phrased and delivered, ideas which were mostly found in practice to be good ones, although there were a few important cases in which it was agreed that variations would be preferable. Meanwhile another photocopy of the script was used as the company's prompt-book, and was marked up with variants as the text developed.

The rehearsals of *Travesties* were followed by nine 'preview' performances (30 May to 8 June 1974) and then by thirty-one ordinary performances of the first production (10 June to 17 August 1974). The Royal Shakespeare Company ran two other plays during the same season at the Aldwych and, although most of the cast of *Travesties* did not perform in the other plays, the leading actor John Wood also played the lead on other nights in *Sherlock Holmes*. The performance text of *Travesties*, which by this time differed considerably from the original script, continued to alter during the earlier performances as audience reaction suggested modifications, some of which returned to the original version, while others diverged further from it. This is not to suggest that the actors felt free to alter the words on their own responsibility in a performance. The changes were made by agreement between author, director, and actors; and once the text was agreed these professional actors could and did achieve a high and consistent level of accuracy in speaking their parts. By the second half of July the text had stabilized into a form approved by author and company, and there was scarcely any variation (Stoppard says) from day to day. This was the final performance text of the production, and on 24 July 1974 I made a tape-recording of a complete performance.

The next stage was the publication of a reading text in the spring of 1975. Stoppard had previously written in the 'Author's note' to his earlier play *Jumpers* (1972) 'In preparing previous plays for publication I have tried with some difficulty to arrive at something called a "definitive text", but I now believe that in the case of plays there is no such animal. Each production will throw up its own problems and very often the solution will lie in some minor change to the text, either in the dialogue or in the author's directions, or both. What follows is a basic version of *Jumpers*'; and in a postscript Stoppard expressed his indebtedness for certain changes to the director Peter Wood (who also directed the first production of *Travesties*) 'whose insight and inventiveness [Stoppard wrote] were a crucial influence on *Jumpers* throughout rehearsals'.[3]

Tom Stoppard, amplifying what he meant by a 'basic text', told me that his intention had been to publish his own preferred text of *Travesties*, the version that he would like to have performed by an ideal cast. The result, which was sent to the publisher in the form of another marked-up photocopy of the original script, incorporated some but not all of the changes made for the performance text, and included some revisions made later. It agreed at some points with the script, at others with the performance text of the first production, and at others again with neither. Flexibility in future productions was encouraged by stage directions which offered optional cuts, and suggested alternative methods of production.

The author continued to encourage textual flexibility during the second production of *Travesties* in the summer of 1975, when the director and most of the actors were the same as before. The stabilized form of the performance text of this second production—of which I again made a tape-recording late in the run on 13 September 1975—generally followed the variants of the first performance text rather than those of the reading text, but there were further developments of verbal detail. There was also one major cut and several minor ones, together with a few lines of additional dialogue newly written in (and in one case removed again).

However, unless Stoppard publishes a revised edition of the reading text, the variations introduced in the second production are unlikely to survive in future productions of *Travesties* by other companies, for these are bound to be based on the original reading text. It is interesting to note in this connection that the Young Vic's 1975 production of Stoppard's *Rosencrantz and Guildenstern are dead*, eight years and many productions after the play was published as a book, followed the published reading text very closely;[4] much more closely, indeed, than the published reading text of *Travesties* was followed by the performance text of its second production.

Let us now compare some extracts from the three main versions of *Travesties*: script, performance text, and reading text. First, a few lines from

---

[3] Stoppard, T., *Jumpers*, London 1972, p. 11.
[4] A performance on 23 Aug. 1975 was compared with the revised Faber text of 1968.

the immense opening monologue of the leading actor, in which Old Carr in 1974 becomes in memory Young Carr in 1917, transcribed from the un-amended author's script (S), my tape-recording of the performance text of the first production (P), and the published reading text (R).

(S) Carr of the Consulate!—first name Henry, that much is beyond dispute, I'm mentioned in the books, certainly the Joyce book, I wouldn't swear to the Lenin and as for the Dada books which tend to be mutually contradictory, a mention would hardly be prima facie—but the name is definitely the goods. For the rest I'd be willing to enter into discussion but not if you don't mind correspondence, into matters of detail and chronology—I stand open to correction on all points, except for my height, which can't be far off, and the success of my performance, which I remember clearly, in the demanding role of Ernest (not Ernest, the other one)—

(P) Carr of the Consulate!—first name Henry, that much is beyond dispute, I'm mentioned in the books. Certainly the Joyce book, I wouldn't swear to the Lenin, and as for the Dada books which tend to be mutually contradictory, a mention would hardly be prima facie—but the name is definitely the goods. For the rest I'd be willing to enter into correspondence but not if you don't mind discussion, on matters of detail and chronology—I stand open to correction on all points, except for my height which can't be far off can it? and the success of my performance, which I remember clearly, in the demand-ing role of Ernest (not Ernest, the other one)—[5]

(R) Carr of the Consulate!—first name Henry, that much is beyond dispute, I'm mentioned in the books.
For the rest I'd be willing to enter into discussion but not if you don't mind correspondence, into matters of detail and chronology—I stand open to correction on all points, except for my height which can't be far off, and the success of my performance, which I remember clearly, in the demanding role of Ernest (not Ernest, the other one)—

The transcripts show that in the performance (P) the actor John Wood followed the author's script (S) with three exceptions. First, he changed the

---

[5] In transcribing the performance texts of these extracts from *Travesties* I have generally copied the author's punctuation in order to simplify comparison with the script and reading text. A rhetorical punctuation would give a closer approximation of the speech as delivered. For example:
'Carr of the Consulate. First name Henry; that much *is* beyond dispute—I'm mentioned in the books. Certainly the Joyce book—I wouldn't *swear* to the Lenin—and as for the Dada books, which tend to be mutually contradictory, a mention would hardly be prima facie . . . but, the *name* is definitely the goods. For the rest, I'd be willing to enter into correspondence, but not if you don't mind dis-cussion, on matters of detail and chronology. I stand open to correction on all points, except for my height (which can't be far off, can it?) and the success of my performance (which I remember clearly) in the demanding role of Ernest . . . *not* Ernest, the other one!' [John Wood on 24 July 1974.]
Even a rhetorical punctuation cannot convey all the nuances of an actor's delivery; it would not, for instance, indicate the differences of pace and emphasis that took place in the delivery of this speech between the first and second productions.

sense of 'I'd be willing to enter into discussion but not if you don't mind correspondence' by saying 'I'd be willing to enter into correspondence but not if you don't mind discussion'. This change was deliberate, and Tom Stoppard comments 'It was just a question of which image seemed marginally more amusing. *I* preferred the idea of Carr liking to talk but not to write letters—J[ohn] W[ood] presumably was thinking that he would not want the *audience* to interrupt, while he would be willing to receive letters later!'[6] Secondly, John Wood said 'on' not 'into matters of detail', no doubt because he felt 'discussion on' sounded better than 'discussion into matters of detail'. (Here Stoppard had amended 'correspondence into' in his copy of the script to read 'correspondence on', for syntactical reasons; but for the reading text he reverted to 'into' because he thought it sounded better after all.) Thirdly, John Wood added 'can it?' to 'which can't be far off'. The actors introduced a good many colloquialisms of this sort into the performance text in order to ease their delivery; but, although Stoppard was aware of these changes, he deliberately kept them out of the reading text.

The reading text (R) followed the unamended script exactly except for a cut of thirty-five words. Stoppard had marked this passage as a cut in his rehearsal copy of the script, but in fact it was not cut in performance; he decided nevertheless to leave it out of the reading text because he 'felt one ought to be getting *on*'. He had also marked 'except for my height, which can't be far off' as a cut in his copy of the script, but this was retained both in performance and in the reading text.

In the second production in 1975 John Wood changed the pace and emphasis of his delivery of this speech, but he repeated the words of the first performance text of 1974 exactly, with the three changes from the script and without the cut made in the reading text. Professional actors prefer a stable text because it simplifies performance, and it is a mark of John Wood's professionalism that he was able to achieve complete verbal accuracy after more than a year.

The main extract from *Travesties*, which is transcribed in the same three versions, is from the first Carr–Bennett dialogue, and comes soon after the passage that we have just considered. The transcripts are printed in parallel, with the speeches numbered for ease of cross-reference; and the notes to the transcripts include Stoppard's own commentary, together with a record of the few changes that were made to Bennett's part for the second production (Carr's part in this extract was not changed).[7]

---

[6] Tom Stoppard's comments on the details of these extracts were made in letters to me of Sept.–Oct. 1975.

[7] On the source of Stoppard's commentary, see n. 6 above. The textual changes from the second production are taken from my tape-recording of 13 Sept. 1975.

S1] BENNETT: A gentleman called, sir. He did not wait.
S2] CARR: What did he want?
S3] BENNETT: He did not vouchsafe his business, sir. He left his card.
(Offers it on a salver)
S4] CARR: "Tristan Tzara. Dada Dada Dada". Did he have a stutter?
S5] BENNETT: He spoke French with a Rumanian accent, and wore a monocle.
S6] CARR: He is obviously trying to pass himself off as a spy. It is a form of vanity widely
indulged in Zurich during a European war, I believe, and adds greatly to the
inconveniences caused by the crowds of real spies who interfere with the flow of
traffic outside the Odeon and the Terrase, and make it almost impossible to get
a table at either. They come for the air, to which I have alluded. It is the reason why
when the rest of Europe periodically heaves and shifts like a snoring Gulliver,
permanent Switzerland fills up with a hodge podge of Lilliputian conspirators.
S7] BENNETT: The phrase may adequately describe him, sir. Certainly he was a small
man. Whether he was also conspiring I could not, of course, tell.
S8] CARR: To masquerade as a conspirator, or at any rate to speak French with a Rumanian
accent and wear a monocle, is at least as wicked as to be one; in fact, rather more
wicked, since it gives a dishonest impression of perfidy, and, moreover, makes the
over-crowding in the cafes, not to mention the interference with the traffic,
gratuitous, being the result neither of genuine intrigue nor bona fide treachery—
was it not, after all, La Rochfoucault in his Maximes who had it that in Zurich in
Spring in wartime a gentleman is hard put to find a vacant seat for the spurious
spies peeping at police spies spying on spies eyeing counter-spies *what a bloody
country even the cheese has got holes in it !!*
(Off the rails again. CARR has, on the above words, done violence to the inside of
a cheese sandwich)
S9] BENNETT: Yes, sir. I have put the newspapers and telegrams on the sideboard, sir.
S10] CARR: Is there anything of interest?
S11] BENNETT: There is a revolution in Russia, sir.

P1] BENNETT: A gentleman called, sir. He did not wait.
P2] CARR: What did he want?
P3] BENNETT: He did not vouchsafe his business, sir. He left his card.
(*Offers it on a salver.*)
P4] CARR: "Tristan Tzara. Dada Dada Dada." Did he have a stutter?
P5] BENNETT: He spoke French with a Rumanian accent, sir, and he wore a monocle.
P6] CARR: Oh, he is quite clearly trying to pass himself off as a spy. It is a form of vanity
widely indulged in in Zurich during a European war, I believe, and adds greatly
to the inconvenience caused by the crowds of real spies who conspire to fill both
the Odeon and the Terrasse, and make it almost impossible to get a table at either.
P7] BENNETT: I have noticed him at the Terrasse, sir, with a friend wearing a brioche in
his left nostril. As to whether he was also conspiring I, of course, could not tell.
P8] CARR: To masquerade as a conspirator, or at any rate to speak French with a Rumanian
accent and wear a monocle, is at least as wicked as to be one. In fact, rather more
wicked. It overcrowds the cafés without offering either genuine intrigue or bona
fide treachery—was it not, after all, La Rochefoucauld in his *Maximes* who had it
that in Zurich in Spring in wartime a gentleman is hard put to find a vacant seat
for the crowds of spurious spies peeping at police spies spying on spies eyeing
counter-spies *what a bloody country even the cheese has got holes in it !!*
(*Throws the remains of a cheese sandwich violently over his shoulder.*)
P9] BENNETT: Yes, sir. (*Cuckoo clock.*) I have put the newspapers and the telegrams on
the sideboard, sir.
P10] CARR: Is there anything of interest?
P11] BENNETT: There is a revolution in Russia, sir.

R1] BENNETT: A gentleman called, sir, He did not wait.

R2] CARR: What did he want?

R3] BENNETT: He did not vouchsafe his business, sir. He left his card.
     (*Offers it on a salver.*)

R4] CARR: "Tristan Tzara. Dada Dada Dada." Did he have a stutter?

R5] BENNETT: He spoke French with a Rumanian accent, and wore a monocle.

R6] CARR: He is obviously trying to pass himself off as a spy. It is a form of vanity widely
     indulged in in Zurich during a European war, I believe, and adds greatly to the
     inconveniences caused by the crowds of *real* spies who conspire to fill the Odeon
     and the Terrasse, and make it almost impossible to get a table at either.

R7] BENNETT: I have noticed him with a group of friends at the Terrasse, sir. Whether
     they were conspirators I could not, of course, tell.

R8] CARR: To masquerade as a conspirator, or at any rate to speak French with a Rumanian
     accent and wear a monocle, is at least as wicked as to be one; in fact, rather more
     wicked, since it gives a dishonest impression of perfidy, and, moreover, makes the
     over-crowding in the cafés gratuitous, being the result neither of genuine intrigue
     nor bona fide treachery—was it not, after all, La Rochefoucauld in his *Maximes*
     who had it that in Zurich in Spring in wartime a gentleman is hard put to find a
     vacant seat for the spurious spies peeping at police spies spying on spies eyeing
     counter-spies *what a bloody country even the cheese has got holes in it!!*
     (*Off the rails again.* CARR *has, on the above words, done violence to the inside of a cheese
     sandwich.*)

R9] BENNETT: Yes, sir. I have put the newspapers and telegrams on the sideboard, sir.

R10] CARR: Is there anything of interest?

R11] BENNETT: There is a revolution in Russia, sir.

P5–8 There is a P version of these speeches on a loose sheet in Tom Stoppard's copy of S.

S6–8 The cuts are indicated in Tom Stoppard's copy of S.

P7   'a friend wearing a brioche in his left nostril': not in S or R, but referred to later in
      the play (p. 61 of the published text). Stoppard comments: 'I think I was wrong to
      drop this [from R]—I thought p. 61 would be funnier if fresh—but the audience
      like to recognise a cross-reference.'
      'As to whether he was also conspiring, I . . .': altered in the second production to
      'As to whether they were also conspirators, I . . .'.

P9   '(*Cuckoo clock.*)': the sound effect used to mark Old Carr's 'time slips'.

S12] CARR: Really? What sort of revolution?

S13] BENNETT: A social revolution, sir.

S14] CARR: A *social* revolution? Unaccompanied women smoking at the Opera, that sort of thing? . . . Are the Romanovs putting milk in their tea?

S15] BENNETT: Not precisely that, sir. It is more in the nature of a revolution of classes contraposed by the fissiparous disequilibrium of Russian society.

S16] CARR: What do you mean, classes?

S17] BENNETT: Masters and servants. As it were. Sir.

S18] CARR: Masters and servants. *Classes.*

S19] BENNETT: (expressionless as always) There have been scenes of violence.

S20] CARR: I see. Well, I'm not in the least bit surprised, Bennett. I don't wish to appear wise after the event, but anyone with half an acquaintance with Russian society could see that the day was not far off before the exploited class, disillusioned by the neglect of its interests, alarmed by the falling value of the rouble, and above all goaded beyond endurance by the insolent rapacity of its servants, should turn upon those butlers, footmen, cooks, valets . . . (parenthetically, Bennett, I see from your book that on Thursday night when Mr. Tzara was dining with me, eight bottles of champagne are entered as having been consumed. I have had previous occasion to speak to you of the virtues of moderation, Bennett: this time I will only say, remember Russia).

S21] BENNETT: Yes, sir. I have put the newspaper and telegrams on the sideboard, sir.

S22] CARR: Is there anything of interest?

S23] BENNETT: The Tzar has abdicated, and resigned as commander in chief of the Russian armies. There is now a Provisional Government headed by Prince Lvov, with Guchkov as Minister of War, Milyukov Foreign Minister and the Socialist Kerensky as Minister of Justice. The inclusion of Kerensky is calculated to recommend the Government to a broad base of the common people, but effective

P12] CARR: Really? What sort of a revolution?

P13] BENNETT: A social revolution, sir.

P14] CARR: A *social* revolution? Unaccompanied women smoking at the Opera, that sort of thing?

P15] BENNETT: Not precisely that, sir. It is more in the nature of a revolution of classes contraposed by the fissiparous disequilibrium of Russian society.

P16] CARR: What do you mean, classes?

P17] BENNETT: Masters and servants. As it were. Sir.

P18] CARR: Oh, masters and . . . Classes.

P19] BENNETT: There have been scenes of violence.

P20] CARR: I see. Well, I'm not in the least bit surprised. I don't wish to appear wise after the event, but anyone with half an acquaintance with Russian society could see that the day was not far off before the exploited class, disillusioned by the neglect of its interests, alarmed by the falling value of the rouble, and above all goaded beyond endurance by the insolent rapacity of its servants, should turn upon those butlers, footmen, cooks, valets . . . (parenthetically, Bennett, I see from your book that on Thursday last when Mr Tzara was dining with me, eight bottles of champagne are entered as having been consumed. I have had previous occasion to speak to you of the virtues of moderation, Bennett: this time I will only say, remember Russia).

P21] BENNETT: Yes, sir. (*Cuckoo clock.*) I have put the newspapers and the telegrams on the sideboard, sir.

P22] CARR: Is there anything of interest?

P23] BENNETT: The Tsar has now abdicated. There is a Provisional Government headed by Prince Lvov, with Guchkov as Minister of War, Milyukov Foreign Minister and the Socialist Kerensky as Minister of Justice, but effective authority has

R12] CARR: Really? What sort of revolution?

R13] BENNETT: A social revolution, sir.

R14] CARR: A *social* revolution? Unaccompanied women smoking at the Opera, that sort of thing? . . .

R15] BENNETT: Not precisely that, sir. It is more in the nature of a revolution of classes contraposed by the fissiparous disequilibrium of Russian society.

R16] CARR: What do you mean, classes?

R17] BENNETT: Masters and servants. As it were. Sir.

R18] CARR: Oh. Masters and servants. *Classes.*

R19] BENNETT (*expressionless as always*): There have been scenes of violence.

R20] CARR: I see. Well, I'm not in the least bit surprised, Bennett. I don't wish to appear wise after the event, but anyone with half an acquaintance with Russian society could see that the day was not far off before the exploited class, disillusioned by the neglect of its interests, alarmed by the falling value of the rouble, and above all goaded beyond endurance by the insolent rapacity of its servants, should turn upon those butlers, footmen, cooks, valets . . . (parenthetically, Bennett, I see from your book that on Thursday night when Mr. Tzara was dining with me, eight bottles of champagne are entered as having been consumed. I have had previous occasion to speak to you of the virtues of moderation, Bennett: this time I will only say, remember Russia).

R21] BENNETT: Yes, sir. I have put the newspapers and telegrams on the sideboard, sir.

R22] CARR: Is there anything of interest?

R23] BENNETT: The Tsar has now abdicated, sir. There is a Provisional Government headed by Prince Lvov, with Guchkov as Minister of War, Milyukov Foreign Minister and the Socialist Kerensky as Minister of Justice. The inclusion of Kerensky is calculated to recommend the Government to a broad base of the

---

P23 The cuts in the earlier parts of this speech were restored in R, but the final cut was not restored. All the cuts are marked in Tom Stoppard's copy of S.

authority has already been challenged by a committee of workers' deputies, or "Soviet", which has for the moment united all shades of socialist opinion. However there is no immediate prospect of the Socialists seizing power, for the revolution is regarded by them as the fulfilment of Karl Marx's prophecy of a *bourgeois capitalist era* in Russia's progress towards socialism. According to Marxist dogma, there is no way for a country to leap from autocracy to socialism: while the *ultimate* triumph of socialism is inevitable, being the necessary end of the process of dialectical materialism, it must, by the same token, be preceded by a bourgeois-capitalist stage of development. When the time is ripe, and not before, there will be a further revolution, led by the organised industrial workers, or "Proletariat", who will assume a temporary dictatorship to ensure the safe transition of the State into a true Communist utopia. Thus, it is the duty of Russian Marxists to welcome the present bourgeois revolution, even though it might take several generations to get through, if the examples of Western Europe and the United States are anything to go by. As things stand, therefore, if one can be certain of anything it is that Russia is set fair to become a parliamentary democracy on the British model, and will honour her obligations to her allies in the struggle against the overweening imperial ambitions of the German tyranny.

S24] CARR: Newspapers or coded telegram?

S25] BENNETT: A concensus of the most recent London dailies and political and humorous weeklies. There are points of disagreement. Some average that the Cossacks will stand firm and rout the insurgents. Others have information that the Tsar and Tsarina have put all their eggs in one basket and fled the country. The Swiss newspapers, true to the national neurosis, have posted men at all the railway stations. If I may quote La Rochfoucault, quel pays saigné, meme le fromage est plein des trous.

S26] CARR: I see. Well, I'm not in the least bit surprised. I don't wish to appear wise after the event, but anyone with half an acquaintance with Swiss café society could see that whenever the rest of Europe periodically heaves and shifts like a fat lady adjusting her stays, Switzerland fills up with a riffraff of refugees, minor royalty, bogus aristocrats, exiles, deserters, spies, counterspies, criminals, radicals, anarchists and artists of all kinds.

S27] BENNETT: Mr. Tzara called, sir. He did not wait.

already been challenged by a committee of workers' deputies, or "Soviet", which has for the moment united all shades of socialist opinion. However there is no immediate prospect of the Socialists seizing power, for, according to Marxist dogma, there is no way for a country to leap from autocracy to socialism: whilst the ultimate triumph of socialism is inevitable being the necessary end of the process of dialectical materialism, it must, by the same token, be preceded by a bourgeois-capitalist stage of development. When the time is ripe, and not before, there will be a further revolution, headed by the organised industrial workers, or "Proletariat", who will assume a temporary dictatorship in order to ensure the safe transition of the State into the true Communist Utopia. It is therefore the duty of Russian Marxists to welcome the present bourgeois revolution, even though it may take several generations to get through, if the examples of Western Europe and the United States are anything to go by. As things stand, therefore, if one can be certain of anything at all, it is that Russia is set fair to become a parliamentary democracy upon the British model.

P24] CARR: Newspapers or coded telegram?

P25-7] BENNETT: A consensus of the most recent London dailies and the political and humorous weeklies, and general rumour put about Zurich by the crowds of deserters, spies, counter-spies, criminals, radicals, poseurs, exhibitionists, artists and riff-raff of all kinds. Mr Tzara called, sir. He did not wait.

common people, but effective authority has already been challenged by a committee of workers' deputies, or "Soviet", which has for the moment united all
shades of socialist opinion. However there is no immediate prospect of the Socialists
seizing power, for the revolution is regarded by them as the fulfilment of Karl
Marx's prophecy of a *bourgeois capitalist era* in Russia's progress towards socialism.
According to Marxist dogma, there is no way for a country to leap from autocracy
to socialism: while the *ultimate* triumph of socialism is inevitable, being the
necessary end of the process of dialectical materialism, it must, by the same token,
be preceded by a bourgeois-capitalist stage of development. When the time is ripe,
and not before, there will be a further revolution, led by the organised industrial
workers, or "Proletariat", who will assume a temporary dictatorship to ensure the
safe transition of the State into a true Communist Utopia. Thus, it is the duty of
Russian Marxists to welcome the present bourgeois revolution, even though it
might take several generations to get through, if the examples of Western Europe
and the United States are anything to go by. As things stand, therefore, if one can
be certain of anything it is that Russia is set fair to become a parliamentary
democracy on the British model.

R24] CARR: Newspapers or coded telegram?

R25-7] BENNETT: A consensus of the most recent London dailies and political and humorous
weeklies, and general rumour put about Zurich by the crowds of spies, counter-
spies, radicals, artists and riff-raff of all kinds. Mr. Tzara called, sir. He did not wait.

S25   'average' (line 2) is a typist's error for 'aver'.

25   There is a version of this speech intermediate in form between S25 and P25 on
a loose sheet in Tom Stoppard's copy of S.

25-7   Of the condensation made for P and R, Tom Stoppard writes: 'S seemed too long
for its own good—the whole Bennett scene I mean. I liked the (Fabergé) *eggs in one
basket* joke but no one understood it: it was too unexplicit. We tried turning "basket"
into "casket", which confused the audience; and finally into "jewel-box", which
was *too* explicit and not funny as a result.'

P25-7 The words 'poseurs, exhibitionists,' cut in the second production.

S28]   CARR: I'm not sure that I approve of your taking up this modish novelty of "free association", Bennett. I realise that it is all the rage in Zurich—even in the most respectable salons to try to follow a conversation nowadays is like reading every other line of a sonnet—but if the servant classes are going to ape the fashions of society, the end can only be ruin and decay.

S29]   BENNETT: I'm sorry, sir. It is only that Mr. Tzara being an artist—

S30]   CARR: If Mr. Tzara is an artist that is his misfortune. I will not have you passing moral judgements on my friends.

S31]   BENNETT: Yes, sir. I have put the newspapers and telegrams on the sideboard, sir.

S32]   CARR: Is there anything of interest?

S33]   BENNETT: The Provisional Government, which is democratic in principle but bourgeois in practice, has now declared its intention to carry on the war, and has gained the sympathy of the British and the French. However, the committee of workers' deputies, or Soviet, consider the war to be nothing more than an imperialist adventure carried on at the expense of workers on both sides. To co-operate in this adventure is to be stigmatised in a novel phrase which seems to translate as a "lickspittle capitalist manservant", unnecessarily offensive in my view.

S34]   CARR: (languidly) I'm not sure that I'm much interested in your views, Bennett.

S35]   BENNETT: Yes, sir. Well, the Soviet has ordered soldiers and sailors to form local soviets, to keep arms out of the possession of the officers, and to ignore the orders of the Provisional Government; all of which has won it the corresponding sympathy of the Germans. However, unity of the Left is not now complete. There is a more extreme position put forward by the Bolshevik party. The Bolshevik line is that some unspecified but unique property of the Russian situation, unforeseen by Marx, has caused the bourgeois-capitalist era of Russian history to be compressed into the last few days, and that the time for the proletarian revolution is now ripe. Furthermore, the Bolsheviks are contemptuous of the peace policy of the Soviet:

P28]   CARR: I'm not sure that I approve of your taking up this modish novelty of "free association", Bennett.

P29]   BENNETT: I'm sorry, sir. It is just that Mr Tzara being an artist—

P30]   CARR: I will not have you passing moral judgements on my friends. If Mr Tzara is an artist that is his misfortune.

P31]   BENNETT: Yes, sir. (*Cuckoo clock.*) I have put the newspapers and the telegrams on the sideboard, sir.

P32]   CARR: Is there anything of interest?

P33]   BENNETT: In St Petersburg, the Provisional Government has announced its intention of carrying on the war. However, the committee of workers' deputies, or Soviet, considers the war to be nothing more than an imperialist adventure carried on at the expense of the workers of both sides. To co-operate in this adventure is to be stigmatised in a novel phrase which appears to translate as a "lickspittle capitalist manservant", unnecessarily offensive in my view, sir.

P34]   CARR: I'm not sure that I'm much interested in your views, Bennett.

P35]   BENNETT: They're not particularly interesting, sir. However, the unity of the Left is not now complete. There is a more extreme position taken by the Bolshevik party. The Bolshevik line is that some unspecified but unique property of the Russian situation, unforeseen by Marx, has caused the bourgeois-capitalist era of Russian history to have been compressed into the last few days, and that the time for the proletarian revolution is now ripe. (*Appassionata.*) Furthermore, the Bolsheviks say

R28] CARR: I'm not sure that I approve of your taking up this modish novelty of "free association", Bennett. I realise that it is all the rage in Zurich—even in the most respectable salons to try to follow a conversation nowadays is like reading every other line of a sonnet—but if the servant classes are going to ape the fashions of society, the end can only be ruin and decay.

R29] BENNETT: I'm sorry, sir. It is only that Mr. Tzara being an artist——

R30] CARR: I will not have you passing moral judgements on my friends. If Mr. Tzara is an artist that is his misfortune.

R31] BENNETT: Yes, sir. I have put the newspapers and telegrams on the sideboard, sir.

R32] CARR: Is there anything of interest?

R33] BENNETT: In St. Petersburg, the Provisional Government has now declared its intention to carry on the war, and has gained the sympathy of the British and the French. However, the committee of workers' deputies, or Soviet, consider the war to be nothing more than an imperialist adventure carried on at the expense of workers of both sides. To co-operate in this adventure is to be stigmatised in a novel phrase which seems to translate as a "lickspittle capitalist manservant", unnecessarily offensive in my view.

R34] CARR (*languidly*): I'm not sure that I'm much interested in your views, Bennett.

R35] BENNETT (*apologetically*): They're *not* particularly interesting, sir. However, the Soviet has ordered soldiers and sailors to ignore the orders of the Provisional Government; this has won it the corresponding sympathy of the Germans. However, unity of the Left is not now complete. There is a more extreme position put forward by the Bolshevik party. The Bolshevik line is that some unspecified but unique property of the Russian situation, unforeseen by Marx, has caused the bourgeois-capitalist era of Russian history to be compressed into the last few days, and that the time for the proletarian revolution is now ripe. Furthermore, the Bolsheviks say the soldiers

---

S33, 35, 37   Cuts and stets marked in Tom Stoppard's copy of S; and 'In St. Petersburg' added at the beginning of S33.

P35   'They're not particularly interesting, sir' altered in the second production to 'Yes, sir' (reversion to S); and the sentence 'Furthermore . . . civil war' cut.

they say the soldiers should actually shoot all the officers and turn the war into a European civil war. However, the Bolsheviks are a small minority in the Soviet, and their leader, Vladimir Ulyanov, also known as Lenin, has been in exile since the abortive 1905 revolution, and is in fact living in Switzerland.

S36] CARR: You astonish me. In Zurich?

S37] BENNETT: Number 14 Spiegelgasse. He is desperately trying to return to Russia to put matters, as he sees them, right, but naturally the Allies will not allow him free passage. Since Lenin is almost alone in proclaiming the Bolshevik orthodoxy, which is indeed his creation, his views at present count for nothing in St. Petersburg, where ostensible Bolsheviks like Kamenev and Stalin are taking a moderate line. A betting man would lay odds of about a million to one against Lenin's view prevailing.

S38] CARR: A concensus of the humorous and intellectual weeklies?

S39] BENNETT: Telegram from the Minister.

S40] CARR: A million to one.

S41] BENNETT: I'd put a pound on him, sir.

S42] CARR: You know him?

S43] BENNETT: I do, sir. And if any doubt remained, the London papers carry the assurance that the man to watch is Kerensky.

that the soldiers should shoot all the officers and turn the war into a European civil war. However, the Bolsheviks are a small minority on the Soviet, and the leader, Vladimir Ulyanov, also known as Lenin, has been in exile since the abortive 1905 revolution, and is in fact living in Zurich.

P36] CARR: You astonish me.

P37] BENNETT: Yes, sir. If one may quote La Rochefoucauld, "Quel pays sanguinaire, même le fromage est plein de trous." It is suggested, sir, that you keep a close watch on Lenin, and try to ascertain his plan.

P38] CARR: A consensus of the humorous and intellectual weeklies?

P39] BENNETT: Telegram from the Minister, sir. Since Lenin is almost alone in proclaiming the Bolshevik orthodoxy, which is in fact his creation, his views count for nothing in St Petersburg, where ostensible Bolsheviks such as Kamenev and Stalin are taking a moderate line. A minister is laying odds of about a million to one against Lenin's view prevailing.

P40] CARR: A million to one.

P41] BENNETT: I'd put a pound on him, sir.

P42] CARR: You know him?

P43] BENNETT: I do, sir. And if any doubt remained, the London papers carry the assurance that the man to watch is Kerensky.

should shoot all the officers and turn the war into a European civil war. However, the Bolsheviks are a small minority in the Soviet, and their leader, Vladimir Ulyanov, also known as Lenin, has been in exile since the abortive 1905 revolution, and is in fact living in Zurich.

R36] CARR: Naturally.

R37] BENNETT: Yes, sir—if I may quote La Rochefoucauld, "Quel pays sanguinaire, même le fromage est plein des trous." Lenin is desperately trying to return to Russia but naturally the Allies will not allow him free passage. Since Lenin is almost alone in proclaiming the Bolshevik orthodoxy, which is indeed his creation, his views at present count for nothing in St. Petersburg, where ostensible Bolsheviks like Kamenev and Stalin are taking a moderate line. A betting man would lay odds of about a million to one against Lenin's view prevailing. However, it is suggested that you take all steps to ascertain his plans.

R38] CARR: A consensus of the humorous and intellectual weeklies?

R39] BENNETT: Telegram from the Minister.
    (*He starts to leave.*)

R40] CARR: A million to one.

R41] BENNETT: I'd put a pound on him, sir.

R42] CARR: You know him?

R43] BENNETT: I do, sir. And if any doubt remained, the London papers carry the assurance that the man to watch is Kerensky.

---

36   Amended in Tom Stoppard's copy of S to read 'Naturally. In Zurich'; but the P version is noted on a loose sheet. Of the development of this speech, Stoppard comments: 'The moment is supposed to be the latter end of a parabola linking a series of references to Switzerland's role as that natural residence of displaced persons, etc., and it never quite paid off as such. The changes reflect various attempts to bring it off.'

37-9 Commenting on why the transfer of material from S37 to P39 was not followed up in R, Stoppard writes: 'This goes back to the cut in S25. I wanted to keep the *fromage* joke, and 37 seemed the natural home for it. Then, to make Carr's subsequent movements clearer in motivation (i.e. going to the Library, etc.) the line "It is suggested that you keep a close watch" etc. was added in rehearsal. [In Stoppard's copy of S a note at the end of S39 adds "He also asks that you find out all you can . . ."] Rhythmically P39 from "Since Lenin" to "moderate line" ought to be cut in performance [in the second production it was cut] but I like the reference to Stalin's "moderate line"—historically true, of course, but evaded in Stalin's history books P *is* better than R—I should have changed it!'

S37, P39, R37 'A betting man' (S, R), 'A minister' (P): Stoppard writes: 'It should be "THE Minister". Again—I now would prefer R to follow P. Because R37 is the way it is, the introduction of "the Minister" is inappropriate—it's really Bennett who, as it were, is "the betting man": i.e. a general abstract proposition, not a comment about what our Ambassador (Minister) thinks.' In the second production the text of P39 was altered to 'Telegram from the Minister, sir. Though he is offering odds of about a million to one against Lenin's view prevailing.'

S37, S40 'million' altered to 'hundred' in Tom Stoppard's copy of S.

The textual variation that comparison of these extracts has brought to light is mostly of a sort that affects the detailed texture of the play rather than its larger structure; not that the verbal variants are therefore unimportant, for many of them affect the meaning of the passages in which they occur, and most of them serve the purpose of making the play more effective in the theatre. But there were also changes on a larger scale, one of which (introduced in the second production) altered the whole balance of the work. This was the deletion of practically the whole of Cecily's political lecture at the beginning of the second act, which had been a disastrous longueur in the first production; freed of its weight, the second half of the play was able to take off with much greater theatrical effect. In the reading text, which was prepared between the first two productions, the author directs that 'The performance of the whole of this lecture is not a requirement, but is an option', and goes on to indicate how much of it might be cut.[8] Following the second production, in which much more of the lecture was cut than had been suggested in the reading text, Stoppard wrote to me, 'I now see less and less virtue in the inclusion of Cecily's lecture either in performance or in print.' Nevertheless the lecture still encumbers the reading text, and it is likely that it will be used, in whole or in part, in future productions of the play.

More large changes were made for the New York production of 1975–6; Stoppard mentioned some of them in a letter written in October 1975:

I have now got around to taking out the new introduction to the Dada scene [which had been introduced in the second production] . . . Furthermore, after some paranoid 'phone calls from New York about 'Broadway Bladder' (a term which possibly has no precedent in the annals of textual bibliography, and refers to the alleged need of a Broadway audience to urinate every 75 minutes) I spent the weekend trying to take 5 minutes out of the first act, and Tuesday afternoon putting the cuts in, and Tuesday evening having misgivings about the result. I have now lost sight of the line where integrity becomes pretentious sanctity of text, and where weakness becomes good sense.

To turn, finally, to the lessons that can be learned from this example of the textual bibliography of a modern play. There is, first, the central importance of the performance text in the development of the work when (as has never been uncommon) the playwright is personally involved in the production of his play. Of course the performance texts of most plays are lost beyond recall, but when a text survives that appears to incorporate any elements of an early performance text we should be ready to recognize and appreciate the performance features. A reading text prepared by the author may have artistic value; but it is not the whole play.

[8] Stoppard, T., *Travesties*, London 1975, p. 66.

Then there is the remarkable flexibility of the performance text when the author collaborates in the production.[9] It is a reminder that what we get in the theatre is a living art: works that are dynamic and developing, not static and completed; plays which evolve with the ideas of the author and are fashioned by the interpretation of the company; performances which are continually affected by the reactions of their audiences.

Again, there is the attention to detail. Here we have seen author and actors manipulating the details of the text, constantly revising and polishing to bring out a meaning here, to get another laugh there; really caring about textual nuances, even though they know that most of them will go straight over the audiences' heads. In the theatre, too, the care given to the text was plain, the actors using all their skills to communicate its subtleties, and doing so with consistent accuracy. Some of this care for detail may, like regular spelling, be a relatively modern phenomenon; but theatrical traditions are celebrated for their longevity, and it is worth remembering that some of the playwrights and actors of the past may also have worked hard and long to get the text exactly right.

There are interesting implications in all this for the textual bibliographer. Take, for instance, the question of the author's intentions. As we have seen, Stoppard said that the reading text of *Travesties* that was published between the first and second productions represents the play as he would like to have it performed by an ideal cast. But in the theatre, when he worked with an actual cast in developing the performance text of the second production, he helped to evolve a version which differed considerably from the published reading text. Stoppard not only accepted this performance version, but he actually preferred parts of it in the production. Yet he says that he is unlikely to incorporate these performance features in his published text. Should a future editor use them, or should he stick to Stoppard's published text?

More fundamentally the textual bibliographer may ask himself what *is* the text of this or any other play? Is it the words written down on the pages of the author's script, or of the company's prompt-book, or of the published reading text, words which each reader has to interpret for himself? Or is it perhaps a tape-recording of the words spoken aloud by actors, when the meaning is interpreted by the listener but is also supplemented and defined by the intonation of the speakers? Or is it a videotape, recording the speech,

---

[9] On 21 Sept. 1975 the BBC broadcast a documentary film about the making of *The boundary* (a television play by Tom Stoppard and Clive Exton which had been written, rehearsed, and transmitted during a single week in July 1975), in the course of which the actor Michael Aldridge remarked: 'It is often very much easier for an actor to go straight to the author to ask a question rather than having to go through the director—without anything against the director, it just is quicker.' To which the other leading actor Frank Thornton added: 'It's marvellous having them [the authors] there, because if there's anything you disagree with, you've got them there to argue with.'

movement, lighting, and all, of an actual theatrical performance, from which the viewer can experience the play as a completed work of art, but with his view limited by what the actors, the director, the camera crew, and the sound recordist make of that particular performance?

As a rule the evidence available to the editors of plays will include reading texts, and occasionally published acting versions or even prompt-books, but not performance texts or videotapes. Since the reading text is what the author wanted people to read and interpret, it may well be the best version to edit, although an acting version might be preferred as offering a closer approach to the realization of the work in the theatre. But in any case the editor should be very clear about what the evidence represents; and he should be prepared, when it includes what may be performance features, to raise his eyes from the play text and to have another look at the play.[10]

[10] Ronald Hayman's *Tom Stoppard* (published by Heinemann, London 1977, while this section was in proof) prints two interviews in which Stoppard discusses his intentions as a playwright, and comments in detail on the development of *Travesties* (including, pp. 9-11, 139-40, Cecily's lecture).

INDEX